Foundations of
Retirement Planning

Financial Advisor Series

C. Bruce Worsham, Editor

Sales Skills Techniques

Techniques for Exploring Personal Markets

Techniques for Meeting Client Needs

Techniques for Prospecting: Prospect or Perish*

Product Essentials

Essentials of Annuities

Essentials of Business Insurance

Essentials of Disability Income Insurance

Essentials of Employee Benefits

Essentials of Life Insurance Products

Essentials of Long-Term Care Insurance

Essentials of Multiline Insurance Products*

Planning Foundations

Foundations of Estate Planning

Foundations of Financial Planning: An Overview

Foundations of Financial Planning: The Process

Foundations of Investment Planning*

Foundations of Retirement Planning

Foundations of Senior Planning

* Courses under development

Financial Advisor Series

Foundations of Retirement Planning

Richard A. Dulisse

The American College Press/*Bryn Mawr, Pennsylvania*

© 2006 The American College Press
270 S. Bryn Mawr Avenue
Bryn Mawr, PA 19010
(888) AMERCOL (263-7265)
www.theamericancollege.edu

Library of Congress Control Number 2006928820
ISBN 1932819371

Printed in the United States of America

To Nancy L. Kooistra
whose wisdom and unconditional friendship are a comfort to me

RAD

Contents

Preface

The mission of this book is to develop your professionalism as a financial advisor who counsels prospects and clients about the need for retirement planning. We intend to do this by teaching you important aspects of the retirement planning process as it is adapted from the eight-step selling/planning process. Each chapter covers one or more concepts relevant to successful retirement planning and/or the skills, techniques, or knowledge that facilitate their use. To gain an understanding of the retirement planning process, you need to read the entire book.

Although much of the text material will be new to you, some will, no doubt, refresh knowledge you acquired in the past. In either case, all of the text material is both valuable and necessary if you aspire to be a successful financial advisor. The benefits you gain from studying the text will be directly proportional to the effort you expend. Read each chapter carefully and answer the essay and multiple-choice review questions for the chapter (preferably before looking in the back of the book for the answers); to do less would be to deprive yourself of the unique opportunity to become familiar with the selling/planning process and all that it entails.

The book includes educational features designed to help you focus your study of the selling/planning process. Among the features found in each chapter are

- learning objectives
- a chapter outline, examples, figures, and lists
- key terms and concepts
- review questions (essay format)
- self-test questions (multiple-choice format)

Features located in the back of the book are a(n)

- glossary
- answers to questions section
- index

Finally, all of the individuals noted on the acknowledgments page made this a better book, and we are grateful. In spite of the help of all these fine folks, however, some errors have undoubtedly eluded our eyes. For these we are solely responsible. At the same time, we accept full credit for giving those of you who find these errors the exhilarating intellectual experience produced by such discovery. Nevertheless, the author acknowledges that any errors discovered are solely his fault.

Richard A. Dulisse

The American College

The American College® is an independent, nonprofit, accredited institution founded in 1927 that offers professional certification and graduate-degree distance education to men and women seeking career growth in financial services. Through a continuum of education program, The College offers professional certification and graduate-degree distance education to men and women seeking career growth in financial services.

At the beginning end of the continuum, the Center for Financial Advisor Education at The American College offers the LUTC Fellow (LUTCF) professional designation jointly with the National Association of Insurance and Financial Advisors [NAIFA] and the Financial Services Specialist (FSS) professional designation. The Center's curriculum is designed to introduce students to the technical side of financial services while at the same time providing them with the requisite sales training skills.

In the middle of the continuum, the Solomon S. Huebner School® of The American College administers the Chartered Life Underwriter (CLU®), the Chartered Financial Consultant (ChFC®), the Chartered Advisor for Senior Living (CASL™), the Registered Health Underwriter (RHU®), the Registered Employee Benefits Consultant (REBC®), and the Chartered Leadership Fellow® (CLF®) professional designation programs. In addition, the Huebner School also administers The College's CFP Board–registered education program, the CFP Certification Curriculum, for those individuals interested in pursuing CFP® certification.

Finally, at the advanced end of the continuum, the Richard D. Irwin Graduate School® of The American College offers the master of science in financial services (MSFS) degree; the master of science in management (MSM) degree with an emphasis in leadership; the Chartered Advisory in Philanthropy (CAP™) professional designation; the Graduate Financial Planning Track (another CFP Board-registered education program), and several graduate-level certificates that concentrate on specific subject areas. The National Association of Estate Planners & Councils has named The College as the provider of the education required to earn its prestigious Accredited Estate Planner (AEP) designation.

The American College is accredited by the Commission on Higher Education of the Middle States Association of Colleges and Schools, 3624 Market Street, Philadelphia, PA 19104; telephone number: (215) 662-5606. The Commission on Higher Education is an institutional accrediting agency recognized by the U.S. Secretary of Education and the Commission on Recognition of Postsecondary Accreditation.

The American College does not discriminate on the basis of race, religion, sex, handicap, or national and ethnic origin in its admissions policies, educational programs and activities, or employment policies.

The American College is located at 270 S. Bryn Mawr Avenue, Bryn Mawr, PA 19010. The toll-free telephone number of the Office of Student Services is (888) AMERCOL (263-7265), the fax number is (610) 526-1465, and http://www.theamericancollege.edu is the home page address. The College welcomes visitors to its 35-acre campus during regular business hours, 8:00 a.m. to 5:30 p.m., Monday through Friday.

Acknowledgments

This book was written by Richard A. Dulisse, LUTCF, CLU, ChFC, RHU, REBC, CASL, CFP, assistant professor of financial planning at The American College.

Special appreciation is extended to Lynn Hayes, director of editorial and production services, whose talent, tenacity, and unparalleled editorial skill transformed an unpolished manuscript into a professional publication. The College also thanks Charlene McNulty for production assistance.

To all of these individuals, without whom this book would not have been possible, The College expresses its sincere appreciation and gratitude.

C. Bruce Worsham
Associate Vice President and Director of
Educational Development
The American College

About the Author

Richard A. Dulisse, LUTCF, CLU, ChFC, RHU, REBC, CASL, CFP, is an author/editor and assistant professor of financial planning at The American College. His responsibilities at The College include writing and preparing text materials for the LUTCF and FSS programs. He also teaches insurance and financial planning courses at The College.

Mr. Dulisse is author of *Essentials of Disability Income Insurance* and *Foundations of Senior Planning*, co-author of *Essentials of Long-Term Care Insurance* and *Foundations of Financial Planning: The Process*, and a contributing author to *Financial Decisions for Retirement*. In addition, he edited *Ethics for the Financial Services Professional* and made extensive contributions to *Essentials of Annuities*. All of these books are published by The American College. Mr. Dulisse also contributes articles to *Advisor Today*, the national magazine distributed to members of NAIFA.

Before joining The College, Mr. Dulisse worked in the life insurance industry from 1979 through 2001. His experience includes 5 years as a life insurance agent—initially with Metropolitan Life and then with New York Life. At New York Life, he also served as a sales manager before becoming a training manager in 1985. As a training manager, he helped implement the company's training curriculum to teach agents product knowledge and selling skills.

Mr. Dulisse earned a BSoc.S degree, cum laude, from The Pennsylvania State University. He also holds both the MSM and the MSFS degrees awarded by The College.

Special Notes to Advisors

Text Materials Disclaimer

This publication is designed to provide accurate and authoritative information about the subject covered. While every precaution has been taken in the preparation of this material to ensure that it is both accurate and up-to-date, it is still possible that some errors eluded detection. Moreover, some material may become inaccurate and/or outdated either because it is time sensitive or because new legislation will make it so. Still other material may be viewed as inaccurate because your company's products and procedures are different from those described in the book. Therefore, the author and The American College assume no liability for damages resulting from the use of the information contained in this book. The American College is not engaged in rendering legal, accounting, or other professional advice. If legal or other expert advice is required, the services of an appropriate professional should be sought.

Caution Regarding Use of Illustrations

Any illustrations, fact finders, sales ideas, techniques, and/or approaches contained in this book are not to be used with the public unless you have obtained approval from your company. Your company's general support of The American College's programs for training and educational purposes does not constitute blanket approval of any illustrations, fact finders, sales ideas, techniques, and/or approaches presented in this book unless so communicated in writing by your company.

Use of the Term Financial Advisor or Advisor

Use of the term "financial advisor" as it appears in this book is intended as the generic reference to professional members of our reading audience. It is used interchangeably with the term "advisor" so as to avoid unnecessary redundancy. Financial advisor takes the place of the following terms:

Account Executive	Financial Planner	Practitioner
Agent	Financial Planning	Producer
Associate	Professional	Property & Casualty Agent
Broker (stock or	Financial Services	Registered Investment
insurance)	Professional	Advisor
Employee Benefit	Health Underwriter	Registered Representative
Specialist	Insurance Professional	Retirement Planner
Estate Planner	Life Insurance Agent	Senior Advisor
Financial Consultant	Life Underwriter	Tax Advisor
	Planner	

Answers to the Questions in the Book

The answers to all essay and multiple-choice questions in this book are based on the text materials as written.

About the Financial Advisor Series

The mission of The American College is to raise the level of professionalism of its students and, by extension, the financial services industry as a whole. As an educational product of The College, the Financial Advisor Series shares in this mission. Because knowledge is the key to professionalism, a thorough and comprehensive reading of each book in the series will help the practitioner-advisor to better service his or her clients—a task made all the more difficult because the typical client is becoming more financially sophisticated every day and demands that his or her financial advisor be knowledgeable about the latest products and planning methodologies. By providing practitioner-advisors in the financial services industry with up-to-date, authoritative information about various marketing and sales techniques, product knowledge, and planning considerations, the books of the Financial Advisor Series will enable many practitioner-advisors to continue their studies so as to develop and maintain a high level of professional competence.

When all books in the Financial Advisor Series are completed, the series will encompass 16 titles spread across three separate subseries, each with a special focus. The first subseries, *Sales Skills Techniques,* will focus on enhancing the practitioner-advisor's marketing and sales skills but will also cover some product knowledge and planning considerations. The second subseries, *Product Essentials,* will focus on product knowledge but will also delve into marketing and sales skills, as well as planning considerations in many of its books. The third subseries, *Planning Foundations,* will focus on various planning considerations and processes that form the foundation for a successful career as a financial services professional. When appropriate, many of its books will also touch upon product knowledge and sales and marketing skills. Current and forthcoming titles are listed earlier in this book.

Overview of the Book

Foundations of Retirement Planning guides the financial advisor through the retirement planning process, explaining the use of fact finders, methods of analyzing facts, presentation of solutions, and calculation of clients' retirement income needs.

Chapter 1 examines 10 critical issues that affect retirement planning today, with an emphasis on the roadblocks to retirement saving. It also discusses the roles and responsibilities of the financial advisor in the retirement planning process. The chapter introduces the eight-step selling/planning process (or sales cycle), including the adaptation of this process to retirement planning. It also discusses the five stages of retirement planning from the client's perspective. Finally, the chapter examines prospecting, retirement planning demographics, and the various age-based market segments for retirement planning.

Chapter 2 identifies the main sources of retirement income, with a special focus on the Social Security system. It also explains the role of Social Security benefits in retirement planning. Next, the chapter considers time-value-of-money concepts and reviews future value and present value calculations. The chapter concludes with a discussion of personal financial statements, including the financial position and cash flow statements, and it explores cash flow analysis, planning, and management, with an emphasis on household budgeting techniques.

Chapter 3 begins with a discussion of goal setting and examines the quantitative assumptions that are required in the retirement planning process, concentrating particularly on the two basic methods for calculating a prospect's retirement income need. The purpose and goals of the initial retirement planning interview are explored, along with three methods to qualify prospects for retirement planning. The chapter also includes a step-by-step explanation of how to use the retirement planning fact finder.

Chapter 4 examines the financial obstacles to successful retirement planning. It discusses the impact of special planning needs—especially college education funding—on retirement planning. It also discusses how Social Security, Medicare, Medicaid, and medical expense and long-term care insurance, as well as other insurance products and risk management techniques, affect planning. The chapter then assesses the impact of income taxation, inflation, and the procrastination of saving on retirement planning.

Chapter 5 focuses on investments and financial products. It considers the four basic approaches to investing, along with the concepts of suitability and risk tolerance, and it identifies the basic types of risk associated with investing. Risk management and investment management techniques, such as diversification, asset allocation, and dollar cost averaging, are examined, as well as financial products used in retirement planning such as mutual funds, annuities, life insurance, stocks, and bonds.

Chapter 6 discusses tax-advantaged retirement plans, examining the basic types of qualified and nonqualified plans in detail. It also addresses the effect of salary reduction on income taxes and the impact of tax deferral on the accumulation of money. There is an in-depth discussion of the traditional IRA, Roth IRA, IRA rollovers, and the rules for the taxation of distributions from IRAs.

Chapter 7 explores wealth management and distribution strategies for retirees. It looks at reasons for and against taking early retirement, along with its effect on Social Security benefits and company-sponsored retirement plans. The chapter explores the roles of Social Security retirement benefits, life insurance, and qualified plan and IRA required minimum distribution rules in retirees' asset distribution planning. Pre- and postretirement investment strategies are covered, as well as the development of effective retirement planning solutions.

Chapter 8, which is devoted to wealth transfer planning and professionalism, opens with a discussion of life insurance beneficiary designations and the five ways that property transfers from owners to survivors at death. The chapter explores the use of basic estate planning techniques and the impact of income in respect of a decedent, and it reviews state regulation of insurance products and federal regulation of securities products. The book concludes with an evaluation of the critical role of ethics and professionalism in the financial advisor's selling/planning activities.

Foundations of Retirement Planning

1

Introduction to Retirement Planning

Learning Objectives

An understanding of the material in this chapter should enable the student to

1-1. Identify the eight steps in the retirement planning process from the advisor's perspective.

1-2. Describe the five phases of the retirement planning process from the client's perspective.

1-3. Describe the critical issues that affect retirement planning.

1-4. Identify the roadblocks to saving for retirement.

1-5. Explain the advisor's role in the retirement planning process.

1-6. List the important characteristics of the silent generation, baby boom generation, generation X, and millennial generation.

1-7. Explain the main objective of prospecting.

1-8. List the four criteria that define a qualified prospect.

1-9. Identify the three demographic generations into which most retirement planning prospects fall.

1-10. List and describe seven sources of retirement planning prospects.

Chapter Outline

INTRODUCTION

It may surprise you to know that retirement planning is a relatively young discipline. Consider this: In 1930, only one in 10 workers was covered by a pension program and Social Security did not exist. For Americans who lived in the early 20th century, "retirement" meant moving from fieldwork to household chores. In the middle of the 20th century, retirement was thought of as a short and sedentary experience. Today's and tomorrow's retirement is thought of as a vibrant and significant time of life, which may last 30 years or longer. Gone are the days of the frail senior sitting in a rocking chair.

Despite its short history, retirement planning has become one of the most crucial aspects of a comprehensive financial plan. According to survey after survey, retirement planning ranks as a top consumer priority.

This chapter will set the stage for your study of retirement planning by identifying the key components of the retirement planning process. It will explore the critical issues that affect retirement planning. The chapter will then

> **Retirement planning has become one of the most crucial aspects of a comprehensive financial plan.**

examine the role of the advisor in helping clients achieve financial security in retirement. Finally, it will discuss marketing demographics and prospecting concepts and sources. ◊

RETIREMENT PLANNING DISCIPLINE

Selling/Planning Process

The selling/planning process is based on a planning philosophy. Over the years, many authors have written about selling and planning the "right" way. In doing so, they have used various terms to describe the right way: relationship, client-centered, counselor, consultative, needs-based, values-based; the list goes on and on. We do not recommend any one method. Instead, we attempt to examine those principles and concepts involved in cultivating a long-term, mutually beneficial relationship with a client.

Because of the nature of the client-advisor relationship, it is both ethically required and financially wise for the financial advisor to thoroughly understand the client's needs and act to fulfill those needs as much as possible. There must be what is known as consultative (client-focused) planning or selling. This approach requires the advisor to gather as much information as possible from the client about the client's needs, goals, interests, and assets in order to put together an investment or insurance package that will best meet the client's needs. Consultative planning or selling is a sound approach to building good relationships with clients.

The selling/planning process is divided into eight steps. The selling process encompasses the (financial) planning process. Within each sale, the advisor should conduct some type of planning. The first two steps are preliminary marketing steps you must complete prior to actual planning. Steps 3 through 8 are the (financial) planning process. These next six steps involve interaction between you and your client. They will be repeated many times because they are the basis for your ongoing working relationship. Knowing what you also want to accomplish and why you want to accomplish it will guide your actions in each step of the process. Figure 1-1 displays the eight steps in the selling/planning process.

Retirement Planning Process: The Advisor's Perspective

Retirement planning follows the same eight steps used in the selling/planning process. Identifying and selecting prospects for individual retirement planning is the first step in a chronological procedure that you need to adhere to and understand to enhance your competency. Below is a more detailed explanation of the selling/planning process as it is adapted to the retirement planning process. Throughout this text, we will refer to these steps as we discuss their importance in retirement planning from the financial advisor's perspective.

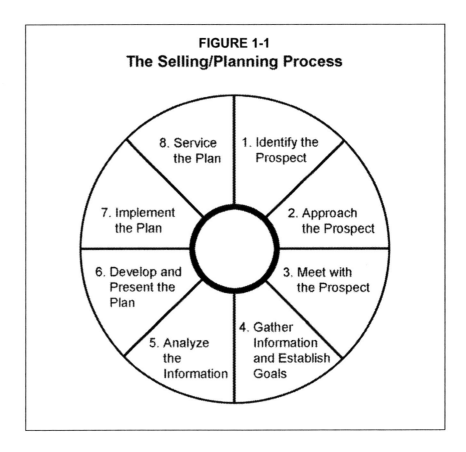

FIGURE 1-1
The Selling/Planning Process

1. Identify the Prospect

Effective retirement planning begins with getting in front of the right prospect. Not only do you want to identify prospects who have a high probability of needing, wanting, and affording your financial products to meet their retirement planning objectives, but you also want to find people who will value you and become a source for repeat business and, more important, for referrals. A systematic approach to prospecting that utilizes various preapproach methods can help you find target markets of potential clients and enable you to market effectively.

2. Approach the Prospect

This step involves getting appointments. You can do this either on the telephone or face-to-face through seminars. If you are successfully cultivating relationships, you will generate more referral-based business. Because of the negative feelings most people have toward telemarketers, cold calling has become more difficult, and referrals are that much more critical.

3. Meet with the Prospect

Meeting with the prospect is the step during which you establish rapport, explain your business purpose, ask some thought-provoking questions, and listen, listen, and listen. The importance of listening cannot be overstated; it is essential when building any relationship. You need to gain prospects' trust and agreement to gather pertinent information about them. In this step, you should outline and discuss an overview of the common problems that people face in retirement planning. You must also let prospects know what you can do for them (in general terms) to solve these problems and help them to see your value. You must answer the prospect's question: Why should I do retirement planning with you? Your final objective in meeting with the prospect is to gain acceptance to proceed to the information-gathering step.

> **In step 3—meet with the prospect—you must answer the prospect's question: Why should I do retirement planning with you?**

4. Gather Information and Establish Goals

Retirement planning requires advisors to listen to their prospects' goals and expectations for retirement. Advisors should not impose their concept of retirement on prospects or assume what they believe to be important is also important to prospects. Prospects have a variety of goals that range from never having to work again to working full-time during retirement. Clearly, advisors have their work cut out for them as they deal with a plethora of expectations and, in some cases, help frame the expectations of their prospects through the education process.

After sorting through their prospects' goals and expectations for retirement, advisors must gather a considerable amount of information about their prospects by using a retirement planning fact finder. They must focus on conducting a financial inventory of retirement assets, savings, and an assessment of the strategies that clients have available to them. For example, advisors must account for all their prospects' resources allocated to retirement, and they must note all opportunities that prospects have available to them such as being able to contribute to a Roth IRA or to participate in a 401(k) plan at their place of work.

5. Analyze the Information

In this step, the advisor looks at the prospect's current situation as well as his or her future goals in order to evaluate the appropriate strategies for that particular prospect. This includes the performance of a retirement needs analysis as well as an analysis of the prospect's financial risk tolerance, risk management strategies, and risk exposures. For example, does the prospect have adequate disability income insurance and long-term care insurance? Do the prospect's current asset allocations adequately achieve his or her financial and/or retirement goals? Is the prospect currently saving enough for retirement? What tax planning and distribution strategies are available to the prospect, and do they make sense for the situation? Advisors need to evaluate and analyze current retirement plan exposures (for example, the penalty tax for premature distributions), current retirement plans, Social Security benefits, and current retirement strategies.

6. Develop and Present the Plan

The advisor should develop and prepare a specific retirement plan tailored to meet the prospect's goals and expectations, commensurate with the prospect's values, attitudes, temperament, and financial risk tolerance. In addition to the prospect's current financial position, the plan should include his or her projected retirement status as it now stands as well as the projected status if the advisor's recommendations are followed. The advisor should also provide a current asset allocation model along with strategy recommendations. Investments should be summarized, and the advisor should recommend an investment policy. The retirement plan should also include an assessment of distribution options and tax strategies. Finally, the plan should include a list of prioritized action items and address issues such as housing and health care.

After developing and preparing the plan, the advisor should present the plan to the prospect and review it with him or her. The advisor should collaborate with the prospect to ensure that the plan meets his or her goals and expectations.

7. Implement the Plan

The advisor should assist the client in implementing the recommendations. This will most likely involve the purchase of financial products that are intended to satisfy the quantitative financial goals established in step 4 of the process. Often this requires the advisor to coordinate with other professionals such as accountants, attorneys, real estate advisors, investment advisors, stock brokers, and insurance advisors.

8. Monitor the Plan

After the plan is implemented, the advisor should periodically monitor and evaluate the soundness of his or her recommendations and review the progress of the plan with the client. The advisor should also discuss and evaluate changes in the client's personal circumstances such as family births or deaths, illness, divorce, or change in job status. Any relevant changes in tax laws, benefit and pension options, and the economic environment should be reviewed and evaluated before the advisor recommends revisions to the plan to accommodate new and/or changing circumstances.

Five Phases of Retirement Planning: The Client's Perspective

Despite the fact that retirement is a moving target that defies a singular definition because it will be different for different people, retirement planning occurs throughout the client's life cycle and is typically evidenced by the following phases:

- savings
- increased preparation and visualization
- decision
- retirement transition and lifestyle
- coping with frailty

Note that the phases tend to be a continuum of experiences that may or may not be demarcated by a singular event.

savings phase

The *savings phase* starts as soon as possible after the client's career begins. During that time, clients will be preoccupied with other competing savings objectives such as buying a home and family-building expenses. The advisor's role in the savings phase is to motivate the client to save for retirement and to educate the client about the importance of starting early. Establishing good retirement savings habits despite the lure of more short-term goals is essential to retirement security because of the miracle of compound interest. Think of clients buying retirement on the installment plan: The sooner they pay, the less it costs. Also, during this period, clients often change jobs, and the advisor's role is to make sure that retirement savings are not cannibalized for other uses. *Rollovers,* tax-free transfers from one tax-qualified vehicle (for example, an employer plan) to another (for example, an IRA) can be a key service the advisor provides for his or her client at this stage.

> The advisor's role in the savings phase of retirement planning is to motivate the client to save for retirement and to educate the client about the importance of starting early.

rollover

increased preparation and visualization phase

The *increased preparation and visualization phase* cannot be identified with any particular age. In fact, the earlier it starts, the better for retirement security purposes. In this phase, the client kicks retirement planning into high gear. Often, the focus on retirement goals is spurred by parents' retirement. At this time, children begin to see the parents' plight and realize they want to emulate the positive and not repeat the negative. In the savings phase, the motivation to plan and save came from the advisor. In the increased preparation phase, it is the client who sees the need to increase 401(k) contributions or make paying off the house before retirement a priority. To initiate the increased preparation phase, advisors should use a retirement income or expenses calculator to identify the amount needed to save for retirement.

In the second part of the phase, clients become even more focused. The concept of what retirement should be begins to crystallize in their minds. Now the need to meet with an advisor becomes more important and possibly more productive. In some cases, clients begin to understand that limiting expenses can be just as important a goal as increasing savings. One strategy advisors often suggest during the visualization phase is to save all raises that are earned in the 5 or 6 years prior to retirement. By putting their salary increase into a 401(k), Roth IRA, or traditional IRA, the clients will not only save more for retirement, but they will also lock in spending habits and learn not to grow their lifestyle and budget—an important lesson for retirement.

decision phase

The *decision phase* is often characterized by the imminent event of retirement. The year before, year of, and year after retirement bring many planning choices and challenges. Clients in the decision phase have often grown tired of their current career. They need to be prepared for a nonworking environment or a phased retirement (discussed in chapter 2). They may look to restructure asset allocation (often unnecessary because certain retirement assets will not be used for 20 or more years in the future). Sometimes they think of moving into retirement because their children have completed college, the clients are becoming empty nesters, or they have received an inheritance. Other times, age drives the decision about when to retire. Advisors should educate clients, however, that health and money are more accurate drivers of the retirement decision. During the decision phase, advisors need to counsel clients on a variety of issues such as pension distributions, when to start receiving Social Security retirement benefits, and how to convert assets into retirement income.

> **Health and money should be the primary drivers of the retirement decision.**

retirement transition and lifestyle phase

The *retirement transition and lifestyle phase* follows immediately after retirement. It is often accompanied by a surge of increased spending on travel and other recreational pursuits and a focus on adapting to a changed environment. Travel, golf, gardening, and volunteer work often occupy the client's calendar. Communications with former coworkers take on a different character. Grandparenting joys may become part of the lifestyle. Advisors must be ready to help with the psychological and emotional needs that accompany these changes. The client-advisor relationship goes beyond financial solutions at this time. Once clients have settled into retirement, advisors must help them adjust their spending plans accordingly. Often, caregiving responsibilities will become the client's "new career." As time passes, the nature of the client's environment also changes. Friends and family may die or move away. Relationships with former coworkers may grow remote. Events with other seniors will take on more importance. By this time, advisors need to help clients decide whether or not to move near family or to a continuing care retirement community. From a financial perspective, clients become more asset rich and income poor.

frailty phase

The *frailty phase* of retirement planning does not depend on any specific age, but is evidenced by dealing with health issues, caregiving for a spouse, and the loss of mobility. Clients in this phase tend to become more lonely and dependent on others. Proximity to medical services and community services becomes more important. Issues such as forfeiting a driver's license and coping with loss dominate clients' lifestyles. At this stage, the advisor can

> **Financial independence can soften the loss of physical independence.**

assist clients by directing them to the appropriate social services. It is also rewarding to advisors to see that their counsel has helped clients to have sufficient resources during retirement. Financial independence can soften the loss of physical independence.

Questions That Define the Retirement Planning Discipline

The essence of retirement planning is to answer clients' diverse questions on a variety of issues. For example, with regard to Social Security, clients are concerned with the inner workings of the system. They will ask what type of benefits it provides and when they should start taking those benefits. They also want to know what lies ahead for the future of the Social Security system. Discussions relating to these questions about Social Security can be found in chapters 2 and 7.

With regard to employer qualified retirement plans, clients desire to maximize the tax efficiencies inherent in these plans. To do so, they need to understand what benefits the employer plans provide. Clients also want to know how nonqualified plans and IRAs can be used to enhance retirement security. Chapters 6 and 7 discuss these issues.

In addition, clients want advisors to answer the question of whether or not the clients can afford to retire. Chapter 3 discusses how to calculate the retirement income need.

Clients are concerned, too, with investment strategies they can use during the accumulation period and the liquidation period. Chapter 5 discusses investment strategies and asset allocation decisions.

Clients are also curious about how different financial products fit into their retirement plan. Chapter 5 examines various types of financial products and investment and risk management concepts.

A major concern for clients entering the retirement period is how to properly plan for distributions from qualified retirement plans. The advisor needs to make clients aware of the available distribution options and to help the clients navigate the maze of choices. Distribution issues are covered in chapter 7.

Insurance products available for retirement are also vitally important. Clients wonder if they will need long-term care insurance and, if so, how much coverage they should purchase. Clients must also understand Medicare and medigap plans. These issues are discussed in chapter 4.

Finally, clients want to know how retirement planning and estate planning intersect because they may seem to have contradictory goals. Estate planning issues are discussed in chapter 8.

Throughout your study, keep in mind that retirement planning is more art than science. Be flexible, and encourage your clients to do the same. Together, you and your client can create a bright future and a successful financial solution to the problem of retirement planning. ◊

CRITICAL ISSUES THAT AFFECT RETIREMENT PLANNING

To better understand the retirement planning discipline, let's look at the different issues an advisor must address. By laying this foundation, the advisor should be able to understand the rules and strategies discussed later in this textbook in the context of the retirement planning environment as it currently exists.

Issue One: Retirement Age

No longer is age 65 a magic number for retirement. A variety of societal, governmental, and personal factors can affect your client's decision about when to retire.

What, then, is retirement age? As a practical matter, the average retirement age (which is slightly over age 62) is irrelevant to the retirement planner. What is important is the retirement age for each individual client.

> Average retirement age is irrelevant to the retirement planner. What is important is the retirement age for each individual client.

Each client has a unique set of personal factors that influence his or her retirement age. Government and employer programs and policies are important. But also important are the client's financial and personal situations, as well as his or her willingness to incur the risk of portfolio performance, inflation, and adverse changes in government and employer policies.

For most clients, specifying a retirement age is based on nonfinancial criteria. If the client indicates the desire to retire at age 64, the advisor's responsibility is to help determine whether that is a financially viable goal. At the same time, the advisor must inform the client of negative aspects of the chosen age. Often, the advisor provides information that causes the client to postpone retirement.

Issue Two: Life Expectancy

Another critical issue that affects retirement is life expectancy. Clients are living longer than prior generations did and, in many cases, living longer than expected. According to the U.S. Census Bureau, there are over 68,000 centenarians. This is double that of the 1990 census. Furthermore, by the year 2050, there are projections that there will be more than 1.1 million centenarians.

Many clients mistakenly look at life expectancy at birth (74.1 years for males and 79.5 years for females) to assess their likelihood of living to a certain age. However, life expectancy at age 65 (85.1 for males and 88.3 for females, according to the Retirement Plans 2000 mortality tables) is much different and a more accurate measure for retirement. Even if clients use accurate life expectancy tables, it is important to remember that many clients will outlive the ages in the tables. In combination, the earlier than expected retirement (issue one) and the increase in longevity (issue two) can be detrimental to retirement financial security.

Issue Three: Financial Preparedness

There is no doubt that some clients are on the fast track to a financially independent retirement and others are swimming upstream. The advisor's job is complex because of the disparity in financial preparedness among the United States population.

> The advisor's job is complex because of the disparity in financial preparedness among the United States population.

Employer-Sponsored Pension Plan Availability

Clients who work for medium- and large-sized employers are typically better prepared for retirement than their counterparts in small firms. One fact of life in retirement planning is that as the size of the organization increases, the chance of having a pension program increases. For example:

- Eighty-five percent of workers at employers with 100 or more employees have an employment-based plan available to them.
- Fifty percent of workers at employers with 25 to 99 employees have an employment-based plan available to them.
- Twenty percent of workers at employers with fewer than 25 employees have an employment-based plan available to them.
- According to the Employee Benefits Research Institute (EBRI), over 25 million employees who work for small businesses are not covered by company retirement plans.

Issue Four: Need for Education and Advisors

In a recent study, more than 90 percent of human resource and financial managers believed that employees are ill prepared to make their own retirement planning decisions. In the same study, 86 percent of human resource and financial managers felt that their employees needed financial advice regarding retirement assets above and beyond the current educational information they were receiving. The managers have the following three primary concerns:

- to help employees make better financial decisions
- to increase plan participation
- to enhance the overall value of benefit packages

Because fiduciary liability concerns often make the plan sponsors hesitant to provide advice, the need for third-party advice becomes increasingly important. This represents a huge opportunity and challenge for financial services professionals. Advisors who can meet this need can provide a necessary service to business clients and also increase their individual client base.

Issue Five: Government Concern

> **Tax preferences for employer pension plans are the single largest government tax expenditure, exceeding subsidies for home mortgages and health benefits.**

One encouraging fact about retirement is that it is currently receiving widespread governmental and consumer support. Tax preferences for employer pension plans are the single largest tax expenditure, exceeding subsidies for home mortgages and health benefits. Roth IRAs, SIMPLE pensions and age-weighted or cross-tested profit-sharing plans are just a few of the newer options in the retirement planning arsenal.

In response to the decreasing rate of saving for retirement among Americans, Congress enacted the Savings Are Vital to Everyone's Retirement (SAVER) Act of 1997 to help consumers realize the importance of retirement savings. The act required the U.S. Department of Labor (DOL) to maintain a public outreach program and convene three bipartisan national retirement savings summits.

The first National Summit on Retirement Savings was in June 1998. The Economic Growth and Tax Relief Reconciliation Act of 2001 (EGTRRA) adopted many of the provisions that had been proposed in this summit.

The second summit was in Washington, DC, from February 27 through March 1, 2002. President George W. Bush and the majority and minority leaders of both houses of Congress were cohosts. Approximately 250 statutory and appointed delegates representing a diverse group of public- and private-sector lawmakers and professionals who work in the fields of employee benefits and retirement savings attended. The common goal of the 2002 summit delegates was to help all Americans retire with security and dignity.

The final summit took place in late February and early March of 2006.

The national summits had the following objectives:

- to advance the public's knowledge and understanding of retirement savings and its critical importance to the future well-being of American workers and their families
- to facilitate the development of a broad-based, public education program to encourage and enhance individual commitment to a personal retirement savings strategy
- to develop recommendations for additional research, reforms, and actions in the field of private pensions and individual retirement savings

In total, these and other changes make it easier and more effective for clients to save for retirement. More important, the government has indicated it is strongly in favor of a policy that will promote retirement savings and retirement security.

Issue Six: Changing Face of Retirement

It is important for advisors to realize that retirement planning is a dynamic environment. Not only do products, services, and tax laws seem to change on a regular basis, but the very nature of retirement is also in flux. Some interesting studies show differences for those planning to retire in the future. For example, surveys show that current workers *expect* to work longer than current retirees worked before they retired. Surveys also show that many baby boomers say they plan to work after they retire because they enjoy working and want to stay involved. In fact, a study found that approximately 15 percent of individuals over age 65 are employed. The trend toward retirees who work is likely to continue as baby boomers retire and a workforce shortage starts to take place.

> **The trend toward retirees who work is likely to continue as baby boomers retire and a workforce shortage starts to take place.**

Another aspect that is changing the nature of retirement is caregiver responsibilities. The retirees of today and tomorrow are increasingly responsible for caring for parents, children, and grandchildren. Caregiving by retirees of aging parents is well documented.

Still another factor in the changing nature of retirement is that current retirees are most likely to identify Social Security as their most important source of income, but current workers are most likely to say that personal savings will be their most important source of income in retirement.

Issue Seven: The Three-Legged Stool

Financial needs during retirement are met from three primary sources, often referred to as the legs of a three-legged stool. The sources are Social Security benefits (discussed in chapter 2), employer-sponsored pension benefits (discussed in chapter 6), and personal savings (discussed in chapter 2). For each client, the advisor must be able to pinpoint benefits available from Social Security and private pensions and encourage the client to maintain an adequate savings program to reach his or her targeted goals. This requires a general knowledge about each of the three sources and extensive specific information about the client and his or her intentions.

Issue Eight: Baby Boomers and Retirement—Demographics Worth Considering

Retirement planning is important for *every* generation—a person is never too old or too young to plan for retirement. Special attention must be paid, however, to the needs of those born from 1946 through 1964, the *baby boom generation*. This generation represents roughly 27 percent of the population and, as it has progressed through the life cycles, it has had a major impact on everything from crowding in grammar schools to the surge in the housing

baby boom generation

Eighty-six percent of baby boomers feel that their generation is not saving enough for retirement; 66 percent say they should have started saving sooner.

market. What will the implications of this demographic tidal wave be on retirement? Consider the following facts:

- According to one survey, 86 percent of baby boomers feel that their generation is not saving enough for retirement.
- Sixty-six percent of baby boomers say they should have started saving sooner.
- Sixty-eight percent of baby boomers admit to not having devoted enough time to planning for retirement.
- The baby boom generation spends freely and has low personal savings rates.

Issue Nine: Roadblocks to Retirement Saving

No matter what the generation, the question remains: Why don't more Americans plan for retirement? After all, the so-called golden years are part of the American dream. The answer lies in the many distractions that hinder retirement savings.

Perhaps the biggest roadblock to retirement planning is the tendency of many working people to use their full after-tax income to support their current standard of living. These people will not have any private savings to supplement Social Security and pension funds. Many of them also may have experienced adversities like unemployment that pushed them into debt. In other cases, a lifestyle that incurs debt can stem from a spendthrift attitude or from the desire to emulate or improve upon their parents' standard of living. Whatever the reason for their lack of retirement savings, clients must follow a budget that allows them to live within their means and that also provides for retirement savings.

A second roadblock to retirement saving is unexpected expenses, including uninsured medical bills; repairs to a home, auto, or major appliance; and periods of unemployment.

> *Planning Note:* The client should create an emergency fund to handle unexpected but inevitable expenses. Approximately 3 to 6 months' income is usually set aside for this objective. (The emergency fund is discussed in more detail in chapter 4.)

Inadequate insurance coverage is a third roadblock to retirement saving. Regardless of whether the component that is lacking is life, disability income, health, home, or auto insurance, many individuals continue to remain uninsured or underinsured. Because the client cannot always recover economically from such losses, one important element of retirement planning

> **Planning Note:** Advisors should conduct a thorough review of their clients' insurance needs to make sure they are adequately covered. Two often overlooked areas are disability income insurance and liability insurance for the professional. Confirm that your clients are adequately protected in both areas.

is protection against catastrophic financial loss that would make future saving impossible. The need for adequate insurance coverage is discussed in chapter 4.

A fourth roadblock to saving for retirement occurs in the case of a divorced client. Divorce often leaves one or both parties with little or no accumulation of pension benefits or other private sources of retirement income. They have only a short time to accumulate any retirement income and are not able to earn significant pension or Social Security benefits. If the marriage lasted 10 years or longer, divorced persons are eligible for Social Security based on their former spouse's earnings record. A spouse may be entitled to the former spouse's retirement benefits if the divorce decree includes a qualified domestic relations order (QDRO). A QDRO is a judgment, decree, or order issued by a state court that allows a participant's retirement plan assets to be used for marital property rights, child support, or alimony payments to a former spouse or dependent.

Another common retirement planning problem is the lack of a retirement plan at the place of employment. Some workers have never had the opportunity to participate in a qualified pension plan because their employer(s) did not provide such benefits.

> **Six in 10 people who changed jobs cashed out their retirement savings instead of rolling them over into another type of plan.**

Workers who have frequently changed employers also face the problem of arriving at retirement with little or no pension. According to the most recent statistics available, six in 10 people who changed jobs cashed out their retirement savings instead of rolling them over into another type of plan.

Another problem that inhibits people from saving for retirement is a lack of financial literacy. Employees have never been properly schooled about investments and finance. For this reason, investment education has replaced health care as the top concern for employee benefit professionals and employees.

> **Planning Note:** Advise clients who change jobs to roll over vested benefits into an IRA or their new qualified plan to preserve the tax-deferred growth on their retirement funds. Advise clients who have recently changed jobs that if they have not met the participation requirements of their new employer's plan, they can make annual tax-deductible contributions to a traditional IRA in those years, regardless of salary.

A final roadblock to the acquisition of adequate retirement savings is the tendency to direct retirement funds for other purposes. (Special planning needs are discussed in chapter 4.) The down payment on a primary residence and/or vacation home and the education of children can consume any long-term savings that people have managed to accumulate. Because reaching these objectives has a greater urgency than planning for retirement, they supplant retirement as a savings priority. Although these objectives are certainly worthy, it is important to remind clients that savings must be carved out for retirement purposes in addition to other long-term objectives.

Roadblocks to Retirement Saving

- Tendency to spend all income
- Unexpected expenses
- Inadequate insurance coverage
- Divorce
- No employer plan available
- Frequent employment changes
- Lack of financial literacy
- Other accumulation needs

> **Saving is possible for only a limited time period, but consumption occurs throughout clients' lives and can drastically increase at any time because of illness or inflation.**

Whatever distractions face your clients, it is important to educate them about the need to plan and save for retirement. Clients must realize that saving is possible for only a limited time period during their life, but consumption occurs throughout their lives and can drastically increase at any time because of illness or inflation. This imbalance makes it essential for clients to save sufficient assets during their working years to ensure that they attain their retirement planning goals. By living below their means before retirement, clients can establish a lifestyle that they can maintain more easily in their retirement years. You can motivate clients to undertake a savings plan by helping them to identify the retirement planning objectives for which they should be striving.

Issue Ten: Retirement Planning Objectives

> **For some people, retirement is the last day they *have* to work, for others the last day they *want* to work, and for still others the last day they *can* work.**

Clients' objectives vary significantly depending on many factors, including health, age, marital status, number and ages of children, differences in the ages of the husband and wife, and personal preferences. Also, a client's objectives vary depending on his or her personal definition of retirement. For some, retirement is the last day they *have* to work, for others it is the last day they *want* to work, and for still others it is the last day they *can* work. Table 1-1 indicates how a surveyed group of CLUs, ChFCs, and members of the Registry of Financial Planning Practitioners believe that their clients would generally rate their retirement planning objectives.

TABLE 1-1
Ranking of Retirement Planning Objectives in Order of Priority

1. Maintaining preretirement standard of living
2. Maintaining economic self-sufficiency
3. Minimizing taxes
4. Retiring early
5. Adapting to noneconomic aspects of retirement
6. Passing on wealth to others
7. Improving lifestyle in retirement
8. Caring for dependents

Other Objectives

In addition to the general retirement planning objectives, your client may have one or more of the following specific retirement planning objectives:

- providing for secure investments—investing assets to minimize potential losses and make the client feel secure about his or her investments
- coping with health care costs—purchasing a Medicare supplement to pay for health care costs not covered under the Medicare program
- continuing the family business—special planning for clients who want to see their business successfully continue after their retirement
- obtaining reasonable value for the sale of a closely held business—maximizing the amount received upon the sale of a business if the client wishes to discontinue operations after retirement
- staying as healthy as possible—ensuring adequate funding for health clubs and other leisure activities ◊

ROLE OF THE ADVISOR IN RETIREMENT PLANNING

Retirement planning is a multidimensional field. As such, it requires that the advisor be schooled in the nuances of many financial planning specialties as well as other areas. Unfortunately, many so-called advisors approach retirement planning from only one point of view (investments, for example). This perspective, that of specializing in just one field, is too limited to deal with the diversified needs of the would-be retiree. A client is better served by a team of advisors who have specialized but complementary backgrounds or by a single advisor who is experienced in a variety of essential retirement topics.

Whether the retirement team or the multitalented individual is the vehicle, the holistic approach to retirement planning is the only way to fully meet the client's needs. Under *holistic retirement planning*, the advisor is required to communicate with clients concerning such diverse topics as

> **The holistic approach to retirement planning is the only way to fully meet the client's needs.**

holistic retirement planning

- the effect of financial well-being on the quality of life
- employer-provided retirement plans
- Social Security considerations
- personal savings and investments
- income tax issues
- insurance coverage
- traditional IRAs and Roth IRAs
- Medicare choices
- tax planning for distributions and other distribution issues
- health insurance planning, including medigap insurance and long-term care insurance
- wealth accumulation for retirement
- selecting a retirement community or another living arrangement
- relocation possibilities and reverse mortgages
- asset allocation and risk tolerance
- wellness, nutrition, lifestyle choices, and other gerontological issues
- assessment of current savings needed to achieve retirement goals

The role of the financial advisor engaged in a retirement planning practice is complicated. This complication arises not only because of the broad-based knowledge needed for the job, but also because the advisor must be able to integrate retirement planning strategies with other financial planning needs such as tax reduction, estate planning, and investment goals.

A word of caution at this point: As stated previously, understanding how to plan for a client's retirement is much more art than science. There is no one-size-fits-all approach to retirement planning. Clients may be single, married, or widowed. They may or may not have children. They may be healthy or unhealthy, happy or miserable, active or sedentary, sophisticated or naive.

A further complication is that retirement planning does not always begin early enough in the financial life cycle. It is a difficult task to plan for a client's retirement when it is too late to influence the client's ability to retire with financial security. Conversely, although planning for relatively young clients opens up a multitude of opportunities, it presents different planning challenges.

Because each client's situation is unique, the advisor must be able to meet a variety of situations creatively and cannot rely on a "formula approach" to solve clients' problems.

Responsibilities of the Financial Advisor

A financial advisor engaged in a retirement planning practice must assume several responsibilities that may not have been a part of his or her traditional financial services practice. These aspects of a retirement planning practice include the following:

- incorporating retirement planning as a segment of comprehensive financial planning. This means the use of financial planning techniques such as fact finding, budgeting, regulating income flow, and rendering investment advice.

- working with other professionals who advise the client. These professionals include the client's lawyer, accountant, banker, investment advisor, and insurance advisor. Communicating with this group offers many advantages, including cultivating a better understanding of the client's needs, providing a team approach for motivating the client to save for retirement, and generating referral sources for future business.

- dealing with relatively young clients. One common mistake is to start retirement planning only after a client has satisfied his or her other long-term responsibilities such as buying a home or educating a child. Financial success in retirement planning is best achieved if clients start saving for retirement at a relatively young age.

> **A common mistake is to start retirement planning only after a client has satisfied other long-term responsibilities.**

- monitoring and/or updating the client's plan. Whether it is part of a comprehensive or multiple-purpose financial plan or is a single-purpose plan, the client's retirement plan needs to be continually monitored and/or updated because of changes in family circumstances (such as job changes, births, deaths, divorces, and the acquisition of inheritances) and/or changes in the tax and economic environment.

- conducting seminars for employers. Many advisors ask employers for time to speak to employees during working hours. The employer sees this as an opportunity to provide a low-cost employee benefit, and the employees appreciate a retirement planning seminar offered by the employer. Advisors who are also designing the employer's qualified or nonqualified retirement plan can point out to the employer that work-sponsored retirement planning seminars help the plan accomplish its main objective—a successful retirement for employees.

- being familiar with available resources. The advisor should be familiar with the various resources available in the retirement planning field. These resources include the National Council on Aging, the American Society on Aging, and the Financial Planning Association, all of which provide newsletters, conferences, and a chance to interact with other advisors. In addition, advisors should make their clients aware of the American Association of Retired Persons (AARP), an organization that provides information on services for the elderly and is a valuable resource for retirement information. Advisors may also want to check the numerous retirement planning Web sites on the Internet.

> ### Internet Help for Advisors and Their Clients
>
> Advisors and practitioners will find the following Web sites useful:
>
> - www.ssa.gov—This site allows individuals to project the benefits they will receive from Social Security; it also provides a great deal of information regarding Social Security.
> - www.EBRI.org—The home page of the Employee Benefit Research Institute presents updates, databases, and surveys that have been recently issued.
> - www.ASEC.org—The American Savings Education Council provides the ballpark estimate calculator that enables people to calculate their savings need for retirement. It also contains links to different financial calculators.
> - www.irs.gov—The IRS Web site offers useful publications on all sorts of retirement issues.
> - www.benefitscheckup.org—This new service allows seniors, their families, and caregivers quickly and easily to identify what programs and services they may qualify for and how to access them.

Motivating Your Clients to Begin Planning for Retirement

Convincing individuals to take retirement planning seriously is often difficult. Sharing the following information may help to motivate your client:

> *To be sure that retirement funds are not depleted early, clients need to plan on beating the odds and living beyond the average life expectancy.*

- Retirement may last longer than planned, because life expectancies continue to rise. From 1981 to 1995, the life expectancy for a 65-year-old increased by almost a full year.
- To be sure that funds are not depleted too early, clients need to plan on beating the odds and living beyond the average life expectancy.
- For most people today, maintaining the preretirement standard of living requires 60 to 80 percent of preretirement earnings.
- Careful planning requires preparing for contingencies. Realistic possibilities include Social Security cutbacks, reductions in company pension benefits, periods of high inflation, and forced early retirement.
- As companies switch to defined-contribution-type plans, more responsibility for retirement planning falls on employees. In many cases, participants must decide how much to save, when to start saving, and how to invest the company retirement money.
- Americans are saving less than ever.
- Starting to save early can mean the difference between success and failure. Assuming a 10 percent rate of return, saving $225 a month beginning at age 40 will result in an accumulation of $300,000 by age 65. At age 50, it will result in an accumulation of only slightly over $94,000.
- Working with a trained professional can help an individual focus on the right issues, prepare a retirement plan, and follow through with it. You as the advisor provide expertise, a fair-minded viewpoint, and motivation. ◊

ASSESSING THE MARKET

Retirement Planning Environment

To better serve clients in the retirement planning process, advisors should be aware of the following factors that help to define the retirement planning environment as we know it today:

- graying of America
- increase in longevity
- changing nature of retirement living

Graying of America

It is estimated that over one in five Americans will be over age 60 by 2040.

The "graying of America" describes the concept of the population aging. Population aging occurs when the proportion of older people relative to younger generations increases. There are approximately 35 million people in the United States aged 65 or older. This currently accounts for about 13 percent of the total population. This older population will double to 70 million by 2030 as the baby boomers start to join this segment. It is estimated that over one in five Americans will be over age 60 by 2040.

Increase in Longevity

It is predicted that one in nine baby boomers (people born from 1946 through 1964) will live to be at least 90. In addition, the number of those 85 years old and older will quadruple by 2050. Consider the following:

- The number of centenarians worldwide is projected to increase sixteenfold by 2050, reaching 1.1 million persons. (The U.S. Census Bureau currently estimates that over 68,000 Americans are over the age of 100, compared with about 35,000 in 1990.) Moreover, life at age 100 is surprisingly healthy.

life span

- Scientists are debating what constitutes the maximum potential *life span* (the maximum potential age of human beings). Most scientists believe it is 120 years (some argue even more!).

Long life is more prevalent in women. Women account for 58 percent of those over age 65, and 70 percent of those 85 or older. In addition, the older population will become more ethnically and racially diverse as time goes by. Of those aged 65 or older now, about 84 percent are non-Hispanic whites. By 2050, that number will be 64 percent. One final important fact: As figure 1-2 illustrates, the longer a client lives, the better his or her chances are to live to a very advanced age.

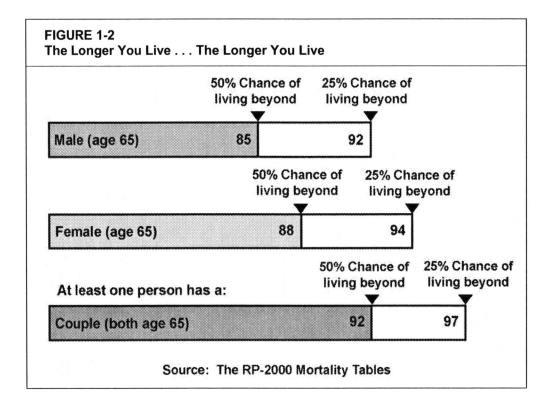

FIGURE 1-2
The Longer You Live . . . The Longer You Live

Source: The RP-2000 Mortality Tables

Changing Nature of Retirement Living

Seniors are better educated, are taking better care of themselves, and are living longer and healthier lives than previous generations. *Active life expectancy* (the number of years a person can expect to live without a disability) is increasing, as well as life expectancy (more than eight out of 10 Americans over the age of 65 are now able to take care of themselves in the routine activities of daily living, an 8.9 percent increase since 1982).

Advisors must keep in mind that the insurgence of over 78 million baby boomers into the retirement landscape promises to change the retirement picture. Totally new patterns of product and service consumption, wealth transfer, travel and leisure, and health management will emerge. Consider, historically, how boomers changed the face of education, housing, and the financial markets at different stages of their life cycle. Why should retirement be any different?

active life expectancy

Baby boomers changed the face of education, housing, and the financial markets at different stages in their life cycle. Why should retirement be any different?

Market Demographics

Demographers often divide the population into age-based segments or cohorts known as generations. Because the process is not an exact science, the dates when a generation begins and ends vary slightly from source to source.

The basis for a demographic generation is the theory that the general population's psyche and behavior are shaped by significant life experiences such as the way people are raised, national and world events, wars, the social and economic climate of the times, and so forth. Although you need to treat each prospect as an individual, generalizations alert you to the different types of attitudes you may encounter from members of each of generation so that you can recognize them quickly and react to them appropriately. Virtually all prospects for retirement planning will fall into one of the first three of the four American generations described below.

American Generations

silent generation

The Silent Generation. There are over 60 million members of the *silent generation*, the population segment born prior to 1946. The silent generation is sometimes referred to as the GI, swing, or mature generation. This generation falls into three groups: preretirees, new retirees, and long-time retirees.

Older members of this generation fought in and lived as adults during World War II. Many helped to shape the socioeconomic direction of America after the war, have been able to accumulate comfortable wealth, and may be remembered as the affluent senior generation. Younger members of this generation are called Depression era or war babies.

Generally, these people have discretionary income, and their children are grown. They often grew up as children in households with one wage earner, and they have retired or will retire as senior adults in households that have two wage earners. They tend to be

- hardworking. They equate success with hard work.
- frugal. Their parents and the Great Depression instilled frugality in them, which has translated into the unprecedented wealth that they carry into their elderly years.
- cautious. As children of the Great Depression parents, they were taught not to take risks.
- self-reliant. They want to be independent and self-reliant and do not want to trust others for their security.

As a whole, the silent generation has benefited from two decades of economic growth following World War II, large increases in Social Security benefit rates between 1968 and 1972, and the explosion in real estate and the value of housing. Members of this generation have deep concerns regarding access to quality health care and asset preservation.

Baby Boom Generation. Over 78 million people born from 1946 through 1964 will reach age 65 from 2011 through 2029. Because its size is so large, this generation can be divided in to two subgroups: older boomers (born from 1946 through 1954) and younger boomers (born from 1955 through 1964).

The members of the baby boom generation often married later, divorced more often, and had fewer children than the generations before them. Baby boomers have higher real incomes than their parents did, but as a group they are poor savers. Many are educating their children and taking care of aging parents. Because of this dual role, they are sometimes referred to as the sandwiched generation. They are

Baby boomers have higher real incomes than their parents did, but as a group they are poor savers.

- spenders. Although baby boomers have more money than preceding generations in their middle years, they tend to spend it. It is not that they do not save at all but that they save less percentage-wise.
- inheritors. It is predicted that baby boomers will be collecting over $9 trillion in inheritances between 1990 and 2030.
- image conscious. Cosmetic surgery, designer clothing, and luxury cars exemplify their passion for image.
- youth oriented. Health, fitness, and laser eye surgery illustrate boomers' desire to remain young forever.

Baby boomers will enter retirement with money saved from their working years and inheritances. They face increasing health care costs, uncertainties about the Social Security system, and fewer adequately funded pension or retirement plans to sufficiently meet their income needs.

generation X

Generation X. Born from 1965 through 1985, members of *generation X* are the children of baby boomers or the younger members of the silent generation. There are about 68 million of them. Sometimes referred to as the baby bust generation, they are

- risk takers. They are ambitious, and entrepreneurial opportunities appeal to them.
- self-oriented. Xers have a "what is in it for me" viewpoint.
- practical. They want something that works; they want a plan with specific steps and a well-defined result.

Because of their self-orientation and practical nature, you can expect them to encourage their silent generation and baby boomer parents to take individual responsibility for retirement, health care, and asset-preservation planning. Also, in the future, look for them to take action regarding planning for their own retirement needs.

millennial generation

Millennial Generation. There are over 75 million people (and growing) in the *millennial generation*—individuals born between 1986 and the present. Although prospects for your retirement products and services will most likely come from the silent generation, the baby boom generation, or generation X, you can begin to have an impact on the generation that will follow. The older members of the millennial generation are now in college or graduate school, or they have begun their working careers.

These young people are the beneficiaries of an information explosion. Many of them were playing computer games by the time they entered kindergarten. They are more affluent teens than their parents were. They believe in short-term savings goals like saving to buy a car. They are consumption oriented and see retirement in the distant future. Nevertheless, they will still look to you for guidance and as an example. Like generations before them, they can learn from history. You may be able to influence them to begin the savings habit with their first jobs.

If you are a parent or grandparent, you can educate these young people about the importance of and the need to save as much as they can, as early as they can. As a financial advisor, you can stress that retirement planning is their responsibility.

Locating Prospects for Retirement Planning

Prospecting Overview

The objective of retirement planning prospecting is to find potential buyers. Reaching that goal requires that you establish organized and systematic procedures. It means following these procedures methodically, thoroughly, and regularly. It entails disciplining yourself well enough and long enough so that the procedures become habitual for you.

> **Successful prospecting is a continual process that you should integrate into all of your selling/planning and service activities.**

Successful prospecting is a continual process that you should integrate into all of your selling/planning and service activities. Being alert to prospecting opportunities at every phase of the selling/planning process will help you maintain a consistent inventory of retirement planning prospects.

To reach the most desirable prospects in the retirement planning marketplace requires the effort to learn facts, develop ideas, and acquire skills—plus a well-organized prospecting plan.

Qualified Prospects

The process of selling any insurance or financial product begins with creating a profile of the typical person who will believe in you and buy your products and services. In other words, you need to define the characteristics of a *qualified prospect.*

qualified prospect

Basically, qualified prospects are people who

- need and value your products and services
- can afford to pay for your products and services
- are insurable or financially suitable
- can be approached on a favorable basis

Let us apply this definition to create a profile of a qualified retirement planning prospect.

Need and Value Your Products and Services. Who needs retirement planning? Although people in their 50s and 60s have a greater probability of needing it than people in their 20s do, poor planning can seriously jeopardize the financial well-being of all individuals during their retirement years. Furthermore, if a person runs out of money during retirement due to inadequate wealth accumulation, he or she will most likely experience a deterioration in the quality of life during retirement.

However, no matter how logical the financial reason for buying products to enhance their retirement security, prospects must have a strong emotional reason to buy. They must value the future financial security and peace of mind that result from adequate retirement funding more than they value other competing needs and desires. In other words, does the prospect *feel* that it is worth the price he or she must pay for these financial products?

Emotional needs are not easily observable. However, there are some characteristics that may indicate that a prospect will value retirement planning advice. We suggest you compile your own list of characteristics, starting with these few examples. Look for people who

> **No matter how logical the financial reason for buying products to enhance their retirement security, prospects must have a strong emotional reason to buy.**

- are implementing a retirement plan or seriously considering one
- own other insurance products such as life, disability income, or long-term care insurance. People who own these types of insurance products demonstrate that they value the concept of risk transfer.
- work for an employer that offers contributory qualified plans such as SEPs, SIMPLE IRAs, or 403(b) plans. In general, people who work for employers who offer such plans are more familiar than the general public with the roles the plans play in retirement planning.

Can Afford to Pay for Your Products and Services. Two of the biggest obstacles to retirement planning are cost and commitment. Note that cost and value are interrelated. For example, a middle-aged couple may say that they cannot afford the financial products involved because they cost too much. You may discover, however, that they own a vacation home. What this couple is really saying is that they value a commitment to retirement funding vehicles less than they value a commitment to funding their other current needs and desires.

> **Two of the biggest obstacles to retirement planning are cost and commitment.**

If you have not done so already, identify the income and net worth ranges you will target in order to avoid affordability issues. Describe any characteristics you will look for that may indicate a prospect's ability to purchase retirement funding vehicles. For example, you might look for the prospect who

- owns a home
- owns a business
- has supplemental policies in place such as a personal articles floater policy on fine jewelry
- has high liability limits on property and casualty insurance
- owns a personal liability umbrella policy

Are Insurable or Financially Suitable

There are many people who want accumulation and investment type products and can afford to pay for them but are unsuitable for one or both of the following reasons:

- They have a greater need for asset and/or income protection products.
- The particular investment product you are marketing does not match their risk tolerance and investment objectives.

For example, if you encounter a married preretired prospect who wants to purchase a deferred annuity or mutual funds but has insufficient life or disability income insurance coverage, you may be risking financial catastrophe for that prospect or family. Many advisors would also argue that long-term care insurance should be in place before investments are purchased. Of course, these higher priority needs present an opportunity to cross-sell the asset or income coverage that is lacking.

On the other hand, you may encounter a prospect who is unsuitable for a risky investment product because he or she has a low risk tolerance and very conservative investment objectives. It would be equally unsuitable to sell a risky investment to such a prospect. The best defense against making this mistake is to use the proper risk tolerance and investment objective assessment tool as part of the fact-finding process. Fact-finding techniques will be discussed in chapter 3.

Can Be Approached on a Favorable Basis. Perhaps the most significant factor in deciding whether someone is a qualified prospect is whether you can meet with this person on a favorable basis.

In general terms, favorable basis means a situation where the advisor is perceived as appropriate (or competent) in the prospect's eyes. It is largely a matter of acceptance and usually implies a good measure of respect, trust, and confidence in the advisor's professionalism. It often evidences itself by the prospect's being at ease with the advisor. It is certainly characterized by a willingness to grant you sufficient and exclusive time to meet with the prospect in an environment that is free of distractions.

Establishing rapport with prospects is important even before your face-to-face meetings with them. For example, if you are making calls on the telephone, you need to be able to project a warm and professional image. If a good reputation precedes you in your target markets, prospects will be more responsive to your request to meet with them.

Once you have established a positive atmosphere and a comfortable working environment with mutual respect for each other's time, the stage is properly set for the initial interview.

> **Establishing rapport with prospects is important even before your face-to-face meetings with them.**

Market Identification Techniques

After determining the profile of a qualified prospect, the next step is to find groups of qualified prospects, or market segments. We will begin our discussion with age-based market segments. Age-based segments are an appropriate place to start prospecting in the retirement planning marketplace because age currently plays a more important role in marketing and selling financial products used in retirement planning than any other demographic factor.

Identifying Market Segments

market segmentation

Market segmentation is a powerful marketing strategy that allows you to customize your approach and presentations based on the common needs and characteristics of the prospects in the segmented market. We have identified four specific demographic groups as American generations, classified primarily according to age. We have also discussed some characteristics and needs that are distinctive to each of the three generations that contain most prospects for retirement planning. Each group has varying degrees of need for your products and services, and each has a different set of planning problems for which you can provide solutions.

Once we have established the common characteristics and needs of the age-based market segments, we will then look at some other useful ways to segment the retirement planning marketplace.

Age-Based Market Segments

From the definition of a qualified prospect described previously, it is easy to conclude that an effective way to segment the retirement planning market is by age. It is only reasonable to assume that you will have greater success with prospects in the age ranges where they typically appreciate the need for retirement planning, can afford to budget for it, are suited to buy the financial products that can facilitate it, and can be approached on a favorable basis. These age ranges are similar to the American generations discussed previously: under age 45 (mostly generation Xers) ages 45 to 61 (mostly baby boomers), and ages 62 and older (mostly the silent generation).

Because the average retirement age in the United States is 62 and this coincides with the age at which workers are eligible to receive early Social Security retirement benefits (although age 65 is the traditional Social Security full retirement age and this will eventually increase to age 67), we will use this age as the line that distinguishes the mid-range age group from the oldest age group. Under our methodology, the age groups are separated into three market segments:

- prospects who see retirement as a distant goal (those under age 45)
- prospects who see retirement as a more immediate concern (those aged 45 to 61)
- prospects who are enjoying retirement or semiretirement (those aged 62 and older)

Under Age 45. As mentioned earlier, prospects in the under-age-45 market segment have traditionally been much less receptive than prospects from the other two market segments to discuss retirement planning. Probably the most universal reason for this reluctance is that people in this market segment consider other needs and wants to be more immediate and important. Examples include saving for a house, buying a new car, saving for a child's education, and securing auto, homeowners, life, and disability income insurance. There is only so much income to spend.

Another reason for the lack of receptivity to retirement planning is that prospects in the under-age-45 market segment perceive it to be a need for people much closer to or actually in retirement. They may believe that they still have plenty of time to plan for retirement.

This is not to say that you should not approach prospects in this market segment. Obviously, people with the discretionary income to purchase financial products may be good prospects. Their income notwithstanding, however, you should look for prospects who

- know a friend or family member who has purchased deferred annuities, mutual funds, stocks, or other investment and savings products
- are in their 40s
- are single or divorced with no dependents
- have high liability limits on their property and casualty insurance
- own a personal liability umbrella policy
- own individual life insurance

The primary goal of retirement planning is to create a nest egg that will last. One of the greatest risks we all face is outliving our resources.

One of the major needs common to prospects in the under-age-45 market is asset protection in the context of retirement and/or estate planning. The primary goal of retirement planning is to create a nest egg that will last. One of the greatest risks we all face is outliving our resources. Prospects with whom you have actually done insurance planning to protect and conserve

---

Retirement Planning for the Under-Age-45 Market

The under-age-45 market may not be your target market, but you should take advantage of the opportunities for approaching this market. Specifically, educate prospects about the risks of waiting too long to start planning for retirement and the associated high costs. Stress to them the power of compound interest, tax deferral, and within qualified plan products, tax deductibility. The information can result in sales opportunities or at least plant the seed for them.

Example: "Mr. and Ms. Prospect, I understand that you feel that you cannot afford to save for retirement right now. However, I would like to give you some information about how certain financial products can help you when you are ready. Would you have any objection to my staying in touch with you from time to time so that when you are ready to take action, you might consider doing it with me?"
("No.")
"Great, I will contact you periodically to see if your financial situation changes, and when you feel that you are ready to start planning for retirement, we can arrange to get together and discuss how tax-favored products can fit into such a strategy. Does that seem fair enough to you?"
("Yes.")
Then put these prospects' names in your call-back file for future contacts.

---

assets make logical prospects with whom to discuss retirement. Proper planning can direct the proceeds of certain financial products to be payable at the death of its owner to a named beneficiary and can provide probate-free assets directly to the heirs of the estate owner. Therefore, it would be wise to at least discuss products such as life insurance and deferred annuities in the context of retirement and/or estate planning.

Ages 45 to 61. This market segment will be the bread-and-butter market for retirement planning for the next several years for a variety of reasons.

First, recall that the baby boomers represent a bulge in the population. Over the next several years, the baby boomer population bulge will dominate the age 45-to-61 market segment, making it the segment with the most prospects by sheer numbers alone.

Second, people in this market segment typically are at their peak income levels. Thus, prospects in the age 45-to-61 segment usually have the means to afford the necessary financial products to facilitate the accumulation and protection of wealth within the context of retirement planning. Therefore, the chances of their qualifying to buy these products and their willingness to act are much better than at the younger ages.

Third, the public generally views annuities, mutual funds, and tax-favored plans such as IRAs as retirement planning components, and ages 45 to 61 are when planning for retirement becomes a front-burner issue. Thus, prospects in this market segment generally have a greater sense of urgency about planning for their retirement than prospects in the under-age-45 market segment.

Another important need among this group is their desire to preserve independence during retirement. When people have self-reliant attitudes, they want to avoid having to depend on government welfare programs and/or their children. You will find this independent, self-reliant attitude among the middle class, especially those who have worked hard to accrue a nest egg for retirement. They are the people who have prepared for their retirement and take great pride in having done so. Again, as we have previously indicated, the purchase of financial products should be a part of any retirement planning discussion.

Individuals in the age 45-to-61 market who might make good prospects are those who

- are saving aggressively for retirement
- are skeptical about the future solvency of Social Security
- have few or no dependent children in the household (empty nesters)

> **Many people in the age 45-to-61 market are under pressure both to save for retirement and to pay for their children's postsecondary education.**

Be aware that many people in this market segment are under pressure to save both for retirement and to pay for their children's postsecondary education. In this regard, they face the same challenges as their under-age-45 counterparts. The difference is that they probably have a higher income and thus a greater ability to pay for financial products.

Age 62 and Older. Prospects in the age-62-and-older market segment generally have the same retirement planning needs as those in the age 45-to-61 market segment, except that prospects aged 62 and older are definitely more sensitive to health care issues, especially those related to Medicare and long-term care. In addition, because the majority of people in the age-62-and-older segment are no longer employed, they have a heightened fear that their monthly income and assets are not going to be sufficient to pay for everything they may want or even need. They fear that a lack of money will force them to depend on relatives, friends, or public assistance and will limit their access to quality long-term care.

Because of their age and retirement status, prospects from the age-62-and-older market are much more concerned about protecting and conserving their assets than younger prospects are. As retirees, these prospects are generally not able to add to their retirement nest egg. Consequently, they readily relate to the risks involved in protecting and outliving their assets. Therefore, as consumers, they are more inclined to purchase financial products such as fixed-interest deferred annuities, immediate annuities, and long-term care insurance.

Targeting a Market

target market

If you can find a market segment that has a communication or network system, then you have a *target market*. The communication system can be formal, such as a newsletter or regular meeting, or it can be informal, such as word-of-mouth within a tightly knit ethnic community. Either way, the communication system or network provides the means by which your reputation as a professional advisor can precede you. In other words, before you personally meet with any prospects in a target market, they will know about your abilities as a financial advisor.

Targeting Markets for Retirement Planning

An extension of age-based target marketing is targeting people in a specific but narrow age range who are also members of an association, service organization, or club. The ideal situation occurs when the majority of the membership is in the chosen age range. For example, if an advisor wants to target preretired prospects aged 45 to 61, he or she may consider targeting a service organization (such as the Rotary, Jaycees, Kiwanis, and so forth) or club (such as a VFW, Elks, or a country club) that has a large membership of people in the desired age range. Besides age range and membership, other common characteristics of the prospect group, such as income range, could help to establish a new target market. If you use this method to target a market, you will need to develop a list of desirable characteristics that you want prospects to possess to guide you in establishing the new target market.

For many advisors, retirement planning is just one of several financial services they perform, so they position the marketing of financial products in a manner consistent with their target market's view of them as advisors. If an advisor's target market is preretired teachers in a large city school district, for instance, he or she will want to position annuities and mutual funds, especially within a 403(b) plan, as part of a strategy for accumulating the teacher's retirement nest egg, and life insurance as a vehicle for safeguarding it.

Target markets enable you to focus on the unique needs of your prospects. Focusing will not only enhance your reputation within the target market as an expert in retirement planning products and services, but it will also allow you to better understand your prospects' needs. With this knowledge, you will soon discover the efficiencies of tailoring a marketing strategy for a large number of prospects with common characteristics and needs.

> Target markets enable you to focus on the unique needs of your prospects.

Prospecting Sources

Once you determine the types of prospects you seek for retirement planning, the next step is to employ useful sources for finding them.

There are many different prospecting sources. We will provide a brief overview of some of the more popular ones that successful advisors have used to locate prospects for retirement planning.

Existing Clients

Most of your existing clients who are in their late 50s and 60s are good candidates for retirement planning. Senior clients who are about to retire or have been retired for a while are good potential clients for products that serve as retirement fund distribution vehicles. If these people are your clients, you already have a professional relationship with them, so it stands to reason that most will be receptive to working with you to further explore their planning needs as they move toward or into their retirement.

Almost every outstanding advisor has a systematic procedure for contacting existing clients to find out if anything in their financial situation has changed, to follow up on previously discussed cross-selling opportunities, or to identify additional needs. Turn these periodic reviews into opportunities to explore retirement planning issues for clients who are still working—update the facts on their current retirement plans, do an analysis, and offer appropriate financial products if they address a need you uncover.

Referrals from Clients/Prospects

It is advisable to pave the way for referrals early in the retirement selling/planning process, preferably during the initial meeting with the prospect. Create the expectation of receiving referrals if the prospect appreciates what you do for him or her. Then, when you ask for referrals, it will not surprise the prospect.

Example: "Mr. and Ms. Prospect, as we work together, if you find what we are talking about to be important and valuable, then give me the opportunity to meet with people you know and care about so that I may help them, too."

The best time to ask is when the prospect indicates an appreciation for you and/or your retirement planning expertise. The prospect's appreciation could be as simple as saying, "I'm so glad you showed me that. I always thought paying taxes on my Social Security retirement benefits was unavoidable." Obviously, if prospects purchase a financial product from you, they have demonstrated an appreciation for the product. Even if prospects do not buy anything, however, inquire about what they found valuable in the retirement planning process. If they have a favorable opinion of you and the process, ask for referrals.

Example: "Ms. Prospect, I know you have decided that you do not need any financial products at this time. May I ask what, if anything, in this process you found to be of value?"
(Wait for a response.)

"That's great. I'm glad I could help you clarify some of the income and health care issues of retirement planning. May I ask who you know who might also benefit from this type of advice?"

Of course, if your prospects have parents who may be in the market for asset preservation products such as long-term care insurance, or who may benefit from owning annuities to either defer their taxes or guarantee a lifetime income, you can specifically ask for their names.

As always, remember to follow up on referrals by providing an update to the referrer to let him or her know how the meeting went.

Satisfied clients can also be an excellent, yet often overlooked, source of referrals. Be sure to put a system in place to regularly ask existing clients for the names of individuals who may be interested in retirement planning.

> **Be sure to put a system in place to regularly ask existing clients for the names of individuals who may be interested in retirement planning.**

Centers of Influence (COIs)

center of influence

By definition, a *center of influence* is an influential person who knows you, has a favorable opinion of you, and agrees to introduce or recommend you to others. A client may become an effective center for you, just as a center may become a client, but this is not necessary to the relationship you need to establish. In general, you will find that COIs are

- active in a community or sphere of influence
- sought out for advice by those within their sphere of influence
- good communicators
- givers, not takers

Good COIs know the people in your target markets, regardless of their occupation or profession. However, some occupations and professions deal directly with your target markets, and finding COIs in these occupations and professions could prove very profitable. Examples include the following:

- elder law attorneys
- CPAs
- fee-based financial advisors
- advisors who sell noncompeting lines of financial products (for example, a property and casualty advisor)
- health care providers
- clergy
- members of a volunteer organization

Also keep in mind that sometimes your best COI is simply a friend or close relative who comes into contact with a lot of people on a regular basis and is personally interested in helping you to succeed in the financial services business.

Once you have identified some possible COIs, you will need to set up meetings with them. Your meeting with a COI is as important as a sales appointment. Therefore, plan your presentation. Keep it brief and consistent with your approach. For example, if you are meeting with a community leader, the goal of your presentation is to show the COI just how he or she can help others by referring them to you. Your approach to accomplish this objective may include the following steps:

- Share the impact that poor retirement planning will have on people who need it and on society in general.
- Illustrate the impact with any personal stories.
- Demonstrate how some financial products can help prevent inadequate retirement planning by providing tax-deferred cash accumulation and guaranteed income.
- Give the COI some practical actions that he or she can take to help.

You will probably want to ask the COI for names of qualified prospects. If so, have a brief written description of how to identify qualified prospects. Although referrals are important, you may find other ways the COI can help you. For example, if the COI is a leader for a senior community service organization, you can approach him or her about doing an educational presentation for the rest of the organization. Be creative.

Networking

networking

Networking is the process of continual communication and sharing ideas and prospects with others whose work does not compete with yours. In turn, their clients might also be shared with you and become your clients.

Most networking groups have the same general rules. Membership is limited to one person from each type of sales background, whether insurance, real estate, mortgage brokerage, or some other sales profession. Each person who attends the meeting is required to bring a prescribed number of names.

Example: The real estate agent member of your networking group just sold a house located in an over-age-55 community that she represents exclusively. She gives you the name of the buyer as a prospect who may be interested in retirement planning. On the other hand, your client may have expressed a desire to live in an independent-living or retirement community and thus would be a good prospect to share with the real estate agent.

If you can find an existing networking group in your community, it might be worthwhile to investigate joining it to provide you with a steady stream of prospects.

Worksite Marketing

Almost every advisor hopes to find a method of prospecting that puts him or her in front of groups of people. Worksite marketing can accomplish this objective.

According to a LIMRA report, *Worksite Marketing of Voluntary Payroll Deduction Products*, over 5 million U.S. firms have fewer than 100 employees. According to government studies, much of future business growth will be in the small business area.

More than half of those interviewed in the LIMRA study said that they preferred purchasing financial products at the worksite. This response reflects a population of workers who lead complex lives and may not want to spend their time away from work meeting with you.

Worksite Marketing and Retirement Planning. You may be asking yourself what worksite marketing has to do with retirement planning. Although it may not be obvious, your activities in the worksite marketplace and your retirement planning activities may actually complement each other.

Retirement planning is long-range planning. To meet long-term goals, you must help your prospects address needs that could keep them from achieving these goals. For example, disability or premature death can destroy the best plans for retirement unless your prospects have a contingency plan. Life and disability income insurance products provide the necessary contingency plans to preserve financial security for individuals (and their beneficiaries) who become disabled or die prematurely.

Worksite marketing gives you access to prospects. Many of these prospects are not currently planning for retirement. By letting them know that you provide this service, you have an opportunity to build long-term client-advisor relationships.

Finally, the workplace is becoming a product distribution center. To this extent, you have the opportunity to market products that will enhance employees' retirement plans. For example, a tax-deferred annuity is an excellent investment vehicle and is often sold in the workplace.

> Although it may be obvious, your activities in the worksite marketplace and your retirement planning activities may actually complement each other.

Seminars[1]

Seminars are a popular prospecting method for retirement planning because they appeal to the demographic age groups most interested in issues related to successful retirement planning: preretirees aged 45 to 61 and retirees aged 62 and over. Some advisors have found that seminars are an extremely effective way to prospect, especially in the seniors market.

Seminars enable advisors to accomplish two key objectives. First, seminars are a means to present financial products in the context of retirement planning to several prospects at one time, resulting in less time needed to conduct one-on-one interviews. Second, seminars cast the advisor as the expert, especially if the advisor plays a significant role in the presentation.

Seminars are not only a source of prospects but also a method for prospecting and marketing financial products. Many successful advisors in the retirement planning marketplace use seminars as their main prospecting tool.

In addition, seminars offer some following advantages:

- Seminars enable you to maximize your time. They are an opportunity to educate and motivate many prospects at once. Consider seminars to be a group version of the first appointment.

- Seminars create a nonthreatening environment in which you can build rapport and credibility with prospects. What other prospecting method allows you to demonstrate your knowledge of the financial problems prospects face and the solutions that you can provide?

- Seminars help you identify qualified prospects. If you use a questionnaire or feedback form, you can pinpoint whom you should call first. In addition, answers to questions can give you insight into prospects' concerns, needs, and questions before you meet them for follow-up appointments.

- To some extent, seminars prequalify prospects. Although you initiate the seminar by inviting the prospects, they confirm their interest by attending and constitute a much better prospect pool than a cold-call list. If you can bring together the right people, ask the right probing questions, offer the right solutions, and present yourself as the professional source for a specialized area of expertise—retirement planning—your seminar will be tremendously successful.

> **If you can bring together the right people, ask the right questions, offer the right solutions, and present yourself as the professional source for retirement planning, your seminar will be successful.**

Lists

Many experienced advisors use this prospecting tool with excellent results. Advisors who have had success with lists note that the key is to select lists that contain prospects who would likely have an interest in retirement planning. For example, a list of American Association of Retired Persons members would certainly contain people who are aged 50 or older. Some financial services companies provide lists to their advisors through market segmentation programs; check with your company to see if one is available. Otherwise, you will want to buy a list from a reputable list vendor.

Prospecting Sources

- Existing clients
- Referrals from clients/prospects
- Centers of influence
- Networking
- Worksite marketing
- Seminars
- Lists

When dealing with a vendor, exercise caution. Here are some points to keep in mind:

- Select lists that reflect your target markets.
- Check to see how recently the data were collected.
- Make sure that the list has current phone numbers.
- Verify the source of the leads.
- Make sure that the list has been "scrubbed." This means that any "do not call" and undeliverable names have been eliminated.
- Check to see if duplicate entries or incomplete names have been deleted.

One final thought on lists: Keep good records so you can evaluate the quality of the leads and compare different vendors until you find the one that gives you the best return on your investment. ◊

CONCLUSION

There is a tremendous opportunity for financial advisors to have a positive impact on millions of Americans' retirement security by using the strategies and techniques presented in this book. Based on the critical issues that affect retirement planning discussed in this chapter, the need for retirement planning is unmistakable. Because of the increased longevity of the American population in general, and the baby boom generation in particular, the retirement planning marketplace will continue to grow steadily over the next 20 to 25 years.

Now that you have a basic overview of the retirement planning landscape, in the next chapter we will examine the major sources of retirement income, the time value of money, and how personal financial statements are helpful to you in the retirement planning process. ◊

CHAPTER ONE REVIEW

Key Terms and Concepts are explained in the Glossary. Answers to the Review Questions and Self-Test Questions are found in the back of the book in the Answers to Questions section.

Key Terms and Concepts

savings phase	life span
rollover	active life expectancy
increased preparation and visualization phase	silent generation
	generation X
decision phase	millennial generation
retirement transition and lifestyle phase	qualified prospect
	market segmentation
frailty phase	target market
baby boom generation	center of influence
holistic retirement planning	networking

Review Questions

1-1. List the steps in the retirement planning process from the advisor's perspective.

1-2. Identify and briefly describe the five phases of retirement planning from the client's perspective.

1-3. Discuss the factors that influence retirement age.

1-4. List eight common roadblocks to retirement planning.

1-5. Explain the importance of the holistic approach to retirement planning.

1-6. Discuss why the retired population is increasing.

1-7. Identify the distinct characteristics of the following American generations:
a. silent generation
b. baby boom generation
c. generation X
d. millennial generation

1-8. Identify the four criteria that define a qualified prospect.

1-9. List the three age-based market segments into which most retirement prospects fall, and briefly describe each segment's retirement planning needs.

1-10. Identify seven popular sources of retirement planning prospects.

Self-Test Questions

Instructions: Read chapter 1 first, then answer the following questions to test your knowledge. There are 10 questions; circle the correct answer, then check your answers with the answer key in the back of the book.

1-1.   Which of the following best describes when the savings phase of retirement planning should begin?

    (A)   upon the client's reaching age 21
    (B)   at the beginning of the client's career
    (C)   when the client purchases his or her first home
    (D)   after the client has his or her first child

1-2.   Which of the following American generations can be described as risk takers, self-oriented, and practical?

    (A)   silent generation
    (B)   baby boom generation
    (C)   generation X
    (D)   millennial generation

1-3.   The marketing strategy that allows the advisor to customize his or her approach and presentations based on the common needs and characteristics of prospects in a particular market is known as which of the following?

    (A)   market penetration
    (B)   market segmentation
    (C)   market share
    (D)   market promotion

1-4.   Which of the following definitions of networking as it relates to the retirement selling/planning process is correct?

    (A)   Networking is the broadcasting of retirement planning infomercials on television and radio.
    (B)   Networking is the competitive relationship among financial advisors who are vying for retirement planning prospects on an ongoing basis.
    (C)   Networking is the continual communication and sharing of ideas and prospects with others whose work does not compete with the financial advisor's.
    (D)   Networking is the obtaining of a steady stream of referrals from clients for whom the advisor has conducted retirement planning.

1-5.   Financial needs during retirement are met by three primary sources. Which of the following is (are) among those three?

    I.   Social Security benefits
    II. Inheritances

    (A) I only
    (B) II only
    (C) Both I and II
    (D) Neither I nor II

1-6.   Which of the following statements concerning active life expectancy is (are) correct?

    I.   Active life expectancy is the number of years a person can anticipate living without a disability.
    II. Although life expectancy is increasing, active life expectancy is actually decreasing.

    (A) I only
    (B) II only
    (C) Both I and II
    (D) Neither I nor II

1-7.   Which of the following statements concerning the age-62-and-older market is (are) correct?

    I.   Now that prospects in the age-62-and-older market are near or in retirement, they have become less concerned about health care issues.
    II. Prospects in this market worry less than younger prospects that their monthly income and assets will be sufficient to cover their needs.

    (A) I only
    (B) II only
    (C) Both I and II
    (D) Neither I nor II

1-8.   All the following are steps in the selling/planning process EXCEPT:

    (A)   Analyze the information.
    (B)   Implement the plan.
    (C)   Ask for referrals.
    (D)   Meet with the prospect.

1-9.   All the following statements regarding the changing face of retirement are correct EXCEPT:

   (A)   Current workers expect to work longer than current retirees did before they retired.
   (B)   Current workers are most likely to say that personal savings will be their most important source of retirement income.
   (C)   The trend toward retirees who work is unlikely to continue.
   (D)   Retirees are increasingly responsible for caring for their parents and children.

1-10.   All the following are advantages of seminars as a prospecting source EXCEPT:

   (A)   They eliminate the need for follow-up appointments.
   (B)   They enable the advisor to reach several prospects at one time.
   (C)   They help the advisor identify qualified prospects.
   (D)   They spotlight the advisor as the expert in a specialized area.

NOTE

1.   For a comprehensive discussion regarding the planning and presentation of seminars, see Richard A. Dulisse, *Foundations of Senior Planning*. Bryn Mawr, PA: The American College Press, © 2004, chapter 3.

2

Retirement Income Sources and Calculations

Chapter Outline

SOURCES OF RETIREMENT INCOME

When we think about retirement income, most of us feel that it will come from one or more of the following sources:

- Social Security
- pensions
- savings

Of course, there are other sources of retirement income. For example, any one of us can win the lottery or inherit a large sum of money. But we cannot plan with any certainty if we rely on chance or the timing of some event.

Some financial advisors use the analogy of a three-legged stool when they speak of retirement income because they feel that approximately one-third of retirement income should come from each of three traditional sources above. This analogy has been a simple and useful starting point for retirement planning.

The majority of your prospects and clients will continue to rely on some combination of Social Security, pensions, and savings to fund their retirements for some time to come. However, the assumption that one-third of retirement income will come from each of the traditional sources may no longer apply.

According to a study by the Social Security Administration (see table 2-1), the four main sources of income for those aged 65 and older are

- Social Security, which makes up 38 percent of their income
- retirement plan benefits, which makes up 21 percent of the aggregate income
- asset income, which comprises 15 percent of income
- earnings from wages, which constitutes 23 percent of income

A small percentage of aggregate income comes from other sources.

TABLE 2-1
Income Sources for People Aged 65 and Over

	Percentage of Aggregate Income	Percentage Receiving Income from Each Source
Social Security	38%	90%
Retirement plans	21	41
Asset income	15	55
Earnings	23	22
Other*	3	10

* Other sources include veterans' benefits, unemployment compensation, workers' compensation, and public assistance.

Source: Income of the Population 55 and Older, 2004, Social Security Administration, March 2005.

Many preretirees are less than optimistic about the future. Many believe that Social Security benefits will be delayed, cut, and fully taxed. Some have failed to make maximum use of their company-sponsored pension plans. And few have saved enough money. As a matter of fact, the median annual income for retirees aged 65 and older in 2004 was $24,509.[1] That figure was virtually unchanged from the 2003 median income level. That means that half of all retirees had incomes above $24,509, and half had incomes below this figure. By comparison, real median household income for all households in 2004 was $44,389.

Rather than looking forward to comfort and leisure in retirement, many people are concerned that they will outlive their resources. They realize that there is a huge gap between what they need and expect in retirement income and what they will actually receive. You need only examine the current status of each of the traditional sources of retirement income to understand these concerns.

> Rather than looking forward to comfort and leisure in retirement, many people are concerned that they will outlive their resources.

Social Security

Almost everyone has a retirement plan—Social Security. Traditionally, for more than 70 years, even people who reached retirement age with no financial assets could generally rely on Social Security. For most Americans, Social Security is the largest single source of retirement income. For low-income families, it may be the only source (see table 2-2). Yet it was never intended to be the sole retirement funding mechanism. Rather, it is and has been intended as the retirement safety net.

TABLE 2-2
Shares of Aggregate Income, by Quintiles of Total Income, 2004 (Printed March 2005)

Source	Lowest	Second	Third	Fourth	Fifth
Social Security	82.6%	84.0%	67.0%	47.0%	19.9%
Retirement plans*	3.5	6.8	15.0	25.5	20.5
Asset income	2.4	3.6	7.4	9.8	18.9
Earnings	1.1	2.3	7.0	14.7	38.4
Public assistance	8.9	1.6	1.0	**	**
Other	1.5	1.7	2.7	2.9	2.4

Percentages may not equal 100 due to rounding.
* Includes private pensions and annuities, government employee pensions, Railroad Retirement, and IRS Keogh and 401(k) payments.
** Less than 0.5%
Source: Income of the Population 55 and Older, 2004, Social Security Administration, March 2005.

Although 38 percent of the aggregate income of individuals aged 65 and older comes from Social Security, actual reliance on Social Security is highly dependent on income. As you can see in table 2-2, if you divide those 65 and over into quintiles of income, those in the lowest quintile receive 82.6 percent of their income from Social Security, while those in the highest quintile receive only 19.9 percent from Social Security. Those in the highest quintile depend as much or more on retirement plans, asset income, and earnings as they do on Social Security.

Social Security was once strictly a pay-as-you-go system. The year's benefits were paid out of taxes collected from workers for that year. Over the years, more was collected in taxes each year than was paid to retirees in benefits. The balance was placed in the Social Security Trust Fund to be invested in Treasury bonds—safe but low-yielding government debt instruments.

> **Any suggestion that the government raise taxes to make up the entire Social Security shortfall fails to recognize the magnitude of the problem.**

The future of the current Social Security program of contributions and payments, however, is the subject of ongoing public policy debate. Any suggestion that the government raise taxes to make up the entire shortfall fails to recognize the magnitude of the problem. Increased longevity and the size of the aging baby boom generation, combined with lower fertility rates for generations that follow, will strain the solvency of the Social Security system. The Social Security board of trustees expects the number of people aged 65 and older, which was 12 percent in 2005, to increase to nearly 21 percent in 2040, and to be 23 percent of the population by 2075. The ratio of workers to beneficiaries will decrease from 3.3-to-1 in 2005 to 2.1-to-1 in 2031. Social Security faces cash deficits in 2017 when payments are projected to be larger than revenue. The Social Security Trust Fund is projected to be exhausted in 2041, absent reform; projected tax revenue would cover 74 percent of projected benefits beyond 2041.

There are proposals under consideration to ensure Social Security's financial viability. Proposed changes in the investment of the fund's assets include investing some or the entire fund in equities (rather than Treasury bonds) or allowing individuals to privately manage a portion of their own contributions.

Medicare is also expected to face cash deficits beginning in the near future. The Medicare Trustees 2005 Annual Report states that Medicare's Hospital Insurance Trust Fund is projected to be exhausted in about the year 2020 absent major reforms in the program. The need for programmatic reform is under serious consideration.

As advisors, we should approach the topic of Social Security objectively. It is likely that Social Security will change. It is equally likely that Social Security will be part of your prospects' and clients' retirement income. Perhaps the approach your prospects and clients can take is to understand the role of Social Security and its potential benefits but to plan and save so that they do not have to rely on it.

Pensions

Pension and retirement plans are the second leg of the retirement planning stool. Although Social Security is the mainstay of most people's retirement income, retirement plan benefits make up 21 percent of the aggregate income. Retirement plans include private and public pensions, 401(k) plans, IRAs, and Keoghs.

Although coverage rates in employment-based plans have not changed much, remaining at about 50 percent over the last 30 years for full-time workers in the private sector, what has changed dramatically is the type of plans that employers are offering. According to a recent survey from the U.S. Bureau of Labor Statistics, during the 1990s alone, the number of workers participating in employer-sponsored defined-benefit plans decreased by 9 percent of the total workforce, while simultaneously the number of workers participating in defined-contribution plans increased by 9 percent. In many cases, employers make retirement plans available but do not contribute to the plans.

There are several important differences between these two types of plans, as indicated in table 2-3. The bottom line is that it is up to the participants in defined-contribution plans to make sure their retirement benefits are adequate, usually by contributing to the plan and often by making investment decisions. In defined-benefit plans, the plan sponsor funds the benefit and is responsible for making sure that the promised retirement benefit will be there when the participant retires.

> Although coverage rates in employment-based plans have not changed much, the type of plans that employers are offering has changed dramatically.

TABLE 2-3
Comparison of Defined-Benefit and Defined-Contribution Plans

Defined-Benefit Plans	Defined-Contribution Plans
Participation usually automatic	Participation often voluntary
Fixed benefit related to pay and/or service or to flat dollar amount	Fixed or variable contribution related to pay or other variable, or to flat dollar amount
Definitely determinable benefits: benefit formula stated in plan	Benefits not definitely determinable: contribution formula stated in plan but benefits dependent on performance of plan assets
Plan sponsor assumes investment risk and reward	Participant assumes investment risk and reward
Flexible funding: turnover, mortality, expected earnings, forfeitures, etc., determine employer contributions	Fully funded: contributions, forfeitures, gain/losses reflected in account balance
Typical distribution: annuity at retirement	Typical distribution: lump sum or annuity at retirement, separation, death, or disability

According to a study by the Pension and Welfare Benefits Administration of the Department of Labor, the number of defined-contribution plans and their participants from the years 1978 to 1998 increased dramatically as a percentage of the total employer-sponsored retirement plans. For example, in 1978, defined-contribution plans constituted 71 percent of all retirement plans; as of 2000, they were 93 percent of all plans. In 1978, defined-contribution plans covered one-third of total plan participants; they now cover 60 percent of total participants. For approximately one-half of all workers with retirement plans, a defined-contribution plan is their only plan.

> Risk and responsibility for retirement income from employment-based plans have shifted from the employers to the employees.

The implications of these statistics are significant: Risk and responsibility for retirement income from employment-based retirement plans have shifted from the employers to the employees.

This may be difficult for some prospects. Some employees have never been covered by employer-sponsored plans. Many others have not taken full advantage of them. It may be too late for some of your prospects to save enough to meet their retirement expectations.

Savings

It is likely that most of your prospects are going to need more money for retirement than they are currently saving. There is little evidence that Americans are saving enough to preserve their preretirement lifestyles in retirement. The retirement income replacement ratio (which is an individual's gross income after retirement divided by his or her gross income before retirement) runs from 75 percent to 89 percent, depending on income and family situation, according to a 2004 study by Aon Consulting and Georgia State University. Preretirement workers—individuals aged 50 to 65—saved at a rate of 2.1 percent or less of preretirement income in 2004. Those in the higher preretirment income ranges ($90,000 to $100,000) saved at a higher level (2.1 percent) than those in the lower income ranges ($20,000 to $60,000), which was less than 1 percent of gross preretirement income.

According to the Committee for Economic Development, all kinds of savings have decreased over the decades. Savings now average less than 2 percent of gross domestic product, down from 4 percent in the 1990s and 8 percent in previous decades. Our nation's prosperity depends on a high rate of savings to provide investment funds for growth. According to the Bureau of Economic Analysis, however, in the aggregate, personal savings as a percentage of disposable personal income fell to 1.8 percent in the year 2004. Misperceptions about retirement and investments may be contributing to the low saving rates. Common mistakes include overestimating investment returns and consequently overwithdrawing funds in retirement, underestimating the needed income to preserve an active lifestyle, expecting too much from Social Security, depending on an inheritance or a spouse's pension, and underestimating longevity.

> **The average American retires with enough total resources to provide only 60 percent of his or her former annual income.**

Those who are saving may not be saving effectively. According to the Congressional Research Service, the median value (half of all families have more and half have less) of retirement savings for workers in America aged 55 to 64 in 2004 was $55,000. The average American retires with enough total resources to provide only 60 percent of his or her former annual income. The problem is more acute for minorities and women. Unfortunately, many retirees may have to rely on their most valuable financial asset, which is the equity in their home, to make up the needed retirement income shortfall.

Many Americans use traditional savings accounts as the primary means of savings for retirement, although investing in mutual funds and 401(k)s is increasing, as evidenced by the increase in workers' participation in 401(k) plans from 44 percent to 55 percent during the 1990s. Individuals who are planning for retirement may have significant resources invested in nonqualified vehicles like cash savings accounts, mutual funds, stocks, and bonds.

These nonqualified investments provide retirees with significant flexibility because the investments have already been taxed. Their sale or surrender may, however, create some negative consequences. Some investments, like certificates of deposits (CDs), have penalties for early surrender. Mutual funds that have appreciated in value may be subject to capital gains taxes. The short-term capital gains reported and taxed annually on these funds are on only the internal transactions, not the appreciated value of the fund shares themselves. Depending on the fluctuation of current interest rates, bonds may be less marketable than desired. Stocks that have appreciated in value are also subject to capital gains tax when sold.

Stocks can be especially problematic. Consider the following example.

Example: An employee worked for a major blue chip company for 35 years before he retired. Every month, he participated in the company's stock purchase plan. Over 35 years, he purchased 1,000 shares of stock for a total investment of $45,000. During that same period, with the continued steady success of the company, he benefited from seven separate stock splits, bringing the number of shares he owns to 12,500. The current value of the stock is $84 a share, for a total value of $1,050,000.

This may not seem like much of a problem, but look at what happens if he decides to liquidate his stock. His basis is only $3.60 per share—his total investment of $45,000 divided by the 12,500 shares he owns. His taxable gain on each share sold is $80.40. Of the $1,050,000 he will realize on the sale, $1,005,000 is taxable as a capital gain.

Earnings

As noted in the Social Security Administration study cited above, 23 percent of the aggregate income of individuals 65 and older comes from earnings—18 percent of that from wages and 5 percent from self-employment. The three-legged stool for funding retirement has given way. The demographic phenomenon of the 21st century: Retirees are working!

bridge job

phased retirement

People are not simply employed one day and retired the next. They are making the transition to retirement through a *bridge job* (a full- or part-time job that involves little responsibility after retiring from a career and before totally ceasing to work) or *phased retirement* (a reduction in hours and commitments rather then a complete removal from the work force). A recent American Association of Retired Persons (AARP) survey confirmed that most baby boomers (80 percent) plan to work at least part-time in retirement.

Future retirees are more likely to work for several economic reasons, including the following:

- The earnings test for Social Security benefits at or beyond full retirement age (FRA) as defined by the Social Security Administration has been eliminated. When a person reaches the age for full Social Security benefits, benefits are no longer reduced because of earnings. Previously, there was a $1 reduction in Social Security benefits for every $2 earned. These changes will encourage people to work after reaching their full Social Security retirement age.
- People are living longer. A woman who retires today at age 65 can expect to live at least 19 more years; a 65-year-old man can expect to live 16 more years. If people continue to retire early and live longer, they have many more years in retirement to fund.
- There is an increased concern about health care coverage, along with an erosion in employment-based retiree health care coverage. Thus, people are likely to continue to work in some capacity to remain covered or to pay for health care coverage.
- Finally, the eligibility age for unreduced Social Security benefits is gradually increasing from 65 to 67 for those who retire in 2003 through 2027 and beyond. (We will discuss this in more detail later in this chapter.)

Seniors continue to work for a variety of noneconomic reasons as well, including the following:

- They enjoy work.
- They feel successful at work.
- They see work as a source of status.
- They need to spend physical and mental energy in a meaningful way.

- They find recreational pursuits unsatisfactory.
- They want to avoid social isolation.
- They want money to buy extras.

Whether a person works or does not work during retirement should be a decision of personal preference, not one of financial necessity. The assistance you provide to your clients today in dealing with the complexities and challenges of comprehensive retirement planning can produce immeasurable qualitative lifestyle enhancements for them tomorrow.

The Advisor's Role

Your prospects are likely to need more money for retirement than they are saving. Moreover, they must evaluate and plan for things that can go wrong in the years ahead.. If retirement were their only goal, planning might be easier. But your prospects may also need to fund college costs for children or care for long-lived parents. Prospects are also facing medical and long-term care costs that are increasing at much higher rates than inflation in general. These issues are discussed in greater detail in chapter 4.

Planning has to occur at all levels. While policymakers are working to restructure Social Security and pensions, your prospects should be taking responsibility for themselves. They should be planning for their futures and saving more. Retirement security is primarily the culmination of a series of personal decisions (or nondecisions) over the course of an individual's lifetime. The most effective retirement savings education will make it clear to people that they hold retirement security in their own hands, and it will motivate them to develop and live by their own personal retirement savings strategy.

You can play a vital role if you understand your market and the issues. As noted in the final report from the 1998 National Summit on Retirement Savings, "We must do a better job of educating the public—employers and individuals alike—about the importance of saving and about the tools available to ensure that we can afford to retire and remain financially independent."

The is a valuable message, and it may help you encourage your prospects and clients to initiate the planning process. Your goal is to build long-term relationships with your clients. You want to be the advisor who plans, reviews, and updates with them.

Example: In approaching prospects about retirement planning, you might say something like "Mr./Ms. Prospect, have you started to plan a strategy for funding your retirement?" or "Are you saving enough money to control the decision to retire when you want and to enjoy the lifestyle that you desire?" ◊

SOCIAL SECURITY: AN OVERVIEW

One of the first steps in any fact finding interview is to determine what coverage is already in place. Most advisors understand that this means asking about group benefits and personally owned policies. But many advisors fail to help their prospects consider the benefits provided by Social Security. Ignoring them, however, can be detrimental to the selling/planning process.

It is safe to say that most people do not fully understand the benefits they have through the Social Security program. Most are aware that it provides benefits at retirement, but many do not know how much to expect or how to estimate what they will receive. Fewer understand survivor benefits or realize that these benefits provide for a surviving spouse only if there are dependent children or if the spouse has reached retirement age. An even smaller number understand the disability coverage offered under Social Security or what it takes to qualify for these benefits.

> **It is safe to say that most people do not fully understand the benefits they have through the Social Security program.**

History of Social Security

The economic depression that was preceded by the stock market crash of 1929 was the longest and most devastating this country has known. It destroyed countless families, stripping them of their possessions, their jobs, and their hopes. The scope and force of its destruction demanded new safeguards against a repetition of the economic evils that caused the disaster. One of the new measures adopted was the Social Security system.

Social Security is an economic welfare plan paid for by both workers and their employers by taxes on income. Its purpose is to help support people when they retire or become disabled and to assist dependents of workers who die before retirement age. Because the objectives of Social Security are similar to those of financial products, such as life and health insurance and savings and investment products, financial advisors should coordinate Social Security benefits with these products in retirement planning with prospects.

Common Misconception about Social Security

> **Some people are under the impression that Social Security alone will meet their protection and retirement needs. In most cases, this will not be true.**

Since the advent of Social Security, people have become increasingly concerned about retirement. Some people still expect Social Security to be a sufficient source of funds on which to live. They fail to consider how they are going to manage their financial affairs when their earnings stop. Some people are under the impression that Social Security alone will meet their protection and retirement needs. In most cases, this will not be true.

Practically speaking, the best hope for people who have not begun to plan for their own retirement is that they will have the good fortune to meet a qualified, properly trained financial advisor who will show them the actual function of Social Security. The message is not new. President Franklin

Roosevelt clearly stated it when Social Security was inaugurated in 1935. President Dwight Eisenhower restated it in 1954 in an address to Congress:

> The Social Security system is not intended as a substitute for private savings, pension plans, and insurance protection. It is rather intended as a foundation upon which those other forms of protection can be soundly built.
>
> Thus the individual's work, his planning and his thrift will bring him a higher standard of living upon his retirement—or his family a higher standard of living in the event of his death—than would otherwise be the case. . . . Hence the system both encourages self-reliance and thrift, and helps to prevent destitution in our national life.

The message is no less valid today. The increases in benefits have changed nothing as far as the purpose of Social Security is concerned. Social Security is a foundation to planning. Augmented benefits are justified by the erosion of buying power, not by the intent of our Congress to provide for all the needs of all people.

Who Is Covered?

Generally speaking, most employees in the private sector, including federal employees hired after 1984 and members of the armed services, are covered by Social Security. The definition of employees is extended to include those who otherwise might be considered to be self-employed, including full-time financial advisors and other classifications of salespeople. Officers of corporations and S corporations are also considered to be employees for Social Security tax purposes.

Since 1951, most self-employed people are included under Social Security. Sole proprietors and partners in a partnership are covered, and the list has been expanded periodically so that it now includes architects, engineers, accountants, dentists, lawyers, medical practitioners, and, most recently, ministers and members of religious orders. In short, almost everyone who is working today is covered by Social Security.

In terms of benefits, there is no difference between employees and people who are self-employed. The difference is in how Social Security taxes—known as FICA, for the Federal Insurance Contributions Act—are paid. For employees, the tax is shared equally by the employer (the amount paid by the employer) and the employee (the amount withheld from the employee's pay). Self-employed workers are responsible for the entire amount. However, self-employed sole proprietors and general partners are permitted an adjustment to income on federal income tax Form 1040 that is equal to 50 percent of their Social Security self-employment tax liability.

In terms of benefits, there is no difference between employees and people who are self-employed.

Only income that is earned as wages is taxable by the Social Security Act. Interest earned on savings or income from investments or capital gains is not income for Social Security tax purposes. Furthermore, not all income is taxable. In any given year, there is a cap on the maximum amount of earnings taxed that is indexed to keep pace with inflation; because benefits are based on contributions, this creates an upper limit on the level of benefits available. ◊

SOCIAL SECURITY BENEFITS

OASDI

The Social Security system provides survivor benefits for the living family members of deceased covered workers; disability benefits for those who are too disabled to work and for their family members, if applicable; and retirement benefits for retired covered workers, their spouses, and minor children, if applicable. The Social Security Administration also administers the Medicare program, which provides medical care to eligible participants. Taken together, these programs constitute the old-age, survivors, disability, and health insurance (OASDHI) program of the federal government. This program is often separated into two broad parts. The first part is the old-age, survivors, and disability insurance (*OASDI*) program. Over the years, OASDI has become commonly referred to as Social Security, and this is the terminology that will be used in this book. The remainder of the OASDHI program is called Medicare.

Eligibility for Benefits

Before looking at specific benefits, it is important to understand who is covered. As mentioned, almost all workers fall under the Social Security system. This does not mean that a worker is automatically eligible for benefits. To be eligible for benefits, an individual must met certain qualifications, based on the amount of time he or she has participated in the system.

There are two categories of qualification under the Social Security system. A person becomes insured by meeting minimum earning requirements under the system for a certain number of calendar quarters, now referred to as credits. A calendar quarter is a 3-month period ending on the last day of March, June, September, and December of each year. The amount that must be earned during the quarter to have it included changes from year to year. In 1980, for example, it was $290. In 2006, it is $970.

To be eligible for Social Security benefits, a person must be either fully insured or currently insured. To be fully insured, a person must have worked for enough quarters in a job or jobs covered by Social Security benefits to meet either of two tests:

fully insured

- A person is *fully insured* if he or she has a total of 40 quarters, or 10 years, in covered work. The work does not have to be in consecutive quarters, and once 40 quarters have been accumulated, the person is fully insured for life.

- If a person has not worked for 40 quarters in covered employment, he or she can still be fully insured if he or she has at least
  - 6 quarters of coverage and
  - one credit for each calendar year after 1950, or has at least as many quarters as the number of years between the year he or she reached age 21 and the year of the disability

currently insured

To be *currently insured*, a person must have earned at least 6 credits (worked for at least 6 quarters) in covered employment during the last 13 quarters prior to his or her death, eligibility for disability benefits, or eligibility for retirement.

maximum taxable wage base

Benefits are based on the covered person's earnings record for earnings reported to Social Security, up to the annual maximum amount reportable. This *maximum taxable wage base* is indexed for inflation each year, and Social Security taxes (FICA) are not charged against amounts higher than the wage base. In 1980, the wage base was $25,900. In 2006, it is $94,200.

primary insurance amount (PIA)

The actual dollar amount of Social Security payments depends on the earnings credited to the worker and the wages earned over his or her covered working years. Benefit levels are subject to legislative change. The amount of benefits a person will receive is currently based on his or her *primary insurance amount (PIA),* which is calculated based on his or her average indexed monthly earnings (AIME). The PIA is the amount paid at Social Security's FRA (full retirement age). To calculate the PIA, individuals must know their AIME, which is based on their earnings history.

The calculation is complicated. Nevertheless, you should be prepared to help your prospects and clients approximate the benefits they can expect from Social Security if they die, become disabled, or retire. Every covered worker now receives an annual statement from the Social Security Administration within a few months of his or her birthday. Various companies, such as Dearborn Financial Services, publish annually updated "Pocket Tables" that include estimates of the three types of Social Security benefits (survivor, disability, and retirement) based on selected amounts of the current year's

TABLE 2-4 **Social Security Benefits Eligibility**			
Insured Status of Beneficiary	**Survivor Benefits Eligibility**	**Disability Benefits Eligibility**	**Retirement Benefits Eligibility**
Fully insured Currently insured	Yes (all) Yes (some)	Yes No	Yes No

income. These estimates are essential if your prospects are to coordinate their Social Security benefits with their private investments, life and disability income insurance, and annuities.

Survivor Benefits

Social Security provides benefits to the survivors of covered workers who meet certain requirements. Available benefits include a lump-sum payment at death, payments to surviving children, payments to a surviving spouse who is caring for dependent children, payments to dependent parents, and payments to an older surviving spouse.

Lump Sum

The surviving spouse or dependent children of a deceased covered worker may receive a lump-sum payment of $255 at the worker's death.

Dependent Children

Children under age 18, or under age 19 if they are still in elementary school or high school, and children over age 18 if they became disabled before age 22 are eligible for benefits if a covered parent dies. College students over age 18 are not eligible. The amount of the benefit is 75 percent of the deceased worker's PIA. These benefits are available if the worker was either fully or currently insured.

Dependent Parents

A dependent parent of a covered worker who is aged 62 or older may qualify for benefits if he or she was receiving at least one-half of his or her support from the deceased worker at the time of the covered worker's death. The benefit is 82.5 percent of the covered worker's PIA for one parent or 75 percent each for both parents, if applicable.

Surviving Spouse with Dependent Children

When a covered worker dies, the surviving spouse, regardless of age, receives benefits if he or she is providing care for a dependent child under age 16 or for a child who became disabled before age 22. These benefits are available if the worker was either fully or currently insured. They end when there are no longer eligible children in the household. For example, the surviving spouse benefit ends when the last child reaches age 16, although the benefits for the child continue until he or she reaches age 18.

Family Maximum

The benefits for a surviving spouse and children are limited. They are subject to a family maximum, which is a cap on the total amount that the surviving spouse and all eligible children can receive.

Blackout Period

Benefits for a surviving spouse who is caring for dependent children end when he or she is no longer responsible for the eligible surviving children. When there are no eligible children, all benefits end until the surviving spouse qualifies for widow(er) benefits. This period of time is referred to as the blackout period.

Surviving Spouse

The surviving spouse of a fully covered worker is eligible for benefits when he or she reaches age 60. If the surviving spouse is disabled, he or she may be eligible for benefits beginning at age 50. These benefits continue until the survivor becomes eligible for full retirement benefits.

Divorced Spouse

If the covered worker has been divorced, his or her former spouse can receive survivor benefits under the same circumstances as the widow(er) if their marriage lasted 10 years or more. The former spouse, however, does not have to meet the length-of-marriage rule if he or she is caring for the covered worker's child who is under 16 or disabled and who is also receiving benefits on the covered worker's Social Security record. The child must be the former spouse's natural or legally adopted child. Benefits paid to a surviving divorced spouse who is aged 60 or older (50 if disabled) will not affect the benefit rates for other survivors who are receiving benefits.

The surviving divorced spouse is also entitled to a survivor's retirement benefit if he or she was married to the covered worker for 10 years and did not remarry before attaining age 60. If the former spouse remarries before age 60, these benefits are not payable unless (and until) the subsequent marriage ends. Remarriage after age 60 does not stop entitlement to these benefits.

Survivor Benefits Statement

The hypothetical statement in figure 2-1 indicates that "total family benefits cannot be more than" the family maximum benefit of $2,164. All benefits paid under the client's earnings record are coordinated so that they do not exceed this amount.

FIGURE 2-1
Sample Survivors Section of Social Security Statement

You have earned enough credits for your family to receive the following benefits if you die this year.

Total family benefits cannot be more than . . .	$2,164 a month
Your child . . .	$ 884 a month
Your spouse who is caring for your child . . .	$ 884 a month
Your spouse who reaches full retirement age . . .	$1,179 a month

---

The child's benefit is fairly straightforward. The child's benefit of $884 shown on the statement is the maximum amount any one child can receive.

In addition, a surviving spouse may be eligible to receive benefits under either the "mother's or father's benefit" or the "widow(er)'s benefit." The "mother's or father's benefit" is available only when the surviving spouse is not entitled to the "widow(er)'s benefit" and is caring for at least one of the deceased worker's children who is under age 16 and receiving the "child's benefit." The maximum amount is the same $884 as that for the "child's benefit."

The widow(er)'s benefit may also be available to the surviving spouse (with or without children) as a retirement benefit at age 60, or at age 50 if he or she is disabled. The Social Security benefits statement lists the amount available when the widow(er) reaches full retirement age, $1,179 as shown in figure 2-1. The widow(er) would receive a percentage of this amount if benefits are received before full retirement. For example, at age 60, the widow(er) would be eligible to receive 71.5 percent of the full retirement benefit amount listed on the statement, which is $843.

Social Security's many caveats and exceptions can be complex. For example, a divorce can result in survivor benefits being paid to both a current and a former spouse. Understanding the nuances of Social Security will allow you to better analyze prospects' and clients' financial situations and demonstrate the necessity to supplement the benefits Social Security provides. It also will show that you have answers to questions and solutions to problems that are important to your client.

Understanding the nuances of Social Security will allow you to better analyze prospects' and clients' financial situations and demonstrate the necessity to supplement the benefits Social Security provides.

Disability Benefits

Many people assume that Social Security will take care of them and their families if they become disabled. To help your prospects and clients plan adequately for their financial needs in case of a long-term disability, it is important that you understand the role Social Security will play.

In general, a person must meet are the following requirements to qualify for Social Security disability benefits: The individual must

- be insured for disability benefits
- be under age 65
- be disabled for 12 months or expected to be disabled for at least 12 months, or have a disability that is expected to result in death
- be so severely impaired physically or mentally that he or she cannot perform any substantial gainful work
- have applied for disability benefits
- have completed a 5-month waiting period

disability insured

To qualify for disability benefits, a worker must be *disability insured*. At a minimum, a disability insured status requires that a worker

- be fully insured
- have a minimum amount of work under Social Security within a recent time period. Workers aged 31 or older must have earned at least 20 credits during the 40 calendar quarters ending with the quarter in which disability occurs. If the disability begins before age 31, separate rules apply. Blind persons are exempt from the recent-work rules and are considered disability insured as long as they are fully insured.

Unlike other forms of disability coverage, Social Security disability benefits may also be received by members of the disabled person's family. In addition to paying benefits to a disabled worker, Social Security may pay benefits to a disabled person's

- children who are under age 18 or under age 19 if attending elementary or high school full-time
- unmarried son or daughter aged 18 or older if he or she has a disability that started before age 22
- spouse who is aged 62 or older
- spouse at any age if he or she is caring for the disabled person's child who is under age 16 or disabled and also receiving benefits
- ex-spouse, if qualified

Benefits for a Divorced Spouse

To qualify for disability benefits, a covered worker's ex-spouse must have been married to the covered worker for at least 10 years, be at least 62 years old, be unmarried, and not be eligible for an equal or higher benefit on his or her own Social Security record or on someone else's Social Security record. Note that the amount of benefits payable to a divorced spouse has no effect on the amount of benefits that either the covered worker or the covered worker's current spouse may receive.

Total Disability

total disability

Total disability is defined by Social Security as the inability to engage in any substantial gainful activity because of a medically determinable physical or mental condition.

The Social Security Administration maintains a list of impairments that are severe enough to mean that a person is totally disabled. If a person's condition is not on the list, the case is determined individually. If, because of the severity of the condition, the person cannot do any kind of work, the claim is approved. This "any occupation" definition of disability is very restrictive and makes it difficult for many people to qualify for benefits.

Social Security disability benefits may be affected if the worker is eligible for workers' compensation or for other federal, state, or local benefit programs, civil service benefits, or military disability payments. Generally, the total payments received from Social Security and any of these other programs cannot exceed 80 percent of the person's average current earnings before becoming disabled.

> Social Security does not take into consideration benefits paid under privately owned or group long-term disability income insurance programs.

Social Security does not take into consideration benefits paid under privately owned or group long-term disability income insurance programs. Most group policies, however, do have an offset provision that reduces their benefits by the amount of any Social Security payments received. This has the effect of drastically reducing the overall benefits received by a disabled person who has a social insurance offset provision in his or her group long-term disability policy. It points out the need for personally owned disability income insurance.

Retirement Benefits

The original purpose of Social Security was to provide retirement benefits for workers. Later, retirement benefits for spouses were added. Today, retirement benefits may be paid to

- a retired covered worker
- the spouse of a covered worker
- the dependent child of a covered worker

To be eligible for any of these benefits, the covered worker must be fully insured.

Covered Worker

A covered worker is entitled to a monthly benefit equal to his or her PIA at full retirement age, which previous to 2003 was 65 and will increase slowly until the year 2027. At that time, the FRA for Social Security purposes will be 67. Reduced benefits are available for those who elect to retire before FRA (see table 2-5).

TABLE 2-5
Social Security Full Retirement and Reductions by Age*

Year of Birth**	Full Retirement Age	Age 62 Reduction Months	Total Percentage Reduction
1937 or earlier	65	36	20.00
1938	65 and 2 months	38	20.83
1939	65 and 4 months	40	21.67
1940	65 and 6 months	42	22.50
1941	65 and 8 months	44	23.33
1942	65 and 10 months	46	24.17
1943–1954	66	48	25.00
1955	66 and 2 months	50	25.84
1956	66 and 4 months	52	26.66
1957	66 and 6 months	54	27.50
1958	66 and 8 months	56	28.33
1959	66 and 10 months	58	29.17
1960 and later	67	60	30.00

Note: An individual can also retire at any time between age 62 and full retirement age. However, if the worker starts at one of these early ages, his or her benefits are reduced by a fraction of a percent for each month before full retirement age.

An important point: There are disadvantages and advantages to taking benefits before full retirement age. The advantage is that the worker collects benefits for a longer period of time. The disadvantage is that benefits are permanently reduced.

* Percentages of monthly and total reductions are approximate due to rounding. The actual reductions are .555 or 5/9 of 1 percent per month for the first 36 months and .416 or 5/12 of 1 percent for subsequent months.

** Persons born on January 1 of any year should refer to the previous year.

Spouse Benefits

The spouse of an eligible covered worker is entitled to benefits beginning at age 62 or earlier if caring for a child who is also entitled to benefits. The nonworking spouse is eligible for an amount up to 50 percent of the covered spouse's PIA, assuming they both retire at their full retirement age. If both spouses have worked throughout their lives, the spouse whose PIA generates the smaller benefit is entitled to the higher of 50 percent of his or her covered spouse's PIA or the benefit generated by his or her own work history.

Example: Dan and Kathy, a married couple, both retire at their full retirement age. Dan's PIA is $1,400 per month when he retires. If Kathy had never worked, she would be entitled to $700 per month, or 50 percent of Dan's PIA at her FRA.

However, suppose that because of Kathy's work history, her own PIA is $1,000. This is more than $700 (one-half of Dan's PIA of $1,400), so she is entitled only to her own retirement benefit and not her spouse's benefit.

Benefits for Divorced Spouse

A divorced spouse can receive benefits on a former husband's or wife's Social Security record if the marriage lasted at least 10 years. The divorced spouse must be 62 or older and unmarried. If the spouse has been divorced at least 2 years, he or she can receive benefits even if the worker is not retired. However, the worker must have enough credits to qualify for benefits and be aged 62 or older. The amount of benefits a divorced spouse receives has no effect on a current spouse's amount of benefits.

Children's Benefits

Dependent children of an eligible worker are entitled to benefits. The definition of a dependent child is the same as the one used for survivor benefits.

Impact of Social Security on Retirement Planning

Today, there is a great deal of uncertainty about the future of Social Security. Growing demands placed on the system by an increasing number of recipients, combined with the spiraling cost of increased benefits, have made many question whether Social Security as we know it can continue to play a significant role in financial planning. Many believe that it will not survive to provide even minimal benefits for today's workers. Discussions are underway to determine ways to ensure its viability. These discussions include shifting the investment responsibility from the government to individuals and giving each worker at least some control over how his or her contributions are invested. Even as these or other changes are made, the prudent financial advisor will assume that the average Social Security benefit will not be enough to provide a satisfactory standard of living.

The prudent financial advisor will assume that the average Social Security benefit will not be enough to provide a satisfactory standard of living.

The changing landscape of Social Security gives you the opportunity to meet with your clients to review its impact on their existing plans. Likewise, any change gives you a reason to contact new prospects who might be affected.

When Social Security was first introduced, there was alarm in both insurance and investment circles. Advisors were apprehensive that potential clients would no longer feel the need to provide for their own retirements. Since Social Security's inception, however, many financial advisors have found that it is a highly effective sales aid when put into the proper perspective.

The government believes that retirement planning is vital. The government's position can be used to convince prospects that it is worthwhile for them to listen to someone who can help them with their planning. Those who listen to knowledgeable, capable advisors—and act accordingly—are the people who will escape the trap of assuming that Social Security will take care of everything when their paychecks end.

Your aim is to help your prospects see the need for income dollars to supplement Social Security. A professional presentation that combines life insurance, disability income coverage, annuities, mutual funds, and other investments can show the prospect how to meet these needs. ◊

OTHER SOURCES OF RETIREMENT INCOME

Social Security and employer-provided retirement plans make up two parts of the major retirement resources that most people have. The third major component is the income provided by the amount of money that retirees have saved and accumulated during their working years. As mentioned previously, the fourth major component in recent years has become earnings. In addition, retirement income funds can also come from a number of sources such as the following:

- capitalizing home equity in the retiree's principal residence by
  - a reverse mortgage
  - sale of the principal residence
- liquidating a business ownership interest
- inheritances
- other forms of support

Capitalizing Home Equity in the Retiree's Principal Residence

For many retired homeowners, the equity in their homes represents the single largest asset they own. These retirees might want to consider strategies such as downsizing to free up cash or using a reverse mortgage. Selling a principal residence and moving to a less expensive residence can capture the equity that they have built up.

Often, a retiree uses this strategy in conjunction with a plan to relocate at retirement. Many retirees choose to move when they retire, seeking warm climates and lower tax rates. The proliferation of retirement communities in places like Florida and Arizona attests to this phenomenon.

Some relocation decisions are based on state income tax considerations, but such decisions should be made with care. States with low income tax rates or no income taxes may have high sales and personal property taxes. They may also have high gift and inheritance taxes that ultimately will more than offset the income tax savings.

Reverse Mortgage

Today's seniors have benefited from the housing market appreciation over the years. Reverse mortgages are a special type of housing loan that allows homeowners over age 61 to convert this equity into cash. This increases cash flow for the senior homeowner to pay for home health or nursing home care, or for whatever else he or she wishes. Payments from a reverse mortgage can be in the form of a single lump sum, regular monthly advances, a line of credit, or a combination of these. There are no payments by the homeowner or any obligation to make repayments as long as he or she lives in the home. Note that the homeowner still retains all homeowner responsibilities, such as real estate and property taxes and maintenance.

Drawing on the equity of a home enables an individual to continue to live in his or her primary residence while using the value of the asset. Furthermore, the monies received from this arrangement are generally not subject to federal income tax.

On the other hand, using the home in this way reduces the possibility of the person's heirs inheriting the house free and clear. Should they decide to retain it, they would have to repay the loan via a traditional mortgage.

Selling a Principal Residence

The ability to exclude $500,000 of gain can make selling their family home an attractive way for a married couple to capture equity for retirement.

There is an income tax break that can make selling the family home and relocating to a less expensive one an extremely attractive way to capture home equity for retirement purposes. Taxpayers may exclude up to $250,000—$500,000 for married couples filing jointly—of gain realized on the sale or exchange of a principal residence. To fully quality for this exclusion, taxpayers must have owned and occupied the home as a principal residence for 2 of the 5 years prior to the sale or exchange.

Liquidating a Business Ownership Interest

Sole proprietors, partnership partners, and owners of small closely held corporations may be counting on the value of their business to help secure their retirement years. Depending on the value of a business to provide retirement income poses at least two problems.

The first, and by far the more serious, is finding a buyer who is willing to pay full value for the business. All too often, a small business is closely tied to the energy, skill, and personal initiative of its owner. Although this assures success while the owner is involved, losing the value of the owner may make the business less marketable.

Planning for the disposition of business interests at retirement is every bit as important as planning for a business transfer caused by death or disability. One alternative is to arrange an installment sale. This can help a qualified buyer make the purchase, while creating an income stream for the retiring owner. If a qualified buyer cannot be found or if the owner wants to continue ownership while retired, he or she may be able to employ others to manage and operate the business, still realizing part of the income.

If a successful sale is made, the business owner faces the second problem—capital gains tax. The profits realized on his or her investment in the business may be subject to the capital gains tax.

Inheritances

For some clients, inheritances will add to their financial security in retirement. According to AARP, only 15 percent of baby boomers expect to receive any future inheritances. The median value of inheritances that boomers have already received is $47,900; less than 2 percent received over $100,000.

It is important to know that the bulk of wealth is concentrated in the hands of the wealthiest 10 percent of the population. It is also important to know that parents are living longer and spending down accumulated assets, or they have annuitized their wealth so that second-generation inheritances are less likely. This does not mean that clients will not receive an inheritance from their parents. It does mean, however, they should not count on inheritances as a financial planning tool.

> Parents are living longer, spending down accumulated assets, or annuitizing their wealth, so that second-generation inheritances are less likely.

Other Forms of Support

There are a variety of other sources of retirement income, as follows:

- life insurance. Receiving life insurance proceeds from a deceased spouse or cashing out a permanent life insurance policy may help to provide retirement security for some individuals. In addition, under the "pension maximization" technique (discussed in chapter 7), life insurance may be used as a substitute for a joint and survivor annuity.
- rental property. Some clients may receive rental income from real estate property they own.
- Supplemental Security Income (SSI). SSI is a benefit program administered by the Social Security Administration that pays monthly income to clients who are 65 or older, blind, or disabled. An individual client who qualifies for the full benefit in 2006 can receive over $600 per month; a couple can receive over $900 per month. In addition, state supplements may increase these amounts, depending on the client's state of residence.

    In a recent year, almost 4 percent of the population aged 65 and older received an average of $4,200 in SSI. Benefits are need based. To qualify, an individual must have limited resources and income (as well as meet other criteria). Assets are limited to $2,000 ($3,000 per couple), but they do not include the home, car, household goods, and other items. The amount of income your client can have each month and still receive SSI depends partly on where the client lives.

The Advisor's Role

Planning for a successful retirement requires making appropriate decisions before and during retirement. The first step in effective decision making is analyzing needs and evaluating options that will meet the needs. You can help your clients at retirement just as you would during the years they were saving and planning for retirement.

As we will discuss in chapter 3, a thorough fact finding interview will help you learn how much income your prospect will need during retirement and how long it must last. During the fact finding interview, you can assess risk tolerance and review risk management strategies. Your review should include determining if adequate life insurance is in force. Without a firm foundation on which to stand, any retirement plan could be rendered useless.

> **Without a firm foundation on which to stand, any retirement plan could be rendered useless.**

During the fact finding interview, you should also determine what your prospects want to pass on to their heirs. Retirement planning naturally leads to estate planning. Assets not consumed during retirement may be left to heirs.

Many of the choices that individuals face at retirement are confusing. This is where you can be of service. By explaining their options, you can help your prospects and clients make informed decisions. But your role may go beyond this. Integrating and timing the distribution of assets at retirement requires an understanding of your prospects' retirement goals as well as the resources available to them. Asset distribution strategies during retirement will be discussed further in chapters 7 and 8. ◊

TIME-VALUE-OF-MONEY BASICS[2]

> **The key to successful long-term planning is time.**

People need to invest their money to accomplish their long-term goals. But the key to successful long-term planning is time. Over time, your prospects can accumulate large sums of money. If you understand the relationship between time and money, you will be in a better position to help your prospects develop the appropriate planning strategies.

time value of money (TVM)

The differences in the value of money over time, due to interest rates either received or paid, relate to the *time value of money (TVM)*. The time value of money is based on the concept that a dollar received today is worth more than a dollar received in the future.

Compound Interest

**simple interest
compound interest**

There are two ways to compute interest. *Simple interest* is computed by applying an interest rate to only the original principal sum. *Compound interest* is computed by applying an interest rate to the sum of the original principal and the interest credited to it in previous periods. In other words, interest compounds as earnings from principal are reinvested, which then generates earnings on its own. Thus, a small sum of money can grow to a substantial amount when interest is compounded, given enough time.

Some words of caution regarding the consequence of compounding: Depending on the type of financial vehicle in which your client's money resides, compound interest can lead to compound taxation. This can frustrate your client and have an erosive effect on your client's attempts to reach his or her retirement planning objectives. You need to be aware of the tax consequences of any recommendations that you make in your professional practice. Chapter 4 will examine income tax rates and tax planning concepts. Chapter 5 will discuss the four different ways that investments can be taxed. For now, however, as we discuss the mathematics of savings and the estimation of future investment values, we will ignore the significance of taxes and concentrate on understanding the basic principles of time and its effect on money.

You can use the mathematics of compound interest to project the impact of time on money—that is, you can calculate the future value of savings. With slightly more complex calculations, you can figure how much your prospects must save for retirement, or you can estimate their living costs over the period of years they expect to be retired.

> **Time is a powerful ally. The more years prospects can allow to work for them, the more likely they are to reach their retirement goals.**

Time is a powerful ally. The more years prospects can allow to work for them, the more likely they are to reach their retirement goals. When interest is being compounded, time makes all the difference.

Estimating the Future Value of Investments

The ability to determine how much money a person will have at the end of a given time period as the result of an investment made today is often important in the retirement planning process. Although some investments do not promise to pay interest at a given rate or at a regular interval, other instruments do make such promises.

Common stocks are an example of the first group of investments, and the calculation of their future value is difficult because of their volatility. CDs are an example of the second group. Their interest rate is known in advance, and determining their future value is considerably easier.

Future Value

compounding

The process by which a dollar today, a present value, grows over time to a larger amount, a future value, is called *compounding*. An increased compound interest rate will increase the future value of a present sum of money, as will an increase in the amount of time during which the money will grow. Decreases in compound interest rates and amount of time will decrease the future value of a present sum of money.

Sometimes very simple and graphic concepts are extremely effective in the approach stage of selling/planning process. Perhaps the most commonly used guide for preliminary wealth accumulation planning is the Rule of 72.

Rule of 72

The Rule of 72. The number 72 can be used as a basis for calculating the approximate number of years that it will take an invested dollar to double in value. To calculate the number of years it will take a dollar to double, divide 72 by the expected annual interest rate. For example, at 8 percent interest, a dollar will double in 9 years (72 ÷ 8 = 9).

To calculate the interest rate required for an investment to double, divide 72 by the number of years the investment is held. Thus, 72 divided by 10 years equals 7.2 percent interest. Therefore, a dollar will double in value if it is invested for 10 years at 7.2 percent.

Although the Rule of 72 is often used for quick estimates, more accurate calculations are usually needed.

Calculating Future Value of a Single Sum

future value of a single sum (FVSS)

The most frequently encountered and easiest to understand application of the time-value-of-money concept involves the *future value of a single sum (FVSS)*. As explained earlier, determining the future value of a sum of money requires compounding, or increasing, the present value at some interest rate for a specified number of years.

The future value of an investment, such as a certificate of deposit, has these two components:

- principal that will be returned at the end of the specified time
- interest that will be earned over the investment period

Future value of a single sum is determined by the following formula:

Future value of a single sum (FVSS) = Initial investment + Interest earned

---

Example 1:   Assume that your client invests $5,000 in a certificate of deposit issued by the local bank. The CD has a maturity of 1 year and an interest rate of 6 percent. What will the value of this investment be exactly one year from today?

FVSS   =   Initial investment + Interest earned
       = $5,000 + (6.0% x $5,000)
       = $5,000 + $300
       = $5,300

A more common method of computing future value is to factor out the $5,000 as shown below. The compound interest rate, 1.060, is found in table A-1, titled "One Dollar Principal," in appendix A:

$$\begin{aligned} \text{FVSS} &= \$5,000 \text{ x } (1 + 6.0\%) \\ &= \$5,000 \text{ x } 1.060 \\ &= \$5,300 \end{aligned}$$

The first method illustrates how future value of a single sum can be segmented into principal and interest; the second method is generally used in actual practice because it can be more easily adjusted to handle more complex problems.

The formula used in Example 1 above works for investments that mature in 1 year, but it is inadequate for longer periods or for investments that experience fluctuations in their rate of return. At maturity, the CD may be exchanged for cash. Alternatively, the investor may decide to reinvest the proceeds by purchasing another CD. Interest rates on CDs typically fluctuate, and the interest rate offered on the new certificate may differ from that offered on the initial investment.

This reinvestment issue presents difficulties for the investor who wished to determine the exact future value of investing in CDs over a long period of time. We can, however, make certain assumptions about future interest rates and thus estimate future value.

Example 2:   Assume that your client invests $5,000 in a CD issued by a bank. The CD matures in 1 year and has a 6 percent interest rate. Assume further that your client plans to continually reinvest in 1-year CDs for a total of 3 years. What will the future value of the investment be at the end of the 3 years?

The correct answer, of course, is that you don't know because the interest rates offered on the CD in the second and third years are unknown. Let's assume, however, that the interest rates in the second and third years will also be 6 percent.

Given this information, we can calculate the return separately for each of the 3 years involved. You will remember from Example 1 that your client will receive $5,300 on a 1-year investment of $5,000 at 6 percent. If the client reinvests this $5,300 for a second year at 6 percent, you can calculate its value at the end of the second year as follows:

$$\begin{aligned} \text{FVSS} &= \$5,300 \text{ x } 1.060 \\ \text{FVSS} &= \$5,618 \end{aligned}$$

The client's $5,000 investment has grown to $5,618 at the end of the second year. If your client reinvests this $5,618 for a third year at 6 percent, the calculation will be

FVSS = $5,618 x 1.060
FVSS = $5,995

Notice the compounding of interest that occurs in Example 2. The interest earned in the second and third years results not only from the original $5,000 investment but also from the interest accrued to date.

Calculating the future value of a single sum year by year becomes burdensome as the number of years increases. An easier way to compute future value is to use the following formula:

FVSS = $I(1 + i)^n$

where   FVSS =   future value of a single sum
       I   =   amount of the initial investment
       i   =   annual interest rate
       n   =   number of years or compounding periods of the investment

This calculation can be performed manually, or you can use a financial calculator, which is programmed with this formula. Simply enter an initial investment amount (often called PV for present value), an interest rate, and the appropriate number of years or compounding periods (called "n"). The calculator then displays the correct future value.

Semiannually, Quarterly, and Daily Compounding

So far, our examples have assumed that interest is paid only once a year, but semiannual, quarterly, and daily compounding are common in actual practice. The key to determining future value for investments that promise semiannual, quarterly, or daily compounding is to segment each year into shorter periods for which interest is to be paid.

Example: If an investment carries an interest rate of 6 percent per year compounded semiannually, the interest rate every 6 months is 3 percent. We must next determine the total number of compounding periods in the duration of the investment. For a 3-year investment, there are six compounding periods. The calculation is

FV = $5,000 $(1 + 3.00\%)^6$
   = $5,000 (1.194)
   = $5,970

By contrast, if the $5,000 were compounded annually at the same rate at 6 percent, the sum after 3 years would be

$$
\begin{aligned}
\text{FV} &= \$5,000 \ (1 + 6.00\%)^3 \\
&= \$5,000 \ (1.191) \\
&= \$5,955
\end{aligned}
$$

Note that when interest is compounded annually, the sum is $15 less than when it is compounded semiannually. Although these calculations can be performed manually, manual calculations quickly become cumbersome and difficult. The use of a business or financial calculator or applicable computer software is highly recommended.

Future Value of Periodic Deposits

Prudent investors often develop a habit of periodically depositing a set amount of money into a savings account or other investment vehicle. For example, your client may wish to deposit $5,000 per year into an investment at the beginning of each year for 5 years, earning 6 percent interest. This scenario describes a future value of periodic deposits (FVPD) problem. Periodic deposits are a series of equal payments made at the beginning of each year (or period) for a specified number of years (or periods).

The formula to calculate the future value of periodic deposits is as follows:

$$
\text{FVPD} = \text{I (FVif)}
$$

where FVPD = future value of periodic deposits
           I   = amount invested each period
          FVif = future value interest factor for the periodic investment (see table A-2, "One Dollar per Annum in Advance," in appendix A)

Example: Assume that your client begins today to deposit $5,000 each year for the next 3 years at an annual interest rate of 6 percent. How much will he have at the end of 3 years?

The factor from the compound interest table (table A-2) for a 6 percent interest rate and a 3-year investment horizon is 3.375. Thus, the future value of the deposits in this example is

Logic dictates that
the higher the interest
rate and the longer
the time horizon, the
higher the future
value will be.

FVPD   = $5,000 x 3.375
       = $16,875

Logic dictates that the higher the interest rate and the longer the time horizon, the higher the future value will be.

Present Value

So far we have discussed compounding—that is, accumulating a known single sum of money at a compound annual interest rate over a specified number of years to determine a future value. Now, rather than moving forward in time and compounding, we will move back in time by discounting a future value to a present value. The process by which a dollar due in the future, a future value, is reduced over time to a smaller amount today, a present value, is called *discounting*. We will use an interest or discount rate to calculate the *present value of a single sum (PVSS)*.

discounting

present value of a
    single sum (PVSS)

Present Value of a Single Sum

Another common question that often arises in retirement planning: How much does a client need to invest today over a period of time to accomplish certain financial objectives or future values?

Example: Your prospect's goal is to have $10,000 at the end of 5 years. How much principal does she have to set aside today at 7 percent interest to accomplish this?

You can make the calculation by using an inverse variation of the compound interest formula $FVSS = I (1 + i)^n$, where future value of a single sum is found by multiplying a current investment amount by 1 plus a specified interest rate over time, and present value is found by *dividing* the targeted future value of a single sum by the future value objective ($10,000) by 1 plus a specified interest rate over time:

PVSS   = $FVSS \div (1 + i)^n$
PVSS   = $\$10,000 \div (1 + .07)^5$
PVSS   = $10,000 \div (1.403)$
       = $7,128

Or the formula can be expressed as

$$PVSS = FVSS \times \left[\frac{1}{(1 + i)^n}\right]$$

where   PVSS   =   present value of a single sum

FVSS   =   future value of a single sum

i   =   compound annual interest or discount rate expressed as a decimal

n   =   number of years over which discounting occurs

$$\frac{1}{(1 + i)^n} = \text{PVSS factor}$$

Because the term $\left[\dfrac{1}{(1 + i)^n}\right]$ in the PVSS formula is the PVSS factor, the PVSS formula can be simplified and written as follows:

PVSS = FVSS x PVSS factor

Thus, you can also make the calculation using the compound discount table titled "One Dollar Principal" (table A-3) in appendix A. The factor for 7 percent for 5 years (.713). In our example this is

PVSS = $10,000 (.713) = $7,130

Note: The difference between the answers of $2.00 ($7,128 versus $7,130) is due to the rounding of numbers within the two tables.

A more difficult problem, and one that is much more common in retirement planning, is determining how much to invest each year or each month to accomplish long-range retirement income objectives. Fortunately, this calculation can also be made using a variation of the formulas we have already studied and the factors from the compound interest tables.

Remember that we calculated a future value of periodic investments using the "One Dollar Per Annum in Advance" table and the formula FVSS = I (FVif). This assumed that we knew how much we wanted to invest each year (I) and needed to calculate what its value would be in the future. This time, we know how much we want to have, but we need to calculate how much to invest to get there.

Example: Your prospect determines that she wants to have $100,000 for retirement in 15 years. She believes she can maintain a steady 7 percent rate of return. How much does she need to save each year?

To determine the amount she needs save each year, you can use division in the formula, drawing the interest factor (if) from the "One Dollar Per Annum in Advance" compound interest table:

$$\begin{aligned}
\text{Annual saving required} &= \text{FVSS} \div \text{FVif} \\
&= \$100{,}000 \div 26.888 \\
&= \$3{,}719
\end{aligned}$$

Thus, your prospect needs to invest $3,719 now and each year to accumulate $100,000 at the end of the 15-year period.

Present Value of Periodic Payments

> Retirees want to know how much money they need to accumulate to generate retirement income and how long a specific sum will last, once accumulated.

Previously, we discussed how to calculate the present value of a single sum that is due or needed at some time in the future. Now we will discuss how to compute the present value of a series of level future payments. This is a present value problem if the payments are made at the beginning of each year.

Retirees want to know how long a specific sum of money will last them, once accumulated. The answers can be found using the factors from the compound discount table titled "One Dollar per Annum" (table A-4) in appendix A.

Example: Suppose your 65-year-old client wants to know how much $200,000 will provide him each year over 20 years during retirement. He feels he can earn 6 percent interest on this money, and he will receive the payments at the end of each year.

To determine the answer, you can use the factors from the compound discount table titled "One Dollar per Annum" (table A-4) in appendix A. In this example, you are trying to solve for the income that a present value ($200,000) will generate over 20 years. You can calculate the answer by dividing the lump-sum present value by the appropriate present value of periodic payments (PVPP) factor that corresponds to the 6 percent interest column and the 20th year.

The formula and calculation are as follows:

$$\begin{aligned}
\text{Annual income} &= \text{PV} \div \text{PVPP factor} \\
&= \$200{,}000 \div 11.470 \\
&= \$17{,}437
\end{aligned}$$

Thus, your client will receive $17,437 at the end of each year for 20 years, but he will have exhausted the present value of $200,000 at the end of 20 years.

Using the Right Tools

The present and future value calculations discussed in this chapter can be done manually; it is useful to have a conceptual working knowledge of how the numbers are derived, but it takes a lot of time and effort to use the tables to locate the appropriate factor and make the calculations. The tables are further limited because they do not provide for rates between half percentage points.

A better idea is to purchase a business or financial calculator or appropriate computer software to complete the complex calculations that you are likely to encounter in the course of individual retirement planning. The proper tools can be valuable in your work with prospects and clients. Anyone who is interested in providing retirement planning services should consider these tools a must. ◊

PERSONAL FINANCIAL STATEMENTS

> **The preparation of organized financial information is an important but often ignored aspect of personal financial and retirement planning.**

The preparation of organized financial information is an important but often ignored aspect of personal financial and retirement planning. Using tools similar to those accountants use to report the financial position and cash flow of businesses, you can help your prospects gain a better understanding of and control over their current finances while helping them focus on priorities for the future.

Personal financial statements that summarize your client's current financial situation as well as those that project future results are useful for planning purposes. In fact, it is difficult to develop a retirement plan and formulate strategies to achieve your client's financial goals without first knowing his or her current financial situation and resources. Moreover, the ongoing analysis of your client's personal financial information is crucial in monitoring whether or nor he or she is achieving his or her financial/retirement goals.

In personal financial and retirement planning, the primary financial statements that you would use to develop a plan for your client are the financial position statement (or balance sheet) and the cash flow statement (or income statement).

pro forma

While your client's current financial position and cash flow statements relate to what has occurred in the past, it is also necessary to prepare pro forma (or projected) financial position and cash flow statements. A *pro forma* statement illustrates what future financial statements are expected to show if certain activities are implemented under specified assumptions. Finally, current financial statements can be compared with past pro forma statements to see if your client is realizing his or her financial goals.

Financial Position Statement

f.nancial position
statement
(balance sheet)

The *financial position statement (balance sheet)* shows your client's (or his or her family's) wealth at a point in time and reflects the results of his or her past financial activities. It contains three basic classifications—assets, liabilities, and net worth—that make up the basic accounting equation:

Assets = Liabilities + Net worth

Financial position statement formats usually group the items that make up assets and liabilities into subclassifications that better enable the advisor to analyze the components of the client's total financial situation and to evaluate the mix of assets and liabilities in relation to the client's objectives. Figure 2-4 shows a typical financial position statement prepared for Jack and Jill Client.

Assets

Assets are items your client owns. It is immaterial whether the items were purchased for cash, financed by borrowing, or received as gifts or inheritances.

fair market value

It is common practice for personal financial position statements to show assets at their current *fair market value*. These values may vary considerably from the original purchase prices. In contrast, business balance sheets list many assets on the basis of adjusted historical costs, net of depreciation.

At a minimum, assets should be subdivided into two categories: financial assets and nonfinancial (or personal) assets. The financial position statement in figure 2-4 separates total assets into three broad categories as follows:

- cash and cash equivalents
- other financial assets
- personal assets

Liabilities

Liabilities are your client's debts. Although the financial position statement in figure 2-4 does not separate liabilities into categories, it is not unusual to see liabilities grouped by the time period in which they must be repaid. For example, the statement might show subtotals for short-term liabilities (due in one year or less), intermediate-term liabilities (due in more than 1 year but no more than 5 years), and long-term liabilities (due in more than 5 years).

The liabilities section of the financial position statement should show all liabilities as of the date of the statement.

Net Worth

Net worth measures your client's wealth or equity at the date of the financial position statement. Increasing this bottom-line figure is one of the primary

FIGURE 2-4
Financial Position Statement for Jack and Jill Client: September 30, 2006

Assets		Liabilities and Net Worth	
Cash, Cash Equivalents	**Current Value**		**Current Value**
Checking accounts/cash	$12,000	Charge accts./credit cards	$ 2,000
Savings accounts		Family/personal/auto loans	16,000
Money-market funds	50,000	Margin/bank/life ins. loans	
Treasury bills		Income taxes (federal, state, local)	
Short-term CDs		Property taxes	
Savings bonds		Investment liabilities	
Other (specify)		Mortgage(s)	220,000
Subtotal	$62,000	Lease(s)	
Other Financial Assets		Child support	
Stock	150,000	Alimony	
Bonds, taxable	90,000	Other (specify)	
Bonds, tax exempt	80,000	Other (specify)	
Mutual funds		Other (specify)	
Other securities		**Total Liabilities**	**$238,000**
Investment real estate			
Long-term CDs		**Net Worth (Total Assets**	
Vested retirement benefits	120,000	**Minus Total Liabilities)**	**$742,000**
Annuities (cash values)			
Life ins. cash values	18,000		
IRAs (Roth/traditional)			
Limited partnership units			
Interest(s) in trust(s)			
Value of business interest			
Other (specify)			
Other (specify)			
Other (specify)			
Subtotal	$458,000		
Personal Assets			
Personal residence	300,000		
Seasonal residence			
Automobiles, other vehicles	80,000		
Household furnishings	50,000		
Boats			
Jewelry/furs	20,000		
Collections (art, coins, etc.)	10,000		
Other (specify)			
Subtotal	$460,000		
Total Assets	**$980,000**	**Total Liabilities Plus Net Worth**	**$980,000**

objectives of financial planning. It is calculated by restating the basic accounting equation as follows:

$$Net\ worth = Total\ assets - Total\ liabilities$$

In other words, net worth is what remains if all your client's assets are sold at their fair market values and all debts are paid. The key to understanding net worth is to realize that it is simply the difference between total assets and total liabilities.

Your client's net worth may increase or decrease during a period of time. Other things being equal, it will increase as a result of any one of the following:

- appreciation in the value of assets
- addition to assets through retaining income
- addition of assets through gifts or inheritances
- decrease in liabilities through forgiveness

The following are examples of actions that have no effect on net worth:

- paying off a debt. The cash account declines by the same amount that the liability declines, leaving the difference between total assets and total liabilities unchanged.
- buying an asset with cash. Total assets remain unchanged because cash declines by the same amount that the other asset category increases. However, commissions and other transaction costs cause net worth to decline because the cash that pays these costs is not reflected in the value of the purchased asset.

> **Net worth is simply the difference between total assets and total liabilities.**

> **Paying off a debt or buying an asset with cash have no effect on a client's net worth.**

Preparing a Financial Position Statement

Because net worth is determined by subtracting total liabilities from total assets, preparing your client's financial position statement involves

- identifying each of his or her assets and liabilities
- valuing each asset and liability as of the date of the statement
- recording the values of assets and liabilities in an appropriate format that shows net worth as the difference between total assets and total liabilities

Valuing Each Asset and Liability as of the Date of the Statement

Assets. Assets (items your client owns) can be categorized in a number of ways. As mentioned earlier, one common approach is to divide your client's assets into two groups—financial assets and nonfinancial (personal) assets.

financial assets

Financial Assets. Financial assets consist of cash and cash equivalents (or liquid assets) and other financial (or investment) assets. Cash and cash equivalents are liquid in the sense that they are either already cash or can be converted into cash relatively quickly with little, if any, loss in value. In addition to cash on hand, cash and cash equivalents include various transactions accounts such as checking, savings and money market deposit accounts, money market mutual funds, and certificates of deposit that mature in the near future (generally, within 1 year). Your clients require cash and liquid cash equivalents to pay daily expenses, provide funds to cover unanticipated emergencies, and provide funds to take advantage of unforeseen investment opportunities that may arise.

Assets classified as "investment assets" for financial position statement purposes represent a variety of assets in which clients may invest to earn a return. Investment assets include

- savings bonds
- other bonds such as corporate bonds; federal, state and local government bonds
- stocks
- mutual funds (excluding money market funds)
- tax-advantaged retirement accounts—IRAs, 401(k) plan accounts, 403(b) plan accounts, and profit-sharing plan accounts
- life insurance cash values
- other managed assets—personal annuities, trusts with an equity interest, and managed investment accounts
- assets generally acquired or held for investment purposes such as futures contracts, stock options, and commodities

nonfinancial (personal) assets

Nonfinancial (Personal) Assets. Nonfinancial (personal) assets include your client's

- primary residence
- other residential real estate
- net equity in nonresidential real estate such as commercial property, rental property, farm land, and undeveloped land
- net equity in privately held businesses
- vehicles such as cars, vans, sport utility vehicles, trucks, motor homes, recreational vehicles, motorcycles, boats, airplanes, and helicopters
- other tangible personal assets such as clothes, household furnishings, appliances, artwork, jewelry, antiques, hobby equipment, and collectibles

Liabilities. Liabilities are debts your client has incurred by borrowing. When your clients borrow, they incur debts that must be repaid in the future—

that is, they incur liabilities. Liabilities are generally identified by the type of debt incurred. The most common types of liabilities clients incur are

- charges for the purchase of consumable goods and services such as rent, appliance repairs, utilities, and medical expenses
- balances for credit cards and other lines of credit
- mortgages and other loans secured by residential property
- installment loans to finance the purchase of items such as automobiles, furniture, and appliances
- other forms of borrowing such as loans from life insurance policies and retirement accounts

Once you have identified your client's assets and liabilities, you must determine a value for each. Assets should be listed on your client's personal financial position statement at their fair market values as of the date the statement is being prepared.

Values must be determined for each of your client's liabilities. Liabilities are valued by using the amount your client owes as of the date the financial position statement is prepared. Likewise, liabilities resulting from mortgages and other types of loans are valued at the outstanding loan balance—that is, the amount of the unpaid principal—as of the date the financial position statement is prepared.

Recording Values of Assets, Liabilities, and Net Worth in Appropriate Format

The final step in the preparation of a financial position statement is to record the values of your client's assets and liabilities in an appropriate format that shows his or her net worth as the difference between total assets and total liabilities.

Cash Flow Statement

cash flow statement (income statement)

The *cash flow statement (income statement)* summarizes your client's financial activities over a specified period of time by comparing cash inflows and cash outflows, and indicating whether the net cash flow for the period is positive or negative. The cash flow statement has three basic components—income, expenses, and net cash flow—that are related as follows:

$$\text{Income} - \text{Expenses} = \text{Net cash flow}$$

The cash flow statement for a given year indicates how your client's financial activities changed his or her wealth (net worth) position from that depicted in the financial position statement at the beginning of the year (the end of the previous year) to that depicted in the financial position statement at the end of the year.

When based on your client's past income and expenses, the cash flow statement (or income statement) gives you a summary of your client's financial activities for a specified period prior to the start of your professional relationship with the client. This information can be used to analyze your client's present financial situation.

On the other hand, a pro forma cash flow statement based on projections of future income and expenses for a specified planning period gives you a means to assess the anticipated impact of various alternative planning strategies on achieving your client's goals. As such, the cash flow statement plays a central role in carrying out the various cash flow management activities in providing financial planning services to clients.

What Is Cash Flow Management?

cash flow management

Cash flow management is another name for the budgetary planning and control process. Financial advisors adopted the change in terminology partly because cash flow management is more inclusive than budgeting. More important, the word "budget" carries negative connotations for many clients, making them less likely to participate in the process.

> The word "budget" carries negative connotations for many clients, making them less likely to participate the process.

Cash flow management consists of three basic components:

- cash flow analysis
- cash flow planning
- budgeting

In practice, the financial advisor may decide to combine the three and consider them a single process.

cash flow analysis

Cash Flow Analysis. *Cash flow analysis*, or income and expense analysis, is the process of gathering data concerning your client's cash flow situation, presenting the data in an organized format (the cash flow statement), and identifying strengths, weaknesses, and important patterns. Cash flow analysis is also a good starting point for you to assist your client in developing goals and objectives. In addition, it reveals inefficient, ineffective, or unusual utilization of resources, highlights alternative courses of action, motivates your client to manage his or her cash flow, and makes family members aware of the need to conserve resources.

cash flow planning
net cash flow

Cash Flow Planning. *Cash flow planning* identifies courses of action that will help optimize net cash flow. *Net cash flow* is defined as the difference between income and expenses. A positive net cash flow is available for any use, whether for consumption, investment, or gifting, although in most financial planning situations, the primary benefit of a positive net cash flow is to provide a source of investable funds.

Cash flow planning can be used as an extension of cash flow analysis. For example, cash flow analysis reveals opportunities for increasing net cash flow by addressing income and expense factors. Cash flow planning then considers what to do with the increase in net cash flow.

budgeting

Budgeting. *Budgeting* is the process of creating and following an explicit plan for spending and investing the resources available to your client. The process works through the establishment of a working budget model followed by a comparison of actual and expected results. Regularly monitoring the budget can enable you and your client to recognize problems as they occur—even anticipate them. Budgeting provides both a means of financial self-evaluation and a guideline to measure actual performance.

Budgeting can uncover money that can be used to insure against financial risks and to save for retirement. It is an opportunity to set the fiscal priorities for the year to come.

A budget can be seen as the way the prospect wants his or her projected cash flow statement to look for the year to come. It is the plan that he or she needs to follow to create the desired future cash flow statement.

The cash flow statement is at the center of the budgeting process. Using the cash flow statement, you and your prospects develop a budget for the next year, which can help them find the money for the new financial priorities they establish. (See sample "Household Budget Summary" in appendix B.)

The following are some general criteria for establishing a budget:

- Make the budget flexible enough to deal with emergencies, unexpected opportunities, or other unforeseen circumstances.
- Keep the budget period long enough to utilize an investment strategy—typically 1 calendar year.
- Make the budget simple and brief.
- Estimate insignificant items.
- Tailor the budget to specific goals and objectives.
- Pinpoint, in advance, variables that may influence the amounts of income and expenses.

Use the following procedure to assist prospects and clients in developing a household budget:

- estimated income. First estimate anticipated total income. Consider all sources—earned income, unearned income (interest, dividends, and so on), and income potential. Income may vary because of expected annual raises and increases or decreases in interest or dividend rates. It is better to underestimate than overestimate if earnings are irregular.

- estimated expenses. Next, estimate expenses. Expenses may vary because of fluctuating living costs, changing tastes or preferences, or changing family circumstances. Determining where money will likely be spent is based on the history of the family's spending habits.
- fixed expenses. Begin estimating expenses by listing all of the family's fixed, or basic, expenses. These are recurring expenses and somewhat unavoidable. Some fixed expenses are regular and are the same amount each month—for example, rent, mortgage payments, taxes, and regular installment payments. Other fixed expenses are recurring but they are variable. Examples are food, clothing, utilities, and transportation.
- discretionary expenses. Once fixed expenses have been determined, the family should list discretionary expenses or expenses that can be prevented or timed through proper budgeting. An expense like dining out can be prevented; a purchase of a new car can be timed.

The advantages of a budget are as follows:

- It creates awareness of total income and anticipated expenditures.
- It gives an accurate picture of where the money goes.
- It facilitates decisions on what is or is not affordable.
- It provides a sense of control and promotes real economic freedom.
- It discourages buying on impulse and spending on unnecessary things.
- It facilitates saving to attain desired financial goals.
- It develops opportunities for investments to be made.
- It allows decisions on how best to protect against adverse financial consequences.
- It encourages peace of mind, thereby reducing stress and conflict.

Finally, a budget plan is only as good as the your client's resolve to stick to it. In developing a budget for retirement planning, it is better to begin conservatively with a plan to which you and your clients know they can adhere. Once the plan is in place and working, clients can add to it. But if the plan fails because it is too ambitious, it will remain dormant and unfulfilled; your client will be discouraged and probably unwilling to undertake the next step.

Preparing a Cash Flow Statement

Although budgeting requires looking to the future, you must first gather past income and expense data from your client to determine his or her present cash flow situation. It is your client's present cash flow situation that provides the starting point for carrying out the three activities of the cash flow management process mentioned earlier: analysis, planning, and budgeting. Financial advisors generally use a cash flow worksheet to gather income and expense data and input it into a computer program that creates the cash flow statement.

Because net cash flow is determined by subtracting total expenses from total income, preparing a cash flow statement for your client involves

- identifying the sources and amounts of gross income your client receives
- identifying the types and amounts of expenses your client incurs
- recording the amounts of income and expense in an appropriate format that shows net cash flow as the difference between total income and total expenses

For a cash flow statement, most financial advisors use a 12-month period. This period is comparable in length to the 12-month period that most advisors use for budgeting.

Recording Amounts of Client's Income and Expenses to Show Net Cash Flow

Jack and Jill Client's cash flow statement in figure 2-5 reflects the year prior to their retirement planning process. Subtracting total expenses from total income reveals the Clients' net cash flow.

If a client's net cash flow is negative, the client can meet this shortfall by a reduction of cash and cash equivalents (a reduction of assets) and/or by borrowing (an increase in liabilities).

A positive net cash flow for a given period can be used to increase assets and/or reduce liabilities, the net result of which is an increase in the client's net worth. When a client's net cash flow is positive, this client can allocate even more financial resources to those areas of discretionary spending such as savings, investments, and an education fund. Prudent use of discretionary cash flow can enhance a client's chances of successful retirement planning.

Analyzing Personal Financial Statements

The benefits of personal financial statements apply to more than just the fact finding interview. When used as part of the fact finding process, these statements help raise questions about what your prospects want to happen in the future and what steps they must take to adequately protect what they have accumulated.

In reviewing personal financial statements, you may make one or more of the following observations about your prospect's current financial situation:

FIGURE 2-5
Cash Flow Statement for Jack and Jill Client for the Period October 1, 2005, to September 30, 2006

Annual Income	Amount
Wages, salary, bonus, etc.: Client	$110,000
Wages, salary, bonus, etc.: Spouse	30,000
Business (self-employment) income	
Real estate rental	
Dividends—investments	3,000
Dividends—close corporation stock	
Interest on bonds, taxable	5,000
Interest on bonds, tax exempt	3,000
Interest on savings accts., CDs	2,000
Interest on loans, notes, etc.	
Trust income	
Life insurance settlement options	
Annuities	
Child support/alimony	
Other sources (specify)	
Total Annual Income	**$153,000**
Housing (mortgage/rent)	$15,500
Utilities and telephone	7,000
Food, groceries, etc.	10,500
Clothing and cleaning	7,000
Federal income and Social Security taxes	27,000
State and local income taxes	4,000
Property taxes	5,000
Transportation (auto/commuting)	8,000
Medical/dental/drugs/health insurance	8,000
Debt repayment	5,000
House upkeep/repairs/maintenance	6,000
Life, property, and liability insurance	13,000
Child support/alimony	
Current education expenses	4,500
Total Fixed Expenses	**$120,500**
Vacations, travel, etc.	4,000
Recreation/entertainment	5,000
Contributions/gifts	1,500
Household furnishings	3,000
Education fund	5,000
Savings/investments	5,500
Other (specify)	5,000
Total Discretionary Expenses	**$29,000**
Total Annual Expenses	**$149,500**
Net Cash Flow (Total Annual Income Minus Total Annual Expenses)	**$3,500**

- There is insufficient current liquidity. Thus, there is not an adequate emergency fund in place.
- A large portion of your prospect's spending is for miscellaneous, discretionary, or frivolous items.
- There is excessive use of credit cards and charge accounts.
- Your prospect routinely receives a substantial income tax refund because too much tax is withheld from earnings.
- Your prospect's investment portfolio is not adequately diversified.
- Your prospect has not been sufficiently committed to saving and investing to achieve his or her financial goals. If not,
  - To what level must your client's rate of saving increase to achieve those goals?
  - Is your client both willing and financially able to make the changes required to achieve this increased rate of saving?
  - Is your client willing to modify either the timing of his or her goals and/or the factors influencing the amount of resources required to achieve them?
- Your prospect has inadequate insurance protection. ◊

CHAPTER TWO REVIEW

Key Terms and Concepts are explained in the Glossary. Answers to the Review Questions and Self-Test Questions are found in the back of the book in the Answers to Questions section.

Key Terms and Concepts

bridge job
phased retirement
OASDI
fully insured
currently insured
maximum taxable wage base
primary insurance amount (PIA)
disability insured
total disability
time value of money (TVM)
simple interest
compound interest
compounding
Rule of 72
future value of a single sum (FVSS)
discounting

present value of a single sum (PVSS)
pro forma
financial position statement (balance sheet)
fair market value
financial assets
nonfinancial (personal) assets
cash flow statement (income statement)
cash flow management
cash flow analysis
cash flow planning
net cash flow
budgeting

Review Questions

2-1. Describe the requirements necessary to become fully insured and currently insured for Social Security benefits.

2-2. Identify the categories of persons who are eligible for Social Security survivor benefits.

2-3. Describe the retirement benefits available under Social Security.

2-4. Explain what happens if the total Social Security benefits for a family exceed the maximum family benefit.

2-5. Explain how a worker's retirement benefits under Social Security are affected if that person elects early retirement.

2-6. Describe the earnings test applicable to the Social Security program.

2-7. Explain how the future value of a single sum (FVSS) is affected by the
a. interest rate used in the calculation
b. number of years used in the calculation

2-8. Using table A-1 in appendix A, calculate the future value of $10,000 in 20 years growing at a constant rate of 8 percent interest.

2-9. Using table A-2 in appendix A, calculate the future value in 25 years of periodic payments consisting of $1,000 annual deposits earning 7 percent interest.

2-10. If your client has $150,000 and wants to take periodic payments at the end of each year for 15 years from an account that earns 7 percent interest, using table A-4 in appendix A, calculate how much the annual periodic payments will be.

2-11. Identify the key components of a financial position statement, and briefly explain what each component represents.

2-12. Identify the various ways in which a client's net worth can increase during a period of time.

2-13. Explain why the following actions have no effect on a client's net worth:
a. paying off a debt
b. buying an asset with cash

2-14. Briefly describe how a cash flow statement is used, and identify its three basic components.

2-15.   Explain the purpose for each of the following components of cash flow management:
a.   cash flow analysis
b.   cash flow planning
c.   budgeting

Self-Test Questions

Instructions: Read chapter 2 first, then answer the following questions to test your knowledge. There are 10 questions; circle the correct answer, then check your answers with the answer key in the back of the book.

2-1.   Which of the following is the correct term for a full- or part-time job involving little responsibility, which a retiree holds after retiring from a career and before stopping work entirely?

(A)   phased retirement
(B)   retirement income credit
(C)   bridge job
(D)   reduced wage base

2-2.   Time value of money is based on which of the following concepts?

(A)   A dollar received today is worth more than a dollar received in the future.
(B)   A dollar received today is worth less than a dollar received in the future.
(C)   Compound interest can lead to compound taxation.
(D)   Compound taxation can lead to compound interest.

2-3.   At a compound annual interest rate of 3 percent, a single sum of $1 will double in value and reach $2 in approximately how many years?

(A)   3 years
(B)   9 years
(C)   18 years
(D)   24 years

2-4.   Which of the following statements concerning the cash flow statement is correct?

(A)   It is based on projections of future income and expenses.
(B)   It has three basic components: assets, liabilities, and net cash flow.
(C)   It classifies annual expenses as either fixed or discretionary.
(D)   It shows a client's wealth (net worth) at a point in time.

2-5. Future retirees are more likely to work than in the past for which of the following reasons?

  I.   People are living longer and thus will have more retirement years to fund.
  II. The earnings test for Social Security benefits at or beyond full retirement age has been eliminated.

  (A) I only
  (B) II only
  (C) Both I and II
  (D) Neither I nor II

2-6. Other things being equal, which of the following changes will increase the future value of a present sum of money?

  I.   an increase in the interest rate used in the compounding process
  II. a decrease in the number of years over which compounding occurs

  (A) I only
  (B) II only
  (C) Both I and II
  (D) Neither I nor II

2-7. Which of the following statements concerning assets is (are) correct?

  I.   For purposes of the financial position statement, it is necessary to know whether assets were purchased for cash, financed by borrowing, or received as gifts or inheritances.
  II. It is common practice to list assets on the financial position statement at their original purchases price instead of their current fair market value.

  (A) I only
  (B) II only
  (C) Both I and II
  (D) Neither I nor II

2-8. All the following are eligible to receive Social Security retirement benefits EXCEPT

  (A) a retired covered worker
  (B) the spouse of a covered worker
  (C) the parent of a covered worker
  (D) the dependent child of a covered worker

2-9.   A client's net worth can increase as a result of all the following EXCEPT

    (A)   appreciation in the value of his or her assets
    (B)   addition to assets through retaining income
    (C)   addition to assets through an inheritance
    (D)   addition to assets by making lifetime gifts

2-10.   All the following statements concerning cash flow planning and/or budgeting are correct EXCEPT:

    (A)   Cash flow planning is identifying courses of action that will help optimize net cash flow.
    (B)   Cash flow planning is effective only when it precedes cash flow analysis.
    (C)   Budgeting is the process of creating and following an explicit plan for spending and investing the resources available to the client.
    (D)   Budgeting provides both a means of financial self-evaluation and a guideline to measure actual performance.

NOTES

1.   U.S. Census Bureau; Income, Poverty and Health Insurance Coverage in the United States: 2004.
2.   For a comprehensive treatment of how to solve time-value-of-money problems using an HP-10BII financial calculator, see Don A. Taylor and C. Bruce Worsham, eds., *Financial Planning: Process and Environment.* Bryn Mawr, PA: The American College Press, © 2005, chapters 6 and 7.

Fact Finding and Goal Setting

<table>
<tr><td colspan="2">

Learning Objectives

An understanding of the material in this chapter should enable the student to
</td></tr>
<tr><td>3-1.</td><td>Describe the importance of goal setting in the retirement planning process.</td></tr>
<tr><td>3-2.</td><td>Identify the assumptions required in the retirement planning process.</td></tr>
<tr><td>3-3.</td><td>Explain the two basic methods for calculating the retirement income need.</td></tr>
<tr><td>3-4.</td><td>Describe the purpose and goals of the initial retirement planning interview with the prospect.</td></tr>
<tr><td>3-5.</td><td>Describe the relevance of the initial retirement planning meeting to the fact finding process.</td></tr>
<tr><td>3-6.</td><td>Explain the three basic methods used to qualify prospects.</td></tr>
<tr><td>3-7.</td><td>Explain the importance of using fact finders for retirement planning.</td></tr>
<tr><td>3-8.</td><td>Identify the major sections of the Retirement Planning Fact Finder, and describe the types of information each of the sections contains.</td></tr>
</table>

Chapter Outline

SETTING RETIREMENT GOALS

Importance of Goal Setting in Retirement Planning

goal setting

    Goal setting in retirement planning is the process of establishing clearly definable, measurable, achievable, and realistic financial and personal objectives toward which the financial advisor can target a prospect's efforts, resources, plans, and actions. Goal setting is critical to creating a successful retirement plan, but few people actually set clearly defined goals. By leading the prospect through the goal-setting process, you not only help the prospect establish reasonable, achievable goals, but you also set the tone for the entire planning process.

Prospects typically express concern about financial topics such as retirement income. Sometimes, prospects are able to enumerate specific prioritized goals, but prospects are more likely to present a vague list of worries that suggest anxiety and frustration rather than direction. Your responsibility as an advisor is to help prospects transform these feelings into goals.

goal prioritization

Another important service of the financial advisor is *goal prioritization.* Goal prioritization is the process of ranking goals according to their importance for the purpose of deciding the order in which to achieve them. Prospects often have competing goals such as saving for retirement and saving for education. As an advisor, you should help prospects rank the importance of these competing goals.

> **Once established, a person's financial goals do not remain static.**

Once established, a person's financial goals do not remain static. What may be entirely appropriate for a young married man with small children may prove quite inappropriate for an executive with college-age children or for a husband and wife approaching retirement.

The Advisor's Role in the Goal-Setting Process

The retirement planning process demands that advisors listen to their prospects' objectives and expectations for retirement. This requires exploring and understanding the prospects' goals, attitudes, and personal preferences. Prospects have a variety of goals that range from never having to work again to working full-time during retirement. Clearly, as an advisor you have your work cut out for you as you deal with a plethora of expectations and, in some cases, help to frame your prospects' retirement planning objectives.

> **Your primary responsibility as an advisor in planning for your prospects' retirement is to make them aware that they are making lifestyle choices that can affect retirement security every day.**

Your primary responsibility as an advisor in planning for your prospects' retirement is to make them aware that they are making lifestyle choices that can affect their retirement security every day. For example, should the prosepct take an expensive vacation or take a moderately priced vacation and save the difference for retirement? You cannot force the client to make lifestyle choices that will provide an adequate source of retirement funds. You can, however, make the prospect aware of the large amount of funds needed for retirement and point out that a spendthrift lifestyle during the prospect's active working years hurts his or her chances of adequately funding for retirement.

Your prospects need to simultaneously save and invest their money for retirement, protect themselves against everyday financial risks and emergencies, and figure out what they want to leave behind for their heirs. Before they can set goals, they must have an idea of what their retirement will look like. Once they envision what they want, they can begin to plan how to get there.

To assist your prospects in the planning process, it is helpful for you to approach retirement planning as an ongoing process of

- defining needs
- setting goals
- implementing strategies to meet goals
- measuring performance
- fine-tuning the process

If viewed this way, the most critical step is getting started. Once a retirement goal is set and a plan is implemented, you and your client can begin the process of evaluating goals and objectives, monitoring and measuring progress, and refining goals and the strategies to accomplish them.

Retirement Expectations

Your first step in retirement planning is to motivate a prospect to work with you. (This occurs in the second stage of the selling/planning process.) Only when a prospect is sufficiently motivated in your first face-to-face meeting will he or she give you permission to proceed. In general, prospects are motivated to take action when they are concerned about their current situation and interested in seeking potential solutions.

The next step in retirement planning is to define retirement for a particular prospect. Although there are some common retirement needs, each prospect has a different idea of what his or her retirement will be. For example, many people look forward to traveling during retirement. Others see themselves moving to warm climates, to cabins on lakes, to the mountains, or to retirement or recreational communities. Still others look forward to having home mortgages paid and living close to family and friends. Some, as we discussed earlier, even plan to work in retirement.

> **You cannot help your prospects plan effectively until you know what they want. And you will not know what they want until you ask them.**

You cannot help your prospects plan effectively until you know what they want. And you will not know what they want until you ask them. You should never make assumptions about what your prospects want. Rather, you should ask them to tell you what they desire their retirements to be. To plan effectively, you must know where your prospects want to live and what they want to do. Once you know your prospect's vision for retirement and which goals are the most important, you can begin to help him or her plan to make the visions a reality.

Within the process of establishing your prospects' goals and expectations for retirement, you must gather a considerable amount of information about your prospects. (Fact finding will be discussed later in this chapter.) You must conduct a financial inventory of retirement assets and assess the strategies that prospects have available to them. Furthermore, you should be prepared to help prospects meet goals that are important to them such as

- maintaining their preretirement standard of living during retirement
- becoming economically self-sufficient
- minimizing taxes on retirement distributions
- adapting to the retirement lifestyle
- taking care of a dependent parent
- handling their own special health needs

In addition, you should be prepared to deal with a variety of attitudes on how long prospects want to work, what their probabilities are for health and longevity, whether the prospects can be disciplined enough to save for retirement, and to what extent they accept investment risk. ◊

ASSUMPTIONS REQUIRED IN THE RETIREMENT PLANNING PROCESS

Retirement Income Needs

Arguably, the most important part of any comprehensive plan for retirement is the estimate of the prospect's retirement income needs, along with the calculation of the savings rate necessary to meet those needs.

retirement income needs

Retirement income needs are typically defined as the total amount of savings that will generate the income required to allow a prospect to sustain the standard of living he or she enjoyed just prior to retirement throughout the retirement period. Generating the needed savings requires the accumulation of a sufficient retirement fund—the bankroll for the retirement years. Stockpiling sufficient savings requires an adequate savings rate, which is either a level annual amount or the percentage of salary that a person must put aside during his or her working years to accumulate a sufficient bankroll.

The methods used to perform a needs and savings analysis can vary considerably. There are a number of privately and commercially available worksheets and computer models that accomplish this objective. Some are available for free at a variety of financial services Web sites; others are sophisticated models that financial services companies provide to their financial advisors. No matter what their origin, most worksheets and computer models leave room for the advisor to insert his or her unique perspective.

Understanding the needs and savings analysis distinguishes you from the crowd and allows you to make more accurate forecasts for your prospects.

This section of the chapter will examine the process involved to arrive at the requisite bottom-line figure. Although it would be impossible to review each worksheet and computer model individually, it is possible to focus on common characteristics and thereby facilitate an understanding of the process. This understanding distinguishes you from the crowd and allows you to make more accurate forecasts for your prospects. To give you an insight into the needs and savings analysis, this section of the chapter will

- examine the assumptions that you must make to arrive at a knowledgeable prediction of your prospect's financial status during retirement, based on his or her unique circumstances
- explore two different methods to determine your prospect's retirement income needs, which will give you insight into the common features of the myriad worksheets and computer models that are available

Many worksheets and computer models enable the advisor to tailor the retirement prediction to a prospect's unique situation by choosing assumptions for future contingencies. Others make the assumption for the advisor and thus eliminate the ability to fine-tune a prediction. Because retirement planning is an art form, not a science, the better models allow the most flexibility by giving the advisor control over assumptions. However, advisors must be equipped to handle the complex task of choosing assumptions effectively.

Assumptions that most worksheets and computer models typically require are the

- rate of inflation the prospect will experience
- age at which the prospect will retire
- age at which the prospect will die
- income requirement for the prospect
- marginal income tax rate applicable now and in the future
- investment return the prospect can expect

> **Both the advisor and the prospect must be comfortable with the numbers to plug into the worksheet if they want a realistic projection.**

Each worksheet and computer model may treat these assumptions differently. For example, many worksheets break down inflation into two categories: preretirement and postretirement. Others make one inflation assumption for both periods. Regardless of how the assumptions are treated, the advisor and the prospect must be comfortable with the numbers to plug in if they want a realistic projection. Let's take a closer look at how to choose the best numbers for your prospect's situation.

Inflation Assumption

One of the most critical assumptions that an advisor must make is the inflation rate that will apply to the prospect. Inflation erodes the prospect's purchasing power over time, making it difficult to maintain economic self-sufficiency during retirement. The effects of this erosion are dramatically illustrated when different inflation assumptions are plugged into worksheets and computer models. For this reason, it is essential to be as accurate as possible when forecasting the rate of inflation that will apply to your prospect.

Forecasting Inflation

The CPI (consumer price index) is the most widely used measure of inflation in the general United States economy. In forecasting inflation, however, the financial advisor must also consider other factors:

- Long-term inflation is the appropriate variable, but published statistical data focus on the annual inflation rate (for example, 1.4 percent in 2004), not the long-term rate.
- There are significant regional variations from the national rate of inflation.
- Medical inflation is twice the national average of the general inflation rate.
- The average "market basket" of goods and services used in measuring the CPI may not be the *average* goods and services that a retiree uses.
- Retirees buy more services than goods. Historically, services have inflated at a higher rate than goods. Thus, even if a national average of inflation is accurate, it may be understated for retirees.
- No matter what statistical data the advisor chooses, it is necessary to remember that a retiree's personal buying habits will affect his or her actual inflation rate.
- Inflation accounts heavily for housing costs. For many retirees, this may be a moot point because they own their houses outright or live in a rent-controlled building.
- Planning for the younger prospect (in his or her late 20s to early 30s) can be troublesome because it requires considering inflation over 60 years or more.

Forecasting the rate of inflation for your prospect would not be an easy task even if you had a crystal ball.

Forecasting the rate of inflation for your prospect would not be an easy task even if you had a crystal ball. Moreover, advisors do not all take the same approach. Most advisors, however, do agree on one issue: adopting a long-term view of inflation because preretirement and postretirement planning can encompass a long period of time. For example, for the period from 1970 to 1999, the inflation index was 4.294 percent. Successful advisors, therefore, are using neither today's relatively low inflation rates nor the double-digit inflation rates of the late 1970s and early 1980s in their forecasts. Advisors can help their prospects better prepare for the financial future by having them focus on a long-term rate.

A second issue that advisors generally agree on is that the assumption should factor in the prospect's risk-tolerance tendencies. A risk-averse prospect will probably want a higher figure projected, whereas a risk taker may feel comfortable with a relatively low inflation assumption.

A third factor to consider is that the inflation assumption can be altered over time to reflect changes in the CPI and the prospect's actual experience. This is not to say that each year the advisor should reinvent the wheel, but it does offer planning flexibility because the retirement model is constantly evolving.

Monitoring Assumptions

Advisors cannot take a once-and-done attitude toward prospects when it comes to sculpting a retirement plan. The plan should be revisited periodically to check the accuracy of assumptions and the effectiveness of meeting the prospect's goals.

Which Inflation Rate Is Best?

Most advisors use inflation assumptions between 3 and 4 percent. The actual rate chosen for a prospect will vary depending on spending habits, current age, and risk-tolerance tendencies. Four percent is common. Some current economic literature indicates that 3.5 percent may be a good proxy for long-term inflation.

A prudent approach is to ask your prospect about the "raise" he or she wants each year in retirement. In other words, by what percentage does the prospect want to increase his or her income each year? The higher the inflation rate (raise), the greater the percentage of salary that your prospect needs to save. Prospects who choose the lowest realistic rate will sacrifice the least amount now. You should warn them, however, that this lack of sacrifice now will affect their future behavior. According to the Bureau of Labor Statistics inflation calculator, a person who retired in 1975 and needed $2,000 a month to live will need around $6,500 a month today just to have the same buying power he or she had in 1975. (The inflation calculator and other important data about the rate of inflation and the CPI can be found at the Bureau of Labor Statistics home page: www.bls.gov.)

> **Prospects who choose the lowest realistic rate of inflation will sacrifice the least amount of salary now. That lack of sacrifice now, however, will affect their future behavior.**

Retirement Age Assumption

Considering the innumerable factors that must be examined, the choice of a retirement date is not the easy task that it may appear to be at first blush. The advisor's role, with the aid of worksheets and computer models, is to calculate the retirement age as realistically as possible for the prospect. Often, a prospect will seek to retire on what he or she considers to be a large amount of money. Unfortunately, that amount is typically not enough. It is up to you to point that out. Because of the impact of inflation and the increase in longevity, delaying retirement may be a more logical situation. In other words, one of the chief functions of the advisor and the retirement worksheet/printout is to foster a realistic attitude in the prospect. This attitude will enable the advisor to better forecast the prospect's intended retirement date.

Longevity Assumption

Ideally, individuals would accumulate enough assets to allow them to live on the interest alone and never have to liquidate the principal. For many retirees, however, this is not a viable strategy. These retirees must liquidate their retirement savings throughout the retirement period. We have already discussed the uncertainty regarding the beginning of retirement. Imagine our dilemma over the uncertainty surrounding the end of retirement—death! As ghoulish as it may sound, the impossible task of predicting the time of their prospects' demise is a real issue that advisors face. Severe mistakes in either direction—too early or too late—can tend to grossly overstate or understate the amount of savings needed to meet a particular retirement goal.

> As ghoulish as it may sound, the impossible task of predicting the time of their prospects' demise is a real issue that advisors face.

Notwithstanding the potential for error, advisors must make their best educated guess concerning their prospects' (both spouses if applicable) life expectancies in order to complete a retirement worksheet or computer model. In many cases, this assumption is generated by the ages at which parents and grandparents have died. This is generally sound thinking because medical studies show a strong relationship between genetics and life expectancy. In addition to family history, factors the advisor should consider are

- the physical condition of the prospect, including the prospect's personal medical history
- life expectancy tables. At the turn of this century, men were expected to live 74.4 years (up from 68.2 in 1980 and 62.6 in 1950), and women were expected to live 79.8 years (up from 76.1 years in 1980 and 67.4 years in 1950). Note, however, that insurance tables tend to understate life expectancy and annuity tables tend to overstate life expectancy. What's more, even if tables are accurate, *one-half of the people outlive the tables' projections.*
- the tendency of higher socioeconomic groups to have longer life expectancies. Many believe this is due in part to easy access to medical care.
- the probability of living from age 65 to a specified age (see table 3-1) (a more accurate measure of life expectancy than life expectancy at birth)

What's an Advisor to Do?

First, the advisor must identify the prospect's expected retirement age. To do this, you must factor in statistical life expectancy information, then adjust the estimate up or down to consider issues such as health, lifestyle, and family history (or use life expectancy calculators). In addition, many advisors feel comfortable adding a "fudge factor" to their life expectancy estimate. If the prospect lives longer than anticipated, the fudge factor will make up for the additional years. If the prospect does not live as long, some excess assets will

TABLE 3-1
Life Expectancy by Age and Gender: United States, 2002

Age	Male	Female
25	51.0	55.8
30	46.3	51.0
35	41.6	46.1
40	37.0	41.4
45	32.6	36.7
50	28.3	32.2
55	24.1	27.7
60	20.2	23.5
65	**16.6**	**19.5**
70	13.2	15.8
75	10.3	12.4
80	7.8	9.4
85	5.7	6.9
90	4.2	5.0

Source: National Vital Statistics Reports, vol. 53, no. 6, November 10, 2004

be left for heirs (which generally is a viable planning goal anyway). At the extreme, some advisors use a life expectancy assumption of age 100 because statistically very few people will live beyond this point. Using this as a conservative estimate will save the advisor from the fatal (pun intended) error of understating life expectancy.

Advisors must guard against overstating the prospect's retirement need to the extent that the annual amount of necessary savings is unattainable. In other words, using unrealistically high life expectancies will create unreasonably high demands on the percentage of salary that must saved and ultimately scare the prospect into inaction because of his or her inability to meet savings schedules.

Income Requirement Assumption

income requirement assumption

The *income requirement assumption* is the advisor's estimate of the level of income the retiree needs to sustain throughout his or her retired life the standard of living he or she enjoyed just prior to retirement. In some cases, this can be measured as a percentage of final salary (called the *replacement-ratio approach*). In other cases, it is the projected retirement budget for a prospect (called the expense method).

replacement-ratio approach

Replacement-Ratio Approach

Some experts believe that between 70 and 80 percent of an individual's final salary will maintain him or her in the style to which he or she is accustomed throughout retirement. Note that postretirement inflation is not factored into the replacement ratio. Instead, it is treated separately. In other words, the worksheets and computer models account for an inflation-protected stream of income separately from the replacement ratio that will be needed in the first year of retirement.

Factors That Influence a Replacement Ratio of Less Than 100 Percent. Support for a replacement ratio of less than 100 percent of final salary rests on the elimination of some employment-related taxes and some expected changes in spending patterns that reduce the retiree's need for income (such as expenditures that will either decrease or disappear in the retirement years). See figure 3-1.

> **In many circumstances, retirees can count on a lower percentage of their income going to pay taxes in their retirement years.**

Reductions in Taxation. In many circumstances, retirees can count on a lower percentage of their income going to pay taxes in their retirement years. Some taxes are reduced or eliminated, and retirees may also enjoy special

---

FIGURE 3-1
Justification of Less Than 100 Percent Replacement Ratio

Patty and Ken Tailor (both aged 64) have a combined salary of $100,000 ($50,000 each) and would like to maintain their current purchasing power when they retire next year. If their anticipated reduced nonwork expenses are offset by increased living expenses (see below), they can maintain their purchasing power by having a retirement income of 80 percent of their salary, as illustrated below.

Working salary		$100,000
Less FICA taxes[1]	$ 7,650	
Less increase in standard deduction[2]	0	
Less tax savings on tax-free part of Social Security[3]	840	
Less state and local tax reduction[4]	1,400	
Less deductible medical expenses[5]	0	
Less reduced living expenses[6]	0	
Less retirement savings[7]	10,000	
Reductions subtotal		19,890
Total purchasing power needed		$ 80,110
Percentage of final salary needed (approximate)		80%

1. Because each earns $50,000, each pays $3,825 in FICA taxes.
2. No increase in standard deduction will occur because they itemize using Schedule A.
3. Patty and Ken will receive $20,000 in Social Security; $3,000 will be tax free, for a savings of $840 at the 28 percent tax bracket.
4. The Tailors will get a sliding scale rebate on their property taxes equal to $1,400.
5. They will not take a medical deduction.
6. The Tailors think any reduced living expenses in retirement from work will be offset by increased retirement expenses.
7. The Tailors had been saving 10 percent of their salary in a 401(k) plan (5 percent each).

favorable tax treatment in other areas. Let's take a closer look at the potential reductions in taxation that are granted to retirees.

Social Security Taxes. FICA contributions (old-age, survivors, disability, and hospital insurance) are levied solely on income from employment. Distributions from pensions, IRAs, retirement annuities, and other similar devices are not considered income subject to FICA or SECA taxes. Hence, for the retiree who stops working entirely, Social Security taxes are no longer an expenditure.

Increased Standard Deduction. For a married taxpayer aged 65 or over, the standard deduction is increased by an additional $1,000 (in 2006). If the taxpayer's spouse is also 65 or older, there is yet another $1,000 increase in the standard deduction ($1,000 for each spouse, or $2,000 total). For a taxpayer over 65 who is not married and does not file as a surviving spouse, $1,250 is added to the standard deduction (in 2006).

Social Security Benefits Exclusion. A married taxpayer can exclude all Social Security benefits from his or her income for tax purposes if the taxpayer's modified adjusted gross income plus one-half of the Social Security benefits does not exceed the base amount of $32,000 ($25,000 for single taxpayers). For others, only part of their Social Security benefit will be untaxed. In this case, the receipt of Social Security benefits may contribute to an increase in the prospect's income taxation. See chapter 7 for a thorough discussion of how Social Security benefits are taxed.

State and Local Income Taxation. In some states, Social Security benefits are fully exempt from state income taxation; in others, some taxation of these benefits might occur. In addition, some states grant extra income tax relief for seniors by providing increased personal exemptions, credits, sliding scale rebates of property or other taxes, or additional tax breaks.

Deductible Medical Expenses. Due to the reduced retirement income level and the increased medical expenses that retirees often face, it might be easier for taxpayers who itemize deductions to exceed the 7.5 percent threshold for deductibility of qualifying medical expenses.

Reduced Living Expenses. In addition to the possible reductions in taxation, certain reduced living expenses may permit retired individuals to maintain their standard of living on a lower income. Let's take a closer look at some of possible reductions in living expenses.

Work-Related Expenses. The costs of appropriate clothing for work, commuting, and meals purchased during work hours are eliminated when a person retires. In addition, other expenses, such as membership dues in some professional or social clubs, may be reduced because of retired status or eliminated if no longer necessary.

Home Ownership Expenses. By the time of retirement, many homeowners have "burnt the mortgage" and no longer have this debt reduction expenditure.

Absence of Dependent Children. When an individual enters retirement, he or she usually no longer has the expense of supporting dependent children. Be cautious, however, because occasionally, retirees—especially those who married later in life—have children who are not self-supporting and will require continued financial support during some of the individuals' retirement years.

Senior Citizen Discounts. Special reductions in price are given to senior citizens. Some reductions, such as certain AARP discounts, are available at age 50. Many businesses, however, require proof of age 65 to qualify for discounts on prescriptions, clothing, and restaurant meals. Discounts typically range from 5 to 15 percent of an item's cost.

No Longer Saving for Retirement. For many retirees, their retirement years are not a time to continue to save for retirement. Cessation of payments to contributory pension plans, lack of eligibility for IRA or Keogh plan contributions, and simply the psychological factor of being retired can sometimes weaken retirees' motivation to save for the future.

> Sometimes, simply the psychological factor of being retired can weaken retirees' motivation to save for the future.

Increased Living Expenses. Some financial advisors are uncomfortable about recommending a planned reduction in income in the retiree's first year of retirement. These advisors believe that certain factors suggest that during the first year of retirement, at least as much, if not more, income will be required to maintain the preretirement standard of living. Let's examine the factors that lead to that conclusion.

Medical Expenses. Without question, medical expenses will increase over time for virtually all individuals. The mere act of aging and the associated health problems generate additional demands for medical services. Even if advancing age does not create an increase in your prospect's demands for medical services, these costs will likely increase because of inflation.

> Even if advancing age does not create an increase in your prospect's demands for medical services, these costs will likely increase because of inflation.

Although retirees are often covered by Medicare and other health insurance, the trend in these coverages has been toward cost containment—defined by the government and the insurance companies as shifting more of the medical cost to the insured through larger deductibles and coinsurance payments. These higher medical expenses are in addition to the increased premiums for the insurance.

Travel, Vacations, and Other Lifestyle Changes. Many retirees expect to devote considerably more time to travel and vacations during retirement than they did during their working years. Increased leisure time, once a scarce commodity, now gives them the opportunity to travel. Vacationing, however, can be an expensive activity. Indeed, an increase in vacation activities represents a rise in the standard of living and will require additional income.

Dependents. As previously stated, parents usually need less income during the first year of retirement because they no longer financially support their children, who typically become self-supporting prior to parental retirement. However, some retirees still have dependents to support. Many parents have children with mental or physical problems who will require long-term custodial and financial care throughout the retirement years. Because medical care, surgical techniques, and drugs are helping to prolong life, other retirees may have to provide for their aged parents who no longer have the wherewithal to do so themselves.

Warning Your Prospects about the Risks

Whether your prospects accept an 80 percent replacement ratio or feel something less is adequate, you should stress that there is no definitive way to determine absolutely if postretirement income should be less than, equal to, or greater than that of the preretirement years.

Estimating financial needs during the first year of retirement is like trying to hit a moving target when you are blindfolded: Your aim is obscured by many unknown variables, and the target is hard to draw a bead on.

Additional Services. As people age, they often need to hire others to perform services that they previously performed themselves. This can include a wide number of physically demanding activities such as cutting the lawn, working on the car, painting the house, climbing ladders to make repairs, and shoveling snow. It may also include hiring individuals for housecleaning or caring for an infirm spouse or other family member. Some physical impairment may require a change in transportation mode—such as taking a taxi instead of public transportation—which will mean an increased expense.

Expense Method

expense method approach

A second way advisors can estimate their prospects' retirement needs in the first year of retirement is by using the *expense method approach*. The expense method of retirement planning focuses on the projected expenses that a retiree will have in the first year of retirement. For example, if a 64-year-old near-retiree expects to have $3,000 in monthly bills ($36,000 annually), then the retirement income for that retiree should maintain $36,000 worth of purchasing power in today's dollars. (See figure 3-2.) If, however, the advisor is working with a younger prospect, the advisor must make (and periodically revise) more speculative estimates of retirement expenses.

FIGURE 3-2
Understanding the Expense Method

Bob and Betty Smith, both aged 64, would like to maintain their current purchasing power when they retire next year. They can do this by having an annual income of $40,860 as illustrated below. Note that the figures are estimates of their expenses during retirement (some are higher than their current expenses and some are lower than their current expenses). Also note that postretirement inflation will be accounted for later.

Estimated Retirement Living Expenses (in Current Dollars)

	Per Month x 12	= Per Year
1. Food	$ 500	$ 6,000
2. Housing		
a. Rent/mortgage payment	400	4,800
b. Insurance (if separate payment)	25	300
c. Property taxes (if separate payment)	150	1,800
d. Utilities	180	2,160
e. Maintenance (if home is owned)	100	1,200
3. Clothing and Personal Care		
a. Wife	75	900
b. Husband	75	900
4. Medical Expenses		
a. Doctor (HMO)	75	900
b. Dentist	20	240
c. Medicines	75	900
5. Transportation		
a. Car payments	130	1,560
b. Gas	50	600
c. Insurance	50	600
d. Car maintenance (tires and repairs)	30	360
6. Miscellaneous Expenses		
a. Entertainment	150	1,800
b. Travel	200	2,400
c. Hobbies	50	600
d. Club fees and dues	20	240
e. Other	100	1,200
7. Life and health insurance	100	1,200
8. Gifts and contributions	50	600
9. State, local, and federal taxes	800	9,600
10. Total expenses (current dollars)	3,405	40,860

The advisor should consider expenses that may be unique to the particular prospect, as well as other more general expenses. As noted for the replacement ratio approach, expenses that tend to increase for retirees include the following:

- utilities and telephone
- medical and dental costs, drugs, and health insurance
- house upkeep, repairs, maintenance, and property insurance
- recreation, entertainment, travel, and dining
- contributions and gifts

Conversely, some expenses tend to decrease for the retiree. These include the following:

- mortgage payments
- food
- clothing
- income taxes
- property taxes
- transportation costs (car maintenance, insurance)
- debt repayment (charge accounts, personal loans)
- child support, alimony
- household furnishings

Ratio versus Expense Method

If your worksheet or computer model gives you a choice of whether to use a replacement ratio or expense amount, consider the following:

- The expense method usually works well for prospects who are at or near retirement because they have a handle on their projected retirement budget.
- The replacement-ratio method usually works well for younger prospects because they do not have a handle on their retirement expenses but can sometimes gauge the standard of living they want to enjoy.

Marginal Income Tax Rates

Marginal income tax rates will affect how much a prospect's taxable savings and investment accumulations will be reduced on an annual basis both prior to and after retirement commences.

Traditional thinking that financial advisors used in the past has been to assume that a retiree's marginal income tax rate will decline because his or her income has declined. This is not always the case. In some cases, a

> **Traditional thinking assumed that retirees' marginal income tax rate would decline because their income had declined. This is not always the case.**

prospect's marginal income tax bracket may actually increase. This could happen due to such factors as a change in filing status from married filing jointly to single, or if total income derived from pensions and withdrawals from savings remains high after retirement while large income tax deductions for a mortgage and taxes on real estate that is sold disappear. Regardless of such changes in prospects' lifestyles, their marginal income tax bracket may remain constant if their advisors have done a good job of helping the retirees accumulate enough withdrawable assets to keep income at the same level before and after retirement, taking into account income from pensions and Social Security.

Some factors to keep in mind regarding future marginal income tax rates are the

- prospect's ability to use tax-sheltered qualified plans and IRAs
- potential future income the retiree is expecting
- inevitable federal tax law changes
- state income taxes that may be applicable to a relocated prospect

Interest Earnings on Savings, Investments, and Assets Earmarked for Retirement

> **With any investment or savings vehicle, it is better to err on the conservative side and underestimate the interest rate.**

As long as your prospect agrees, the long-term rate assumed for retirement assets should be no more than 4 percent above the average inflation rate. With any investment or savings vehicle, it is better to err on the conservative side and underestimate the interest rate of return. Although trends from the recent past may give you an idea of what interest rate to assume, there is no guarantee that a vehicle will continue to perform in the future as it has in the past. The assumption you use must be realistic if you plan to rely on it to develop a plan for your prospect.

The following are some factors to consider in this process:

- the historical return of the retirement portfolio with which the prospect is comfortable
- the prospect's inclination to invest more conservatively (and consequently have a lower rate of return) as he or she approaches retirement and after retiring
- the prospect's tendency to invest too conservatively in the qualified plan at work
- the likelihood that the prospect will be given an inheritance from parents
- the possibility of the prospect's receiving a lump-sum payment for retirement
- the advisor's investment recommendations

Other Assumptions

In addition to making assumptions concerning inflation, retirement age, longevity, the amount/percentage of final salary determined to be enough to maintain the appropriate standard of living (replacement ratio), marginal income tax rates, and investment returns, financial advisors must

- consider the total financial resources available to the prospect for use during retirement
- project the amount and level of savings needed from today until retirement age

These considerations, along with the aforementioned assumptions can help an advisor to develop a retirement plan to address a prospect's specific situation.

Total Financial Resources Available to Prospects

A retiree's income generally comes from a combination of three sources: Social Security, pensions, and personal savings. Because you are trying to determine the amount of personal savings necessary to supplement Social Security and pensions, you must first estimate the benefits your prospect expects to receive from these two sources. After you estimate the benefits from Social Security and pensions, you should look at what your prospect has personally saved. Seeing what your prospect has personally saved for retirement will not only tell you how much is currently available to supplement Social Security and pensions, but it will also help you determine the annual rate at which your prospect has been saving.

Most of your prospect's personal retirement savings will be in employer-sponsored retirement plans, savings accounts, CDs, deferred annuities, mutual funds, and stocks and bonds. The amount of savings your prospect has invested in each of these vehicles depends on such factors as his or her age and level of risk tolerance. You will need to assess the current and potential value of each of these assets. You must then factor those values into the overall amount of retirement income these assets may generate.

Also, do not overlook the use of assets such as home equity during retirement. Your prospect may be able to convert this source of personal savings into a reverse mortgage (see chapter 2), or alternatively, he or she may be able to cash out some of the equity by moving to a less expensive residence.

**retirement
income gap**

Retirement Income Gap. The difference between the amount of money your prospect must accumulate to reach his or her retirement income goal and the amount he or she expects to have from all sources is the *retirement income gap*. Each situation involves different variables, but at a minimum, your prospect should seek a savings target that reconciles the retirement income gap.

Projected Amount of Savings by Retirement Age

> Once you determine the amount of saving that your prospects can realistically accumulate, you will be in a better position to develop a plan to reach (eliminate) the retirement income goal (gap).

Projections of retirement savings using different assumptions can be generated by a financial calculator or financial planning software. The goal is to have a projection that reaches the target amount of savings using realistic assumptions. Once you determine the amount of savings your prospect can realistically accumulate, you will be in a better position to help him or her develop a plan for reaching (eliminating) the retirement income goal (gap). If your prospect cannot reach a retirement income goal, then you need to help him or her adjust the goal downward.

Level Rate. One way to assist your prospects in reaching their retirement accumulation goals is to determine the annual level amount of savings needed henceforth, based on an average interest rate. This is easy for the prospect to understand. As we will see later in this chapter, however, the initial amount of savings needed in the early years of this accumulation strategy may be more than the prospect's budget allows. The alternative is an approach that begins today with a lower annual savings amount and then increases the savings amount according to the prospect's increased income.

step-up rate

> The step-up rate typically corresponds to the prospect's projected growth rate in compensation, thus keeping the rate of savings at a constant percentage.

Step-up Rate. Many financial planning models look at savings as a percentage of income, whereby the amount saved each year increases as salary increases. Some models have the added flexibility of a *step-up rate*, which is the percentage growth in the prospect's annual allocation to savings. The step-up rate typically corresponds to the prospect's projected growth rate in compensation, thus keeping the rate of savings at a constant percentage. In other words, prospects can increase retirement savings in a painless way by bolstering savings with future salary increases. To best predict this rate, the advisor should review employment contracts, salary scales, and salary history. Such a review will inform the advisor about expected increases in the prospect's income.

Summary

The advisor must elicit from and discuss with the prospect all the assumptions used to determine retirement income and accumulation needs. This is done during the fact finding process, which will be examined in detail later in this chapter. How these assumptions apply to a prospect's specific quantitative and qualitative retirement goals will be explained in conjunction with a retirement planning fact finding form. The income replacement ratio method of determining a prospect's retirement need will be demonstrated in an example that uses several interest rate tables.

In subsequent chapters, we will discuss preretirement planning strategies, investment management techniques, and financial products that can be implemented to help your prospects eliminate the retirement income gap. ◊

MEETING WITH THE PROSPECT

In this section, we will return to the third component in the selling/planning process within the context of retirement planning. We will explore effective techniques to interview prospects, along with methods to explain the need for retirement planning. Finally, we will discuss alternative retirement funding sources, as well as several approaches to qualify prospects.

Preparing for the Interview

What to Expect in the Retirement Planning Interview

The retirement selling/planning process is much the same as that for any individual financial product sale. That is, you need to identify and approach prospects, meet with them, and conduct effective fact finding to establish a financial need in the initial interview. Then you should schedule a second interview in which you recommend the appropriate financial product(s), such as investments or insurance products, to help meet that need. You should consider financial products within the context of retirement planning and/or as components of a broader, more comprehensive financial plan.

Retirement Planning Process Steps 3 and 4

Part of your job as a financial advisor is to guide prospects through steps 3 (meet with the prospect) and 4 (gather information and establish goals) of the general selling/planning process (discussed in chapter 1) by executing the same due diligence you would expect if you were the buyer. This process, as it relates specifically to retirement planning, involves (but is not limited to)

- meeting personally with the prospect
- explaining the need for retirement planning
- discussing the potential inadequacy of traditional retirement funding sources
- discussing financial products as part of the retirement funding solution
- qualifying the prospect
- gathering information and establishing goals
  - fact finding
  - compiling financial information
  - feeling finding
- identifying the need
- quantifying the need
- securing a discovery agreement

In the remainder of this chapter, we will address in detail each of these topics in the order listed above.

Initial Interview

The purpose of the initial interview is to establish the foundation for a collaborative relationship with the prospect, not to make a sale. In fact, many successful advisors have said that if you collect the information from the prospect during the initial interview, including his or her needs, values, feelings, goals, and objectives, as well as facts and figures, this will result in much less resistance to making sales and implementing solutions. The systematic process of building a lasting client-advisor relationship begins with this initial meeting and is made up of the following four steps:[1]

- establishing rapport and credibility
- utilizing effective communication techniques
- identifying the prospect's needs, wants, qualifications, and concerns
- reaching an agreement to work together to address the prospect's needs, wants, and concerns

Establishing Rapport

Client building begins with establishing rapport. People want to work with professionals who create meaningful relationships with them and listen to what they want to accomplish. If you develop rapport and credibility in the process of exchanging information, the product options and amounts you recommend will more likely reflect the prospect's real needs and values. For prospects to buy any products from you, they must first trust you. Trust is the intangible aspect of selling that an advisor must cultivate and earn. You must prove that you are there to help prospects, not simply there to sell them something. Thus, your objective in the initial interview is to establish rapport by creating an environment that promotes prospect openness by

> **Trust is the intangible aspect of selling that an advisor must cultivate and earn.**

- alleviating the prospect's concerns
- responding to the prospect's social style
- communicating effectively with the prospect
- mutually agreeing to an agenda for the interview

Alleviating the Prospect's Concerns. You must remove the barriers that can create tension between you and your prospect during an initial meeting if rapport is to be established. These barriers include

- distrust of salespeople in general
- fear of making a decision
- resistance to change
- reluctance to commit his or her time
- real time constraints

Being aware of prospect tension can help you identify opportunities to alleviate it and to establish rapport. Here are some tips:

- Do not impose. Schedule your initial meeting at times that are convenient for the prospect.
- Watch your verbal pace. Talk in an unhurried, businesslike manner. Never interrupt when prospect speaks. Listen carefully to what he or she says. As we will discuss shortly, listening is your best tool.
- Remember nonverbal behavior. You might be surprised to learn that as little as 7 percent of a first impression is based on what is actually said. The remaining 93 percent is based on nonverbal behavior, such as physical appearance, body language, voice quality, and tone.
- Encourage the prospect to talk. Having the prospect talk is not only a great tool for getting feedback, but it is also a common way for the prospect to relieve stress. Encourage the prospect to do most of the talking.
- Control your anxiety. Several studies have shown that a person who is already anxious becomes even more so when talking to someone who displays nervousness or anxiety.

Establishing rapport is your responsibility.

social style

Responding to the Prospect's Social Style. Establishing rapport is your responsibility. That means that you should be able to detect what each prospect wants in a client-advisor relationship and adapt your responses to his or her respective needs.

Psychologist Dr. David Merrill divided individuals into those four *social styles*:

- driver
- expressive
- amiable
- analytical

According to Dr. Merrill and Roger H. Reid, "We all say and do things as a result of certain habit patterns, and people make predictions about us because they come to expect us to behave in a particular way—the fact is that even though each of us is unique, we tend to act in fairly consistent, describable ways. All of us use habits that have worked well for us, habits that make us comfortable, and these habits become the social style that others can observe."[2]

The American population is approximately evenly divided among the four social styles. Each person has a dominant social style, and that style influences the way he or she behaves. People will tend to seek out social situations that reinforce their behavior and avoid situations that cause discomfort.

People are like thermostats; they are constantly seeking to reach a state of equilibrium or comfort. As soon as another person enters the picture,

As advisors, we can achieve better communication when we understand the other person and treat him or her the way he or she wants to be treated.

tension results, and each person must reestablish his or her balance and comfort zone. The challenge for each of us is to determine the right amount of tension and stress that will provide the proper balance. As advisors, we can achieve better communication when we understand the other person and treat him or her the way he or she wants to be treated.

When you adapt to the prospect's social style, you make the person feel at home and less threatened. By listening and observing carefully during the first few minutes of the interview, you get an idea of how to treat the prospect.

Table 3-2 summarizes the characteristics of each social style and indicates how you can best respond to establish rapport with a person who has that style. Listen carefully and observe your prospect to determine which set of characteristics best describes him or her; then build rapport by responding in the appropriate way throughout the interview.

TABLE 3-2
Responding to Social Styles

Social Style	Style Characteristics	How to Respond
Driver	• Forceful, direct • Will not waste time on small talk • Is motivated by a desire for power • Is controlling	• Be efficient. • Move right along. • Support his or her conclusions and actions. • To encourage decisions, provide options and probabilities.
Expressive	• Outgoing, enthusiastic • Enjoys telling about personal projects and dreams • Is motivated by a desire for recognition • Is energizing	• Be interesting. • Take time to listen. • Support his or her visions and intuitions. • To encourage decisions, provide testimony and incentives.
Amiable	• Easygoing, dependent • Enjoys telling about personal relationships • Is motivated by a desire for approval • Is supportive	• Be cooperative. • Find areas of common involvement. • Support his or her relationships and feelings. • To encourage decisions, provide assurances and guarantees.
Analytical	• Logical, quiet • Is uncomfortable with small talk • Is motivated by a desire for respect • Is systematic	• Be accurate. • Stick to an agenda. • Support his or her principles and thinking. • To encourage decisions, provide evidence and service.

Communicating Effectively with Prospects

effective
communication

Failing to hear
what your prospect
is really saying can
cost you dearly.

To help solve prospects' problems, advisors must be effective communicators. Some advisors think *effective communication* means only that they have to be able to explain financial products to prospects. Obviously, that is important, but one of the most critical aspects of being an effective communicator is learning also to be an effective listener. Failing to hear what your prospect is really saying can cost you dearly. Developing good listening skills will result in increased sales and the sense of a job well done.

active listening

Active Listening. Your goal as an advisor should be to become an active, understanding listener—one who attempts to understand the prospect from the prospect's perspective. *Active listening* has occurred if you can state in your own words what the prospect has said and meant to communicate, and the prospect accepts your statement as an accurate reflection of what he or she said and felt.

The most important
part of communication
is listening.

To become an active listener, you must believe in the importance of each prospect's needs. Then you must commit to hearing and understanding what each prospect is saying. Your prospects are more likely to accept your recommendations if you demonstrate an interest in them as individuals, listen to their hopes and dreams, and help them prioritize their goals. In other words, the most important part of communication is listening.

Questioning. In any fact finding session, you will ask questions and your prospects will answer them. If you can help your prospects feel comfortable talking about themselves, you will learn what is important to them. The more you know about your prospects' feelings, the better job you can do. Asking questions and being an active listener allows you to control the direction of the fact finding conversation without being too obvious about it. Prospects then feel they are a part of the process.

The intangible by-product of establishing rapport, tuning into and responding to the prospect's social style, and actively listening during the interview process is enhancing your credibility to the prospect. Your credibility, combined with your compassion and understanding, will eventually lead to the prospect's trust in you. Once a prospect trusts you, he or she will be willing to do business with you. Winning a prospect's trust does not come easily. You have to work hard to achieve it, so be patient. ◊

INTERVIEWING THE PROSPECT

Your job in the selling/planning process is ongoing. You will spend considerable time with the prospect to determine his or her financial goals and objectives—the prospect's needs. After this is complete, you will use the information you have gathered—the facts and feelings that you have discussed—to make recommendations. Each meeting with the prospect should accomplish specific objectives.

The beginning of the initial interview sets the tone for the entire meeting by establishing expectations for both you and the prospect. Therefore, in the introductory phase of the interview, the first order of business is to establish an agenda.

Establishing an Agenda

It is a good idea to follow a predetermined agenda for each fact-gathering session. This lets the prospect know what is expected of him or her and reduces anxiety and discomfort about what will happen during the meeting. It is wise to involve your prospect in setting the agenda.

> **Setting proper expectations for the meeting helps establish rapport and gets the initial interview off to a positive start.**

Setting proper expectations for the meeting helps establish rapport and gets the initial interview off to a positive start. You can reduce any early tension in an interview with a prospect whom you have never met before by outlining your approach to retirement planning. Explain the following steps of the selling/planning process:

- Establish goals and objectives.
- Identify existing resources to meet these goals and objectives.
- Analyze the gap between goals and objectives and the existing resources.
- Develop a plan for bridging the resource gap.
- Implement the plan.
- Service the plan.

You should have an agenda for every sales meeting. To present the agenda you should do the following:

- Communicate what you intend to accomplish during the meeting.
- Explain how you will work with the prospect.
- State the benefit for the prospect.
- Check for the prospect's acceptance.

In the initial planning session, you might propose the agenda by saying something like this to the prospect:

Purpose	*What You Say*
Communicate what you intend to accomplish during the meeting.	During this meeting, we will discuss some retirement planning issues that may concern you.

Explain how you will work with the prospect.	First, I'll tell you a little about who I am and the company I represent.
	We'll also talk about the need for adequate retirement funding.
	Then we'll talk about your concerns, goals, and desires regarding retirement planning.
	Next, we will look at your current financial status in regard to your current cash flow, current savings and investments, and potential sources of retirement income.
	Finally, I'll identify any problems or gaps in your current retirement plan.
State the benefit for the prospect.	That way, you can determine whether it will be of value for us to move ahead and develop a retirement planning strategy tailored for you.
Check for acceptance.	How does that sound?

By proposing the agenda in this way, stating the benefit to the prospect, and checking for acceptance, you are sharing control of the interview with your prospect, which helps to establish rapport. It may be advisable to reassure the prospect of your continuing commitment to the process.

Example:	"If in the course of our work together, we discover that you have a need for financial products within a plan for funding retirement, I'll assist you in devising a customized plan that addresses your individual concerns. I'll then help you to implement that plan and promise to monitor and service it in the future."

After you present your agenda, ask for any other concerns that your prospect wishes to discuss. Write them down, and be sure to cover these concerns in your discussion. Do so even if the concerns do not fall under categories you had on your agenda. Your prospect's input is an important step in the open exchange of data and feelings.

Explaining the Need for Retirement Planning

The transition from the exchange of amenities and acknowledgment of the agenda to the qualification portion of the interview takes a relatively short time, during which you describe yourself, your services, your company, and the common problems facing individuals today in financing the increasing costs of retirement.

This part of the initial interview deals with explaining, in general terms, the need for adequate income during retirement. You can use various methods to accomplish this objective. For example, you can discuss the widespread financial problem of the need for sufficient retirement funding. You can caution against depending too heavily on financing alternatives like government programs and qualified plans to solve the problem, pointing out how low-yielding taxable investments may hamper prospects' cash accumulation goals during their working years and noting that postretirement employment may not be desirable or even possible. You may then describe briefly how certain financial products can help to alleviate the looming retirement funding problem. You should select some appropriate concept papers to give to the prospect to reinforce these points.

Clarifying Motives and Goals

> **Your first meeting with a prospect is both an opportunity and a challenge. The opportunity is to address the prospect's interest in retirement planning. The challenge is to develop a climate of cooperation.**

Your first meeting with a prospect is both an opportunity and a challenge. The opportunity is to address the prospect's interest in retirement planning. The challenge is to develop a climate of cooperation so you can learn enough about the prospect's financial planning goals and buying motives in order to individualize a plan of action that best addresses his or her circumstances.

In setting the stage to explain the need for retirement planning, you may want to take time to establish what the prospect knows and what the prospects thinks he or she knows about retirement planning. For example, one advisor simply asks, "What does the word 'retirement' mean to you?" Asking this or a similar question is a great way to begin a discussion of retirement concepts and to establish certain definitions used for such concepts as tax deferral, the cost of retirement, and what various government and pension programs do and do not provide. It also uncovers the prospect's assumptions about the myths and misunderstandings about retirement planning. You should also elicit feedback from the prospect regarding his or her level of knowledge about financial products and seek insight into the prospect's understanding of retirement planning goals. Only when you are speaking the same language as the prospect can you begin to comprehend the prospect's objectives in purchasing any financial products as components of a balanced retirement plan.

Methods

To enhance your credibility with your prospect, it is important that you explain why he or she may need to consider purchasing financial products to implement a successful retirement plan. This discussion often leads to the use of other tools and techniques (which, of course, must be approved by your company's compliance department) that you as an advisor can draw upon to help you. These various tools and techniques should be in the retirement planning presentation binder that you may develop for your use.

Visuals

Visuals are a compelling presentation technique. People tend to listen actively to what is being said when they are involved in the communication; it is your responsibility to ensure that your prospect is involved and actively listening throughout the fact finding process. Asking questions and soliciting the prospect's opinions while he or she looks at visuals keeps the prospect involved in the process. The physical act of placing visuals in front of the prospect helps to direct the discussion and focus the prospect's attention.

Keep in mind that any materials presented to the prospect must have your company's prior approval.

Third-Party Substantiation

In addition to simple pictures, your company probably has preapproved marketing brochures, product fact sheets, and even third-party testimonials available for your use. Become familiar with these and selectively decide which ones to include in your retirement planning presentation binder.

Statistical Evidence

Many advisors use charts, graphs, and statistics about the cost of retirement funding in light of increasing longevity in the United States today. Other relevant resources are magazine articles and PowerPoint presentations. You need to develop and update your own inventory of suitable materials to appeal to the prospect's emotions regarding financial security and his or her potential need for retirement planning financial products.

Real-Life Stories

Some advisors also find it useful to develop a repertoire of real-life stories and case histories that they can draw upon to illustrate the usefulness of mutual funds, annuities, and insurance products in retirement planning. Although this technique may not be appropriate for every advisor—some are better story-tellers than others—it is one more resource in your inventory of tools and techniques to market these products. Recounting an actual situation in which the need for emergency funds arose suddenly prior to retirement and how life insurance cash values were used, or how an annuity product provided guaranteed income or life or long-term care insurance premium dollars after retirement, can help to heighten a prospect's personal awareness about the need for proper planning.

The Problem: Ensuring Adequate Retirement Income

Americans' increased longevity has intensified the need for adequate funding of their income during retirement.

As mentioned previously in this chapter, Americans' increased longevity has intensified the need for adequate funding of their income during retirement. People in this country who live to age 65 can expect to live an average of 18 more years. With increased longevity comes the greater probability of depleting the personal financial reserves accumulated over a lifetime of saving. How will your prospects be able to adequately fund their retirement?

The answer for most individuals (and their families) depends on the level of income prior to retirement.

Sources of Retirement Income[3]

There are many misunderstandings regarding retirement income and the resources available to generate it. As a financial advisor, you must be prepared to educate prospects on the shortcomings of the various personal, employer-sponsored, and government financing alternatives for retirement income. This process will often require you to dispel the misconceptions about the effectiveness of these alternatives as adequate retirement funding vehicles. Most individuals' retirement income will come from one or more of these sources:

- Social Security
- pensions
- personal savings
- earnings

Of course, there are other sources of retirement income, including

- capitalizing home equity in the retiree's principal residence through
  - a reverse mortgage
  - the sale of the principal residence
- liquidating a business ownership interest
- inheritances
- other forms of support

During the early part of the initial interview, you should incorporate the text, charts, and graphs presented in chapter 2 that address the sources of retirement income into your discussion of the general need for retirement planning. As mentioned previously in this chapter, you would also include some discussion about financial products, investment strategies, or income-tax-minimizing techniques that are integral components of a coordinated retirement plan. This would usually include the presentation of concept papers and product fact sheets. You may also use printouts of retirement planning software presentations that highlight the need for early and adequate retirement planning. ◊

QUALIFYING THE PROSPECT

> **The more time you spend with qualified prospects, the greater number of them you will convert into clients.**

After you have discussed the need for retirement planning in general, you should make sure that your prospect and his or her spouse, if applicable, will qualify for the purchase or issue of financial products that will be needed to implement the plan before (or while you are performing) personal information gathering. In the ideal scenario, qualified prospects are identified before private face-to-face meetings are established. Many successful advisors prequalify prospects on the telephone once they have agreed to an appointment. It is advisable to ask the kind of questions that will preliminarily qualify the prospect for the appointment. However, in many instances, a face-to-face meeting occurs before you know for certain whether or not you are dealing with a qualified prospect. These meetings take time. The more time you spend with qualified prospects, the greater the number of them you will convert into clients.

To increase chances of converting a qualified prospect into a client, keep in mind the four characteristics of a qualified prospect that we discussed in chapter 1. Qualified prospects for financial products are people who

- need and value your products and services
- can afford to pay for your products and services
- are insurable or financially suitable
- can be approached on a favorable basis

If these four conditions are satisfied, then you have a potential client. If at any time during the interview you discover that these four conditions are not satisfied, you should have a contingency strategy either to pivot to another product, outline a plan for future contact with the prospect when he or she is better qualified, or gracefully exit the interview and move on.

> **You must have a barometer of the prospect's finances to determine if there are sufficient funds to afford products you recommend.**

By virtue of the fact that you have obtained the interview, let us assume that you approached the prospect and are meeting with him or her on a favorable basis. Whether or not the prospect satisfies the remaining three qualification criteria has yet to be determined. Thus, it is helpful for you to have a sense of the prospect's perception of a need for retirement planning that may lead to purchasing an investment or insurance product, and his or her ability to make such a purchase. Therefore, you must have a barometer of the prospect's finances to determine if there are sufficient funds to afford products you recommend. Whether or not the prospect satisfies these three qualifying criteria will become apparent as you gather information in the initial interview. As each criterion is fulfilled, you should mentally check it off so that you will know that the prospect is qualified to purchase financial products that you may recommend as part of the retirement plan.

Regardless of the extent of the information you acquire, you must keep several points in mind regarding your professional responsibility. You should always complete a fact finder of some sort within the context of any financial product sale. At the same time, you need to maintain a certain degree of flexibility, depending on the circumstances under which you made the appointment with the prospect. This is because many, but certainly not all, financial products can be sold as retirement planning vehicles. For example, you could be meeting with a prospect to discuss using an immediate annuity as a guaranteed funding vehicle for long-term care insurance. In this case, a guaranteed income for funding retirement is not the prospect's concern, so only the relevant segments of a comprehensive retirement planning fact finder would have to be completed in order for you to adequately address your prospect's needs.

There are three basic methods used to qualify prospects:

- using the Personal Retirement Planning Review for a general retirement planning assessment and attempting a preliminary discovery agreement prior to a full retirement planning analysis
- using an abbreviated or modified retirement planning fact finder to address a concern or dominant need that does not require a full retirement planning analysis
- proceeding directly into personal information gathering using a comprehensive retirement planning fact finder

Let's examine each of these methods.

Personal Retirement Planning Review

After you have discussed in overall terms the need for retirement planning, consider the following approach to increase the amount of time you spend with current qualified prospects:

- Begin to qualify your prospect with a general retirement planning qualifying form.
- Attempt a preliminary discovery agreement or trial close before conducting a full retirement planning analysis.

Afterwards, you would use a comprehensive retirement planning fact finder, which we will discuss in detail in the next section of this chapter.

The Personal Retirement Planning Review is a short and simple qualifying fact finder designed to uncover a prospect's predisposition or potential objections to retirement planning. It can also serve as an additional motivator to purchase financial products. The use of this mini fact finder is optional, but you may find it helpful. A copy is included here for your use, but please be sure first to obtain your company's approval.

Personal Retirement Planning Review

Prepared for: _____

1. Retirement Preferences
    When do you plan to retire? (When did you retire?_____
    Where do you plan to live when you retire?_____
    Do you expect to maintain your preretirement standard of living in retirement?   Yes   No
    Do you believe you are sufficiently preparing (prepared) financially to enjoy
        the lifestyle you prefer during retirement?   Yes   No

2. Savings and Investments
    Are you satisfied with the amount of money you currently have accumulated?   Yes   No
    Are you currently saving and investing enough to reach your retirement goal?   Yes   No
        If no, do you feel you need to increase your savings?   Yes   No
    Are you willing to increase your savings to meet your retirement goals?   Yes   No
    Have you recently been forced to dip into savings?   Yes   No
        If yes, why was it necessary_____
    Are you concerned with reducing the taxes you pay on your savings?   Yes   No

3. Risk Tolerance and Risk Coverage
    Into what risk category or categories would you consider yourself to be
        included?
    1. High risk? (Aggressive)   Yes   No
    2. Balanced risk? (Some aggressive, some conservative)   Yes   No
    3. Conservative? (Little or no risk)   Yes   No
    Do you feel you have sufficiently addressed your need for
    1. Life insurance coverage?   Yes   No
    2. Disability income coverage?   Yes   No
    3. Long-term care insurance?   Yes   No

4. Goals for Retirement Resources
    During retirement, do you want to be financially able to
        A. Leave an estate to your children?   Yes   No
        B. Provide long-term care for any dependents?   Yes   No
        C. Help pay for your grandchildren's education?   Yes   No
    Would you want to be certain that your assets are not depleted during
        retirement?   Yes   No
    Are you willing to consider purchasing additional financial products to help you
        reach your retirement goals?   Yes   No

The answers to the questions in the Personal Retirement Planning Review will help you discern whether the prospect feels motivated to take action to improve retirement security and meet financial goals. In other words, the answers give you enough information to make an initial judgment about whether you should proceed with the prospect into the more detailed retirement planning fact finder.

Some of the reasons that prospects cite for buying financial products have to do with their perceptions of the benefits associated with owning such products. It is important to remember that the purchase of any financial product is not always just about dollars and cents; it is often also emotional. Consequently, this is something about which you need to be sensitive as you ask feeling finding questions in the interview.

> **Remember that the purchase of any financial product is not always just about dollars and cents; it is often also emotional.**

Preliminary Discovery Agreement

By the time you have successfully discussed the need for retirement planning and asked the prequalification questions, you should expect that a qualified prospect is ready to take the next steps toward planning for retirement that may involve purchasing financial products. These steps begin with the completion of a more thorough fact finder and feeling finder so that you can determine a financial need and recommend an appropriate product or products. Therefore, at this juncture, you may consider using a trial close or *preliminary discovery agreement.*

preliminary discovery agreement

Example: "Mr. and Mrs. Prospect, based on your answers to my questions up to this point, it is apparent that you want to take action to ensure a financially secure and comfortable retirement. You also indicated that you would consider taking appropriate action to reach your retirement goals. If I can design a plan that would enable you to accomplish these goals at an affordable cost to you, would you be interested in working together to construct such a plan?"

If the answer is yes, you have a qualified prospect with whom you can proceed. You should use a transitional phrase (see below) in which you gain the prospect's permission to ask for confidential information. You should then proceed to complete the Retirement Planning Fact Finder (see appendix C).

(If the answer is no, or not positive enough, you should explore tactics for handling prospects who fail to qualify and pivoting strategies, depending on the type of situation you encounter.[4])

Dominant Need Situation

A second alternative may occur in which you preliminarily qualify the prospect using the Personal Retirement Planning Review form and then proceed to an abbreviated or modified retirement planning fact finder or your company fact finder because an obvious planning concern or dominant need arises that does not require a full retirement planning analysis. Thus, depending on the prospect's preconception of the purpose of your meeting or willingness to purchase a specific financial product, you may find it advisable to begin to take an application for the appropriate type of product at this point in the initial interview. This situation is the exception rather than the rule in the typical selling/planning process; however, it may happen.

Example: Suppose you meet with a conservative retired prospect who was referred to you. This prospect, who has some money in low-yielding taxable savings and tax-free investment accounts, seeks tax deferral along with a higher return on her money. In this case, you may sell a fixed-interest deferred annuity and not explore every facet of her retirement funding resources. Although the prospect's main concern is receiving a better rate of return on her money, you still need to conduct fact finding to determine the suitability of a fixed-interest deferred annuity in the context of the other financial products that she owns. It may involve obtaining only some basic personal and financial data, but you must explore the prospect's current situation to justify the financial suitability of any product you sell.

Flexibility is a key consideration in conducting a successful interview with potential clients.

As stated earlier, flexibility is a key consideration in conducting a successful interview with potential clients. However, in the example above, you would still need to ask the prospect questions regarding desired areas of annuity benefits, as well as the basic personal information questions in the fact finder you will need to complete the annuity application. Thus, if the prospect clearly views a financial product, such as an annuity, as a single-product need and shows positive buying signs, then sell the product now, rather than jeopardize the opportunity to make the prospect your client. If, however, based on your sales experience and judgment, you think the prospect is more interested in a comprehensive retirement plan that may or may not include an annuity, move into more thorough fact finding using a transitional phrase such as those that follow.

Direct Transition

In the third alternative, immediately after a general discussion of the need for retirement planning and the possible need for financial products within that plan, instead of completing any additional qualifying questions, you could bypass the Personal Retirement Planning Review altogether and proceed directly into personal information gathering using your company's more comprehensive retirement planning fact finder or the one in appendix C. Regardless of which qualifying method you use, it is always advisable to make a smooth transition from one segment of the interview into the next.

Transitional Phrase

You can achieve a seamless transition from a general discussion to actual fact finding by asking for the prospect's permission to proceed.

Example: "For me to do a proper job analyzing your potential retirement (financial) well-being, I'll need to ask you some personal questions. I can assure you that the information I gather will be held in the strictest confidence. With this in mind, is it all right to proceed?"

Note that it might be necessary to schedule a second interview to complete the fact finder. This decision is a judgment call that is based on the following factors: how well you know the prospect, how well educated he or she is about retirement planning issues, how long the previous segments of the interview have taken, and how tired the prospect is.

> Selling financial products to unqualified prospects is unethical because it may cause them more financial harm than good; it may also expose you to legal liability.

Summary

Selling financial products to unqualified prospects is unethical because it may cause them more financial harm than good; it may also expose you to legal liability. Thus, it is in the best interest of all parties to use one of the three procedures above to make certain that the prospect is qualified before recommending a financial product. ◊

THE FACT FINDING PROCESS

After you have qualified the prospect and obtained a preliminary discovery agreement, the actual fact finding and feeling finding portion of the retirement planning process can be a continuation of the initial interview, or it can be a separate interview. This is your option. It is important, however, to remember that the prospect might be tired. The discussion of finances can be exhausting. You need to make certain that your prospect is still alert and attentive to your questions if you decide to continue the initial interview into the fact finding process.

One approach to the financial needs analysis is deductive, while the other is inductive.

Total Financial Needs Analysis to the Dominant or Single Need— the Deductive Approach

deductive approach
The *deductive approach* uses a thorough and lengthy fact finding form that encompasses all the prospect's financial needs. This method covers life, disability income, and long-term care insurance; investment, estate, and education planning needs; and retirement income needs. The process requires quantifying these various financial planning needs and asking the prospect to prioritize them. The category of needs with the highest priority should be determined first. You should then address this most important category of needs by selling the prospect the appropriate product or products that meets that category.

Dominant or Single Need to Total Financial Needs Analysis—the Inductive Approach

inductive approach
The *inductive approach* is the converse of the broad information gathering described above. This method starts with a dominant or single need, such as the need for an annuity to reduce the current taxation of the prospect's savings. It then widens into a full-blown comprehensive financial needs analysis that identifies and prioritizes several financial planning needs. This may occur only after the dominant or single need has been covered by a particular product sale, and it could take several interviews to complete. Sometimes, however, as discussed previously under the "Dominant Need Situation," the dominant or single need product, such as a deferred annuity, may be the only product you ever sell to the prospect, and a total financial needs analysis may never transpire.

We do not necessarily endorse one approach over the other. Your company can provide you with guidance in this area that is consistent with its own marketing strategy and suitability requirements. Some companies that use the inductive or dominant needs approach focus on preapproaching prospects for specific financial products as a door opener in the preretirement or seniors market in the hope of becoming involved in the prospect's retirement planning. Other companies that use the deductive or comprehensive financial planning approach attempt to position the sale of financial products somewhere in the sequence of financial planning needs. For purposes of our discussion, we have chosen the fact finding and feeling finding questions that can be used with either approach to enhance your retirement planning sales opportunities.

Fact Finders

fact finder

There are numerous *fact finders* available for collecting data. Your company has probably already provided you with several that you are using. Nevertheless, we have included a Retirement Planning Fact Finder in appendix C that you are welcome to use with the permission of your company's compliance department. The point to remember about using a fact finder is not to limit yourself to asking just factual and quantitative questions. You should also ascertain your prospect's feelings and values. Asking only the factual questions will not involve your prospect and will not reveal his or her important feelings and values. Values are a person's beliefs and attitudes about a given subject. Feelings reflect a person's values. When you learn about your prospect's dreams and aspirations, you begin to understand him or her. Values are the basis of a person's behavior, and they influence an individual's priorities in life. Discovering your prospect's priorities is the key to understanding what he or she will spend time and money to achieve. Be sure to record the feelings and values revealed during the fact finding process.

> Discovering your prospect's priorities is the key to understanding what he or she will spend time and money to achieve.

Involving the prospect in the fact finding segment of the selling/planning process gives him or her an ownership interest in your financial product recommendations. The very process of discussing and examining feelings leads the prospect to self-discovery. In fact, the prospect is far more likely to spend more time and money on financial products associated with a plan that he or she played a role in designing.

Your prospect must collaborate in the process. Because the prospect is potentially buying your financial products and services, he or she should make that decision based on knowledge obtained from you during the interview. This involves more than just being told what type of product is the best one for him or her. By making a knowledgeable decision to buy, the prospect develops a sense of ownership in the planning process and will truly become your client for other products.

A formal retirement planning fact finder can be divided into four distinct components. The first three are discovery components you should complete with the prospect. The fourth section is for your use only. Whether or not you complete the fourth section in the prospect's presence or after your meeting depends on how comfortable you are using interest tables and performing retirement income need calculations. The four fact finder components are as follows:

- personal data and retirement goals
- quantitative data
- retirement income sources
- calculations and interest tables

As you proceed through the instructions for using this fact finder, keep in mind that it is meant to be a self-contained vehicle for gathering facts, figures, and feelings from a prospect to quantify and qualify the need for financial products, especially as it relates to retirement funding. This requires eliciting personal financial information from the prospect and using several planning assumptions. So that a financial calculator or computer software that illustrates complex time-value-of-money concepts is not needed, this fact finder incorporates interest tables to calculate the prospect's retirement income need. However, because planning assumptions must take into account the inflation rate, interest rates, and the prospect's life expectancy, you should regard the resulting figures as only an estimate of what may actually be sufficient when the prospect retires. Consequently, once you have estimated the retirement income need, you should meet with your client periodically to make any necessary adjustments to the plan.

> Once you have estimated the retirement income need, you should meet with your client periodically to make any necessary adjustments to the plan.

Note: All page numbers referred to in the Retirement Planning Fact Finder in appendix C are the internal page numbers in the fact finder itself, not the page numbers in this textbook.

Personal Data and Retirement Goals

Most questions in the Personal Data and Retirement Goals section of the Retirement Planning Fact Finder are closed-ended and designed to learn simple information that the prospect can easily identify or remember. Many questions in this section begin with "Who is," "When did you," "When do you," and "What are" or "What is." These questions can be asked and answered rapidly. There are also several open-ended questions that require the prospect to consider what he or she would like to do in retirement or reflect on what retirement means to him or her personally.

Questions on fact finder pages 2 and 4 that are marked with an asterisk indicate, as the footnote explains, that these questions also appear on the Personal Retirement Planning Review form in this chapter. This is to remind you that if you used that form to qualify the prospect prior to using the Retirement Planning Fact Finder, you will not ask these same questions again. However, if you make the transition directly from the general discussion of the need for retirement planning to the fact finder, the questions on pages 2 and 4 are useful qualifying questions that you should ask early in the retirement planning fact finding process.

Spaces are provided to fill in the prospect's and spouse's names, dates of birth, Social Security numbers, phone numbers, and children's names, ages, and locations. There is also a question that asks for the names, addresses, and phone numbers of the prospect's professional advisors (that is, attorney, accountant, insurance advisor, bank or trust officer, and securities broker). Additional questions ask about the documents prepared and the services performed by these advisors.

The questions in the Retirement Goals—Assumptions subsection of page 2 are important because they form the basis upon which all calculations of retirement assets and income will be based. For example, it is necessary to know whether a spouse is to be included in this plan, and if so, when the prospect and spouse plan to retire (or have retired). The question on the number of retirement years for which to plan is important because it affects all retirement income calculations regarding how long resources will be required to last. Likewise, accuracy is important regarding the average rate of inflation. You will use this percentage throughout the entire pre- and postretirement periods to ensure that the prospect's future income remains equivalent to what it is today in real or inflation-adjusted dollars. Refer to fact finder table 2 on page 13 of the fact finder for sample inflation rates in the last 3-, 5-, 10-, 15- and 20-year periods to help the prospect select a realistic rate. Approximately 2.5 percent is the average of all the rates found in that table. You and the prospect should determine an average whole number inflation rate and write it in the blank space provided in fact finder table 2. You should also write it in the space provided in question 2 on page 2 of the fact finder.

For questions 3 and 4 on page 2, you need to obtain from the prospect an average rate of compound interest before taxes that can be applied to all savings and investment vehicles before and after retirement begins. An alternative is to calculate the growth of each savings or investment vehicle individually using different rates of interest. This can be confusing to the prospect and cumbersome for you, however, so avoid it if possible. It may be easier for you to use the same interest rate before and after retirement if the prospect agrees.

For questions 5 and 6 on page 2, you have to determine the prospect's average income tax rate. This is important because in reality, all gross income from wages, pensions, taxable savings, and investments, either before or after retirement, will be reduced by this average percentage of expense. Average tax rate is not the same as a person's marginal tax bracket. Marginal tax bracket is the percentage of income taxation applied to the last dollar of income received. Average or effective tax rate percentage is determined by dividing the actual dollar amount of income taxes paid in a year by total income received.

Example: If a single person earns $50,000 in income and pays a total of $8,000 in taxes for the year, his or her average tax rate is $8,000 ÷ $50,000 = 16 percent. Using current rates, the individual's marginal tax bracket is probably 25 percent.

The difference in the two rates is because individuals are allowed to take reductions from gross income for a personal exemption amount, tax-qualified plan contributions, and itemized deductions. You do not have to be a tax expert to determine a prospect's average tax rate. Just find out the total income taxes

Questions on what retirement means to the prospect and the desired standard of living in retirement will give you insight into the prospect's priorities concerning postretirement lifestyle.

the prospect paid in a recent year, (from his or her W-2 form or federal income tax return) and divide it by the prospect's gross income.

There are also several questions in the Retirement Goals—Qualitative section on page 2 that ask about the prospect's recreational activities and where he or she plans to live in retirement. The questions on what retirement means to the prospect personally and the desired standard of living in retirement will give you insight into the prospect's priorities concerning his or her post-retirement lifestyle. There is also a question regarding whether or not any children will be involved in the financial decisions about retirement planning. If so, it is good to discover this early so that you can invite them to be part of subsequent interviews, if appropriate.

All these questions will take only a few minutes to answer and are a good warm-up for the more difficult questions that follow.

Transitional Phrase. You should then make the transition into the next section of the fact finder by letting the prospect know that answers to questions about personal details will help you get a clearer understanding of his or her present financial situation.

Example:	"I appreciate your cooperation in providing the answers to personal details about you and your family, as well as your general retirement goals. Now with your permission, I'd like to ask you some questions about your finances that are necessary for me to get a clear picture of where you stand so that any recommendations I may make will be suitable for your situation. If you have no objection, may I continue?"

Quantitative Data

The objective of this section of the Retirement Planning Fact Finder, which begins on page 3, is to have the prospect provide information about his or her assets and liabilities, most recent cash flow statement, current financial status, investment objectives, and risk tolerance. If the prospect has not already prepared a cash flow statement, he or she may have to obtain the information by looking at income tax records, checkbook receipts, and other documents.

The questions in this section of the fact finder are mostly closed-ended factual questions that ask for a number or percentage, or they are questions that require a "yes" or "no" answer that may have to be combined with an open-ended question to help clarify reasons behind the quantitative data. The answers help you to qualify the prospect and determine the motivation to buy financial products, such as deferred annuities, that will enhance the prospect's financial situation in retirement.

This section of the fact finder asks for personal financial information. Even though you have already told the prospect that you need this information and why, completing this section may take a considerable amount of time, especially if there are no existing financial statements. Meanwhile, you are gradually building trust with the prospect as he or she answers each question.

A key question to ask in the Quantitative Data section is at the top of page 5, immediately after determining the prospect's net cash flow. Asking the prospect what percentage of total annual income received today he or she will require to live comfortably in retirement forces the prospect to begin to realize just how much he or she needs to accumulate from available financial resources to generate the desired income when his or her working life ceases. The percentage of income needed in retirement should then be multiplied by the total gross income today (ascertained from the cash flow statement on fact finder page 4) to calculate what amount of income will be necessary during retirement. This amount should be expressed in today's dollars before taxation.

You may have to help the prospect be realistic in setting a goal for income during retirement. A good rule of thumb is that retirement income should equal about 75 percent of preretirement income to maintain the standard of living after retirement. A goal of less than 75 percent usually means a lower standard of living; a goal of more than 75 percent usually means a higher standard of living after retirement. This will, of course, vary depending on the prospect's individual retirement plans, goals, and financial circumstances.

> The commitment from the prospect for the amount he or she can budget to save can be a "range of affordability" rather than a specific dollar amount.

Obtaining a Dollar Commitment for the Amount That the Prospect Can Afford. While completing the quantitative section of the Retirement Planning Fact Finder, you should obtain a dollar amount commitment from the prospect that he or she can afford to budget to save for retirement. It does not have to be a specific dollar figure *per se*. It can be a "range of affordability" in terms of monthly or annual cost. Therefore, if the prospect indicates that he or she feels the need to increase savings to reach the retirement income goal, you should discuss this need while all the financial information is still fresh in everyone's mind.

Example: "Mr. or Ms. Prospect, assuming you have a need to increase your savings for retirement, I would like you to consider how much you could comfortably afford on a monthly basis to address that need. I don't expect you to have a specific dollar figure in mind, but if you have some idea of

> what you can afford, I assure you I will do every-
> thing possible to customize a plan that fits within
> your budget. Does this make sense to you?"

Alternatively, depending on the prospect's age and retirement status, an increase in savings may be inappropriate because saving has ceased. The prospect may be retired and interested in conserving or growing the assets he or she has accumulated, or at least improving the return on his or her money. Therefore, you may want to ask this question on page 5: "Do you have any funds on hand now that you might want to invest?" If the answer is "yes," then you should ask how much the prospect would consider investing. If the answer is "no," you will have to probe further using questions on page 8 in the Current Investments subsection of the Retirement Income Sources section to uncover assets in taxable income, poorly performing savings, or investment vehicles that could be reallocated to tax-deferred financial products.

By the time you have completed the quantitative section of the fact finder, you should have set the stage for the all-important Retirement Income Sources section.

Transitional Phrase. Again, you should smooth your progression into the next section of the interview with a transitional phrase. Confirm the prospect's annual and monthly cash flow amounts so that you are both in agreement on the figures. Confirmation of figures is a good way to signal the completion of this section of the fact finder. At this point in the interview, you may want to thank the prospect for his or her cooperation.

Example: "You've been very cooperative and forthcoming with information about your personal finances, and I appreciate your help. Now I'd like to ask you some questions that explore your possible retire-ment income sources. This information will allow me to calculate where you stand today in relation to tomorrow's retirement income goal that you have expressed. Does this sound reasonable?"

Retirement Income Sources

This section of the fact finder is the longest and consists of the most questions. It is essential to complete it thoroughly and accurately in order to estimate the prospect's retirement income. It begins with three categories of retirement income summary sections on page 6. The first two income summary categories include inflation-indexed income derived from Social

Security and the other five retirement income sources listed underneath. The third summary category includes fixed income derived from all of the retirement income sources listed below except Social Security. The summaries of inflation-indexed and fixed-income sources of retirement income are derived from information determined in the six subsections on pages 7 through 11. These subsections are

- Social Security Benefits (page 7)
- Pension and Other Funded Income Payments (page 7)
- Current Investments (page 8)
- Deposits and Earnings (page 9)
- Distribution Options (page 10)
- Income and Expenses in Addition to Living Requirements (page 11)

After completing each subsection on fact finder pages 7 through 11, you should go back to the summary sections on page 6 and fill in the correct total for each source of inflation-indexed and fixed income.

The totals of retirement income from each of the six subsections except Social Security are referred to as "sources," as in retirement income sources. The total projected Social Security retirement income is a separate category that is shown in line 1-1 on page 6. All inflation-indexed income derived from each of the remaining five subsections (lines 1-2 through 1-6) is totaled on the line SOURCE 1. All fixed income derived from each of the five subsections, excluding Social Security, is totaled on the line Total of SOURCES 2 + 3 + 4 +5 + 6. The projected income from Social Security should be expressed in today's dollars. The other inflation-indexed income and estimated fixed income from each of the other five sources should be expressed in the actual future dollars anticipated at the prospect's retirement. These five sources constitute the Total Fixed Income (total of SOURCES 2–6). The Total Fixed Income amount should be converted into Total Inflation-Adjusted Fixed Income. The procedure for doing this is explained in the retirement funding calculation example on page 3-50. This will become the category 3 retirement income source, which is the last line on page 6 of the fact finder. Later, the numbers for the prospect's estimated income from Social Security (line 1-1), the total Other Inflation-Indexed Income (SOURCE 1), and the total Inflation-Adjusted Fixed Income (SOURCES 2 through 6) can be copied into their proper boxes in the Client's Figures column of the Retirement Income Calculation Worksheet on fact finder page 12.

Social Security Benefits. The information requested here is straightforward. You should enter the estimated Social Security retirement benefit for the prospect and spouse, if applicable, and indicate the age at which retirement benefits will begin. This information is available from the Social Security benefits statement mailed each year to all participants from the Social Security administration. It can also be requested online at www.ssa.gov. The total of these numbers (on line 1-1 of fact finder page 7) should be in today's dollars because it will be indexed automatically to reflect changes in the CPI. You should also enter this same dollar amount on line 1-1 of the retirement income summary on fact finder page 6.

Pension and Other Funded Income Payments. This subsection consists of annual projected future income from employer-sponsored defined-benefit pension plans, deferred-compensation arrangements, or taxable trust income. The age when benefits will start and the number of years they will be paid should be entered for each separate source, if any. The income derived from this source is presumed to be fixed, not increasing. If it is indexed for inflation at retirement, it should be totaled at the bottom of this subsection (line 1-2 of page 7) and added to other inflation-indexed income dollar amounts (if any) on page 6, line 1-2, to be included as a component of the SOURCE 1 total because it is automatically inflation indexed.

Most defined-benefit plans are not indexed once payment commences, so they should be entered in the SOURCE 2 amount, which will consist of a flat dollar future figure. Many defined-benefit plans may, however, show a projected retirement income figure that will be indexed each year until the prospect's retirement, at which time it will remain fixed. You can obtain this figure from the prospect's current pension benefit statement, which will be expressed in today's dollars. To calculate it at tomorrow's dollars payable at retirement, take the payment in today's dollars and use fact finder table 1 on page 13 to increase it to the expected payment at retirement, assuming a given rate of inflation. For example, if the prospect has $1,000 per month of benefits on his statement and has 15 years remaining until retirement, use the factor found in fact finder table 1 assuming a 3 percent inflation rate, and multiply $1,000 by 1.558 to arrive at $1,558 of income expected from this source at retirement. Then enter $1,558 in SOURCE 2 on fact finder page 7, and also in the SOURCE 2 dollar amount of the summary of fixed income on page 6.

Current Investments. This subsection of the fact finder may be the most cumbersome for the purpose of determining the annual income generated for use in retirement. The inventory of current investments gives you a clear picture of what asset types the prospect owns, how much of each one, and what interest rate each one is earning. This can be extremely valuable information for the possible reallocation of investment or savings dollars away from poorly performing taxable investments and into a tax-deferred product such as a single-premium deferred annuity that is consistent with the prospect's risk tolerance and investment objectives. Therefore, this section of the fact finder can be useful in a dominant needs sales situation when you want to get a total picture of a prospect's current asset allocations. It will help you to better determine the

> The inventory of current investments can be valuable information for the possible reallocation away from poorly performing taxable investments into a single-premium deferred annuity.

prospect's investment diversification needs so that you can more responsibly recommend the most suitable annuity product. Now we will calculate retirement income from resources listed in this subsection of the fact finder.

First, notice that there are six columns. The first column is the tax category, which requires you to indicate whether the investment is taxable (T), tax free (TF), deductible tax deferred (TD), nondeductible tax deferred (ND), or a Roth IRA (R). The second column is the asset class, where you will list the type of each investment. Next, ask the prospect the current value and rate of return for each investment. Using the rate of return (before taxes or after taxes, depending on the tax category of the investment) and the number of years until retirement, estimate the future value of only those investments that will be utilized in retirement to generate income. The after-tax rate of return on an investment can be estimated by reducing the pretax interest rate by the average tax rate found on page 2 of the fact finder. For example, an 8 percent pretax rate of return and a 15 percent average tax rate will generate an after-tax rate of return of about 7 percent (8% x .85 = 6.8%, rounded to 7%). The future value of a single sum is then calculated by using the fact finder table 1 factor on page 13 corresponding to the assumed interest rate and the years of accumulation until retirement. Thus, if $100,000 today grows at 8 percent tax-deferred compound interest for 15 years, multiply $100,000 by the factor in fact finder table 1, which is 3.1722, to find the future value of $317,220. Then, in the last column on the right in the Current Investments section on page 8, indicate what amount of the future value the prospect will use to generate income (all of it, none of it, or only a fraction of it).

Income from investments can be calculated on either a capital-retention basis or a capital-liquidation basis. Instructions for calculating income without depleting the capital are under the heading "How to Calculate the Fixed Income from Investments." For example, if the prospect has $100,000 for use in retirement that is earning an average of 8 percent interest, it will generate $8,000 per year in income before taxes and not deplete the principal sum ($100,000 x .08 = $8,000). You should then enter this figure, $8,000, as the SOURCE 3 dollar amount on page 8 and as the SOURCE 3 dollar amount of the fixed-income summary section on page 6.

This income is fixed, meaning it will not increase. A more realistic method of calculating retirement income is to consider the need for the income to increase each year while in retirement. This involves assuming an inflation rate as well as an earnings rate. It also involves using factors from fact finder table 4 on page 15, titled "Retirement Income Multiplier/Divisor Factors."

Instructions for calculating capital liquidation on an inflation-indexed basis over a finite period of retirement are under the heading "How to Calculate the Inflation-Indexed Income from Investments" on fact finder page 8. For example, if income in real dollars is desired for a finite period of time in retirement, such as 20 years, then use the retirement income multiplier/divisor factors from fact finder table 4. Assuming an interest earnings rate of 8 percent and an inflation rate of 3 percent, to receive 20 years of income, divide the investment capital sum of $100,000 by 13.23. Thus, $7,558 is the inflation-indexed (real) income amount that will be generated each year for 20 years, at which time the capital sum will become exhausted. Thus, you should enter $7,558 on line 1-3 of fact finder page 8, and on line 1-3 of page 6.

What that means is that the actual dollar amount of the payment will increase by the rate of inflation each year but have the same purchasing power as when the payments began, which would usually be when retirement begins. This method is the more responsible one for calculating retirement income needs because inflation is a fact of life; therefore, income in retirement must increase to keep pace with it. It is important, however, to note that this method of using a lump sum of money to generate retirement income will deplete funds that are earmarked to provide income at the end of the assumed period of time that retirement is expected to last.

> **Inflation is a fact of life; therefore, income in retirement must increase to keep pace with it.**

Also, notice that some of the totals lines in this and the next three subsections have a "+" sign to the right of them. This, as the explanatory footnote says, indicates that the totals may include tax-free income that will need to be converted to taxable equivalent amounts. In this way, we can regard all income in retirement as taxable for the sake of simplification and express the shortfall of income on a uniform basis, thus making it more understandable to the prospect. Therefore, any tax-free income receivable during retirement should be converted to its taxable equivalent amount using the prospect's average tax rate and the instructions and example at the bottom of page 11 of the fact finder. The conversion of any tax-free amounts marked with the plus sign should be done before transferring them to their respective SOURCE or line in the summary sections on fact finder page 6.

Deposits and Earnings. This subsection separates the prospect's deposits and earnings into five types of investments. For each type of investment, you should ask the prospect the amount of annualized deposits being made and whether the deposits will increase each year with the rate of inflation. Then, using either the annual rate of interest that applies to each type of investment or the assumed rate of interest from fact finder page 2, estimate the lump-sum value of each future sum that can be used to generate income at retirement. Use either fact finder table 3 (Annual Accumulation Factors: One Dollar per Year in Advance) alone or in conjunction with fact finder table 1.

Example: Assume a prospect is depositing $3,000 per year into a nondeductible tax-deferred annuity. Also assume the average earnings rate is 8 percent and that there are 15 years until retirement. If the deposits remain level, multiply the factor from fact finder table 3 for an 8 percent accumulation rate over 15 years:

29.324 x $3,000 = $87,972

However, if the deposits grow by 3 percent per year, you can use fact finder table 1 to estimate the average dollar amount of deposits for 15 years, and then multiply that figure by 29.324. The approximate inflation adjustment to $3,000 deposits for 15 years can be found using the 3 percent column of fact finder table 1. Take the factor that appears in this column that corresponds to the mid-point year between today and year 15, which is assumed to be the number of years until the prospect retires (year 8). Multiply that factor (1.2668) by $3,000. Next, multiply that amount by 29.324 from fact finder table 3, which equals $111,443, the approximate lump-sum value accumulated by making deposits of $3,000 that increase by 3 percent per year for 15 years and earn 8 percent interest each year:

1.2668 x $3,000 x 29.324 = $111,443

Then determine the projected income generated at retirement from the lump sum accumulated, using either the capital-retention method or the capital-liquidation method discussed previously. Thus, $111,443 multiplied by .08 will provide a level income of $8,915 every year in retirement. This number will constitute the SOURCE 4 dollar amount at the bottom of fact finder page 9, and you should also enter it as the SOURCE 4 dollar amount on page 6.

If, on the other hand, $111,443 is divided by 13.23, which is the retirement income divisor factor from fact finder table 4 for 8 percent interest, 3 percent inflation, and a 20-year liquidation period, $8,424 will be generated in inflation-indexed dollars during the 20-year retirement. You should enter this indexed income from deposits and earning should on line 1-4 at the bottom of fact finder page 9 and on line 1-4 of page 6.

Distribution Options. This subsection totals the annual distributions of income from required minimum distributions, annuity payouts, and life insurance products that the prospect will receive during retirement. These income amounts can be fixed and/or level, depending on their source. Add together those distribution options that are fixed income and write the total dollar amount as SOURCE 5 at the bottom of fact finder page 10. Also transfer the total to page 6 as SOURCE 5 in the summary of fixed income.

Total the sources of distribution options income that may be indexed to inflation, and enter the dollar amount on line 1-5 at the bottom of page 10; also enter that amount on page 6, line 1-5, in the summary of indexed income.

Income and Expenses in Addition to Living Requirements. This subsection is a catch-all for annually received income sources that the fact finder has thus far not addressed. The exact amount of income from some of these sources may be hard to predict. For instance, the sale of a business that may take place 15 years in the future may generate a large sum of investable capital that the prospect can use to help fund retirement. However, the sale price may be impossible to determine accurately, so you will have to work with the prospect to arrive at a reasonable estimate. Other annual sources of income may be temporary. You must exercise judgment as to whether or not you can count on these sources to be consistent during retirement. Total the sources that apply as additional funds are expected per year.

From this amount, subtract any additional major expenses such as the annual mortgage payments needed to purchase a retirement home. Again, some of these expenses may also be temporary, and they may be offset by temporary additional income amounts. But identify those that are deemed to be permanent, and subtract them from additional income. Finally, list the total amount of net fixed additional annual income or expenses as either a positive or negative number, and enter it on fact finder page 11 as the SOURCE 6 dollar amount. Also enter it on page 6 as SOURCE 6. For those amounts that are net indexed additional annual income or expense amounts, list the total as either a positive or negative number, and enter it on page 11 as the line 1-6 dollar amount. Also transfer it to page 6, line 1-6.

Before concluding the interview, you should return to fact finder page 6 and confirm the amount of total Social Security benefits in today's dollars. Then total all inflation-indexed income on lines 1-2 through 1-6. This represents Other Inflation-Indexed Income from SOURCE 1. Also, add fixed retirement income SOURCES 2 through 6 to find Total Fixed Income. Although it may be apparent that a shortfall in retirement income exists, depending on the prospect's situation, it is wise to refrain from discussing products or solutions until the next interview. In any event, the final section of the fact finder, Calculations and Interest Tables, is for your use only and is discussed below.

> During fact finding with the prospect, it is wise to refrain from discussing products or solutions.

Calculations and Interest Tables

This section of the fact finder, pages 12 through 15, consists of a retirement income calculation worksheet and four tables (to which we have previously referred). Three of the tables contain interest factors used in the calculation of an additional retirement income need. This section of the fact finder can best be understood by using an example.

Calculating the Retirement Funding Requirement. Financial advisors need to show prospects the annual or monthly savings required to meet their retirement funding goal. The calculation lends itself to several time-value-of-money concepts that are simplified here to focus on the practical application of these concepts within retirement planning. A worksheet that generates a good approximation of the retirement funding required should contain the following:

- annual gross income goal at retirement in today's dollars
- annual Social Security benefits in today's dollars
- other inflation-indexed income
- total inflation-adjusted fixed income
- an assumed inflation rate
- the number of years until retirement
- the number of years in retirement
- an assumed investment rate of return

The following example describes the calculation process. The replacement-ratio method of calculating the required retirement income is demonstrated. The example illustrates the eight inputs above, and it includes an explanation of how they are derived from the Retirement Planning Fact Finder to determine the income needed at retirement. There is also a detailed explanation of the rationale and procedure for each step of the calculation.

First in this example, the prospect's current annual income ($75,000) is multiplied by a percentage of income with which he or she will be comfortable during retirement. This can range from 50 to 100 percent; 60 percent is shown in the example. This result ($45,000) will produce the prospect's gross annual retirement income goal, which must be expressed in today's dollars.

Next, from the gross annual retirement income goal, subtract the prospect's estimated Social Security retirement income ($21,200), which can be found on the prospect's annual Social Security statement. Again, this number is expressed in today's dollars because under current assumptions, the Social Security retirement benefit will increase in accordance with the CPI. The result is the adjusted annual retirement income goal—in this example, $23,800.

Multiply this figure by the appropriate inflation factor in fact finder table 1 that corresponds to the inflation rate the prospect has chosen and the number of years until retirement. As a guideline, most advisors use a rate in the 3 percent to 4 percent range. Three percent is shown in the example below; factor 1.558 is under the 3 percent column in fact finder table 1 and the row that corresponds to 15 years until retirement. The result determines the first-year retirement income needed, which is $37,080 in this example.

Example:

Current annual income	$75,000
Multiplied by percentage of income needed	x 60%
1. Annual retirement income goal	$45,000
2. Minus projected annual Social Security benefits in today's dollars	−$21,200
Equals adjusted annual retirement income goal (in today's dollars)	$23,800
Multiplied by inflation factor for 15 years at 3%	x 1.558
Equals first-year retirement income needed	$ 37,080
Multiplied by the average inflation factor during 20 years of retirement	x 1.3439
Equals the inflation-adjusted annual retirement income goal	$49,832
Future accumulation of $167,176 / 13.23 (retirement income multiplier/divisor factor from fact finder table 4) = $12,636	
3. Minus other inflation-indexed income	− $12,636
Equals preliminary retirement income shortage	$37,196
4. Minus total inflation-adjusted fixed income	$−7,441
Equals net annual retirement income shortage (approximately)	29,755
Multiplied by retirement multiplier factor for 20 years in retirement	x 13.23
Equals additional accumulation needed	$393,659
Divided by annual accumulation factor for 15 years (fact finder table 3)	÷29.324
Equals annual savings required to reach retirement funding goal	$13,424

Assumptions:

5. Annual inflation rate = 3%
6. Years until retirement = 15
7. Years in retirement = 20

Next, you must adjust the first year retirement income need by the average inflation rate that is anticipated over the 20-year period of retirement. You can estimate this amount by finding the factor from fact finder table 1 that corresponds to the midpoint year of retirement. The midpoint between years 1 and 20 is 10. Thus, the factor from fact finder table 1 under the 3 percent inflation column for year 10 is 1.3439; $37,080 x 1.3439 = $49,832—the inflation-adjusted annual retirement income goal.

From this figure, subtract all other inflation-indexed income (SOURCE 1) and inflation-adjusted fixed income (SOURCES 2 through 6), based on their expected values at retirement. In this example, the SOURCE 1 value is $12,636, which is arrived at by applying several factors to certain accumulation assumptions. Specifically, assume that the prospect is depositing 4 percent of income into a tax-sheltered annuity at work and that the employer is matching it with another 2 percent of income. That means that 6 percent of $75,000, or $4,500 per year, is accumulating at an average assumed compound interest rate of 8 percent. However, this contribution is linked to the prospect's salary, so it is assumed to be increasing with the rate of inflation. There are several steps involved to estimate the approximate result (on an annual basis).

First, you must multiply $4,500 deposited for 15 years by the average 3 percent inflation rate factor for 15 years in fact finder table 1. The factor applied is for the midpoint between today, year 1, and 15 years from today, which would be year 8. This factor, 1.2668, is then multiplied by $4,500, which equals $5,701. This is assumed to be the average annual deposit that is approximately equal to $4,500 growing each year for 15 years at a 3 percent inflation rate. Next, $5,701 is multiplied by the annual accumulation factor from fact finder table 3 for deposits made each year for 15 years at 8 percent interest. That factor is 29.324. Thus, $5,701 multiplied by 29.324 equals $167,176. This result, $167,176, is then divided by 13.23, which is the appropriate retirement divisor factor in fact finder table 4 for an 8 percent interest accumulation rate, a 3 percent inflation rate, and a 20-year (capital liquidation) period of retirement. This results in $12,636 of other inflation-indexed income, which you should enter in the Client's Figures column on the retirement income worksheet in the box next to Other Inflation-Indexed Income (SOURCE 1). Subtracting $12,636 from $49,832 results in a preliminary retirement income shortage of $37,196.

Next, you should divide the total amount of fixed income in SOURCES 2–6 on page 6 of the Retirement Planning Fact Finder by the average inflation factor for the retirement period to arrive at an estimated inflation-adjusted fixed income figure. This is necessary to ensure that all retirement income reflects the erosion of purchasing power caused by inflation while the prospect is retired. For example, if the prospect expects a fixed $10,000 per year at retirement from investments, divide $10,000 by the average inflation factor for 20 years of retirement, which is the factor in fact finder table 1 for the midpoint year (year 10). Thus, $10,000 divided by 1.3439 equals $7,441, which is the 3 percent inflation-adjusted or real-dollar income equivalent of $10,000 for 20 years of retirement. Enter the $7,441 amount in the Client's Figures column, on the worksheet in the box next to Total Inflation-Adjusted Fixed Income (SOURCES 2-6 Adjusted for Inflation). Subtract this amount from the preliminary retirement shortage of $37,196 to find the net annual retirement income shortage.

Calculation Note: Table 4 in the fact finder (Retirement Multiplier/Divisor Factors) works in two ways. It shows factors for compound interest rates of 4 percent, 6 percent, 8 percent, and 10 percent, with inflation rates of 1 percent to 5 percent, for 5-, 10-, 15-, 20-, and 25-year periods. When a lump sum of dollars ($167,176) is divided by the respective factor (13.23) based on three retirement planning assumptions, (8 percent compound interest, 3 percent inflation, and 20 years of retirement, in this case), the result ($12,636) shows the annual retirement income that will be generated in real or inflation-adjusted dollars. Conversely, when a shortfall of income in real dollars must be filled with income that will not be eroded by inflation, then the desired annual income or shortfall is multiplied by the respective factor shown in fact finder table 4 to arrive at the lump sum that the prospect must accumulate to generate the desired annual retirement income. This will be demonstrated below.

> **Calculating an inflation-adjusted fixed income figure is necessary to ensure that all retirement income reflects the erosion of purchasing power caused by inflation.**

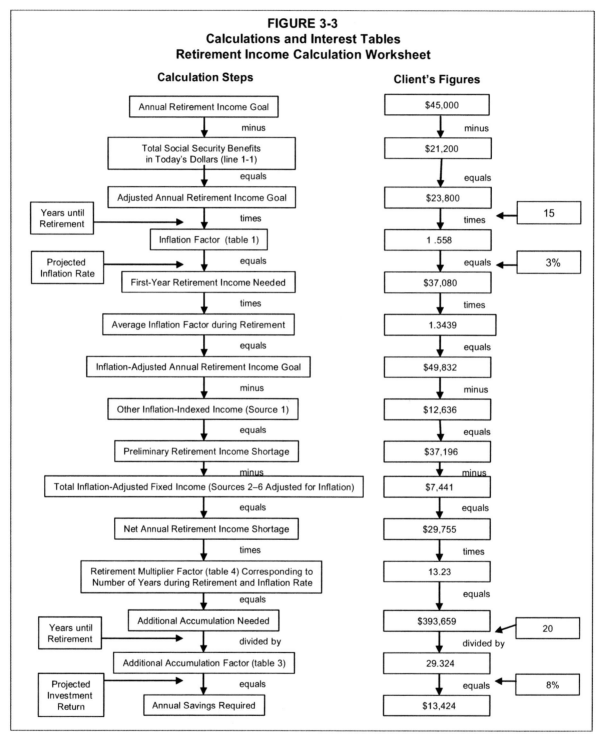

FIGURE 3-3
Calculations and Interest Tables
Retirement Income Calculation Worksheet

Assumes an average annual net rate of return on a 20-year retirement. Retirement begins at age 65. (Taxes not considered.) Rate of return is hypothetical, for illustrative purposes only, and does not represent actual performance of any product.

Thus far, in this case, there is a net annual retirement income shortage of $29,755. A calculation is needed to determine the sum of capital that must be accumulated by the beginning of retirement that will generate $29,755 in inflation-adjusted dollars throughout the 20-year retirement period. To find the capital sum required, *multiply* $29,755 by factor 13.23, which is the factor from fact finder table 4 that corresponds to 8 percent compound interest and 3 percent inflation for 20 years of retirement. The result is $393,659, which is the additional sum of money that the prospect needs to accumulate over the next 15 years, assuming an 8 percent compound interest rate before taxes and a 3 percent inflation rate, to produce $29,755 in constant purchasing power each year.

To determine how much the prospect must save each year to reach this $393,659 accumulation goal, refer to fact finder table 3. This table shows accumulation factors for $1.00 deposited each year in advance for a given number of years at various assumed compound interest rates. A capital sum desired at some future year can be divided by these factors based on years of accumulation and net compound interest rate to determine the annual savings required to reach the desired future sum. Thus, $393,659 is divided by factor 29.324 in fact finder table 3 under the 8 percent interest column in the 15 years row. The result, $13,424, is the level annual savings amount required to accumulate $393,659 earning 8 percent for 15 years. The result of dividing $13,424 by 12, which is $1,119, is the approximate level monthly deposit the prospect must make to reach his or her desired retirement income goal based on the above cited current assumptions and inputs.

You can also include the step-up rate of savings required for the first year, beginning immediately. You can calculate this by dividing the $13,424 level annual savings required by the inflation rate factor for the midpoint between today and 15 years when retirement will begin. The factor is 1.2668 in the 3 percent column of fact finder table 1 corresponding to year 8 The result of dividing $13,424 by 1.2668 is $10,597, which would be the first year's contribution. The contribution would increase by 3 percent each year to correspond to increases in earnings that are assumed to increase at the rate of inflation.

Summary

When you have completed all three information-gathering sections of the Retirement Planning Fact Finder, you should be equipped to analyze the information so that you can design an appropriate plan and recommend products that are consistent with the prospect's goals and objectives. Because you may have collected an enormous amount of data during the fact finding process, it may be a good idea to review and confirm each section as you complete it. Or you may choose the close of the interview as the best time to review all the information you have recorded. You should summarize your interpretation of the prospect's feelings about retirement planning issues and

> **Because you may have collected an enormous amount of data during the fact finding process, it may be a good idea to review and confirm each section as you complete it.**

give him or her a chance to agree with your assessment or to clarify any aspects you may not have accurately understood.

The point at which you complete the retirement income calculation worksheet is a matter of choice. One approach is to apply the information from the Retirement Income Sources section of the fact finder (pages 6 through 11) and use the worksheet after your meeting with the prospect. In this way, you can carefully calculate what the prospect needs to fill the retirement income gap and make specific product recommendations at that time. However, as mentioned previously, flexibility is the key to successful interviewing, and if you feel comfortable enough to use the retirement income calculation worksheet in the presence of the prospect, then by all means do it. If you take this latter approach to quantifying the additional retirement income needed, make sure you show it to the prospect and include a reference to it in the verbal discovery agreement (discussed below) before you conclude the meeting.

By reviewing the facts and feelings that you have recorded, you not only check your understanding of what the prospect has told you, but you also show the prospect that you were paying attention to what he or she said. Be sure that the prospect concurs with your interpretation of his or her feelings. A retirement plan or product recommendation will not be effective if it is based on inaccurate information or on assumptions that you, rather than the prospect, have made.

Mutual Agreement to Work Together

The fact finding process is often a very complex one. More than one meeting may be necessary before the entire process is complete. At the beginning of any subsequent meetings, be sure to review and confirm the information gathered at the previous meetings. Always be sure that you and the prospect are thinking along the same lines.

Discovery Agreement

discovery agreement

Finally, many financial advisors conclude the initial fact finding interview by summarizing the prospect's goals in writing. This practice, known as the *discovery agreement*, can also be done verbally. When the discovery agreement is verbal, you should ask the prospect to acknowledge that he or she has a financial need and elicit from the prospect a willingness to work together with you toward seeking financial solutions within the framework of his or her budget that address the retirement planning concerns discussed throughout the interview.

The agreement to work together toward mutually acceptable solutions to the prospect's financial concerns establishes a climate of trust and partnership.

It is more effective, however, to send a letter subsequent to the meeting that not only acknowledges the substance of what you and the prospect discussed, but also provides a blueprint for proceeding through the next step(s) in the selling/planning process. This implied contract is essential in building a true client-advisor relationship. The agreement to work together toward mutually acceptable solutions to the prospect's financial concerns establishes a climate of trust and partnership. ◊

CHAPTER THREE REVIEW

Key Terms and Concepts are explained in the Glossary. Answers to the Review Questions and Self-Test Questions are found in the back of the book in the Answers to Questions section.

Key Terms and Concepts

goal setting	social style
goal prioritization	effective communication
retirement income needs	active listening
income requirement assumption	preliminary discovery agreement
replacement-ratio approach	deductive approach
expense method approach	inductive approach
retirement income gap	fact finder
step-up rate	discovery agreement

Review Questions

3-1. Explain why goal setting is important to the financial/retirement planning process.

3-2. List the six assumptions that an advisor must make in the retirement planning process.

3-3. List the reasons why is it difficult to forecast an inflation assumption for a prospect.

3-4. Identify and discuss some reduced living expenses that a retiree may encounter.

3-5. List and discuss some living expenses that may increase for the retiree.

3-6. Describe how the replacement-ratio method can be used to estimate a prospect's retirement income.

3-7. Describe how the expense method can be used to estimate a prospect's retirement income.

3-8. Explain the main purpose of the initial interview in a two-interview sales approach.

3-9. Identify the important components of steps 3 and 4 in the retirement planning process.

3-10.	List the four social styles, and identify the characteristic that best explains what a prospect with a particular style is motivated to achieve.

3-11.	Describe some of the sales presentation tools and techniques that an advisor can use to explain the need for retirement planning.

3-12.	Briefly explain the three methods used to qualify prospects.

3-13.	Identify the four distinct components of a formal retirement planning fact finding form.

3-14.	Identify and briefly describe the implied contract an advisor should secure at the conclusion of the fact finding interview that represents mutual consent between the advisor and the prospect to continue working together.

Self-Test Questions

Instructions: Read chapter 3 first, then answer the following questions to test your knowledge. There are 10 questions; circle the correct answer, then check your answers with the answer key in the back of the book.

3-1.	Which of the following expenses is likely to increase for retirees?

(A)	Social Security taxes
(B)	work-related expenses
(C)	medical expenses
(D)	home ownership expenses

3-2.	The approach to information gathering that uses a fact finding form that first broadly covers all the prospect's financial needs and then narrows the discussion to prioritized dominant needs is the

(A)	deductive approach
(B)	inductive approach
(C)	single-need approach
(D)	dominant-need approach

3-3.	In estimating retirement savings, which of the following corresponds to the prospect's projected growth rate in compensation, thereby keeping the rate of savings at a constant percentage?

(A)	step-up rate
(B)	capitalization of equity
(C)	accumulation factor
(D)	standard of living

3-4. The difference between which of the following best decribes the retirement income gap?

(A) age 65 and the prospect's life expectancy
(B) the deductibility threshold and the excess above that threshold for qualifying medical expenses
(C) the amount of money that is necessary to reach the retirement income goal and the amount anticipated from all available sources
(D) the estimated inflation rate and the long-term inflation rate

3-5. Which of the following statements regarding the goals of retirement planning is (are) correct?

I.   Retirement planning has become less important today because of changes in our socioeconomic institutions and because most people now anticipate working at least part-time during their retirement years.
II. The primary responsibility for an advisor in planning for prospects' retirement is to make them aware that they are making lifestyle choices about their retirement security every day.

(A) I only
(B) II only
(C) Both I and II
(D) Neither I nor II

3-6. Which of the following statements concerning the level of income that a retiree needs to sustain throughout his or her retired life is (are) correct?

I.   The replacement ratio method usually works well for prospects at or near retirement because they can closely approximate their retirement income budget.
II. The expense method generally works well for younger prospects because they cannot accurately estimate their retirement expenses but they can determine the standard of living they want to enjoy during retirement.

(A) I only
(B) II only
(C) Both I and II
(D) Neither I nor II

3-7. Which of the following statements concerning forecasting the rate of inflation is (are) correct?

    I. The inflation assumption rate chosen depends on the prospect's spending habits, current age, and risk tolerance.

    II. The lower the inflation rate projected, the greater the percentage of salary the prospect needs to save for retirement.

    (A) I only
    (B) II only
    (C) Both I and II
    (D) Neither I nor II

3-8. All the following are assumptions required in the retirement planning process EXCEPT

    (A) retirement age assumption
    (B) longevity assumption
    (C) income requirement assumption
    (D) insurability assumption

3-9. To establish rapport in the initial interview, an advisor must create an environment that promotes prospect openness by doing all of the following EXCEPT

    (A) alleviating the prospect's concerns
    (B) responding to the prospect's social style
    (C) talking most of the time to the prospect
    (D) mutually agreeing to an agenda for the interview

3-10. All the following are considered major sources of retirement income EXCEPT

    (A) marginal income
    (B) personal savings
    (C) Social Security benefits
    (D) pension distributions

NOTES

1. These topics are discussed here in an abbreviated manner. For a more comprehensive discussion of these interviewing techniques, see Johni R. Hays, ed., *Essentials of Annuities*. Bryn Mawr, PA: The American College Press, © 2004, chapter 3.
2. "Personal Styles and Effective Performance," David W. Merill and Roger H. Reid, © 1999 CRC Press LLC.
3. See pages 2.2 through 2.10 of this text for sources of retirement income.
4. For a more comprehensive discussion of these interviewing techniques, see Johni R. Hays, ed., *Essentials of Annuities*. Bryn Mawr, PA: The American College Press, © 2004, chapter 3.

4

Financial Obstacles to Successful Retirement Planning

Learning Objectives

An understanding of the material in this chapter should enable the student to

4-1. List the special planning needs that can create obstacles to successful retirement planning.

4-2. Identify financial products and concepts available to help fund a college education.

4-3. Describe the basic benefits provided by medical expense insurance, Medicare, and medigap for long-term care (LTC) expenses.

4-4. Identify and describe the different levels and types of long-term care.

4-5. Identify the common long-term care insurance provisions and define common long-term care insurance terms.

4-7. Explain the concept of transfer of risk as a risk management technique.

4-8. Explain why life insurance and disability income insurance play important roles in retirement planning.

4-9. List and explain the risks associated with property ownership.

4-10. Describe the impact that income taxation has on planning for retirement, and identify income tax reduction strategies to handle it.

4-11. Explain the effect of inflation on purchasing power.

4-12. List and describe financial management techniques for dealing with inflation.

4-13. Explain the impact that the procrastination of saving has on funding for retirement.

Chapter Outline

SPECIALIZED PLANNING NEEDS

specialized financial planning goals

In addition to the major planning areas that pertain to almost every client, there are a number of more *specialized financial planning goals*. The most important of these specialized goals in terms of the number of people it affects is college education funding. The other specialized areas worthy of mention are those that can be categorized as financial planning for special circumstances. These areas typically include planning for

- divorce
- terminal illness
- nontraditional families
- job or career change
- job loss, including severance packages
- dependent parents who need long-term care (LTC)
- other dependents with special needs
- the purchase of a first home
- the purchase of a vacation or second home

An important part of the retirement planning process is recognizing the need for contingency planning. Reaching long-term goals requires your prospects to look at all the life events that may interrupt their planning strategies or divert money from retirement savings.

Your prospects can plan for some life events and integrate them into an overall long-term plan. For example, parents who want to plan for college educations can make this goal part of their overall long-term planning.

On the other hand, people do not plan to divorce or to have ailing parents to care for. But these events happen. Statistically, one in two marriages fails. And as life expectancy increases, parents will live longer. The longer parents live, the more likely it is that they will need care.

Your prospects and clients can protect themselves against the financial consequences of some life events. They can purchase adequate amounts of life and disability income insurance or LTC insurance for themselves and their parents.

In analyzing specialized financial planning goals, however, keep in mind that the choices your client makes regarding one component of a financial plan will often affect other components. For example, if both retirement planning and education funding are priorities, you need to help your client balance the two.

After fact finding, you should have a clear picture of the assets and/or discretionary income your client has available to fund both goals. If assets and/or income are insufficient for this purpose, he or she may have to tighten the budget, earn more income, or modify one or both goals. If goal modification is the choice, your client may have to forego plans to retire at age 60 if he or she wants to send children to college. This may require postponing retirement to age 65 or even 70. Moreover, your client may also have to compromise on his or her children's choice of colleges or their lifestyle while attending college. This may mean that the children have to attend the less expensive state university instead of the elite private university, or that they have to live at home and commute to a junior college for the first 2 years before transferring to a 4-year university. These are some of the compromise choices your client may have to make to achieve a balance between two priority goals.

This chapter begins with a discussion of college education funding because it is an expensive life event that can be planned. However, you should not

> **Keep in mind that the choices your client makes regarding one component of a financial plan will often affect other components.**

overlook the other life events that occur. Ignoring them does not make them go away. Later in this chapter, the following obstacles to successful retirement planning, along with some suggested actions your clients can take to overcome them, will be discussed:

- health care costs during retirement
- income taxes
- other insurable financial risks
- inflation
- procrastination

College Education Funding[1]

If your client wants help in developing a funding plan for specific objectives, such as children's college educations, it is important to have a quantifiable determination of his or her financial risk tolerance. You can determine this through a questionnaire such as those use in conjunction with the sales of mutual funds or variable life insurance policies. (The topic of financial risk tolerance is discussed in chapter 5.) This specific objective may require either funding that is separate from the funding allocated to long-range objectives, such as capital accumulation for retirement or temporary allocations of all or part of the client's financial resources.

> **Clients often delay funding college expenses because they have no idea what those expenses will be in the future.**

Clients often delay funding college expenses because they have no idea what those expenses will be in the future. Without precise information, you can estimate these expenses from existing studies, such as those conducted by The College Board (www.collegeboard.com), which publishes estimates of the average college costs for 2-year and 4-year public and private colleges. College cost estimates will enable you to project the total education expenses for each child. Therefore, you should use them with clients whenever possible. Although no one knows with precision what future rates will be, any meaningful estimates of future college costs must assume an inflation rate.

Along with the estimated tuition cost in today's dollars and the tuition inflation rate, you should list the child's name and age, the number of years until the child begins college, and the number of years the child is expected to attend college. All existing capital and monthly income allocated for the specific purpose of college funding should also be listed. The growth rate of these earmarked funds should be recorded.

In addition, you may want to ask your client some questions regarding education funding such as

- How do you plan to pay for your children's college educations?
- Have you made contingency plans to fund your children's college educations if you become disabled or die before they reach college age?
- Have you considered all potential resources available to fund college?

As a financial advisor, you should determine whether your client's financial resources can be supplemented by other help, such as scholarships; part-time work; loans from federal, state, or family sources; and wills, trusts, and other gift programs by grandparents or other relatives. Help may be expected from a previous spouse. You should explore all possible sources in an effort to reduce or even eliminate the client's share of anticipated costs. This will free investment capital and cash flows for allocation to the client's other financial objectives.

Education Needs

consumer price index (CPI)

> **The vast majority of families accumulate far too little money for college by the matriculation date.**

Most clients with children understand the need to save for college and are aware that college costs have risen at a faster pace than the *consumer price index (CPI)*. Still, the vast majority of families accumulate far too little money for college by the matriculation date. They usually have to cut back on living expenses, borrow money, tap into retirement assets, or seek additional employment to meet the funding need. Often, they lower their sights and target schools that are less expensive rather than the ones best suited to their children's needs. Consequently, planning to meet the costs of higher education has become a necessity for most parents.

The cost of higher education has increased dramatically, particularly at private colleges and universities. For example, it may cost $30,000 to $40,000 or more per year in tuition, fees, and room and board for a student to attend some private colleges. This can result in a tremendous financial drain for a family with college-age children; yet it is a predictable drain that can be prepared for by setting up an education fund.

The size of the fund obviously depends on the number of children, their ages, their educational plans, any scholarships and student loans that may be available to them, and the size of the family income. It also depends on the family's attitude toward education. Some people feel they should provide their children with all the education they can profit from and want. Others, however, feel that children should help earn at least a part of their educational expenses themselves. What types of schools the children plan to attend also has a considerable bearing on the costs involved.

> **When planning for your client's specialized goals, your primary task is to help him or her develop a way to fund them.**

An investment fund for educational needs is often a relatively long-term objective, and the hope is that the fund will not be needed in the meantime. Thus, wider investment latitude seems more justified than in the case of an emergency fund to secure a more attractive investment yield. All that is really necessary is for the funds to be there by the time each child is ready for school.

Calculating the Funds Needed

When planning for your client's specialized goals, your primary task is to help him or her develop a way to fund them. The steps for calculating the funds needed for any type of specialized financial planning goal are as follows:

1. Estimate the annual or total cost of the goal in today's dollars.
2. Determine the date in the future when the funds will be needed.
3. Apply an inflation rate to the dollar estimate from step 1 and project it to the date in the future determined in step 2.
4. Determine the amounts of capital and/or income currently available for funding the goal, assign a compound growth rate to those amounts, and project them to the date in the future determined in step 2.
5. Compare the projected amounts currently available from step 4 to the inflation-adjusted estimated cost from step 3. To the extent that the estimated cost from step 3 exceeds the projected amounts currently available from step 4, a shortfall of funds is indicated.

As a component part of your client's financial plan, you should develop and include strategies for funding the shortfall.

If your client has college education funding as a specialized financial planning goal for which additional capital is needed, you should summarize these needs. The summary should include the total amount of dollars needed to fund the desired goal that you calculate during the analysis stage of the selling/planning process. You should compare this dollar amount to how much of that goal your client's current plan provides.

Example: Suppose that your clients have a goal to fund their children's college education, which requires that they accumulate an additional $200,000 over the next 15 years. You project that they will accumulate $95,000 at their current rate of saving. This shows a shortfall of $105,000 if your clients make no change in their current plan:

Total capital needed for college	$200,000
Current plan provides	95,000
Additional capital required	105,000

If there is a disparity between the amounts, you and your client can work together to develop solutions to meet the client's goal. In the example above, it is necessary to calculate the additional amount needed per year (shown in today's dollars) to fund this goal based on an assumed rate of return such as 6 percent interest. You should then summarize several funding alternatives to meet the extra amount needed, in addition to having your client continue the existing savings plan. The funding alternatives could include the following modes of payment and amounts:

- additional lump sum $43,813
- additional monthly level savings $359
- additional monthly inflated savings (amount $123
  shown is for the first year only; this amount
  must be increased annually by an assumed
  inflation rate of 3 percent)

(Bar graphs that depict how the increasing accumulations of cash will meet the needed cash accumulation goal for college funding are helpful in illustrating alternatives. Creating these bar graphs is simple, using the financial planning software available today.)

Finally, you should assemble a list of all possible sources of funds that your client may not yet have considered. If, in the example above, all financial aid programs, student loans, home equity loans and lines of credit, scholarship sources, student employment income, and gifts from family members, such as grandparents, have already been factored into the calculation, along with all current education income tax credits and deductions, then the remaining amount needed to fill the funding deficit would have to come from financial vehicles and products.

You can incorporate the following list of sources and tax benefits into your recommendations for college funding:

- Coverdell education savings accounts. Formerly known as education IRAs, these accounts allow donors (parents, grandparents, or anyone else) to contribute up to a maximum of $2,000 per child per year into an education fund. Although the contribution is not deductible, earnings are not taxed as long as the funds are used to pay elementary, secondary, or postsecondary education expenses.
- traditional IRA, Roth IRA, simplified employee pension plan (SEP), and SIMPLE plan distributions. Withdrawals from these individual retirement plans that are made to pay "qualified higher education expenses" for the taxpayer, the taxpayer's spouse, and the child or grandchild of the taxpayer or the taxpayer's spouse are exempt from the usual IRS early withdrawal penalty, which is generally 10 percent of the amount withdrawn. Qualified education expenses include tuition, fees, books, supplies, and equipment required for enrollment in a postsecondary education institution.
- employer-sponsored qualified retirement plan loans and distributions. Qualified plan loans are tax free as long as they are repaid within the allotted time period. Distributions are subject to income taxation and the IRS early withdrawal penalty.
- qualified tuition programs (Sec. 529 plans). These programs are tax-advantaged approaches to saving for college expenses. Funds accu-

mulated grow tax deferred. Also, distributions are tax free as long as the proceeds are used for qualified education expenses such as room, board, tuition, books, and supplies. Available in almost all states, plans can take two forms: prepaid tuition plans and savings plans. Approaches vary, but *prepaid tuition plans* sponsored by states or qualified educational institutions generally allow parents to purchase tuition credits at current prices, thus locking in a child's tuition rate years in advance of enrollment. Sec. 529 savings plans typically allow investment in mutual funds. Their returns are not tied directly to tuition inflation at a particular college, but the potential returns exceed the inflation protection.

- education savings bond programs. Series EE U. S. savings bonds are exempt from state income tax, making them especially appealing to higher-income-bracket clients. Interest from these bonds is either totally or partially exempt from federal income taxation if used for tuition and fees. The tax-exempt feature phases out for joint filers with modified adjusted gross income (MAGI) above $94,700 and for single taxpayers with MAGI above $63,100 for 2006, and it is indexed for inflation.

- Hope scholarship tax credit. A tax credit of up to $1,650 (in 2006) per student per year is allowed for tuition and related expenses incurred during the first 2 years of postsecondary education. The credit equals 100 percent of the first $1,100 of qualified tuition and related expenses, and 50 percent of the next $1,100 of tuition and fees.

- lifetime learning tax credit. A credit is allowed for up to $2,000, calculated as 20 percent of the first $10,000 of tuition and other qualified education expenses. (In 2006, both credits were phased out for MAGIs from $45,000 to $55,000 for single filers and $90,000 to $110,000 for joint filers.)

- deductibility of interest on education loans. As a result of the Taxpayer Relief Act of 1997, some interest on education loans is now deductible even if your client does not itemize deductions. The available deduction is a maximum of $2,500. For the year 2006, it is subject to a phaseout for single filers between $50,000 and $65,000 of MAGI and for joint filers between $105,000 and $135,000 of MAGI.

- employer's educational assistance program. Under this program, an employer can pay for an employee's tuition (both graduate and undergraduate), enrollment fees, books, supplies, and equipment, and these benefits are excluded from the employee's income up to $5,250 per year (for 2006).

Table 4-1 summarizes the highlights and attributes of the various income tax benefits related to higher education covered in this section.

TABLE 4-1
Highlights of Tax Benefits for Higher Education for 2006

	Hope Scholarship Credit	Lifetime Learning Credit	Coverdell Education Savings Account[1]	Traditional, Roth, SEP, and SIMPLE IRAs[1]	Student Loan Interest	Qualified Tuition Programs[2] (Sec. 529 Plans)	Education Savings Bond Program[1]	Employer's Educational Assistance Program[1]
What is your benefit?	Credits can reduce the amount of tax you must pay		Earnings are not taxed	No 10% additional tax on early withdrawal	You can deduct the loan interest	Earnings are not taxed	Interest is not taxed	Employer benefits are not taxed
What is the annual limit?	Up to $1,650 per student	Up to $2,000 per student	$2,000 contribution per beneficiary	Amount of qualifying expenses	$2,500	Determined by sponsor	Amount of qualifying expenses	$5,250
What expenses qualify besides tuition and required enrollment fees?	None		Books, supplies, equipment Room and board if at least halftime student Payments to state tuition program	Books, supplies, equipment Room and board if at least halftime student	Books, supplies, equipment Room and board Transportation Other necessary expenses	Books, supplies, equipment Room and board if at least halftime student	Payments to Coverdell ESAs Payments to qualified tuition program	Books, supplies, equipment
What education qualifies?	1st 2 years of undergraduate	All undergraduate and graduate[3]						
What are some of the other conditions that apply?	Can be claimed on 1st 2 years tuition and related expenses Must be enrolled at least halftime in a degree program		Can contribute to Coverdell ESAs and qualified tuition program in the same year Must withdraw assets by age 30		Must have been at least halftime student in a degree program	Distribution excluded from gross income Hope and lifetime learning credits permitted in the same year but not for the same expenses	Applies only to qualified series EE bonds issued after 1989 or series I bonds	

1. Any nontaxable withdrawal is limited to the amount that does not exceed qualifying educational expenses.
2. Exclusion is extended to distributions from qualified tuition programs established by an entity other than a state after December 31, 2003.
3. For Coverdell education savings accounts, qualified elementary and secondary school expenses are also permitted (grades K–12).

Financial products could include

- savings accounts
- certificates of deposit
- mutual funds
- brokerage accounts (including stocks and bonds)
- annuities
- life insurance products

Legal instruments such as the following can also contain financial products used for education funding:

- Uniform Gifts to Minors Act (UGMA) accounts and Uniform Transfers to Minors Act (UTMA) accounts. These accounts are frequently used for smaller gifts that fall within the annual gift tax exclusion ($12,000 in 2006). They offer simplicity, the benefits of management, income tax shifting, and other trust characteristics without the cost of drafting a trust. Note that a *kiddie tax* applies to children under 14 in 2006, increasing to age 18 in 2007. It allows up to $850 (in 2006; indexed for inflation) of unearned income in accounts such as these to be received income tax free, taxes the next $850 at 10 percent, and applies the parents' tax rate to additional amounts.
- Sec. 2503(c) trusts. These trusts are useful to take advantage of the annual gift tax exclusion. A married couple can contribute up to $24,000 per year per child to a 2503(c) trust gift tax free. Because this type of trust can accumulate income, delay payment of principal, and then allow disbursements during the college years, it is an ideal method where larger amounts are involved.
- Sec. 2503(b) trusts. The 2503(b) trusts require that all income be paid at least annually to the beneficiaries. This type of trust is also eligible for the annual gift tax exclusion and allows delayed payment of principal until college funding is needed. It differs from the 2503(c) trust in two ways. First, the 2503(b) trust requires that all income be paid out each year, whereas the trustee of a 2503(c) trust can decide to accumulate it. Second, the 2503(b) trust can retain funds beyond the beneficiary's age of majority, while the 2503(c) trust requires that all principal and income be distributed to the minor at age 21.

Your recommendations of financial products and funding vehicles will depend on your client's risk tolerance and time horizon.

Your recommendations of financial products and funding vehicles will depend on your client's risk tolerance and time horizon, and they must be suitable for the specific situation. As with any component of the personal financial plan, you must present a choice of funding products and concepts that you think your client will find acceptable. Otherwise, your client may not implement the concepts you recommend, in which case everybody loses.

Remember Insurance Protection and Risk Management Needs

Before leaving our consideration of college funding, at least one point is worth repeating. No plan will succeed if it is not funded. For this reason, making sure that the parents have adequate life and disability income insurance is a critical part of any college funding plan.

Review your clients' life and disability income insurance programs with the need for college funding in mind. There should be appropriate coverage to ensure their children's educational funding even if a parent dies or becomes disabled.

Also, you should address other forms of risk management, such as adequate liability, property, medical expense insurance, and, depending on their age, LTC insurance coverage for the parents of children for whom college planning is being undertaken before saving for college is initiated. The financial disaster that can occur from any of these perils can sidetrack college funding as well as retirement planning. ◊

HEALTH CARE COSTS DURING RETIREMENT

One of the most challenging and formidable obstacles to the financial security of today's retirees is the spiraling cost of health care in the United States. Consider the following statistics:

- Life expectancy for men and women who reach age 65 is 16 and 19.4 years, respectively.[2]
- Although estimates vary, a couple retiring at age 65 without private health insurance from a former employer can expect to pay significant out-of-pocket health care costs during their retirement years. One study estimates out-of-pocket health care costs of $190,000 over 15 to 20 years for a couple who retires in 2005. This estimate excludes the costs of LTC or over-the-counter medicines.[3]

> At age 65, people face at least a 40 percent lifetime risk of entering a nursing home at some point, and about 10 percent will have a stay of 5 years or longer.

- At age 65, people face at least a 40 percent lifetime risk of entering a nursing home at some point, and about 10 percent will have a stay of 5 years or longer.[4]
- The average daily rate in 2005 for a private room in a nursing home was $203 ($74,095 annually), and a semi-private room cost $176 a day ($64,240 annually).[5]
- The average length of a nursing home stay is about 2.4 years.[6]
- At an average daily rate of $203, an average nursing home stay of 2.4 years costs about $178,000.

In this section we will briefly discuss medical expense insurance, Medicare, and Medicare supplement insurance programs that provide health care benefits for the retiree. Then we will look at the issue of LTC and the extent to which these three types of insurance programs provide potential LTC benefits for retirees. We will examine the financial threat that LTC poses for retirees and discuss how long-term care insurance (LTCI) can be used to protect their liquid assets during retirement.

Medical Expense Insurance

Continued Employer-Provided Coverage

Almost one-third of retired employees may have some type of employer-provided coverage to supplement Medicare. Although coverage can also be continued for retirees' dependents, it is often limited only to spouses. Retired employees under age 65 usually have the same coverage as the active employees have. Coverage for employees aged 65 or older (if included under the same plan), however, may be provided under a Medicare carve-out or a Medicare supplement. Some employers furnish coverage to supplement Medicare in a manner similar to what is provided by one of the standard Medicare supplement policies discussed later.

> **Because of increasing benefit costs, many employers have lowered or eliminated retiree medical expense benefits, or they are considering such a change.**

Because of increasing benefit costs, many employers have lowered or eliminated retiree medical expense benefits, or they are considering such a change. However, many employers also feel that there is a moral obligation to continue these benefits. As a result, most employers are not altering plans for current retirees or active employees who are eligible to retire. Rather, the following changes will apply to future retirees:

- eliminating benefits for future retirees
- shifting more of the cost burden to future retirees by reducing benefits, providing lower benefit maximums, covering fewer types of expenses, or increasing copayments
- adding or increasing retiree sharing of premium costs after retirement
- shifting to a defined-contribution approach to fund retiree benefits (for example, an employer might agree to pay $5 per month toward the cost of coverage after retirement for each year of the employee's service)

Medical Expense Coverage for Long-Term Care

Group and individual medical expense insurance primarily covers acute medical care for illness or injury. However, coverage often includes some very limited benefits for services rendered by licensed medical practitioners (such as physicians, nurses, and therapists).

Medical expense policies also frequently contain a specific exclusion for custodial care, the most common form of care required by the elderly and others with chronic physical and cognitive impairments. The custodial care exclusion is defined broadly to eliminate coverage for the following:

- assistance with activities of daily living (ADLs) (ADLs are defined later in this chapter under the heading "Chronically Ill Person.")
- services that do not seek to cure or are provided during periods when the patient's medical condition is not changing
- services that do not require continued administration by trained medical personnel

Note that insurers will sometimes pay for LTC (convalescent care) expenses that are not otherwise covered as long as this care is a less expensive alternative to covered services under a policy (such as hospitalization).

Overview of the Medicare System

> For some people, Medicare will fall far short of answering their LTC needs.

Many seniors depend on Medicare to finance their health care costs. For some people, the system will prove adequate for their medical health care needs. For others, Medicare will fall far short of answering their LTC needs. As a financial advisor, your knowledge of the Medicare system is important in giving advice to seniors. Understanding what is covered and what is not covered under the Medicare system will enable you to educate seniors about their needs and to offer solutions to fill those needs.

Medicare

Medicare is a federal program administered by the Center for Medicare and Medicaid Services (CMS) that provides health care coverage for more than 37 million seniors and disabled individuals. Its coverage rules are uniform throughout the country. The same set of rules applies whether a person resides in Alaska or Florida. The Medicare program consists of four parts: Part A, Part B, Part C, and the new prescription drug plan, Part D.

Medicare Part A: Hospital Insurance

Medicare Part A provides coverage primarily for inpatient hospital care. It also provides hospice care and limited coverage for skilled-nursing home and home health care.

Most seniors become eligible for Part A coverage when they reach full retirement age and become entitled to Social Security retirement benefits. Some seniors, such as those who have not earned the mandatory number of credits for Social Security benefits, enroll on a voluntary, premium-paying basis.

Medicare Part A coverage is provided without cost to seniors who are eligible for Social Security benefits. In other words, there are no premium payments for most seniors.

Inpatient Hospital Care. Except for the "deductible" and "coinsurance" amounts that the patient must pay, Medicare helps pay for inpatient hospital service for up to 90 days in each "benefit period." The 90-day benefit period starts again with each spell of illness. A benefit period is a way of measuring the patient's use of services under Hospital Insurance. The patient's first benefit period starts the first time the patient receives inpatient hospital care after Hospital Insurance coverage begins. A benefit period ends when the patient has been out of a hospital or other facility primarily providing skilled nursing or rehabilitative services for 60 days in a row (including the day of discharge). After one benefit period has ended, another will start whenever the patient again receives inpatient hospital care. Table 4-2 indicates what Medicare Part A inpatient hospital coverage includes.

TABLE 4-2
Medicare (Part A) Coverage

Medicare Part A hospital insurance covers inpatient care.
Coverage includes

• Semiprivate rooms	• Xrays
• Diagnostic procedures	• Skilled rehabilitation
• Anesthesia	• Hospice care
• Operating room costs	• Posthospital skilled nursing facility
• Recovery room costs	care under specific conditions and
• Blood	limited time periods

Lifetime reserve days are extra hospital days to use if a patient has a long illness and needs to stay in the hospital for more than 90 days in a benefit period. Each person has only 60 lifetime reserve days.

Medicare Coverage of Long-Term Care. There are provisions in Medicare Part A that pay for the cost of care typically associated with LTC, namely skilled-nursing facility care and home health care. For this reason, we will take a closer look at these two benefits so you can explain them to a prospect who may have questions. In addition, because many LTCI policies cover hospice care, we will look at the hospice benefits that Medicare provides.

Skilled-Nursing Facility Care. Medicare Hospital Insurance helps pay for inpatient care in a Medicare-certified skilled-nursing facility following a hospital stay if the person's condition requires nursing or rehabilitation services that can be provided only in a skilled-nursing facility.

It is important to point out, however, that many skilled-nursing facilities in the United States are not Medicare certified. Moreover, it is necessary to meet both of the following conditions to qualify for Medicare coverage in a certified skilled-nursing facility:

- The person's attending physician must prescribe a stay in a Medicare-certified skilled-nursing facility for a condition that (1) was treated in a hospital within the past 30 days or (2) started while Medicare-covered services were being received in a skilled-nursing facility for another reason.
- The person must have been in a hospital at least 3 consecutive days (not including the day of discharge) before being transferred to the skilled-nursing facility.

If a person qualifies, the schedule of benefits and copayments shown in table 4-3 applies.

TABLE 4-3 **Medicare Skilled-Nursing Facility Coverage**	
Days	**Insured Pays**
1–20	$0.00
21–100	$119 per day in 2006 (total of $9,520)
101+	Full cost

Covered items and services include the following:

- room and board in semiprivate accommodations (private rooms covered only if required for medical reasons)
- nursing services (except private-duty nurses)
- use of facility supplies and equipment, such as oxygen or wheelchairs
- medications ordinarily furnished by the facility
- diagnostic or therapeutic items or services
- rehabilitative services such as physical, occupational, or speech therapy
- medical social services
- dietary counseling
- ambulance transportation, when necessary, to the nearest supplier of needed services that are not available in the skilled-nursing facility

Medicare does not cover custodial care services (discussed later in this chapter) unless the person is in need of daily care that can be administered only by a medical professional.

Home Health Care. If the person needs skilled health care at home for the treatment of an illness or injury, Medicare pays for covered home health services furnished by a Medicare-certified home health agency that specializes in giving skilled-nursing services and other therapeutic services, such as physical therapy, in the home. In addition, Medicare will pay 80 percent of the cost of durable medical equipment such as walkers and wheelchairs.

Medicare pays for home health visits only if the

- care needed includes intermittent skilled-nursing care (not 24-hour care)
- person is confined to home
- person is under the care of a physician who determines the patient needs home health care and sets up a health plan to provide the care
- person's condition is improving
- home health agency providing the services is Medicare certified

If all of these conditions are met, either hospital insurance or medical insurance will pay for medically necessary home health services.

Hospice Benefits. Hospice benefits are available under Part A of Medicare for beneficiaries who are certified as being terminally ill persons with a life expectancy of 6 months or less. The benefit period consists of two 90-day periods followed by an unlimited number of 60-day periods. These periods can be used consecutively or at intervals.

Although a hospice is thought of as a facility for treating the terminally ill, Medicare benefits are available primarily for services provided by a Medicare-certified hospice to patients in their own homes. However, inpatient care can be provided if needed by the beneficiary. In addition to including the types of benefits described for home health care, hospice benefits include drugs, bereavement counseling, and inpatient respite care when family members need a break from caring for the ill person.

There are modest copayments for some services.

Medicare Part B: Optional Medical Insurance

Medicare Part B covers physician and surgeon services in addition to outpatient hospital care. It also covers a variety of other specified services, including physical therapy, as shown in table 4-4.

Medicare Part B is an optional program for which premiums are charged. Most seniors have these premiums automatically deducted from their Social Security benefits. For the year 2006, the monthly premium for Medicare Part B coverage is $88.50. Despite annually scheduled increases in cost, Part B premiums are considered a bargain for the coverage they provide. General tax revenues subsidize 75 percent of the costs.

Most seniors enroll automatically in Medicare Part B when they apply for Social Security and Medicare Part A benefits. There is no separate application.

> Despite annually scheduled increases in cost, Medicare Part B premiums are considered a bargain for the coverage they provide.

TABLE 4-4
Medicare (Part B) Coverage

Medicare Part B is an optional health coverage program available to seniors. Coverage includes

- Physician visits
- Surgeon fees
- Physical therapy
- Speech therapy
- Mammograms
- Ambulance transportation
- Durable medical equipment

- Prosthetic devices
- Outpatient services
- Limited home health care under specific and restricted conditions (no more than 8 hours per day for up to 21 days)

There is no nursing home coverage.

Gaps in Medicare Parts A and B Coverage. There are gaps in the Medicare program, including copayments and deductibles (see table 4-5). Many services are not covered. The purchase of a supplementary policy has been a traditional way to cover some of these gaps. Medicare Advantage (Part C) offers some insureds a second alternative. Neither option provides adequate LTC coverage.

Medicare Advantage (Part C)

All Medicare Advantage plans are required to provide the current Medicare benefit package (excluding hospice services) and may offer supplemental benefits. Such plans may provide more preventive services and charge lower copayments. However, they are generally restricted to participating providers (physicians, hospitals, nursing homes, and so on).

> If insureds are comfortable with managed care, their enrollment in Medicare Part C offers a way to free premium dollars for other needs, including LTCI products.

Again, such plans generally do not provide LTC coverage. Short-term nursing home care covered by Medicare and the patient's Medicare HMO is usually available only in participating facilities. If insureds are comfortable with managed care, their enrollment in Medicare Part C offers a way to free premium dollars for other needs, including LTCI products.

Prescription Drug Insurance (Part D)

Prescription Drug Insurance offers a standard benefit to most participants. Part D pays no LTC benefits.

Medicare Supplement Insurance

Medicare supplement insurance

Medicare supplement insurance policies, often called medigap policies, are designed specifically to cover deductibles and any coinsurance payments under Medicare (as shown in table 4-5). Most policies pay 100 percent of

---

TABLE 4-5
Medicare Gaps (Applicable in 2006)

During a hospital stay, Medicare Part A does not pay for

- the yearly $952 deductible
- a coinsurance amount of $238 for each day of hospitalization more than 60 days and up to 90 days for any one benefit period
- a coinsurance amount of $476 for each day of hospitalization more than 90 days and up to 150 days for any one benefit period past a 150-day hospitalization
- the first three pints of blood, unless replaced during foreign travel

During a stay in a skilled-nursing facility, Medicare Part A does not pay for

- a coinsurance amount of $119 for each day in the facility more than 20 days and up to 100 days for any one benefit period
- anything for a stay of more than 100 days

For doctors, clinics, laboratories, therapies, medical supplies and equipment, Medicare Part B does not pay for

- the $124 yearly deductible
- 20 percent of the Medicare-approved amount
- 15 percent above the Medicare-approved amount if the provider does not accept assignment
- routine examinations and testing
- treatment that is not considered medically necessary
- vaccinations and immunizations
- prescription medication that can be self-administered
- general dental work
- routine eye and hearing exams
- glasses or hearing aids

For home health care, Medicare Part A does not pay

- for 20 percent of the approved cost of durable medical equipment or approved nonskilled care
- anything for nonmedical personal care services

---

inpatient hospital care expenses after Medicare benefits are exhausted for an additional 365 days. These additional days are limited to 365 over the individual's lifetime.

There are 10 standardized policies that are referred to as plans A through J, or participants can opt for Medicare Part C. Plan A spells out a set of core benefits that are enhanced in the other medigap policies. This basic core benefit package provides

- Part A hospital coinsurance for days 61 through 90 ($238 in 2006)
- Part A hospital coinsurance for days 91 through 150 ($476 in 2006)

- 365 hospital days after Medicare benefits have ended
- Part B doctor bill 20 percent coinsurance after the annual $124 deductible is met
- payment for the first three pints of blood yearly

Beginning in 2006, two new standard plans (Plans K and L) also became available. These two plans do not include the entire core benefit package. Both plans call for the covered insured to assume more cost sharing under Medicare Parts A and B except for the part B deductible. There is a limit of $4,000 (Plan K) and $2,000 (Plan L) on annual out-of-pocket spending under Medicare Parts A and B.

> **Medigap coverage will be unnecessary for most seniors who enroll in a Medicare Advantage program.**

Medigap coverage will be unnecessary for most seniors who enroll in a Medicare Advantage program.

Medicare Supplement Insurance and Long-Term Care

Some of the standard Medicare supplement policies in the marketplace provide limited benefits for services that could be described as long-term care. For example, some provide up to $1,600 per year of at-home assistance with activities of daily living for persons who are recovering from illness, injury, or surgery at home or at any other location other than a hospital or skilled-nursing facility. Policies with these benefits will not pay for more than seven 4-hour visits in any week and no more than $40 of reimbursement for any visit.

Long-Term Care

long-term care (LTC)

> **Long-term care is more than just nursing home care.**

The definition of *long-term care (LTC)* seems to have grown more complex over the years. Because of the public misconception of LTC, it is important to emphasize that LTC is not simply nursing home care. It is much more than that. LTC can best be defined as the broad range of medical, custodial, and other care services provided over an extended period of time in various care settings due to a chronic illness, physical disability, or cognitive impairment. Examining this definition closely will help you understand and explain LTC to your prospects and clients.

In 2005, there were over 5 million people aged 85 or older. As you might expect, the number of people in this group is expected to grow rapidly. It is projected that there will be over 7 million people aged 85 and older by the year 2020 and over 20 million by 2050. As we mentioned earlier, the average daily rate in 2005 was $203 for a private room in a nursing home and $176 for a semi-private room; the average length of stay is about 2.4 years. These statistics reflect the need for and high cost of long-term care.

The need for long-term care is compounded by significant changes in family structure and lifestyle that have been occurring over many years. There are more women in the workplace, fewer children, more divorces, and greater distances between family members. This change in what has been called the "nuclear family" limits the amount of informal care that the elderly receive from their families. The result is an increasing dependence on organized formal care and the need for funds to provide this care.

Another significant factor compounding the need for long-term care is the increase in the longevity of the elderly. This is due to advances in medical science and health maintenance. This increased longevity will place an ever growing burden on LTC providers. It is anticipated to continue to drive up the costs of care far in excess of the general inflation rate. As the over-age-65 population continues to grow and to live longer, it is only logical that there will be a considerable need for funds to provide for the increased health, medical, and custodial care that goes along with the aging process.

Many people think that Medicare will pick up a large amount of these expenses. Many people also assume that if Medicare doesn't cover these expenses, then private medical or Medicare supplement policies will pay for LTC. Both of these assumptions are incorrect.

Current expenditures for LTC facility costs exceed $100 billion per year and are increasing. Home care costs are estimated to cost Americans more than $35 billion per year. By 2020, LTC facility costs alone are expected to exceed $200 billion.

Although these payments come from a variety of government, insurance, and private sources, Medicaid is the primary funding source for LTC in the United States, accounting for about 40 percent of all LTC facility payments.

The Medicaid Program

Medicaid is a joint federal and state program to provide medical assistance to the poor. Although it provides extended-care assistance to seniors who have extremely limited resources and no insurance, these benefits come at a terrible price. To qualify for Medicaid, an individual must be impoverished. Assets accumulated over a lifetime must be "spent down." When only minimal assets remain, the Medicaid program will step in to cover the costs of care. Most people find the prospect of becoming destitute—spending down all of their assets to qualify for Medicaid—distasteful at the very least. But, unfortunately for some, it may be the only solution.

The price paid for Medicaid coverage is more than financial. Clearly, there is also a psychological price to pay for impoverishment. Moreover, many commentators point out that a quality of care issue is often involved. Health care providers participating in Medicaid must accept Medicaid payments made to them as payment in full. Medicaid reimbursement rates are usually lower than the rates paid by LTC insurers or by private patients, and therefore this often translates into a lower quality of care.

Sidebar notes:

Increased longevity is anticipated to drive up the costs of long-term care far in excess of the general inflation rate.

Medicaid

Although Medicaid provides extended care assistance to seniors who have extremely limited resources and no insurance, these benefits come at a terrible price.

The Solution: Long-Term Care Insurance

Most people find the prospect of becoming destitute—spending down all of their assets to qualify for Medicaid—distasteful at the very least. But for some, it may be the only solution. Using personal savings and assets, relying on family, borrowing, or charity are all unlikely or unacceptable solutions to this problem.

long-term care insurance (LTCI)

This leaves *long-term care insurance (LTCI)* as the most viable option for most people. Premiums can be budgeted and assets can be legitimately protected from the ravages of LTC costs. Living standards can be maintained for healthy family members while those needing it can receive the quality care they desire.

The only sensible answer to financing the costs of LTC is to transfer the risk to an insurance company. This solution provides many advantages:

- Clients are able to preserve their independence.
- The healthy spouse's financial security and independence can continue.
- Funds will be there to pay for greater than normal medical and custodial care costs during prolonged periods of time when personal health is declining.
- There are alternatives for at-home care.
- Benefits are available when needed; care is not delayed because it might cause financial hardship.
- Clients have the freedom to choose from among various LTC options.
- Wealth and assets that have accumulated over a lifetime are preserved for a spouse, children, charity, or other purposes.

Long-term care insurance should be an integral part of any discussion of retirement planning.

LTCI should be an integral part of any discussion of retirement planning. It is insurance against the deterioration of accumulated assets that had been planned for a secure retirement.

Effect of HIPAA Legislation

Health Insurance Portability and Accountability Act of 1996 (HIPAA)

The *Health Insurance Portability and Accountability Act of 1996 (HIPAA)* established standards for LTCI and helped to stabilize the industry, which until that time had little uniformity. It also made the tax treatment of LTCI policies more favorable if they met prescribed standards. In most cases, the imposition of these federal standards resulted in broader coverage. Policies issued on or after January 1, 1997, generally must meet the federal standards to be considered tax qualified, while policies in force before January 1, 1997, generally are grandfathered and automatically qualify for tax benefits.

Eligibility for Favorable Tax Treatment

To ascertain whether an LTCI policy will receive favorable income tax treatment under HIPAA, it is necessary to understand the meaning of several terms.

Qualified LTCI Contract. HIPAA provides favorable income tax treatment to a *qualified LTCI contract.* This is defined as any LTCI contract that meets all the following requirements:

qualified LTCI contract

chronically ill person

- chronic illness definition. A *chronically ill person* is one who has been certified by a licensed health care practitioner as meeting one of the following requirements:
  - The person is expected to be unable to perform, without substantial assistance from another person, at least two *activities of daily living (ADLs)* for a period of at least 90 days due to a loss of functional capacity. HIPAA allows six ADLs:
    - □ eating
    - □ bathing
    - □ dressing
    - □ transferring from bed to chair
    - □ using the toilet
    - □ maintaining continence

    (A tax-qualified LTCI policy must contain at least five of the six ADLs.)
  - Substantial supervision is required to protect the individual from threats to health and safety because of severe cognitive impairment.

activities of daily living (ADLs)

- chronic illness certification. A licensed health care practitioner must at least annually certify that the insured remains chronically ill.
- no medical necessity trigger. A licensed health care practitioner's recommendation alone cannot trigger benefit payments.
- 90-day expectation of disability. A licensed health care practitioner must certify that ADL dependency is expected to last at least 90 days.
- guaranteed renewable. The contract must be guaranteed renewable.
- no cash value. The contract does not provide for a cash surrender value or other money that can be borrowed or paid, assigned, or pledged as collateral for a loan.
- coordination with Medicare. The contract cannot pay for expenses that are reimbursable under Medicare or would be reimbursable except for the application of a deductible or coinsurance amount.

- qualified long-term care restriction. The insured must receive services that help him or her perform ADLs or that provide substantial supervision for cognitive impairment.
- consumer protection provisions. The contract must comply with various consumer protection provisions.
- life insurance/LTCI combination product. A qualified LTCI contract can include that portion of a life insurance contract that provides LTCI coverage by a rider or as part of the life contract as long as the above criteria are satisfied.

**qualified LTC
services**

Qualified LTC Services. HIPAA defines *qualified LTC services* as necessary diagnostic, preventive, therapeutic, curing, treating, and rehabilitative services, and maintenance or personal care services that are required by a chronically ill person and are provided by a plan of care prescribed by a licensed health care practitioner.

Benefit Eligibility

All tax-qualified LTCI contracts use the same two criteria, known as benefit triggers, to determine whether an insured is chronically ill and eligible for benefits. The insured is required to meet one of the two criteria. The first criterion, or benefit trigger, is that the insured is expected to be unable, without substantial assistance from another person, to perform at least two (out of six) ADLs for a period of at least 90 days due to a loss of functional capacity.

The second criterion or benefit trigger is that substantial services are required to protect the person from threats to health and safety due to extensive cognitive impairment.

Federal Income Tax Provisions

Premiums. A tax-qualified LTCI contract is treated as accident and health insurance. With some exceptions, costs for LTC services, including insurance premiums, are treated like other medical expenses. That is, people who itemize deductions can deduct unreimbursed LTC services, including insurance premiums, in excess of 7.5 percent of adjusted gross income (AGI). However, there are limits on the amount of personally paid LTCI premiums that an individual can claim as medical expenses. These limits, which are based on a covered person's age and subject to cost-of-living adjustments, are shown for 2006 in table 4-6. Medical expense deductions cannot be taken for payments made to a spouse or relative who is not a licensed professional with respect to such LTC services.

TABLE 4-6
LTCI Deductible Premium Limits for 2006

Age	Annual Deductible Limit per Covered Individual
40 or younger	$ 280
41–50	530
51–60	1,060
61–70	2,830
Over 70	3,530

Benefits. Policies pay benefits in one of two ways. Some policies provide benefits on an indemnity (per diem) basis. This means that the full daily benefit amount is paid, regardless of the actual cost of care. For example, if the daily cost of a nursing home is $150 and the insured has a maximum daily benefit amount of $200 under an indemnity (per diem) policy, then the full $200 daily benefit will be paid. The majority of newer policies pay benefits on a reimbursement basis. Such contracts reimburse the insured for actual expenses up to the specified policy limit. For instance, in the previous example, if the insured has a reimbursement policy instead of an indemnity (per diem) policy, only $150 per day would be paid instead of the $200 daily benefit that the indemnity (per diem) policy would pay.

Under HIPAA, an LTC recipient will receive benefits income-tax free when they are paid from a tax-qualified policy of the reimbursement type. Indemnity (per diem) policy benefits are also free from income taxation up to $250 per day in 2006 (this amount is indexed annually for inflation), regardless of whether the insured received actual qualified LTC services. However, any indemnity (per diem) benefits the insured received in excess of $250 per day are not tax free unless it can be shown that the qualified LTC services he or she received actually equal those benefits.

In other words, if the cost of qualified LTC services equals or exceeds the LTCI benefits received, the benefits are tax free. If the LTCI benefits received from a tax-qualified policy exceed the cost of qualified LTC services, the amount in excess of $250 per day (in 2006) is taxable income.

Long-Term Care Insurance Model Act

Among other functions, the National Association of Insurance Commissioners (NAIC) provides states with model minimum policy standards. These are known as model acts. The model legislation focuses on two major areas—policy provisions and marketing.

The legislation consists of a model act that is designed to be incorporated into a state's insurance law and model regulations that are designed to be

Although NAIC model legislation establishes guidelines for minimum policy standards, insurance companies still have significant latitude in many aspects of product design.

adopted for use in implementing the law. Because most insurance companies sell essentially the same LTCI product everywhere they do business, the NAIC guidelines are often, in effect, adhered to in states that have not adopted the legislation.

It is important to make two points. First, the model legislation establishes guidelines. Insurance companies still have significant latitude in many aspects of product design. Second, many older policies are still in existence that were written prior to the adoption of the model legislation or under one of its earlier versions.

Types of Care Covered

There are many types of care for which benefits may be provided under an LTCI policy. By broad categories, these can be identified as facility care, assisted-living, and home and community-based care. An LTCI policy may provide benefits for one, several, or all of these types of care.

facility care (nursing home)

Facility Care (Nursing Home). Facility care (nursing home) encompasses

skilled-nursing care

- *skilled-nursing care*—daily nursing care ordered by a doctor and provided continuously by skilled medical personnel

intermediate care

- *intermediate care*—occasional nursing or rehabilitative care that must be performed by skilled medical personnel

custodial care

- *custodial care*—assistance with ADLs

assisted-living facility care

Assisted-Living Facility Care. *Assisted-living facility care* is provided in facilities that care for individuals who are no longer able to care for themselves but do not need the level of care provided in a nursing home.

community care

Community Care. LTCI policies usually provide benefits for people who remain in the community. These benefits are available for a variety of programs and services such as the following:

- home health care—care by a provider who comes to the insured's home, usually on a part-time basis. This can be skilled care, including nursing care, physical therapy, and other similar services, or unskilled care to help with ADLs. Some companies offer benefits to pay a family member who provides home health care.
- adult day care—care in a long-term facility or through a special program in the community. Adult day care provides a location where individuals receive assistance with daily living needs and they benefit from socialization and special programs. Skilled medical care is often available on call.

- homemaker companion or home health aide—usually an employee of a home health care agency who assists with homemaker services such as cooking, laundry, shopping, cleaning, bill paying, or other household chores
- caregiver training—training for a family member or friend in how to give safe and effective care so that an insured in need of care can remain at home
- respite care—care that offers temporary relief to family members who are providing care for someone in their own home. The insured is placed in a long-term facility temporarily, usually overnight or for a weekend, to relieve the at-home provider.
- hospice care—special kinds of care and emotional support given to individuals who have been diagnosed with terminal illnesses. These services can be in an inpatient facility or in the person's home.
- therapeutic devices—special equipment or devices, such as a ramp for a wheelchair or bathtub grab rails for which some policies will pay, which are needed to help a person remain in the community for as long as possible

Contract Provisions and Benefits

Although the trend has been toward standardization of LTCI contracts, there are still significant differences among policies. This is especially true when comparing older, existing contracts to the ones being issued today.

> **The way benefits are defined has an impact on when they will begin, how much will be paid, and how long they will last.**

Different policies define the benefits that will be paid in different ways. The method used has an impact on when benefits will begin, how much will be paid, and how long benefits will last. Some policies have specific requirements that must be met before benefits become available.

Elimination Period. The elimination period in an LTCI policy is the amount of time, usually expressed as the number of days, the insured will pay for services before the policy benefits begin.

Maximum Daily Benefit. LTCI policies pay benefits for the covered services up to a daily maximum amount stated in the policy. The insured elects this amount at the time the policy is purchased.

When purchasing LTCI, the applicant selects the level of benefit he or she desires up to the maximum level the insurance company will provide. Benefits are often sold in increments of $10 per day up to frequently found limits of $200 or $250 or, in a few cases, as much as $400 or $500 per day.

Maximum limits may be different for nursing home care and community-based care. The maximum limit for community care is often a factor of the nursing home care benefit.

Inflation Protection. Most states require an LTCI policy to offer some type of automatic inflation protection. The applicant is given the choice to select this option, decline the option, or possibly select an alternative option. If the applicant selects the automatic-increase option, the cost of the option is built into the initial premium, and no additional premium is levied at the time of an annual increase. As a result of the NAIC model act and HIPAA, the standard provision in almost all policies is a 5 percent benefit increase that is compounded annually over the life of the policy. Under this provision, the amount of a policy's benefits increases by 5 percent each year over the amount of benefits available in the prior year.

A common alternative that many insurers make available is based on simple interest, whereby each annual automatic increase is 5 percent of the original benefit amount.

Maximum Duration of Benefits. Most insurers require the applicant to select the benefit period, and they make several options available. For example, one insurer offers durations of 2, 3, and 5 years, as well as lifetime benefits. In most cases, a single benefit period applies to long-term care, no matter where it is received. A few policies, however, have separate benefit periods for facility care and home health care. There are also a few policies, usually the indemnity (per diem) type, that specify the maximum benefits as a stated dollar amount such as $100,000.

There are two ways that the benefit period is applied in the payment of benefits. Under one approach, benefit payments are made for exactly the benefit period chosen. If the applicant selects a benefit period of 4 years and collects benefits for 4 years, the benefit payments cease. The other approach, most commonly but not exclusively found in reimbursement policies, uses a pool of money. Under this concept, there is an amount of money that can be used to make benefit payments as long as the pool of money lasts. Daily benefit payments from the pool of money cannot exceed the maximum daily policy benefits.

Renewability. LTC policies currently being sold are guaranteed renewable, which means that an individual's coverage cannot be canceled except for nonpayment of premiums. Although premiums cannot be raised on the basis of a particular insured's claim, they can (and often are) raised by class of insureds.

In addition to the basic benefit provisions, LTC policies can contain a number of other contract provisions.

Waiver of Premium. The contract may or may not include a provision for waiver of premium. If it is included, it is important to know how many days must elapse before this benefit becomes effective.

Shared Benefit. A few insurers use the concept of a shared benefit when a husband and wife are insured under the same policy or with the same insurer. Under this concept, each spouse can access the other spouse's benefits. For example, if each spouse has a 4-year benefit period and one spouse has exhausted his or her benefits, benefit payments can continue by drawing on any unused benefits under the other spouse's policy. In effect, one spouse could have a benefit period of up to 8 years as long as the other spouse receives no benefit payments.

Nonforfeiture Options. Most companies give an applicant for LTCI the right to elect a nonforfeiture benefit, and some states require that such a benefit be offered. With a nonforfeiture benefit, the policyowner will receive some value for a policy if the policy lapses because the required premium is not paid in the future.

The most common type of nonforfeiture option, and the one almost always available in tax-qualified policies, is a shortened benefit period. With this option, coverage is continued as a paid-up policy, but the length of the benefit period (or the amount of the benefit if stated as a maximum dollar amount) is reduced. A company may also offer a reduced paid-up policy or partial benefits as another alternative, or a return of a portion of the premium if a policy is dropped after a given number of years.

Restoration of Benefits. Many policies written with less than a lifetime benefit period provide for restoration of full benefits if the insured received less than full policy benefits and has not required LTC for a certain time period, often 180 days. If a policy does not have this provision, maximum benefits for a subsequent claim are reduced by the benefits previously paid.

Alternative Plans of Care. Many policies provide benefits for alternative plans of care, even though the policy might not cover the types of care. For example, a policy that a covers nursing home care only might provide benefits for care in an assisted-living facility if these benefits are an appropriate and cost-effective alternative to care in a nursing home. As a general rule, the alternative plan must be acceptable to the insurance company, the insured, and the insured's physician.

Limitations of Coverage

All policies have some outright exclusions. The common exclusions are for illness, treatment, or medical condition arising out of war, participation in a felony, service in the armed forces, attempted suicide, aviation if a person is a non-fare-paying passenger, alcohol or drug addiction, and mental or nervous disorders (this does not permit the exclusion of Alzheimer's disease). Many policies issued today specifically state that they do cover organically based cognitive impairments, including Alzheimer's disease, senile dementia, and Parkinson's disease.

Policies are usually issued with some form of preexisting-condition exclusion clause. This provides that there will be no coverage for any condition for which the insured was treated within a certain time frame. Usually, the preexisting-condition exclusion is for 6 months before and after the policy's coverage takes effect.

There are great variations in coverage and in premiums. Generally, no company will issue coverage beyond age 80 or 85.

Premium

> **The vast majority of LTCI policies have premiums that are payable for life and determined by the insured's age at the time of issue.**

The actual premium is determined by several factors, including gender, age, medical history, and benefits. The vast majority of LTCI policies have premiums that are payable for life and determined by the insured's age at the time of issue. A few insurers, however, offer other modes of payment. Lifetime coverage can sometimes be purchased with a single premium. Some insurers offer policies that have premium payment periods of 10 or 20 years or to age 65, after which time the premium is paid up. These policies are particularly attractive to applicants who do not want continuing premium payments after retirement.

Designing the Plan

Your objective is to help the prospect get the best value for his or her money through an effective plan design. Plan design is a balancing act between the prioritized coverage needs of the prospect and his or her premium commitment. One way to approach this task is to begin with the basic coverage design, creating an "ideal plan." Then, using the premium commitment and the prospect's priorities, begin adjusting the plan to create an optimal solution that will best meet his or her priorities within the specified premium commitment.

Potential LTCI Product Recommendations: Basic Coverage Design

When considering LTCI insurance products to fill your clients' needs, your basic coverage design solution should answer six important questions to determine the amount of insurance and the premium for the policy:

- When will benefits start? (elimination or waiting period)
- How much will be paid? (maximum daily benefit)
- How long will benefits last? (benefit period)
- Where will care be given? (comprehensive or facility-only policy)
- Will policy benefits periodically increase? (inflation protection)

- How will the policy be treated for tax purposes? (tax-qualified or nonqualified policy)

Decisions can be made about each aspect of the coverage by referring to the information you gathered in the fact finding process.

Analysis Worksheets

You may want to use some type of analysis worksheet to help you and your prospects understand the various options and choices available in different policies. There are several sources of worksheets available to you.

Many state insurance departments have released *Consumer Guides to Long-Term Care Insurance*. Most of these publications include analysis worksheets. You can write or call the state department for more details.

Combination Products

Today, prospects can choose from several different insurance products to cover LTC expenses. Of course, the most widely recognized and utilized is the individual LTCI policy that provides benefits on either an indemnity (per diem) basis or a reimbursement basis. Additionally, there are several combination products that package other insurance coverage with LTCI. Under these package products, life insurance, disability income insurance, or an annuity is combined with LTCI to provide customized solutions to a variety of prospects' needs and goals. These combination products have been referred to as hybrid products, linked policies, blended polices, or packaged policies. ◊

OTHER INSURABLE FINANCIAL RISKS

The previous section discussed LTC expenses. The following discussion will concentrate on the remaining factors to consider in analyzing and calculating your client's needs in the major areas of personal insurance planning. It will also address the concept of an emergency fund.

Insurance Planning and Risk Management

insurance planning and risk management

Insurance planning and risk management is the analysis and consideration of your client's financial exposure because of the following factors:

- mortality—survivor income and capital needs analysis
- morbidity—impact of ill health
- property—loss of value
- liability—legal exposure
- business—loss due to business involvement

This category of financial planning goals recognizes most people's desire to protect themselves and their families against the risks they face in everyday life. Risk management consists of three steps:

- identifying exposure to loss of income or property
- evaluating the nature of each contingency, including the probability of occurrence and maximum loss potential
- selecting the best tools for managing the risk

Of the three steps, risk identification is the most critical. Failure to identify a risk can lead to the possibility that the client will inadvertently be forced to assume an exposure to loss. These risks can arise from the possibility of

- medical care expenses
- long-term care expenses
- premature death losses
- disability income losses
- property and liability losses
- unemployment

These risks, the consequences of which can be adequately insured against occurring or can be managed, represent the primary focus of financial planning that the client should typically address before pursuing capital accumulation and investment goals for retirement security. Overexposure to each of these risks can negatively affect a client's retirement plans or even totally thwart them. It is your responsibility to help your prospects and clients understand the extent of the risks they face and the dangers the risks pose. Only then can you help them transfer the risks to your company through the use of insurance products.

Use of Insurance in the Financial Planning Process

You must analyze your client's current insurance holdings to determine exposure to potential loss of income or assets. There are three basic ways to deal with such exposures:

- Your client can bear the risk of the entire loss himself or herself (self-insurance or retention).
- Your client can pay another to assume the risk for him or her (shifting the risk through insurance).
- Your client can utilize some combination of these strategies.

Transferring Risk

The concept of transferring risk is the foundation on which all insurance is based.

The concept of transferring risk is the foundation on which all insurance is based.

All assets have value. An asset's value can be its current value (what it is worth today) or a future value (what it will be worth at some future time). Today's value is usually easy to determine. It is the price that someone is willing to pay to own the asset. Future value, on the other hand, depends on any number of variables, many of which are outside the owner's control.

Insurance is how people protect themselves from the risks associated with the loss of valuable assets. Homeowners, auto, and business insurance will indemnify the insured for some or all of the value of the losses of each type of asset. Without insurance, the insured carries the entire risk and potentially suffers the entire loss. With insurance, the risk of loss is transferred to an insurance company for a small premium.

Medical Care Expenses

Medical care expenses represent a potential financial disaster to any individual or family if they are not insured. The unexpected nature of both illnesses and accidents fosters in many individuals the need to know that if either should strike, financial ruin will not be added to their family's problems. For personal financial planning, it may be helpful to divide family medical care costs into three categories, as follows:

- "normal" or budgetable expenses. These are the medical expenses the family more or less expects to pay out of its regular monthly budget such as the annual out-of-pocket deductibles and copayments associated with routine visits to physicians, expenses of minor illnesses, and small drug purchases.
- "larger than normal" expenses. These are medical expenses that exceed those that are expected or budgetable. If they occur, they probably cannot be met out of the family's regular income. To meet such expenses, most people need insurance. The cutoff point between normal and larger than normal expenses depends on the family's circumstances.
- "catastrophic" medical expenses. These are expenses so large that they cause severe financial strain on a family. They are important to plan for because they are potentially so damaging. Again, the dividing line between larger than normal losses and catastrophic losses depends on individual circumstances. One family, for example, may feel that uninsured medical expenses of over $1,000 in a year would be a severe financial strain. Another family, however, with a larger income and an emergency fund, may feel that it could tolerate uninsured medical expenses of several thousand dollars. There really is no way for you to know in advance just how large catastrophic medical expenses might be. Because they could be very large, clients should plan for that possibility and insure themselves accordingly.

Medical Care Expense Insurance

There is little need to convince most people of the need to protect themselves and their families against medical care costs. Medical expense coverage is a necessity.

Most people have coverage provided to them by their employers. However, some have to rely on individually purchased plans or state or federally subsidized plans; many have no coverage at all. As a financial advisor, keep in mind the following general points regarding the acquisition of medical expense insurance coverage:

- Clients' medical expense coverage should include major medical coverage for $1 million or more.
- Be sure that any internal policy limits are in line with customary hospital and medical expenses in the client's geographical area.

Potential Medical Expense Insurance Product Recommendations. To the extent that your clients' coverage is inadequate, your product recommendations should be based on their individual financial goals and/or family situation. When considering medical expense insurance products to fill your clients' needs, you should design solutions according the following factors:

- affordability
- amount of annual deductibles
- amount of copayments for respective types of benefits
- amount of annual out-of-pocket limit for claims
- amount of aggregate policy limit payable on claims
- selection of benefits that are most relevant to the client's individual and family needs

Sources of Protection against Medical Care Expenses. The following are the major sources to which clients may look for coverage of medical care costs:

- health insurance
    - employer-provided medical expense coverage (including self-insured plans, Blue Cross–Blue Shield plans, insurance company comprehensive medical expense plans, health maintenance organization plans, preferred provider organization plans, and point-of-service plans)
    - individual medical expense insurance (including hospitalization/surgical expense insurance plans, and major medical plans such as stand-alone, supplementary, and comprehensive plans)
- health savings accounts
- other assets available to the family

Premature Death Losses

A major planning objective for most people is to protect dependents from the financial consequences of death. Some people also are concerned with the impact of their deaths on their business affairs. The following financial losses may result from a person's death:

- loss of the deceased's future earning power that would have been available for the benefit of his or her surviving dependents
- incurrence of costs and other obligations arising at death
- increase in expenses for the family
- loss of tax advantages
- loss of business values because of an owner's or key person's death

Role of Life Insurance

Life insurance provides family financial security. Life insurance can help survivors maintain their standard of living after a wage earner is gone. Through life insurance, the resources needed to pay the continuing expenses of the living beneficiaries will be available.

Life insurance can even uniquely serve the dual role of providing retirement income for the insured if living, or for the insured's spousal beneficiary if the insured dies prior to retirement.

As a financial advisor, your role regarding the marketing of life insurance is twofold. First, you must help your prospects and clients understand the financial problems and needs their death will create. Second, you must encourage them to solve those problems and meet the needs of their survivors.

Sometimes, identifying the needs is easy. At other times, especially in the advanced planning markets of business insurance and estate planning, the needs can be complex; the complexity is exacerbated by complications of tax law, conflicting needs, and multiple objectives.

Although each individual and family is unique, with its own set of financial goals and objectives, the following areas of life insurance planning are common concerns to most families:

- final expenses
- mortgage liquidation or payment
- debt cancellation
- education funding
- family income
- retirement planning
- business needs
- estate taxes

Not every prospect has all these needs. Each prospect will want to approach insurance planning and purchasing differently. It is your job to ask your prospects questions that will stimulate their thinking. By asking about each area listed above, you will encourage them to identify their primary concerns as you help them to determine their needs.

> **Many people fail to see the need to insure the most valuable asset they have—their ability to earn a living.**

Most people readily see the need to protect themselves from the loss of their most expensive tangible assets such as their home or car. However, they often fail to apply the same common sense to insuring the most valuable asset they have—their ability to earn a living. Like any other asset, a person's earning capacity has an economic value that can be measured and protected.

Premature Death Losses/Survivor Needs

To properly address a family's specific itemized life insurance needs, it is necessary to calculate the extent of the existing potential losses in terms of survivor cash needs today and income needs for each of the remaining years of your client's (and spouse's, if applicable) life expectancy.

Cash Needs. First, you must total the lump-sum cash needed to pay for such items as final expenses, a readjustment fund, mortgage and debt cancellation, children's education, and estate settlement costs for the deceased. Then you must subtract that amount from existing capital resources available from the government, your client's employer, savings, and existing in-force life insurance. If there is a shortage of capital to cover cash needs at death, you should note it accordingly.

Income Needs. Indicate the annual income the surviving spouse and other dependents need in the event of the other spouse's death, and subtract the projected total income available from all resources from this amount. Note any shortage of annual income needed for survivors today, as well as for years projected into the future, based on agreed upon interest earnings and inflation assumptions. Add the income need shortage to any cash need that may exist to determine the total amount of capital required to solve the deficit funding of survivor needs.

Human Life Value

The human life value concept is an important alternative to the needs-based approach to the determination of life insurance required. Human life value is the fundamental basis for the purchase of life insurance, although there are also other methods for determining the amount of life insurance an individual should purchase based on specific needs.

One method of determining how much life insurance a person should carry is called the human life value approach. It is based on the proposition that a person should carry life insurance in an amount equal to the capitalized present value of his or her net earnings. Under this theory, a person should capitalize this economic value at an amount large enough to yield, at a reasonable rate of interest, an income equal to the family's share of those earnings.

The technically accurate method of computing the monetary value of a person involves an estimate of the individual's personal earnings for each year from his or her present age to the date of retirement, taking into account the normal trend of earnings and inflation. From each year's income, the cost of self-maintenance, life insurance premiums, and personal income taxes is deducted. The residual income for each year is then discounted at an assumed rate of interest and against the possibility of its not being earned. The sum of the discounted values for each year of potential income is the present value of future earnings or the monetary value of the life in question. That is, as we explained in chapter 2, the present value is what some money to be received in the future is worth today. It is equivalent to the given sum to be received in the future, discounted (reduced) by an interest rate that represents the interest that could be earned on that money if it was received today instead of in the future.

Example: Julia is a 35-year-old woman who earns a gross salary of $35,000. After taxes and self-maintenance, her net income is approximately $25,000. This is her annual economic value to her family.

Of course, we anticipate that Julia will work and contribute to her family for more than 1 year. If she continues to work until she retires at age 65, she will have worked another 30 years. Even if she receives no raises during that period, her net economic contribution to the family will be $750,000 (30 x $25,000).

Will it take $750,000 to replace her $25,000 of net earnings each year? An amount of $403,527 invested at 5 percent interest will produce $25,000 annually while depleting the capital amount at the end of 30 years. (This example assumes that a 5 percent return is the net after-tax earnings realized.)

However, what happens if we factor in an inflation rate of 4 percent into this equation?

If $25,000 is compounded at 4 percent annually, Julia's economic value at age 65 will be $77,966. Cumulatively, over the next 30 years, the potential total economic value to Julia's family will be $1,402,123. How much would it take to replace her economic human life value, including inflation?

The present value of money needed to replace her future stream of earnings, assuming 5 percent interest earned on the capital, is $655,701.

Potential Life Insurance Product Recommendations

Any life insurance product that you recommend should be compatible with your client's affordability, suitability, and planning priorities.

Any life insurance product recommendations you propose should be compatible with your client's affordability, suitability, and planning priorities. Because life insurance protection is one of the fundamental building blocks in the financial planning pyramid that is of paramount importance in protecting the financial security of so many families today, you should make every effort to provide your clients with as much life insurance coverage as possible, given their financial resources. This involves experimenting with alternative product options for your clients to consider.

For example, if your client has a need for $1 million of life insurance and is in his or her early 30s, term insurance only or a combination of some permanent and mostly term insurance may be most appropriate. As with other components of the financial plan, you should develop several alternatives for your clients and let them choose the one they are most comfortable in purchasing.

Disability Income (DI) Losses

Another major planning objective should be protection from financial losses arising out of disability, whether it is total (either temporary or permanent) or partial. Disability, particularly total and permanent disability, is a serious risk almost everyone faces. Surprisingly, it is often neglected in financial planning.

The statistics in table 4-7 show that the odds of death during an individual's working years are much less than the odds of a significant long-term disability (one lasting more than 90 days). This is something for the young family man and woman to think about.

TABLE 4-7 Probability of Disability vs. Death	
Age	**Ratio of Disability to Death**
30	2.31 to 1
35	2.21 to 1
40	1.95 to 1
45	1.69 to 1
50	1.53 to 1
55	1.33 to 1
Source: Commissioners' Disability Individual Table A and CSO Mortality Table	

The financial losses from disability generally parallel those resulting from death. An important difference from the consumer's viewpoint, however, is that there is a wide range of possible durations of total disability—from only a week or so to the ultimate personal catastrophe of total and permanent disability. Virtually all experts agree that clients should pay the greatest planning attention to protecting themselves against long-term total and permanent disability rather than being unduly concerned with disabilities that last only a few weeks. For example, depending on individual circumstances and resources, it is often much more economical for a family to rely on their emergency fund for shorter-term disabilities than to buy DI insurance to cover such disabilities.

> **Total and permanent disability of a family breadwinner is actually a much greater financial catastrophe than the breadwinner's premature death.**

The total and permanent disability of a family breadwinner is actually a much greater financial catastrophe than the breadwinner's premature death. This is because as a disabled person, the breadwinner remains a consumer, whose consumption needs may even increase because of the disability, and because other family members, especially a spouse, must devote at least some time to caring for the disabled breadwinner as long as he or she is alive. In fact, total and permanent disability has been graphically described as a "living death."

Role of DI Insurance

Most people obtain the majority of their money from personal earnings. Because earnings are the foundation of financial security, disability income insurance—protection against the interruption of the steady flow of earnings due to accident or illness—is a cornerstone of financial planning.

Insurance products protect against financial catastrophe from a number of different sources. For most people, the values protected are generated in one way—earned income. Life insurance replaces income that was generated by the efforts of the deceased insured. Disability interrupts or ends a person's ability to earn income, but the person does not die. Life insurance proceeds are not available to replace the income generated by the disabled person.

Even if a disability is relatively short, the absence of income affects the lifestyle of the disabled person and his or her family for a long time. Depending on the length of a disability and a family's lack of preparation for it, it can postpone or shatter a person's plans for a financially secure retirement. Therefore, a natural consideration in the retirement planning process is evaluating your prospect's income needs during disability.

Addressing the Impact of DI Losses

To calculate your client's needs in the event of disability, list the total household monthly income objective at the level needed today and at the inflation-adjusted income levels that are anticipated until at least your client's (and spouse's, if applicable) retirement age. From this amount, you need to subtract the spouse's available income (if any) and group DI insurance in force, any personally owned DI insurance, any assets that can be used to provide income, and any government benefits to be factored in if so desired. If a shortage exists today, you should address it by recommending the appropriate amount of monthly DI insurance benefit.

If your analysis of your client's income needs reveals a shortage in funding, you should recommend the appropriate amount of monthly DI insurance.

Potential DI Insurance Product Recommendations. When considering DI insurance products to fill your clients' needs, you should design solutions according to the following factors:

- affordability
- length of elimination period
- duration of benefit period
- total, residual, and/or partial benefits
- appropriate definition of disability
- contract's renewability provision
- inclusion of riders regarding
  - future purchase options
  - inflation protection
  - social insurance supplements

Property and Liability Losses

Property and liability losses can hinder a family's plans for a financially secure retirement.

All families are exposed to the risk of property and/or liability losses. These types of losses can hinder a family's plans for a financially secure retirement. For planning purposes, it is helpful to consider property exposures and liability exposures separately because somewhat different approaches may be used for each.

Property Losses

Ownership of property brings with it the risk of loss to the property itself—direct losses—and the risk of indirect losses arising out of loss or damage to the property—consequential losses.

Direct and consequential losses to property can result from a wide variety of perils, some of which, such as fire, theft, windstorm, and automobile collision, are common, while others, such as earthquake and flood, are rare except in certain geographical areas.

The kinds of property that individuals and families own that may be exposed to direct loss include the following:

- primary residence
- summer home
- investment real estate
- furniture, clothing, and other personal property
- automobiles
- boats and aircraft
- furs, jewelry, silverware, and fine art
- securities, credit cards, cash, and the like
- professional equipment
- assets held as an executor, trustee, or guardian
- assets in which the person has a beneficial interest

Some of the consequential losses that may arise out of a direct loss to such property are the

- loss of use of the damaged property (including additional living expenses while a residence is being rebuilt, rental of a substitute automobile while a car is being repaired, and so on)
- loss of rental income from damaged property
- depreciation losses (or the difference between the cost to replace damaged property with new property and the depreciated value, called "actual cash value," of the damaged property)
- cost of debris removal

Many property losses are comparatively small in size, but some are of major importance. As with DI losses and medical care expenses, what constitutes a "small" loss depends on the resources and attitudes of those involved. Also, like DI and medical expense exposures, a financial planning decision needs to be made as to how much property loss exposure your client should assume and how much he or she should insure. Another decision is what property to insure against what perils.

Liability Losses

By virtue of almost everything clients do, they are exposed to possible liability claims made by others. These claims can arise out of their own negligent acts, the negligent acts of others for whom they may be held legally responsible, liability they may have assumed under contract (such as a lease), and the liability imposed on them by statute (such as workers' compensation laws).

Some of the exposures that may result in a liability claim are

- ownership of property (for example, residence premises or a vacation home)
- rental of property (for example, a vacation home)

- ownership, rental, or use of automobiles, boats, aircraft, snowmobiles, and so on
- hiring of employees
- other personal activities
- professional and business activities
- any contractual or contingent liability

> **Most people may not realize all the liability exposures they have and may not protect themselves against the possibility of very large claims.**

Most people realize the financial consequences that could occur as a result of liability claims against them. However, they may not recognize all the liability exposures they have and may not protect themselves against the possibility of very large claims. Like medical expenses, there really is no way a person can know in advance just how large a liability loss he or she may suffer. Judgments and settlements for $1 million and more are not unusual by any means. Therefore, prudent financial planning calls for assuming that the worst can happen and providing for it through the purchase of additional liability coverage with an umbrella liability insurance policy.

Addressing Property and Liability Losses

To address your client's potential property and liability losses, you must analyze his or her exposures to the types of direct and consequential property losses discussed above, seeking to minimize loss exposures in a manner that is consistent with the client's budget, risk tolerance, and financial goals. You should note any changes in existing insurance coverage that are necessary to enhance your client's protection against property and liability risk exposures, and consider these changes when you are developing your plan recommendations.

You should recommend to your clients that they have the most complete insurance against property and liability loss exposure that they can afford and educate them about the dangers of ignoring these risks.

Unemployment

Unemployment has received greater attention in recent years as many capable persons have lost their jobs because of various economic uncertainties. Unemployment is a financial risk to families that cannot be insured. However, a reasonable emergency fund can help prevent the problem of temporary unemployment from becoming a crisis by giving the family time to adjust before disturbing their other investments and directly affecting retirement plans.

Emergency Fund

You should recommend to your clients that they establish an emergency fund as a risk management tool to meet unexpected expenses not planned for in the family budget; to pay for the "smaller" disability income losses, medical expenses, and property losses that insurance purposely does not cover; and to provide a financial cushion against such personal problems as prolonged unemployment.

The size of the emergency fund varies greatly and depends on such factors as the client's family income, number of income earners, stability of employment, assets, debts, insurance deductibles and uncovered health and property insurance exposures, and the family's general attitudes toward risk and security. The size of the emergency fund can be expressed as so many months of family income—typically 3 to 6 months.

By its very nature, the emergency fund should be invested conservatively. There should be almost complete security of principal, marketability, and liquidity. Within these investment constraints, the fund should be invested to secure a reasonable yield, given the primary investment objective of safety of principal. Logical investment outlets for the emergency fund include

| By its very nature, the emergency fund should be invested conservatively. |

- bank passbook savings accounts (regular accounts)
- bank and mutual fund money market accounts
- short-term United States Treasury securities
- United States savings bonds
- life insurance cash values

The careful client also may want to have some ready cash available for emergencies, even if it is noninterest earning. ◊

IMPACT OF INCOME TAXES ON RETIREMENT PLANNING

Income taxes have a far-reaching effect on retirement planning. In addition to income taxation of wages, which reduces an individual's income and consequently his or her potential retirement savings, unearned income in many of the financial vehicles that clients use to save for retirement is taxed each year as funds within them grow. Also, as the sums of money within these taxable accounts get larger, the income taxation on those larger sums increases as well. Thus, income taxes directly reduce the net amount of money that clients would otherwise potentially accumulate for use during retirement. Therefore, a working knowledge of income taxation is necessary to minimize the adverse effect that it can have on clients' retirement planning goals.

Income Tax Rates

Income tax rates are based on the level of taxable income and filing status of the individual taxpayer. There are four different filing categories for individuals:

- married individuals filing jointly and surviving spouses
- heads of households
- unmarried individuals other than surviving spouses and heads of households
- married individuals filing separately

Regardless of the filing category, the basic process to determine taxable income and the amount of income tax owed is the same. The following components are used in computing income taxes:

gross income

- gross income. *Gross income* refers to all wages, salaries, commissions, alimony received, taxable pensions, IRA distributions, rents, royalties, the taxable portion of annuity payments, and many other items defined by the IRS. Gross income also includes capital gains (or losses), dividend income, and net business income for individuals who are self-employed.

adjusted gross income (AGI)

- adjustments to income. Certain amounts are subtracted directly from gross income to arrive at *adjusted gross income (AGI)*. These amounts include deductions for contributions made to a Keogh plan, simplified employee pension (SEP), savings incentive match plan for employees (SIMPLE), or individual retirement account (IRA) (if eligible).
- itemized expenses. Once AGI has been computed, taxpayers can deduct certain approved expenses. These include medical and dental expenses in excess of 7.5 percent of AGI, eligible mortgage interest, gifts and contributions to charity, and state and local income taxes paid.
- personal exemptions. In addition to the specific deductions already made, the tax code allows individuals to take a flat deduction for themselves and for their dependents who are not reported on other tax returns.
- taxable income. Taxable income is the amount of income to which the appropriate income tax rate is applied. It is the income that remains after all the adjustments and deductions listed above have been applied.

Income Tax Credits

income tax credits

Once the taxable income has been calculated and the income tax rate applied, the taxpayer can reduce the amount of income tax due if he or she qualifies for any income tax credits. *Income tax credits* are items that can be subtracted directly from the amount of income tax owed to determine the amount of income tax that has to be paid.

The discussion above is a summary of how federal income taxes are calculated. Later in this chapter we will explore some ways that your clients can reduce the income taxes they owe. But first we should take a look at state income taxes and the impact they have on your clients.

State Income Taxes

Frequently, taxpayers will add the state tax rate to their federal tax rate bracket and assume this is the total income tax rate they must consider in evaluating investment alternatives. However, a person with a 28 percent marginal federal income tax rate and a 6 percent state income tax rate is not actually in a 34 percent combined income tax bracket. Rather, the correct total is 32.32 percent, because the state income tax paid is a deduction against federally taxable income so long as the taxpayer itemizes deductions for federal income tax purposes. Thus, the federal income tax is reduced. The following formula can be used to determine the precise combined tax rate:

State tax rate x (1 – Federal income tax rate) + Federal income tax rate
= Combined income tax rate

or

$$
\begin{aligned}
(.06 \times .72) + .28 &= \text{Combined income tax rate} \\
.0432 + .28 &= .3232 \\
&= 32.32\%
\end{aligned}
$$

> **The income tax rate is not applied to gross income. It is applied to taxable income after adjustments, expenses, and the personal exemption.**

It is important to note that the income tax rate is not applied to gross income. It is applied to taxable income after adjustments, expenses, and the personal exemption. A nominal tax rate of 28 percent, therefore, is not equal to 28 percent of gross income. Still, for illustrative purposes, it is convenient to add the federal and state income tax rates together to demonstrate the income tax savings potential.

Tax Reduction Strategies

Generally, all taxpayers, especially those with high incomes, can benefit from six income tax reduction strategies that are created by current tax law. These six strategies are

- adjustments to income
- income tax deductions
- tax-exempt income
- income tax credits
- income tax deferral
- income tax shifting

Adjustments to Income

Income tax law allows taxpayers to adjust or reduce their current gross income by the amount of certain allowable expenditures like alimony paid and contributions to qualified retirement plans. Contributions to qualified retirement plans do not eliminate taxes, but they do reduce the taxation of current gross income, thus deferring payment of income tax until the time funds are actually used. The following example illustrates why you should encourage prospects to take advantage of the tax-qualified retirement plans available to them.

Example: Your client contributes $3,000 to his qualified plan, which reduces his taxable income for the current year by $3,000. If his marginal income tax rate for federal and state taxes is 30 percent, he or she has saved $900 in tax. Although setting aside $3,000 reduces spendable income by $2,100, it leaves the full $3,000 to earn interest and compound the growth of both principal and interest for the future.

Income Tax Deductions

The IRS allows taxpayers to reduce their taxable income by taking certain deductions. Income tax deductions are designed to recognize certain needs like health care or to encourage positive social action. For example, deductions are allowed for medical expenses above a certain percentage of the individual's AGI. The tax deduction for mortgage interest seeks to stimulate taxpayers to purchase homes. Donations to charities support organizations that help the community. By providing favorable income tax treatment, the government supports and encourages these activities.

Two other itemized deductions from income deserve mention:

- state and local taxes. The only deductible taxes are state and local income taxes, state and local real property taxes, and personal property taxes. Income tax deductions for consumer interest were phased out in 1991. (Loan interest on individually owned life insurance is considered consumer interest and, therefore, is generally no longer deductible as consumer interest.)
- allowable interest paid. Certain mortgage interest and certain investment interest are the only types of interest that are deductible.

  Mortgage interest paid on the mortgage for a principal residence and/or a second home is deductible as long as the mortgage does not exceed both of the following:
  - $1 million in aggregate debt
  - $100,000 in home equity debt

  Under these rules, a homeowner who borrows against the equity in his or her home or second home generally is permitted to fully deduct the interest on the smaller of (1) $100,000 ($50,000 if married filing separately) or (2) the total of the home's fair market value reduced by the amount of its home acquisition debt and grandfathered debt. (If the loan proceeds are for investment, business, or other deductible purposes, then the loan can exceed these limits and the interest may still be deductible.) These rules apply to second mortgages and home equity loans taken after October 13, 1987. Interest on home loans and mortgages arranged prior to that date that exceed the above limits are considered grandfathered and continue to be fully deductible.

Tax-Exempt Income

Over the years, federal income tax legislation has identified certain types of income that are not subject to income taxes. This income comes from a wide variety of revenue sources:

- cost basis of immediate annuity payments
- child support payments
- individually owned disability income insurance benefits
- health and accident insurance proceeds
- interest on bonds issued by states and cities
- casualty insurance proceeds
- life insurance death benefits
- welfare benefits
- workers' compensation payments
- personal injury claims settlements
- divorce property settlements

Some items on this list are fully exempt from taxation. Several other items can be partially exempt. For example, a specific exemption is allowed for the taxpayer and each of his or her dependents. In addition, certain investment income is exempt from federal income taxes.

Personal Exemption. For each individual, spouse, and dependent, there is a personal exemption. This is an amount that increases slightly each year and is available to each individual regardless of his or her income, but it is available only once each year. A person who is claimed as a dependent on another taxpayer's return is not allowed a personal exemption on his or her own return. For example, if a dependent child has taxable income, the child cannot apply a personal exemption to that income because he or she can be claimed on the parent's tax return.

Income Tax Credits

Once gross income has been reduced by the allowable adjustments and deductions, the taxpayer has arrived at his or her taxable income. For some taxpayers, using certain tax credits can further reduce their tax liability.

A tax credit is more
desirable than either
a tax deduction or a
tax exemption.

A tax credit is more desirable than either a tax deduction or a tax exemption. A $200 tax deduction or exemption reduces income taxes only by $200 multiplied by the taxpayer's marginal federal income tax rate. For example, assuming a 25 percent marginal federal income tax rate, a $200 deduction is worth only $50, or $150 less than the value of a tax credit. A $200 tax credit actually reduces income tax due by the full $200. Currently, the major individual income tax credit available is the child care credit.

Income Tax Deferral

Unlike an income tax deduction, which causes an immediate reduction in taxable income, an income tax deferral allows an individual to delay or defer including certain income in current taxable income. Income tax on the specific income may be deferred for several years but ultimately will have to be paid in some future year.

Examples of income tax deferrals include the 403(b) tax-deferred annuity programs available to employees of public schools and certain nonprofit organizations, executive-deferred compensation programs, 401(k) salary reduction plans, and cash value accumulations in deferred annuities or permanent life insurance policies. In addition, income tax deferrals apply to the earnings on money invested in qualified or tax-favored retirement plans that are eligible for a deduction for the amount contributed to them such as corporate pension and profit-sharing plans, Keogh plans, and traditional IRAs. The advantage of tax deferral is that the growth in money compounds periodically without being reduced by income taxes.

Income Tax Shifting

Under certain conditions, tax laws allow taxpayers to shift or transfer their obligation to pay income tax on specific income to another taxable entity. Shifting the tax obligation from a taxpayer with a high marginal income tax rate to one with a lower marginal income tax rate can reduce the total tax income liability.

If income-producing property is transferred from any source to a child under age 14 in 2006 (age 18 in 2007 and thereafter), the income may be taxed in the parent's tax bracket. Children beyond these respective ages are taxed at their own marginal income tax rate.

Alternative Minimum Tax (AMT)

When a significant portion of taxpayers' income is from ventures or financial activities that receive preferential tax treatment, or when taxpayers maximize their use of the deductions and exemptions available to them, their income tax liability may be considerably reduced. To help restore tax equity, the laws provide for an alternative minimum tax (AMT). The AMT is aimed at corporate and noncorporate taxpayers whose high incomes result from tax preference items that include certain itemized deductions, and tax-exempt interest, for example.

Some of the preferences must be recomputed and added back into income. This may require a recalculation of adjusted gross or taxable income. In effect, taxpayers who benefit from these tax preference items must compute their taxes according to the ordinary method and the alternative method and pay the higher income tax that results from either method.

Using Form 1040 to Find Selling/Planning Opportunities

You can use individual income tax returns to learn a great deal about a client's financial situation and, more important, how to improve that financial situation.

Individual income tax returns are the closest thing to a personal income statement that most individuals prepare. You can use these returns to learn a great deal about a client's financial situation and, more important, how to improve that financial situation. The following are some key areas on the federal income tax Form 1040 that you should examine for potential selling/planning opportunities:

- dependents. If there are dependents, is there a need to discuss education funding?
- wages and salaries. Look for what is missing, like deductions for a 401(k), SEP, or tax-deferred annuity. Is the client maximizing all the opportunities available?
- dividends and interest. This may provide clues to portfolio diversification and risk tolerance. Could the current allocation of assets be improved?
- capital gains and losses. Do these favor the capital loss or the capital gain side? Use Schedule D to determine trade frequency and holding periods. If the client is making many trades, look for longer horizons to minimize transaction costs. With whom does the client trade? Is this business you should have?
- rents, royalties, partnerships, estates, and trusts. Look at Schedule E to determine the types of investments the client owns. If there are losses from real estate and partnerships, question the economics of the losses. Although they may have some advantages, the overall net economic effect of owning the property over a specified holding period should determine whether it is worth keeping, or selling and reinvesting the proceeds elsewhere.
- IRA deductions. Does the client qualify to take income tax deductions for contributions to a traditional IRA? If so, is it because of low income or because there is no other tax-qualified retirement plan available?

- Keogh plans. If the client is self-employed and not contributing to a Keogh or SEP, is it feasible to set one up?
- alternative minimum tax. If the client is liable for the AMT, what is the cause? Could you help structure or time items to avoid the AMT or reduce the client's overall income taxation?
- overpayment of taxes. Is too much tax being withheld from the client's income? If so, can you help find a better way to use the money? There are also some things to look for on Schedule A.
- medical expense deductions. If there are substantial medical deductions, should you review the client's medical expense coverage?
- charitable giving contributions. What are the size and nature of the charitable donations? Would it be better for the client to contribute appreciated assets because the appreciation that has taken place since the assets were purchased would not be taxed?

Special Income Tax Rules for Qualified Plans

There are several income tax rules that apply to distributions from qualified plans. For example, with a few exceptions for special circumstances, there is a tax penalty for withdrawing funds from a qualified plan before age 59 1/2. There are also minimum distribution requirement rules after age 70 1/2 that are quite complex. We will explore the tax rules for qualified plans in greater detail in chapters 6 and 7.

Important Income Tax Planning Concepts

Your familiarity with two pairs of income tax concepts will be useful in conversations with prospects and their advisors, and it will assist you in using your company's retirement planning software.

pretax income

The first pair of concepts is pretax income and after-tax income. *Pretax income* refers is income that has not yet been subjected to income taxes. When asked what their annual income is, most people will respond with a gross, or pretax, amount.

after-tax income

After-tax income is more meaningful for most financial analyses. *After-tax income* is the income that remains after taxes have been paid. After-tax income is what most people refer to as their take-home pay. The financial analysis methodology underlying retirement planning compares after-tax income needs with after-tax resources.

marginal income tax rate

Another pair of valuable concepts is marginal and effective income tax rates. The *marginal income tax rate* is the rate at which an individual's next dollar of income will be taxed. The concept of marginal income tax rate is useful in evaluating the tax benefit to be derived from additional income or deductions.

Example: If a single individual with a gross income of $50,000 is in a marginal rate bracket of 25 percent, his or her next dollar of income will be taxed at 25 percent.

effective income tax rate

Effective income tax rate is determined by dividing the taxes actually paid into an individual's gross pretax income. The concept of effective income tax rate is useful to determine the amount of income left over after taxes for savings and retirement income planning.

Example: An individual who earned $50,000 of gross income paid $10,000 in income taxes. The effective income tax rate is 20 percent, compared to a marginal income tax rate of 25 percent.

As you might expect, most software packages that perform financial analysis require the user to input a tax rate. In most instances, the effective income tax rate provides a more meaningful analysis of an individual's income tax situation than the marginal income tax rate does. ◊

INFLATION

Causes of Inflation

inflation

Inflation is an economic condition created by too much demand chasing after too few goods and services. When government fiscal policy and the Federal Reserve System create too much money relative to the products available for purchase, prices inevitably rise. The rise in prices causes labor to demand higher wages and investors to demand higher returns on capital.

Inflation is measured by various indices. The most widely known of these are the consumer price index (CPI) and the wholesale price index (WPI). The CPI measures prices paid for goods by households at the retail level. The WPI measures prices paid for wholesale farm products, processed foods and feeds, and industrial commodities. Table 4-8 provides a brief history of inflation.

What Inflation Means

What does inflation mean for your retirement planning clients? It means a loss of purchasing power. Inflation destroys value.

When the technical discussion is said and done, what does inflation really mean for your retirement planning prospects and clients? It means a loss of purchasing power. In simple terms, inflation destroys value. A dollar set aside today will not, if inflation continues, purchase as much next year as it will today.

TABLE 4-8
A History of Inflation

The Consumer Price Index is the government's statistical measure of the changes in the prices of goods and services bought by urban wage earners and clerical workers. It is commonly used to measure the rate of inflation.

Year	Index*	Percentage Increase	Purchasing Power of the Dollar
1983 (base)	100	—	$1.00
1984	104	4.35%	.95
1985	109	3.6	.91
1986	110	1.9	.90
1987	114	3.6	.86
1988	119	4.1	.83
1989	124	4.8	.79
1990	131	5.4	.75
1991	137	4.2	.72
1992	141	3.0	.69
1993	145	3.0	.66
1994	149	2.6	.65
1995	153	2.8	.64
1996	157	3.0	.62
1997	161	2.3	.60
1998	164	1.8	.59
1999	167	2.2	.58
2000	173	3.3	.56
2001	177	2.8	.55
2002	180	1.6	.54
2003	184	2.3	.52
2004	191	3.8	.50
2005	197	3.4	.48

U.S. Bureau of Labor Statistics purchasing power of the dollar is rounded off to the nearest cent. U.S. City average. Urban wage earners and clerical workers: Base year index of 100 is divided by the index for the year in question.
* Rounded to the nearest whole number.

In effect, everyone feels inflation, but it is most devastating to people with fixed incomes. To help you understand its impact, consider the following example.

Example: Mary Alexander retired at age 65 with a fixed annual pension of $24,000 a year and savings of $200,000 that she kept in a bank savings account at 3 percent annual interest. Her home was paid for, and she lived comfortably on only $20,000 a year, putting the excess $4,000 in her savings account for a rainy day.

For the first 4 years of Mary's retirement, it looked like she was doing well, even though inflation had raised her expenses. By year 5, her expenses exceeded her income; each year, the problem got worse. At 85, Mary was still in excellent health, but her income had remained fixed, her expenses kept rising with inflation, and she had to withdraw more dollars from her savings each year. Her lifestyle and peace of mind are threatened in her golden years by the effect of inflation. (See table 4-9.)

TABLE 4-9
Inflation's Effect on a Retired Person

Years	Fixed Income	Inflation-Adjusted Expenses 1986–2005	Net Effect on Savings Gain/Loss	Total Life Savings Account Balance Earning 3% Interest
1	$24,000	$20,380	$3,620	$209,729
2	$24,000	$21,114	$2,886	$218,994
3	$24,000	$21,980	$2,020	$227,645
4	$24,000	$23,035	$965	$235,468
5	$24,000	$24,279	($279)	$242,245
6	$24,000	$25,299	($1,299)	$248,174
7	$24,000	$26,058	($2,058)	$254,499
8	$24,000	$26,840	($2,840)	$259,209
9	$24,000	$27,538	($3,538)	$263,341
10	$24,000	$28,307	($4,307)	$266,805
11	$24,000	$29,156	($5,156)	$269,498
12	$24,000	$29,827	($5,827)	$271,581
13	$24,000	$30,364	($6,364)	$273,174
14	$24,000	$31,032	($7,032)	$274,126
15	$24,000	$32,056	($8,056)	$274,052
16	$24,000	$32,954	($8,954)	$273,051
17	$24,000	$33,481	($9,481)	$271,477
18	$24,000	$34,251	($10,251)	$269,063
19	$24,000	$35,553	($11,553)	$265,235
20	$24,000	$36,762	($12,762)	$260,047

Table 4-10 also illustrates the concept of how inflation erodes purchasing power. An individual with a monthly income of $1,000 today will require $1,217 of income in 5 years in order to keep pace with a 4 percent inflation rate. In 30 years, the income needed will increase to $3,243. Meanwhile, the purchasing power of the individual's $1,000 of income today will erode to $815 in 5 years and to $294 in 30 years.

TABLE 4-10
Effect of 4% Inflation on Financial Objectives

Age	Income at Today's Value	Increased Monthly Income Required	Purchasing Power of Fixed Income
40	$1,000	$1,000	$1,000
45	1,000	1,217	815
50	1,000	1,480	665
55	1,000	1,801	542
60	1,000	2,191	442
65	1,000	2,666	360
70	1,000	3,243	294
75	1,000	3,946	240
80	1,000	4,801	195
85	1,000	5,841	159

Inflation and Financial Decision Making

Increases in prices of goods and services are a fact of life that consumers in the United States have come expect. The effect that inflation has on the price of items we use every day is something that we all have become accustomed to coping with.

The effect of inflation on investments, however, is less obvious than its impact on prices. Although it may be more difficult for the average family to recognize at first, in the long run, the influence of inflation on savings and investments can be just as devastating as escalating prices.

Your prospects need to make good financial decisions, despite the level of inflation. Knowledgeable advisors help their prospects and clients design programs that will reduce unnecessary exposures to inflation.

Regardless of national economic policy, individuals can and must act to minimize the negative effects of inflation on their personal financial programs. If you convince your prospects how serious their exposure to inflation is and suggest effective means to minimize this risk, you will indeed provide a valuable service.

The following financial management techniques will help your clients deal with inflation:

> *If you convince your prospects how serious their exposure to inflation is and suggest effective means to minimize the risk, you will indeed provide a valuable service.*

- saving consistently. In the long run, a firm commitment to regular, consistent savings is an essential financial discipline to lessen the effects of inflation. (Note, too, that as inflation pushes wages and salaries higher, the dollar amount of your client's emergency fund should also continue to grow.)

- using interest-bearing checking accounts wherever possible. You should encourage your clients to move non-interest-bearing checking accounts to accounts that earn interest.

- repositioning assets. Your clients should consider transferring all savings that exceed their emergency fund into well-diversified portfolios of assets that are likely to grow more rapidly than the rate of inflation.

- reducing income tax withholding. Clients might want to reduce the number of exemptions used for withholding taxes from paychecks. The extra money can be automatically deposited monthly into mutual funds so the money can grow but be liquid at the same time. Furthermore, the earnings can then be directed into the purchase of additional necessary financial products.

  (You can direct your clients to the Internal Revenue Service Web site at www.irs.gov where there is a "withholding calculator" that helps people fine-tune their personal exemptions so that less money is withheld from their pay. The number of exemptions can be adjusted by submitting an updated W-4 form that can be obtained from the employer's human resources department.)

- minimizing taxes. Higher income caused by inflation puts many wage earners into higher tax brackets. You can make your clients aware of the importance of thinking about the impact of taxes and what they can do to eliminate unnecessary taxation.

- avoiding the "join the crowd" philosophy. Your clients should avoid the tendency to overreact to the economic perils of inflation by investing in high-risk, speculative ventures. Incurring excessive market risk or default risk is never a prudent response to inflation.

- avoiding long-term fixed income investments. These investments are especially susceptible to the perils of inflation; therefore, clients should avoid them.

- reviewing insurance coverage annually. As the value of your client's assets increases, so does the need for higher limits on homeowners and other property insurance. Life and disability income insurance coverage that adequately protect these higher income and living expense levels is equally important. LTCI should contain an inflation rider to adjust the maximum daily benefit annually to keep pace with the increasing cost of long-term care.

- using credit wisely. When borrowing is necessary, clients should shop for credit carefully. Significant variations in loan terms and charges are more common in periods of high inflation. Because the banking business has become so competitive, shopping for banking services is a smart approach.

- taking advantage of income-building opportunities. Your clients should try to identify and react to opportunities that can result in increased income. For example, additional formal or technical education is often a key contributor to increased compensation.

> **Incurring excessive market risk or default risk is never a prudent response to inflation.**

- managing all investments prudently. Your clients should make the time to manage all financial and nonfinancial investments carefully. Carelessness proves to be especially painful in an inflationary economy. Sharing your knowledge with clients of the financial concepts and technical tools discussed in this textbook should lead to their making better financial decisions. ◊

DANGER OF PROCRASTINATION

When should your prospects start planning and saving for retirement? Because it is likely that they will have to reach their retirement goals by making small investments in regular amounts, they must begin saving early to make compound interest work and to enable their money to grow for the long term.

The importance of investing early also applies to how early in the year they make their investments. Investing at the start of the year gives money a full 12 months to grow.

> **It takes discipline to save regularly. Beginning a savings plan often means balancing current lifestyle against future needs.**

It takes discipline to save regularly. Beginning a savings plan often means balancing current lifestyle against future needs. Unexpected emergencies can arise to compete for savings dollars. Moreover, deviating from a regular saving schedule may cost money. Prospects will lose earnings because they will miss the full benefit of compounding on the investments they delayed or skipped.

Cost of Waiting

It is easy to postpone starting a plan of savings in favor of current spending needs. Often, you will find your competition is not with other forms of investments. Rather, it is the prospect's choice of spending today versus saving for tomorrow. The following three examples may help you convince prospects that they lose by waiting to save or by interrupting their savings.

Example 1:   Kim and Chris are both aged 25. Kim decides to start saving $2,000 each year, Chris wants to wait. After 7 years, Chris finally starts to save $2,000 annually. At the same time, Kim decides to stop saving and let her account accumulate interest. If both accounts earn 10 percent interest compounded annually, what will their account balances be in years to come?

At the end of 40 years, Kim's account is just $4,204 less than Chris's, yet Kim's total cash outlay was $14,000 versus $66,000 for Chris.

Example 1: Cost of Waiting (Estimated Return: 10%)		
End of Year	**Kim's Balance**	**Chris's Balance**
5	$13,432	$0
7	$20,872	$0
10	$22,780	$7,282
15	$44,740	$25,159
20	$72,055	$53,950
30	$186,892	$174,995
40	$484,750	$488,954

Postponing the start of a savings plan costs money at retirement. One of the greatest advantages of starting as early as possible is the compounding of the earnings.

Example 2: Has a prospect ever said, "I want to wait to start saving until next year"? By waiting, the prospect loses the benefit of compounding on the contributions that are delayed.

The table below shows the yield that is lost by waiting 1 year. It assumes an annual contribution of $2,000 made at the same time each year from selected current ages until age 65 at a 10 percent investment yield.

In this example, waiting 1 year to start a plan does not cost the $2,000 the prospect might have put in. For a 25-year-old person who waits until age 26 to begin a savings plan, it costs as much as $90,000 by age 65.

Example 2: Waiting 1 Year to Start Saving		
Age	**Accumulation**	**Lost Earnings**
25	$973,704	
26	$883,185	$90,519
30	$596,254	
31	$540,048	$56,206
35	$361,887	
36	$326,988	$34,899

Example 3: Some prospects begin to save for retirement, then skip deposits when their budgets are strained or when they use funds to satisfy unplanned current needs or desires. To understand the power of compounding is

to understand that the effect of interrupting a regular savings plan is also compounded. The table below illustrates the financial incentives to invest earlier versus later in a year.

Suppose your 35-year-old prospect places $5,000 a year into an investment that earns 8 percent interest that is tax-deferred and is compounded annually. If she regularly invests this amount until retirement, she will have $611,729 (column 1) at age 65.

Consider the effect of a 5-year interruption in her savings plan. Such an interruption might occur if she used the $5,000 to help fund her daughter's college education.

By making regular deposits each year, your prospect will accumulate $31,680 at the end of 5 years or by age 40. If this amount is left to earn interest until she retires without making any further deposits after year 5, she will have $216,957 (column 2) accumulated at age 65. However, if your prospect resumes her regular deposits at age 45 after a 5-year interruption in making deposits, she will then have a total of $464,072 (column 3) at age 65.

Example 3: Does It Matter When You Contribute To An IRA?						
Age	Regular Deposits	Column 1 Accumulations	Stopped Deposits	Column 2 Accumulations	Interrupted Deposits	Column 3 Accumulations
35	$5,000		$5,000		$5,000	
36	5,000	$ 5,400	5,000	$ 5,400	5,000	$ 5,400
37	5,000	11,232	5,000	11,232	5,000	11,232
38	5,000	17,531	5,000	17,531	5,000	17,531
39	5,000	24,333	5,000	24,333	5,000	24,333
40	5,000	31,680		31,680		31,680
41	5,000	39,614		34,214		34,214
42	5,000	48,183		36,951		36,951
43	5,000	57,438		39,907		39,907
44	5,000	67,433		43,100		43,100
45	5,000	78,227		46,548	5,000	46,548
50	5,000	146,621		68,394	5,000	100,074
55	5,000	247,115		100,493	5,000	178,721
60	5,000	394,772		147,657	5,000	294,279
61	5,000	431,754		159,470	5,000	323,221
62	5,000	471,694		172,228	5,000	354,479
63	5,000	514,830		186,006	5,000	388,237
64	5,000	561,416		200,886	5,000	424,696
65	5,000	**$611,729**		**$216,957**		**$464,072**

The 5-year interruption will cost your prospect $147,657 in lost dollars accumulated for retirement. This amount is determined by subtracting $464,072 in column 3 from $611,729 in column 1. In the world of compound interest, persistence definitely pays!

The Advisor's Role

You may already use examples like those above during the early planning stages with your prospects. These examples point out the importance of starting to save early and saving on a regular basis.

Most prospects are aware of the power of compounding interest and the cost of waiting, at least conceptually. But there are ways that you can assist your clients in reaching their retirement goals by helping them to see all the areas that call for planning.

It is a mistake to ignore any of the life events that can interrupt retirement saving. Therefore, help your clients plan for their children's college funding, career and job changes, and the need to care for aging parents. These events all have a potential impact on retirement planning that you should not ignore.

Ignoring life, disability income, and property and liability insurance planning may lead to an interruption in savings if money is needed to replace lost or damaged property or if one of the wage earners dies or becomes disabled.

> **It is better to start with small regular savings than to set an unattainable goal and stop short of reaching that goal.**

You can help prospects and clients set realistic and attainable goals. It is better to start with small regular savings than to set an unattainable goal and stop short of reaching that goal.

Finally, you should periodically review your client's plans. These reviews serve two purposes. First, you can determine if your clients' needs have changed. If they have, you can work with your clients to make the necessary adjustments in their long-term plans. Second, the review serves to monitor your clients' progress. By helping your clients plan for their retirement and monitoring their progress, you build the relationship of a trusted advisor. ◊

CHAPTER FOUR REVIEW

Key Terms and Concepts are explained in the Glossary. Answers to the Review Questions and Self-Test Questions are found in the back of the book in the Answers to Questions section.

Key Terms

specialized financial planning goals	Medicare supplement insurance
consumer price index (CPI)	long-term care (LTC)
Medicare	Medicaid

long-term care insurance
   (LTCI)
Health Insurance Portability
   and Accountability Act
   of 1996 (HIPAA)
qualified LTCI contract
chronically ill person
activities of daily living
   (ADLs)
qualified LTC services
facility care (nursing home)
skilled-nursing care
intermediate care

custodial care
assisted-living facility care
community care
insurance planning and risk
   management
gross income
adjusted gross income (AGI)
income tax credits
pretax income
after-tax income
marginal income tax rate
effective income tax rate
inflation

Review Questions

4-1.   List common examples of specialized financial planning needs that can create obstacles to successful retirement planning.

4-2.   Identify the financial and legal products and vehicles that can be used to help fund a college education.

4-3.   Describe the extent to which long-term care is usually covered under employer-provided medical expense insurance.

4-4.   Briefly describe the extent to which Medicare pays LTC benefits.

4-5.   Explain the LTC benefits that Medicare supplement insurance pays.

4-6.   List and briefly describe the types of care commonly found in today's LTCI policies.

4-7.   List and briefly describe the basic and optional benefits in today's LTCI policies.

4-8.   Identify six common losses or risks that should be considered in insurance planning and risk management.

4-9.   Describe why life and disability income insurance are important to successful retirement planning.

4-10.   Explain the effect that income taxation has on planning for retirement.

4-11. List six income tax reductions strategies that can be used to minimize income taxation.

4-12. Explain the effect that a 4 percent inflation rate has on the purchasing power of a retiree living on a fixed income.

4-13. Identify and explain five strategies to help limit exposure to inflation.

4-14. Explain the effect that procrastination can have on the accumulation of funds for retirement.

Self-Test Questions

Instructions: Read chapter 4 first, then answer the following questions to test your knowledge. There are 10 questions; circle the correct answer, then check your answers with the answer key in the back of the book.

4-1. Which of the following specialized financial planning goals is the most important in terms of the number of people it affects?

(A) job or career change
(B) college education funding
(C) dependent parents who need long-term care
(D) terminal illness

4-2. Before qualifying for benefits under a tax-qualified LTCI policy, an insured must be cognitively impaired or expected to require substantial assistance to perform two or more activities of daily living (ADLs) for a period of at least which of the following?

(A) 30 days
(B) 60 days
(C) 90 days
(D) 120 days

4-3. Which of the following is the most effective means of reducing income taxes?

(A) tax exemption
(B) tax deduction
(C) tax deferral
(D) tax credit

4-4. Which of the following is the most critical aspect of risk management?

(A) identifying exposure to loss of income or property
(B) evaluating the probability of occurrence
(C) calculating the maximum loss potential
(D) selecting the best tools for managing the risk

4-5. Which of the following statements concerning medical expense insurance coverage is (are) correct?

I. Group and individual medical expense insurance primarily covers acute medical care for illness or injury.
II. Medical expense policies frequently contain a specific exclusion for custodial care.

(A) I only
(B) II only
(C) Both I and II
(D) Neither I nor II

4-6. Which of the following statements concerning today's LTCI policies is (are) correct?

I. The policies are guaranteed renewable, which means that an individual's coverage cannot be canceled except for nonpayment of premiums.
II. Few states require an LTCI policy to offer some type of automatic inflation protection.

(A) I only
(B) II only
(C) Both I and II
(D) Neither I nor II

4-7. Which of the following statements concerning the effects of inflation is (are) correct?

I. Inflation increases prices.
II. Inflation increases purchasing power.

(A) I only
(B) II only
(C) Both I and II
(D) Neither I nor II

4-8. All the following statements concerning Medicare payments for long-term care are correct EXCEPT:

   (A) Medicare hospital insurance helps pay for inpatient care in a Medicare-certified skilled-nursing facility under certain conditions.
   (B) Medicare pays some benefits for covered home health services furnished by a Medicare-certified home health agency.
   (C) Custodial care is available under Medicare even if the insured patient needs no other level of long-term care.
   (D) Hospice benefits are available under Part A of Medicare for terminally ill insured persons with a life expectancy of 6 months or less.

4-9. LTCI policies typically limit or exclude coverage for all the following reasons EXCEPT

   (A) preexisting conditions
   (B) alcohol or drug addiction
   (C) Alzheimer's disease
   (D) attempted suicide

4-10. All the following are financial consequences that usually occur as a result of a working family member's death EXCEPT

   (A) loss of the deceased's future earning power
   (B) incurrence of costs and other obligations arising at death
   (C) decreased expenses for the family
   (D) loss of tax advantages

NOTES

1. An overview of college education funding is discussed in this section. For a more comprehensive discussion college funding, see *Foundations of Financial Planning: The Process*. Bryn Mawr, PA: The American College Press, © 2004, chapter 8.
2. A Statistical Profile of Older Americans Aged 65+, U. S. Department of Health and Human Services, August 2004.
3. The Rising Cost of Health Care and Your Retirement, Fidelity Investments, 2005.
4. AHIP, A Guide to Long-Term Care Insurance, 2004.
5. 2005 MetLife Market Survey of Nursing Home & Home Care Costs.
6. CDC/NCHS Health Care in America, Trends in Utilization; U.S. Department of Health and Human Services; January 2004.

5

Investments and Financial Products

<table>
<tr><td colspan="2">

Learning Objectives

An understanding of the material in this chapter should enable the student to
</td></tr>
<tr><td>5-1.</td><td>List and describe the investment opportunities and products that compete for investment dollars.</td></tr>
<tr><td>5-2.</td><td>Describe the four basic approaches to investing.</td></tr>
<tr><td>5-3.</td><td>Explain the concepts of suitability and risk tolerance.</td></tr>
<tr><td>5-4.</td><td>Describe three methods to gauge an investor's risk tolerance.</td></tr>
<tr><td>5-5.</td><td>Explain the basic types of risks associated with investing.</td></tr>
<tr><td>5-6.</td><td>Explain the risk-return trade-off.</td></tr>
<tr><td>5-7.</td><td>Explain how diversification can be used to manage risk.</td></tr>
<tr><td>5-8.</td><td>Describe asset allocation and dollar cost averaging.</td></tr>
<tr><td>5-9.</td><td>Define mutual funds and explain how they work.</td></tr>
<tr><td>5-10.</td><td>Explain the advantages of mutual funds.</td></tr>
<tr><td>5-11.</td><td>Explain the purpose of a prospectus.</td></tr>
<tr><td>5-12.</td><td>Briefly describe the three basic types of deferred annuity products.</td></tr>
<tr><td>5-13.</td><td>Describe the role of life insurance in retirement planning.</td></tr>
</table>

Chapter Outline

SAVING AND INVESTING

As stated earlier, there is a great deal of concern that Americans are not very good at saving money. Most of us save and invest only a small portion of our incomes. Enticed by easy credit and low down payments, we tend to buy today on credit rather than save and buy tomorrow with cash.

Individuals who are setting aside money are confronted with a range of investment and savings opportunities, each of which is competing for savings dollars. The advantages and disadvantages of different investment opportunities overlap. Your prospects and clients must consider several factors to determine if an investment is appropriate These factors are

- risk
- time horizon
- liquidity
- transaction costs
- tax consequences
- competing investment opportunities

Risk

Individuals who are willing to accept higher risks expect higher returns.

Simply stated, risk is the possibility of losing money. When speaking of investing, risk often refers to price fluctuations or the volatility of total return. In general, there is a positive correlation between risk and expected return. Individuals who are willing to accept higher risks expect higher returns. Conversely, those who are averse to risk usually invest in safer vehicles that typically produce lower returns.

Time Horizon

Time horizon is the amount of time an investment will be left in place before it is used. Short-term, intermediate, and long-term investing require different strategies. Clients should consider the investment time horizon when selecting the investment vehicle that is best for them.

Liquidity

Liquidity refers to how quickly an asset can be converted into cash with little or no reduction in value. Each client should determine the amount of funds to keep readily available to meet cash needs without liquidating long-term investments. These funds should be available for emergencies or to use when opportunities arise.

Transaction Costs

Some investments, such as stocks, bonds, and mutual funds, carry sales charges, fees, and administrative costs. Others, such as real estate, require a great deal of the client's time and still have sales and administrative costs. An investor should consider the total cost of investing to determine real total return.

Tax Consequences

Taxes, like transaction costs, can reduce the total earnings an individual receives from an investment. Clients must evaluate the income and capital gains tax consequences of any investment. Because taxes affect returns, it is best to express total returns on an investment on an after-tax basis.

Competing Investment Opportunities

The distinction between institutions and the products they offer has faded dramatically.

In addition to the other factors to consider in determining whether or not an investment is appropriate is the range of opportunities and products that compete for the investment dollar. Each type of investment has its own advantages and disadvantages. Adding to the confusion is that the distinction between institutions and the products they offer has faded dramatically. Banks offer mutual funds, annuities, and life insurance. Insurance companies market mutual funds, including money market accounts.

Banks and Savings and Loan Institutions

Banks and savings and loan institutions offer convenience and safety of principal for most of their accounts. They provide high liquidity but pay relatively low rates of return.

Real Estate

Long considered one of the most secure and sound long-term investments, real estate generally requires a large single lump-sum investment and has the disadvantage of being relatively illiquid. Income-producing real estate, like rental property, can generate a stream of income as well as long-term appreciation.

Life Insurance Companies' Products

Although life insurance's primary function is to protect against the financial hardships caused by death, permanent insurance does provide an accumulation component that can be an integral part of your client's retirement plan.

The advent of universal life—and more recently the proliferation of variable life products—offers options that replicate other investment opportunities. Many insurance companies also offer annuities and other products that provide low-risk investment opportunities with tax-favored growth and guaranteed returns.

Corporate-Issued Securities

Many people view individual stocks and bonds issued by corporations as a means of providing significant capital growth opportunities and dependable income. In exchange for growth opportunities, however, owning individual corporate securities exposes clients to higher levels of risks.

Government-Issued Securities

Available in many different types and maturities, federal government securities give clients a high degree of security and varying degrees of liquidity and return. State and local bond issues are rated for their safety and often offer tax-free benefits.

Mutual Funds

Mutual funds provide the opportunity to invest in a diversified portfolio of securities under the management of a professional fund manager. The structure of mutual funds makes them highly liquid, and the diversification of the fund's portfolio reduces some of the risks. Your clients can select from a wide range of fund types and pick the ones that are suitable for them, taking into account their personal investment objectives, risk tolerance, and time horizon.

To make appropriate recommendations, you must understand the nature of your client's investment objectives, the products available to meet these objectives, and your client's risk tolerance.

Summary

What this means is that all individuals, whether they are making large or small investments, have a seemingly unlimited number of options from which to choose. Your job is to help your prospects and clients sort through the different options available and to recommend the ones that meet their specific needs and objectives. To make appropriate recommendations, you must understand the nature of your client's investment objectives, the products that are available to meet these objectives, and your client's risk tolerance. ◊

APPROACHES TO SAVING AND INVESTING

Saving for retirement often competes with other financial needs. The road to retirement is not always smooth, and the demands for a family's money are many and varied. This means that the retirement plan must maximize every dollar while remaining flexible enough to meet changing demands.

To accomplish these seemingly conflicting goals, retirement funds can be accumulated in four broad categories of saving and investment vehicles:

- pretax
- tax-free
- tax-deferred
- after-tax

Each of these categories has its own specific strengths and shortcomings; a well-designed plan will incorporate all four types to provide maximum flexibility.

Pretax

Pretax retirement savings are known as qualified plans. A qualified plan is one that meets the IRS's nondiscrimination, funding, and fiduciary guidelines for employer-sponsored retirement programs. Contributions made to the retirement fund are made with pretax dollars. No tax is paid on the money set aside until it is withdrawn from the retirement plan.

Most company defined-contribution retirement plans such as profit-sharing plans and 401(k) plans, fall into the pretax savings category. Other employer-sponsored tax-favored retirement plans, such as 403(b) plans (tax-sheltered annuities) offered to teachers and employees of other not-for-profit organizations, and SEP (simplified employee pension) plans are also in the pretax savings category of investment plans. Also included are qualifying contributions to IRAs. We will look at all of these programs in more detail in chapter 6. For now, the important concept to understand is the value of investing in them.

Money set aside in a qualified plan is not taxed at the time it is earned. Because the income is deferred until retirement, so is the tax that would normally be paid on it. In effect, the government is loaning the investor the amount of the tax due until retirement. To make it even better, this "loan" is interest free.

Example: Mary Johnson earns $57,000 a year as a computer technician. Her marginal income tax rate is 25 percent. She sets aside $200 a month in her company's qualified retirement plan. Mary does not pay tax on the $2,400 annually when she files her federal income tax return. Thus, she pays $600 less in taxes now because of the retirement plan.

> We can look at this as $600 that the federal government has allowed Mary to use until she retires. In addition, she may realize additional savings on her state and local taxes. These savings are a strong incentive for her to maximize the amount she sets aside in her company's plan.

Some companies offer another reason to maximize contributions to a qualified plan. Often, a company will offer to match an employee's contribution to a retirement plan up to a certain percentage. For example, a company may offer to match $.50 for every dollar an employee contributes up to 6 percent of the employee's salary.

Employees who have this kind of offer available to them should generally be encouraged to participate in the company plan at least to the extent needed to maximize the employer's contribution. The immediate increase in the employee's investment in the example given is 50 percent—hard to beat in any other investment vehicle.

The downside to investments in qualified retirement plans is a lack of liquidity. Once money is contributed to a qualified plan, it is difficult to access until retirement. The government imposes severe penalties for the early withdrawal of funds from qualified plans, and because taxes are deferred on the money at the time it is deposited, the amounts withdrawn are fully income taxable. Thus, the qualified plan participant is discouraged from using this money for anything other than its intended purpose, which is, of course, to provide retirement income.

Tax-Free

The second type of investment to consider is an investment that grows free of federal income taxation. Some securities that come to mind for retirement planning purposes are tax-free municipal bonds and tax-free money market funds. Several tax-free accumulation vehicles (as mentioned in chapter 4), such as Sec. 529 qualified tuition plans and Coverdell education savings accounts, and certain interest on Series EE U.S. savings bonds are geared toward education funding. The Roth IRA, which is also a tax-free vehicle that can contain various types of securities that might otherwise be taxable, will be discussed in chapters 6 and 7.

Money deposited into tax-free savings vehicles is not income tax deductible. However, it can be withdrawn at retirement totally income tax free. This concept is attractive to many clients who appreciate the simplicity, and it is especially beneficial to clients in higher income tax brackets.

When assisting clients in evaluating the potential merit and appropriateness of tax-free investments, it is necessary to examine the concept of taxable equivalent yield. Usually, tax-free investments, such as municipal bonds and tax-free money market funds, will pay a lower rate of interest than their taxable counterparts. For example, distributed corporate bond yields are higher than municipal bonds yields, but the income is reportable on Schedule B of the IRS individual federal income tax Form 1040. No such income tax is due on municipal bonds. If an individual is in a 35 percent marginal federal income tax bracket, it may be advantageous to purchase the tax-free bond. It depends on the respective yields of the two types of securities being compared. To understand the concept of taxable equivalence, we must apply a simple formula, plug in the variables, and calculate a comparison.

The formula for determining the taxable equivalent yield is as follows:

Tax-exempt yield ÷ (1 – Marginal income tax bracket) = Taxable yield

Example:	Your client, Billy, is in the 35 percent marginal income tax bracket. If he is considering a corporate bond with a yield of 10 percent and a municipal bond with a yield of 7 percent, which would be more beneficial, assuming they possess the same degree of risk? If we plug the variables into the formula above, the result is as follows:

Tax-exempt yield ÷ (1 – Marginal income tax bracket) = Taxable yield
       7% ÷ (1 – .35) = Taxable yield
       7% ÷ .65 = 10.77%

The taxable equivalent yield of the municipal bond for Billy is 10.77 percent. If we reverse the formula, it looks like this:

Taxable yield x (1 – Marginal income tax bracket) = Tax-exempt yield
       10.77% x (1 – .35) = Tax-exempt yield
       10.77% x .65 = 7%

What that means is that if Billy buys a corporate bond that pays 10 percent, or $1,000, after paying taxes on the $1,000 in the 35 percent marginal income tax bracket ($350), the net yield on the taxable bond will be 6.5 percent, or $650 ($1,000 – $350 income tax). Therefore, if all else is equal, the income-tax-free investment that yields a net of 7 percent is more profitable for Billy because the taxable corporate bond would have to pay 10.77 percent or more to outperform the municipal bond at the 35 percent marginal income tax bracket.

Generally speaking, the higher your client's income tax bracket, the more appealing tax-free investments will be.

Tax-free investments are a powerful retirement planning tool. They are, however, not appropriate for everyone. For instance, they usually do not generate as much after-tax interest to people in lower marginal income tax brackets. This is because an investor in a 15 percent marginal income tax bracket would usually earn more net interest after paying the income tax on a higher yielding taxable investment than he or she would earn on a much lower yielding tax-free investment. However, tax-free investments are an option that may make sense as part of a well-rounded retirement planning strategy. Generally speaking, the higher your client's income tax bracket, the more appealing tax-free investments will be.

Tax-Deferred

The third type of savings or investments that should be included in a comprehensive retirement plan is typically purchased with after-tax dollars. Income taxes on the accumulation in these financial products, however, are deferred until the funds are withdrawn. Permanent life insurance, deferred annuity products, and noncoupon bonds, including U.S. savings bonds, are in this category. Under current tax law, the accumulation of cash values in life insurance and deferred annuity products is tax favored. No income tax is paid until the accumulated cash is withdrawn. When funds are withdrawn, the gain in the contract (the amount withdrawn in excess of the premium paid) is taxable as current income.

Example: Your client invests $3,000 a year, which earns 8 percent interest per year. Table 5-1 shows how much

TABLE 5-1
Tax-Deferred Versus Taxable Savings

Year	25% Tax Bracket	Tax Deferred
1	$ 3,180	$ 3,240
2	6,551	6,739
3	10,124	10,518
4	13,911	14,600
5	17,926	19,008
10	41,915	46,936
15	74,018	87,973
20	116,978	148,269
25	174,469	236,863
26	188,117	259,052
27	202,584	283,016
28	217,919	308,898
29	234,175	336,850
30	251,504	367,038

Source: Investment Company Institute.

faster it would grow in a tax-deferred account, such as a deferred annuity product, compared with an account whose interest is taxed annually at 25 percent and the income tax paid from the money in that account.

The value of tax deferral is obvious. Money that would have been paid in taxes remains in the policy to appreciate. Through the compounding of principal and interest, the earnings generated can be significant.

After-Tax

Other investment products that should be in a sound retirement plan are after-tax investments. These are investments that are made with income that has already been taxed and thus offer no favorable income tax advantages.

The advantage of after-tax investments is that they provide a flexible source of cash to meet preretirement needs when necessary. A well-developed financial plan anticipates emergencies and short-term savings objectives. These are best met by investments that are liquid, giving the client maximum flexibility. The amount of flexibility and liquidity depends on the specific type of investment product, not on IRS income tax penalties. Cash investments, such as savings and money market accounts, are the most liquid. CDs are highly liquid but usually involve a penalty for early withdrawal.

| An increasing tax burden is the price that clients who invest in after-tax vehicles pay for flexibility and liquidity. |

A major disadvantage of after-tax investments is that although they consist of deposits from earnings dollars that have already been taxed, the unearned income in the form of interest in these accounts is taxed each year. This taxation occurs whether or not the interest is withdrawn or left in the account to compound periodically. As the balances of these accounts grow, therefore, so does the taxation on their earnings. This increasing tax burden is the price that clients who invest in after-tax vehicles pay for flexibility and liquidity.

The Advisor's Role

Every product you sell has value and a place in financial and retirement planning. There are advantages and disadvantages to consider in each of them. Your job is to help your prospects and clients determine the best way to meet their objectives. Neither you nor they should be allowed to act on presuppositions not related to the specifics of their unique situations. ◊

SUITABILITY AND RISK TOLERANCE

suitability

Suitability and risk tolerance are closely related. *Suitability* refers to whether or not a specific investment is appropriate for a particular prospect or

risk tolerance

client. *Risk tolerance* can be defined as the degree to which your prospect or client is willing to accept risk.

Suitability

> **Perhaps no part of an advisor's job is more important— or more demanding— than determining the suitability of a product.**

Perhaps no part of a financial advisor's job is more important—or more demanding—than determining the suitability of a product. It is a difficult task for a number of reasons. It requires the advisor to consider the prospect's or client's current financial position, investment objectives, time horizon, and age, as well as his or her temperament and tolerance for risk, and then to recommend the appropriate financial product to achieve a desired objective. It goes beyond simply determining what the prospect or client wants.

It is not enough that an investment is safe, or highly rated, or well known, or issued by a company with a good reputation. The investment must fit the needs and investor profile of the person for whom it is being recommended. It is your responsibility to obtain enough information about your prospect or client and his or her situation to make certain that the product is suitable.

Suitability is also a moving target. There is no absolute rule on which to rely. Each case depends on the situation of the individual involved. It requires a subjective judgment that goes further than the specific facts of the case.

Example: Your prospect, Barry, is a 70-year-old retiree. He is living on Social Security retirement benefits and has no other source of income. He has $20,000 set aside in a savings account. Barry's physical condition is deteriorating, and he spends most of his time at home watching television. On a talk show, he hears about a new mutual fund your company handles that is setting the world on fire. He calls you and wants to invest his $20,000 in the fund. You tell him about the risks involved, but he is determined. Should you sell him shares in the fund?

Based on the facts above, the answer would be no. No matter how much Barry wants the investment, it is not suitable for his needs. His age, physical health, time horizon, and lack of financial resources all suggest that a volatile, risky investment is not in his best interest, no matter how enthusiastic he is about it.

Some investments have a built-in suitability rule. For example, some limited partnership investments set minimum financial standards that must be met before a person can make an investment. The purchase of a share in a limited partnership program may require the prospect or client to have a minimum net worth of $100,000 and a specified level of income. Rules like these are designed to protect investors who cannot afford to take significant losses if the investment fails.

Determining suitability, however, should go beyond adhering to the special requirements of some products. The advisor must do everything he or she can to assure that the products a prospect or client buys are appropriate for his or her needs and risk tolerance.

Risk Tolerance

You see varying degrees of risk tolerance every day in property and casualty policies, as some clients opt for very low deductibles while others choose very high deductibles. Those who opt for the higher deductibles take the risk of greater out-of-pocket costs at the time of a loss in return for lower current premiums.

Risk Spectrum

We can make an analogy to a scale when measuring risk. For simplicity's sake, let's assume this risk measurement scale ranges from zero to 100. Some of your clients will stand at zero and others at 100, but most will fall somewhere in between. Those who stand at zero are extremely risk averse. The closer the client moves to 100, the greater degree of risk tolerance. Those who stand at 100 can be viewed not only as completely tolerant of risk but also as risk seekers. Those who stand somewhere in between can be considered risk tolerant in various degrees.

Clients need to recognize where they stand on the scale. As an advisor, you must understand both the scale itself and the fact that different clients have different degrees of risk tolerance. Some recommendations are appropriate for clients who are willing to accept risk but inappropriate for those who are risk averse. Prudent marketplace practice dictates that advisors should assume that most clients are risk averse. This assumption automatically adds a level of caution to any recommendation.

> **Prudent practice dictates that advisors assume that most clients are risk averse. This adds a level of caution to any recommendation.**

Risk Tolerance Assessment Techniques

Given the importance of a client's tolerance toward risk, how does the advisor make an assessment? Although there is no one absolute way, we suggest the following three methods to gauge a client's risk tolerance:

- investment philosophy test
- examination of investment history
- review of investment objectives

Investment Philosophy Test. An investment philosophy test (often referred to as an investor profile) aims at uncovering a client's risk tolerance through a series of questions. The test usually takes the form of a questionnaire, with a scoring device that quantifies a client's preference for a conservative, moderate, or aggressive investment strategy.

Examination of Investment History. The past is often considered the prologue to the future. One way to gauge a client's risk tolerance is to examine the type of investments the client made in the past. For example, clients who placed their savings solely in CDs would, in all likelihood, have a very low level of risk tolerance.

Review of Investment Objectives. Another way to gauge risk tolerance is to ask your client about his or her financial objectives with follow-up questions designed to uncover the client's feelings about various topics related to risk. These follow-up questions would typically concern safety of principal, tax reduction, and asset appreciation strategies. Other follow-up questions would probe the client's feelings regarding the need for liquidity, generation of current income, and inflation. The client's answers to both the financial objective(s) and follow-up questions give the advisor a source of information from which to infer the client's risk-tolerance level.

The Advisor's Role

Before making any specific investment recommendations, you must determine your client's specific investment objectives, time horizon, and the degree of risk he or she is willing to accept. Once you have ascertained this, you have narrowed the range of investments that will fit your client's situation.

Moreover, you must be certain to comply with all the regulatory disclosure requirements involved in the sale of any security or financial product. You must also make sure that your client fully understands the features, benefits, and drawbacks of any investment product before he or she purchases it. ◊

MANAGING RISK

Understanding Risk

One measure of risk is the extent by which returns fluctuate from one period to the next.

Another term for risk is volatility, and one measure of risk is the extent by which returns fluctuate from one period to the next. All investment and savings vehicles carry some element of risk. We see this as the market value of investment and savings vehicles rises or falls over time. Risk cannot be eliminated, but if it is understood, it can be managed.

The total risk to which your clients are exposed can be divided into two categories:

- systematic risk
- unsystematic risk

There are other investment risks that are more difficult to categorize that will not be discussed in this text.

Systematic Risk

systematic risk

A *systematic risk* is a risk that affects the entire market, not just one business or industry. Systematic risks are associated with investing in general. Some examples are

- market risk
- inflation risk
- interest rate risk
- reinvestment risk
- currency risk

Market Risk. To the extent that stock and bond values have a tendency to move with the market, they are affected by market risk. Market risk is the risk that general market conditions will affect the value of a particular stock or bond.

Inflation Risk. Inflation reduces purchasing power. To experience real gains, your client needs returns in excess of inflation. Inflation risk is the risk that inflation will erode your client's purchasing power and perhaps the value of the asset itself.

> **Rising interest rates generally cause bond prices to fall, whereas falling interest rates usually cause bond prices to rise.**

Interest Rate Risk. The risk that interest rate changes will cause changes in the value of securities is known as interest rate risk. Bonds are particularly sensitive to interest rate risk. An inverse relationship exists between interest rates and bond values. Rising interest rates generally cause bond prices to fall because investors expect to be paid the higher interest rate.

Reinvestment Risk. The risk that your client will not be able to reinvest earnings from a current investment in another investment of equal price that yields the same return is reinvestment risk.

Currency Risk. The value of the dollar relative to foreign currency may affect an investment. This is known as currency risk.

Unsystematic Risk

unsystematic risk

An *unsystematic risk* is unique to a single business or industry. These are specific risks associated with an underlying investment, not with the market as a whole. Examples of unsystematic risks are

- business risk
- regulation risk
- financial risk
- default risk
- country risk

Business Risk. The riskiness of the specific business includes the speculative nature of the business, the management of the business, and the philosophy of the business. Different of types of businesses will have different levels of risk.

Business risk can also be thought of as the uncertainty of income. Companies with fluctuating income levels, such as auto manufacturers, have higher business risk.

Regulation Risk. The risk that changes in the law, such as zoning changes or changes in the tax rates, will have an adverse effect on an investment is known as a regulation risk.

Financial Risk. The capital structure or extent to which a firm relies on debt may cause an investment to be more or less risky. High debt may be problematic. On the other hand, no debt may mean that a firm is not taking advantage of appropriate opportunities.

Default Risk. Default risk is the possibility that the organization in which an investment is made will go bankrupt or will experience financial strains that cause it to default on its obligations. (This type of risk is also called credit risk.)

Country Risk. The risk international investments face that is unique to each country, including political and economic risks, is known as country risk.

Managing Risk

Each investment opportunity presents advantages and corresponding disadvantages. Keeping in mind that risk cannot be entirely eliminated, we might think of a particular investment's advantages and disadvantages as a set of weights that balance the benefits to be derived against the risk associated with achieving those benefits.

In choosing investment opportunities, there are tradeoffs between possible benefits and risks. In general, riskier investments tend to experience wide fluctuations because their reactions to market movements are above average. Investors expect higher returns as the level of risk increases. Investors also try to estimate the downside risk of an investment.

Assessing the level of risk a client is willing to take is a skill that requires the ability to ask the right questions and listen carefully to answers. It is a process of elimination, starting with questions that define the general investment categories your client finds acceptable, then narrowing the choices to a few specific investments.

Risk-Return Trade-off

> **The expected reward from an investment is directly related to the risk it bears.**

All investment and savings vehicles carry some element of risk. A basic tenet of finance is that the expected reward from an investment is directly related to the risk it bears. The greater the risk, the greater the expected return should be.

It is critical that your clients clearly understand the risks associated with a proposed investment. Your clients should expect to earn a higher return than what they would realize on a less risky investment only if they are willing to assume the higher risk.

Occasionally, a client may be enticed by the promise of very high returns, failing to recognize the speculative nature of the investment and the possibility that he or she could lose the entire amount invested. In these cases, the advisor must focus the client on the risks inherent in the investment and help him or her find opportunities that are more suitable.

Investment Risk Management

There are several tools to help estimate and manage risk. Perhaps the most important tool is diversification.

Diversification

diversification

Diversification is a portfolio management technique that is designed to minimize the impact of any one security, investment, or asset category on overall portfolio performance. It is possibly the single most important tool for managing risk. It takes advantage of the relationship between asset categories and investments within an asset category.

Diversification can be accomplished in at least three ways. Your client could

- hold a variety of assets across several categories of assets. For example, he or she may own real estate, stocks, bonds, mutual funds, and so on.

- hold alternative assets within each category of assets. For example, a client who invests in common stocks may own a number of different stocks.
- purchase assets that mature or can be sold at different times

In effect, diversification means that your client does not put all his or her money into one investment. Instead, he or she invests across asset categories to take advantage of the relationships between investments and to minimize risk.

Establishing several asset categories and selecting investments for those categories is not diversification if each one of the categories is designed for investments that have similar risk and return profiles as the investments in other categories. True investment diversification occurs only when a portfolio is composed of several asset categories, each one of which is designed for investments with risk and return profiles that are dissimilar to the profiles of investments in other categories. Thus, a downward movement of investments in one asset category is, ideally, offset by an upward movement of investments in another asset category.

In reality, it is difficult to establish asset categories whose performance will be exactly opposite but in the same proportion all the time. With most diversified portfolios, clients select investments for several asset categories that, while not perfectly dissimilar in terms of the risk and return profiles of the investments, offer better protection than if the portfolios consisted of several asset categories whose investments have fairly similar risk and return profiles.

Diversification is necessary not only among asset categories but also within each category. A portfolio with a large-cap-stocks category should not hold both General Motors and Ford. Diversification requires avoiding excessive concentration in an industry. Similarly, it requires avoiding concentration across asset categories. If the client holds stock in General Motors, he or she should not also hold General Motors bonds. The diversification requirement cannot be stated in terms of fixed allocation percentages but instead depends on the facts and circumstances of each asset category, as well as the individual investments within each category. It also depends on such factors as the purposes of the portfolio, the amount of portfolio assets, and financial and economic conditions.

Finally, you should caution your client about investing too heavily in investments that are closely aligned with his or her occupation. The reason is that if the industry collapses, then not only would there be a drop in the value of the client's portfolio, but he or she might also be out of a job. It is tempting for clients to want to invest in industries with which they are familiar, but they should do so with caution. They should always adhere to the principle of diversification, no matter how strong the temptation to do otherwise. ◊

If a client invests too heavily in investments closely aligned with his or her occupation, in addition to a drop in the value of the client's portfolio if the industry collapses, he or she might be out of a job.

MANAGING INVESTMENTS

Investment Strategies

Over the years, many strategies have been advanced to attempt to manage risk by picking winners. Some strategies are based on the risk management tools discussed above. Others are less scientific. Some are active strategies that require the investor's time to monitor. Others are passive strategies. We will give one strategy in particular—asset allocation—special emphasis in this chapter, along with the methodical periodic investment technique known as dollar cost averaging.

Asset Allocation

asset allocation

Asset allocation is a portfolio management technique that allows the client to spread investment risk across different types of investments in a planned and predetermined way. Asset allocation is a strategy to create proper diversification. Correctly used, asset allocation is an excellent way to protect assets and experience consistently favorable overall investment returns.

Over the course of any investment period, macroeconomic factors have an effect on an investment program's success or failure. These factors are difficult to predict for the short term, and they are almost impossible to predict for any long-range period. Therefore, advisors and clients need to follow an investment strategy that will lessen the impact of uncontrollable fluctuations of the general economy. The process of asset allocation is one such technique.

Example: Your client, Rose, wishes to benefit from the potential growth of a bull market in stocks, but she wants a portion of her money in more secure issues. In other words, she wants to be aggressive, but not with all of her investment dollars.

To achieve the balance she desires, Rose decides to invest 40 percent of her funds in an aggressive, small company stock fund, but she elects to balance that investment by putting 40 percent in a government bond fund, leaving the remaining 20 percent for a money market fund. She has allocated her assets in a way that allows her to benefit from both an aggressive investment and a conservative one, at least partially offsetting the risks involved with the volatility of the stock fund.

Consider what her investments might look like at the end of the year. Assume she invested $2,000—$800 in the stock fund, $800 in the bond fund, and $400 in the money market account—and then reinvested all the earnings. The stock fund performed very well, and at the end of the year her shares have a net asset value of $1,112. The bond fund also increased in value to $860, and the money market account grew to $425. At the end of a year, the value of her investment has risen to $2,397.

What has happened to her allocation formula? Based on the performance of her investments, Rose has lost the balance that she started with. The stock fund now represents 46.4 percent of her investment, the bond fund only 35.9 percent, and the money market account only 17.7 percent.

What should Rose do? Her funds can be automatically rebalanced. This will be discussed shortly.

That above example illustrates the basic premise of asset allocation management, and many investors use this approach without even thinking about it, electing to spread their investments across more than one type of fund or security. In actual practice, an asset allocation approach, whether intentional or not, is more complicated and requires more active management.

There are many ways to allocate or divide invested assets. What is right for your prospects and clients depends primarily on three factors:

- investment goals
- tolerance for risk
- investment time horizon

For example, if a prospect is 50 years old, comfortable with normal fluctuations in investment markets, and has 15 years until retirement, investment choices might include a sizable percentage of growth-oriented mutual funds. The middle investment stage in figure 5-1 illustrates this. However, if only 5 years remain until retirement, or the prospect has little risk tolerance, investment allocations might include more stability such as like fixed-income investments. The late investment stage in the asset allocation model illustrates this. The asset allocation model offers opportunities to experience and retain gains through more stable allocations of fixed income and money market investments.

But what if your prospect is younger and just starting to invest? This investor would typically lean heavily toward growth investments, assuming he or she has suitable risk tolerance. The early investment stage in figure 5-1

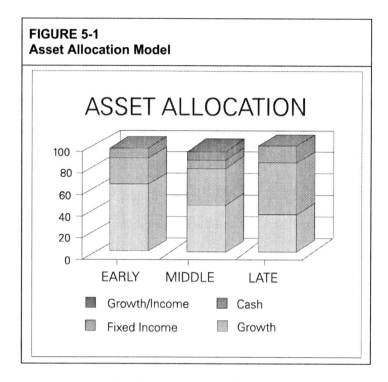

FIGURE 5-1
Asset Allocation Model

depicts an approximately 60 percent asset allocation in growth-oriented investments because time works in the investor's favor.

In each example, investment opportunity is balanced with investment
risk and time horizon. Historical rates of return suggest diversification. Asset
allocations work to produce favorable overall investment returns, manage
macroeconomic risk factors, and enable your clients to reach long-term
financial goals.

Many investment companies now provide rebalancing services for their
family of funds or variable products. In *rebalancing*, companies use computers
to allocate each periodic payment or transferring existing assets into the
appropriate accounts to maintain the original percentage balances your client
had selected. This does not mean, however, that your role is unnecessary.

Asset allocation approaches give you the ideal reason to contact and meet
with your clients. If their accounts are not being managed automatically, they
will need and appreciate your help to determine how existing assets should be
reallocated or into which funds new money should be invested. Even when the
money is being automatically distributed to maintain the selected balance, you
should meet to discuss the appropriateness of the allocation formula in light of
any changes in your client's situation or in market conditions.

Reallocation of Assets. In the concept known as *reallocation of assets*,
an investor takes the value accumulated in one asset and reallocates it to meet

rebalancing

> Asset allocation
> approaches give you
> an ideal reason to meet
> with your clients. They
> will need your help
> to determine how
> existing assets should
> be reallocated or
> into which funds
> new money should
> be invested.

reallocation of assets

some other need. For example, if a client takes a home equity loan to pay off expensive credit card debt, he or she is using part of the value in the home to increase monthly cash flow. Reducing the excessive interest expense the client pays frees up additional cash that can then be allocated to reducing total debt more quickly or to investing in a retirement funding program.

Other forms of asset reallocation can significantly improve your clients' planning for retirement. When analyzing prospects' or clients' finances, you should always look for ways to maximize the value they are getting from their current saving and investment programs. It makes sense to reallocate assets to

- reduce current taxes
- change from taxable to tax-deferred or tax-deductible investments
- meet more than one planning objective

Example:	Your client, Ralph, is investing regularly in income taxable mutual funds and has accumulated a significant nest egg over the years. He may be eligible for a traditional IRA but is not taking advantage of the opportunity, feeling that he just cannot afford it. You might suggest transferring some of the money invested in the nonqualified mutual fund to an IRA. The advantages of such a transfer may be a reduction in taxes.
	The contribution of $3,000 to a traditional IRA reduces Ralph's current income taxes by lowering taxable income. (We are assuming in this example that Ralph is fully eligible for a tax-deductible IRA. We will discuss eligibility later in this text.) If Ralph's income tax rate is 33 percent, the tax deferral is $999.
	In addition, transferring $3,000 from a taxable investment to the traditional IRA defers taxes on the earnings. Instead of paying tax on the earnings of the mutual fund, Ralph defers taxes until retirement, even if the same mutual fund is used for the IRA investment.

Of course, there is a downside to the concept the example above illustrates. Making a transfer from a taxable mutual fund to an IRA limits the liquidity of that money. The withdrawal of funds from an IRA may subject it to the 10 percent penalty tax on the early withdrawal of retirement funds. The withdrawal from the original investment may also be subject to ordinary income and/or capital gains tax on its appreciation. Finally, the withdrawal may be subject to surrender fees or sales charges. Before a decision is made to transfer the funds, you and your client need to carefully consider these factors.

Reallocation of Current Spending. One way to find the money necessary to help fund retirement is through a reallocation of current spending. By working with prospects and clients to examine their spending habits, you can help them focus on ways to reduce their current discretionary spending to make funds available for the future.

Reallocation of current discretionary spending is often not easy. Many people are already spending more than they earn, relying on easy-to-obtain credit to spend now against what they hope will be higher income in the future. If your clients are truly concerned about the future accumulation of wealth, they must change this pattern.

Convincing clients to begin retirement planning by altering their current spending habits will not happen overnight. Even if they change their spending habits, they may face significant accumulated debt. This debt, with its high interest rate, can be self-defeating. Reducing it slowly is expensive. A substantial part of each payment goes to interest, with only a small amount applied to the principal balance.

One way your clients can reverse the trend is to start investing in the future even if only on a small basis. By implementing a modest plan for the future, you can help them refocus on their priorities, spending for the future first. This can be especially effective if the investment plan is based on an automatic monthly withdrawal directly from the client's checking account. Most insurance and mutual fund companies make this option available. An automatic withdrawal plan assures that a monthly deposit to the plan, no matter how modest, will be made, and the client will see his or her savings for the future begin to accumulate.

Another way your clients can reverse the trend of spending now instead of saving for the future is to control their current spending through debt consolidation. A low-interest home equity loan, for example, used to pay off a number of accumulated high-interest credit card debts, will reduce the amount of interest being paid for credit each month. Of course, this approach works only if the client has the discipline to control the future use of his or her credit cards.

> **Convincing your clients to begin retirement planning by altering their current spending habits will not happen overnight.**

Repositioning for Protection. Repositioning assets to purchase life insurance is an excellent way to meet more than one financial objective. Transferring funds from an investment vehicle into a permanent life insurance product may be a way to meet a client's life insurance protection needs through the insurance's guaranteed death benefit, while at the same time providing the tax-deferred accumulation of cash values.

When considering repositioning or reallocating assets, it is important that there be a clear and compelling reason to change from one financial vehicle to another.

When considering repositioning or reallocating assets, it is important that there be a clear and compelling reason to change from one financial vehicle to another and that all transaction costs are considered. Switching from one mutual fund to another without being able to show a distinct advantage and financial benefit is known as churning, and churning is illegal.

Likewise, borrowing against an existing life insurance policy to purchase a new one or surrendering one policy to purchase another is known as replacement. Replacement is generally viewed as not being in the client's best interest. Borrowing money to invest is a risky and sometimes illegal practice. It should not be encouraged. Often, the earnings anticipated in the investment do not keep pace with the interest paid on the borrowed funds, leaving the client in a worse financial situation than before he or she borrowed the funds. When working with a client to reallocate existing assets, look for assets that are not being maximized. Make sure that you understand the purpose of the asset as it is currently invested. Then explore the pros and cons of moving it to serve other purposes.

Dollar Cost Averaging

dollar cost averaging

Dollar cost averaging, an investment strategy that can help to minimize investment risk, is a technique for methodical, periodic investing. It does not guarantee profit or protect against market losses, but it does tend to level out changes in the market. Dollar cost averaging is like investing on the installment plan. For a small, regular investment, your client can start to build a large portfolio that can grow over an extended period of time.

The key ingredients of dollar cost averaging are discipline and consistency.

How Dollar Cost Averaging Works. Basically, dollar cost averaging levels off the ups and downs in the market and turns them to the investor's advantage. It is a low-risk technique that will fit into most clients' comfort zones. The key ingredients are discipline and consistency.

Instead of trying to time the highs and lows of the market, the client invests the same amount of money in a mutual fund, variable life insurance equity account, or a variable annuity at regular intervals over a period of time. Because the plan is to ride out the ups and downs, what the mood of the market is when your client begins makes little difference in the end results achieved.

Example: May invests $100 per month in a mutual fund. The first month the shares sell at $10 each. She invests $100 and receives 10 shares. The next month the market drops and—taking an extreme example—the fund goes down to $5 a share. May invests $100 and receives 20 shares. The next month the market rebounds and her fund is back to $10 per share. May again receives 10 shares for her $100 investment

Result: May now owns 40 shares of the fund after a $300 total investment. However, with an ending market price of $10 per share, her shares are actually worth more than she paid for them, as shown in table 5-2.

Total investment = $300
Current value: 40 shares x $10 per share = $400

TABLE 5-2
Dollar Cost Averaging: Fluctuating Market

Systematic Investment	Share Price	Number of Shares Acquired
$100	$10	10
100	5	20
100	10	10
$300		40

Average cost per share: $7.50 ($300 ÷ 40)
Average price per share: $8.33 ((10 + 5 + 10) ÷ 3)

The average price per share over the 3 months is $8.33—$25 divided by three investments. The average cost per share over the 3 months is $7.50—$300 divided by 40 shares.

The important point to make with your clients is that dollar cost averaging requires discipline. They cannot stop making the systematic investment when the market drops. In the long run, persistence and adherence to the plan are what will make it work.

You can appreciate the savings you clients can achieve with the dollar cost averaging method. Using dollar cost averaging, a share's average cost is usually lower than its average price. This is illustrated in the example above. The advantage to your client is that the fixed investment purchases more shares when the price is low.

Dollar cost averaging is most effective in volatile markets. When the market experiences sharp changes, the positive effect of dollar cost averaging is most obvious.

Dollar cost averaging is most effective in volatile markets.

Dollar cost averaging works even better if the periodic investment is spread among several investment options. For example, your client could further diversify his or her holdings by allocating the money among three or four mutual funds in the same family of funds. Some experts claim that dollar cost averaging is not prudent when an investor puts all his or her money into only one particular fund. In that case, the investor is hoping that the one fund selected will perform well.

When discussing dollar cost averaging with prospects and clients, remind them that it is a technique for regular, systematic investing and it does not guarantee them a profit or protect them against losses if the market drops. It is simply a way to take advantage of the normal fluctuations of the market over a period of time.

There are no sure bets. Investing has its risks. By using appropriate strategies, your client can minimize those risks. Systematically investing money over a long period of time in products that offer professional management and diversification can help clients develop large nest eggs for retirement, or for any other wealth accumulation goal.

Dealing with Sudden Wealth

Your clients may come into sudden wealth in one of many ways. Two common ways are inherited wealth and life insurance proceeds. We will discuss them briefly from the perspective of helping clients invest the funds they receive from these two sources.

Inherited Wealth

In many ways, inherited wealth is similar to any other form of sudden wealth. If the inheritance is in the form of cash, the person who inherits it may need help to decide the most appropriate way to invest the inheritance to maximize its future value.

People who inherit wealth other than cash, such as stocks and other securities, often cling to these investments for sentimental reasons. For example, a widow or widower may continue to hold a particular stock because it was acquired by the deceased spouse. The widow or widower may have little or no knowledge of securities but trusts the deceased spouse's wisdom in building the portfolio. He or she may feel that selling the security would question the deceased spouse's wisdom. Many widows and widowers stubbornly watch a major holding steadily deteriorate to near worthlessness because they cannot bear to be disloyal.

In *The Money Game,* Adam Smith spoke eloquently about the tendency to hold stock because of a sentimental attachment. His advice: "Just remember that the stock doesn't know you own it."

> **Adam Smith's advice about holding stock because of a sentimental attachment: "Just remember that the stock doesn't know you own it."**

Sentiment is a strong emotion, and your initial approach in situations like this may determine whether an individual will trust you and accept your advice. On the other hand, you can provide a valuable service to your prospects and clients by uncovering potentially wasteful uses of money.

For example, many people with very sizable sums of money have their investments tied up in real estate. These holdings can be extremely valuable, offering significant tax advantages, substantial income, and strong growth potential. Alternatively, the real estate investments may be completely inappropriate for the individual who has immediate cash or income needs.

You may also discover sizable sums in holdings of individual securities that were appropriate for the deceased but are not in keeping with your client's risk tolerance. If you have learned about your client's wants and needs, you should be able to help the client evaluate the suitability and financial balance of his or her holdings based on current circumstances.

An objective third-party viewpoint can be immensely beneficial in confronting the problem of sentimental attachments to investments. Armed with the proper information, you can prepare a report on how well or how poorly the current investment fits the particular situation. For instance, suppose that you are working with a recipient of inherited wealth who has expressed a desire for increased income. Assume further that the individual has a large sum of money in an investment that is providing only minimal income, perhaps 2 percent, but that has appreciation potential. Certainly, that investment is ill advised for this individual, even if you believe the investment itself is a good one.

> **When advising prospects and clients on the disposition of inherited assets, keep the income tax consequences in mind.**

When advising prospects and clients on the disposition of inherited assets, keep the income tax consequences in mind. Under the provisions of the existing estate tax laws, the cost basis of inherited property is stepped up to the asset's current market value. This means that heirs can usually sell inherited assets soon after a deceased owner's death without creating prohibitively large capital gains tax consequences.

In simple terms, cost basis is the price paid for an asset. When the asset is sold, the taxable gain is the difference between its selling price and its basis.

Example: Matt buys 100 shares of stock for $2,500. Ten years later, he sells the stock for $10,000. The gain is $7,500—the sale price of $10,000 less the $2,500 cost basis.

If, however, Matt leaves the stock to his niece, no income tax will be due when the stock is transferred by reason of death, and the niece's cost basis in the stock will be stepped up to $10,000. If she sells the stock for $10,000, she will realize no gain. Therefore, no income tax will be due.

People who inherit assets that are inappropriate for their investment goals or risk profiles can dispose of the assets and reinvest the proceeds in more suitable vehicles without adverse income tax consequences. By explaining how cost basis is stepped up, you can show your prospects and clients when they have an important investment window of opportunity.

Life Insurance Proceeds

Few opportunities for your financial services are as natural and well received as those that are tied to money acquired from life insurance policy death claims. Often, a beneficiary receives a lump sum that is a much greater amount of money than he or she is accustomed to handling. Determining where and how to use such sums is not easy. This is especially true if the funds are critical to maintaining the beneficiary's lifestyle, as is often the case with life insurance proceeds.

After paying the immediate expenses associated with the deceased's death and assuring that there are sufficient funds for short-term cash needs, the beneficiary must view the remaining funds as an important financial resource for the future. Both insurance settlement options and alternative investments should be given careful consideration to determine the best possible choices to meet the beneficiary's long-term needs.

Investment Planning for Beneficiaries. Reaching out to a client's family when a death occurs requires sensitivity and delicacy. It is a time when friends, neighbors, and family members are all giving advice to your client—some of it sound, some of it unsound. If a person is already your client, you should have developed and maintained the relationship of trust necessary to make your counsel even more valuable during the difficult time following the death of a loved one.

After fact finding, you should uncover various investment needs or income problems, and then you should review the types of investments that might best address these needs. It is not difficult to demonstrate, for example, that a balanced mutual fund is a relatively conservative, fully managed method to attain the surviving spouse's capital appreciation and income goals.

You should also remind the surviving spouse that because he or she is now the sole head of the family, there will be expenses and perhaps additional taxes when he or she dies. There may be a need to increase the surviving spouse's life insurance to cover the estimated costs of final expenses, probate costs, estate taxes, and other associated estate settlement expenses. There may be a further need to guarantee income for minor children.

You should evaluate all of these considerations—as well as others—in a comprehensive fact finder. It is important that the plan you recommend addresses both immediate needs and long-range goals. ◊

OVERVIEW OF INVESTMENT AND FINANCIAL PRODUCTS

Mutual Funds

mutual fund

Of all the retirement planning options available, mutual funds are the most common. *Mutual funds* are investment companies that pool investors' money and invest it according to the objectives of the fund. Investors can purchase full or even partial shares, making mutual funds an excellent investment vehicle for small investors and those making regular periodic investments. Mutual funds and mutual-fund-like accounts underlie most of the retirement programs, or they are options within specific programs, including variable life and annuity products.

Millions of people invest in mutual funds each year. In addition, separate accounts—similar to the mutual fund concept—are at the heart of variable life and annuity products and 401(k) products.

Some advantages of mutual funds are

- professional management
- diversification
- liquidity and guaranteed marketability
- ease of investing

Professional Management

The professional money managers of the mutual fund take the pool of money collected from shareholders and invest it in a wide variety of stocks, bonds, and other securities. Securities are specifically selected to meet the fund's investment objectives. Money managers continually make expert decisions on what and where to buy, what and when to sell, and when to hold, based on extensive research.

Diversification

The investment objective of each mutual fund determines which securities are to be purchased for that fund. Investors can achieve further diversification by investing in funds with different investment objectives. Your client can split his or her money between a stock fund and a bond fund, for example, to gain additional diversification.

Liquidity and Guaranteed Marketability

Mutual funds are highly liquid. An investor's shares can be redeemed or purchased back by the fund itself, creating an immediate market for them.

Ease of Investing

Many mutual funds cater to small investors by allowing them to invest modest amounts. Because shares are sold in fractional units, your clients can make regular investments, often through automatic checking account debits. This not only makes investing easy, but it also provides the built-in advantage of dollar cost averaging, which we discussed previously.

How Mutual Funds Work

Mutual funds generally operate with these five interrelated components:

- investment company
- management/investment advisor
- custodian
- transfer agent
- underwriter

Investment Company

investment company

Every *investment company* is regulated by the Investment Company Act of 1940. There are three types of investment companies: open-end funds, closed-end funds, and unit investment trusts.

open-end company

A mutual fund is sometimes referred to as an *open-end company* because it generally stands ready to issue new shares whenever someone wants to make a purchase and to buy back (redeem) its shares when a shareholder wants to sell them.

> All mutual funds must meet minimum net worth and shareholder limits and have a clearly defined investment objective.

Before a mutual fund can be started, it must meet minimum net worth and shareholder limits and have a clearly defined investment objective. The board of directors of the fund is responsible for setting investment policies. Board members are elected by the shareholders and have a fiduciary responsibility to operate the fund for the shareholders' benefit. The directors can be sued and held personally liable if they are

- self-serving
- involved in a conflict of interest
- grossly negligent
- acting in a way that is clearly contrary to the shareholder's best interest

The primary responsibility of the board of directors is to see that investments are in keeping with the stated objectives and policies of the fund. Although all directors share the full burden of this responsibility, the board may appoint certain directors to serve on an investment advisory committee to concentrate on this vital activity.

Fund Manager/Management Company

**fund manager/
management
company**

The board of directors of the mutual fund hires a *fund manager* or *management company* to manage the day-to-day operation of the fund. A majority of the fund's shareholders, as well as the directors, must approve the contract between the fund and the company each year.

The duties of the management company go beyond the business of handling the fund's investments. For example, the management company usually provides and pays for the fund's office facilities, the salaries of its employees, and statistical and research information. For these services, the management company's annual fee is usually one-half of 1 percent of the average net assets of the fund. This fee percentage generally decreases at certain specified levels as the size of the mutual fund increases.

The main task of the management company is to manage the mutual fund's investments. It performs this duty strictly on direction from the fund itself. It must adhere to the fund's basic investment objectives.

Custodian

custodian

The law requires that the assets of the mutual fund, the securities and cash, be held by an independent *custodian*. The custodian—usually a commercial bank named by the directors—receives a fee for its services but has no voice in the investment decisions.

Transfer Agent

transfer agent

The *transfer agent* is responsible for the mutual fund's record keeping. The transfer agent issues shares and confirmation statements, redeems fund shares, and sends out fund distributions. Like the fund custodian, the transfer agent is paid a fee for the services provided. The transfer agent and fund custodian can be the same entity.

Underwriter

underwriter

The *underwriter*, also known as the sponsor or distributor, is responsible for marketing shares of the mutual fund to the public. The underwriter is compensated by adding a sales charge to the price of each share sold.

Many funds, like many of those marketed by life insurance company subsidiaries, sell their shares directly to the public through registered representatives of their own exclusive broker/dealer firms established specifically for that purpose. A registered representative is an advisor who engages in the sale of individual stocks, bonds, and options and has obtained a general securities license from and has registered with the National Association of Securities Dealers (NASD).

It is important to understand that an investor purchases an unallocated, undivided interest in a mutual fund's portfolio rather than a specific investment.

net asset value

Mutual funds raise capital by selling new issues of common stock shares that have equal voting and dividend rights. It is important to understand that an investor purchases an unallocated, undivided interest in the fund's portfolio rather than a specific investment. As a practical matter, most funds have minimum initial and subsequent investment amount requirements. An investor may purchase or redeem full or fractional shares.

Share Value. The value of a share is determined on a daily basis. The total value of the fund's assets is divided by the number of outstanding shares. This yields the *net asset value* of a share:

$$\frac{\text{Total asset value}}{\text{Total number of shares}} = \text{Net asset value per share}$$

The price of mutual fund shares fluctuates based on net asset value rather than on supply and demand.

All funds must determine their net asset value at least once each business day. The price of mutual fund shares fluctuates based on the net asset value rather than on supply and demand pressures. When a mutual fund receives an investor's instructions to redeem shares, the fund pays the investor the net asset value of his or her shares as of the next valuation.

Fund prices can be found on the financial pages of many newspapers. Generally, the price per share is reported in the following two columns:

bid price

- bid. The *bid price* is the net asset value per share. This is the redemption price for a share of the fund.

asked price

- asked. The *asked price* is the price that a consumer actually pays for a mutual fund share. This is the public offering price, which includes any applicable sales charges.

Sales Charges

sales charge

The *sales charge* of a mutual fund is referred to as its load. This is an unfortunate term. NASD limits the maximum load on any transaction to 8.5 percent. Some fund organizations offer different classes of shares within a fund. For example, the Class A share may have a front-end sales charge. Class B shares of the same fund might have a back-end contingent deferred sales charge. Other classes might use other load structures.

When working with prospects and clients, you should be able to explain the following terms as they apply to mutual fund sales charges:

- front-end load
- back-end load
- no load
- 12b-1 fees

front-end load

Front-End Load. A fund with a *front-end load* is one that includes a sales charge as part of the purchase price at the time of purchase. The cost of purchasing a share of a front-end-loaded fund is equal to the net asset value of the share plus the sales charge. Shares are redeemed at net asset value.

back-end load

Back-End Load. Some funds charge a contingent deferred sales charge (CDSC), or a *back-end load*. This is a charge imposed at the time shares are redeemed when the investor withdraws funds from the account. These charges are often used instead of front-end loads and decrease over a period of time, typically 1 to 6 years. Generally, if money is transferred from one fund to another in the same family, no charge is imposed.

no-load fund

No-Load Fund. A *no-load fund* has neither a front-end sales charge nor a contingent deferred sales charge. It may, however, charge an annual percentage of assets to cover distribution costs.

12b-1 fee

12b-1 Fee. A *12b-1 fee* is an asset-based sales charge to cover the fund's distribution services, which include any activity or expense intended to result in the sale of fund shares. Named after the federal regulation that allows them, 12b-1 fees are used as an alternative to front-end charges. Funds that charge 12b-1 fees are required to disclose that long-term shareholders may pay more in sales charges than they would have paid with front-end fees.

Prospectus

prospectus

The mutual fund sales process begins with the registered representative's giving the potential investor a prospectus. A *prospectus* provides detailed information about a mutual fund. It is a written document that describes the key aspects of a security being sold and the company issuing the security. The prospectus details certain limits on how that fund may invest. The fund's self-imposed restrictions also cover other important points. These provisions, once adopted, may not be changed without the affirmative vote of a majority of the shareholders. To alter any of its stated provisions is illegal.

> The purpose of the prospectus is to give possible investors information to help them make an informed decision about the security's investment potential.

The purpose of the prospectus is to give possible investors information to help them make an informed decision about the security's investment potential. A registered representative should never attempt to sell an investment without reviewing the prospectus. It must be given to an investor before or during the sales process and before he or she can buy into the fund. Likewise, your prospects and clients should never buy a security without first reading the prospectus.

Common Types of Mutual Funds

Mutual funds fall into different categories. The category into which a fund falls tells the investor something about the fund's objectives. Reading the prospectus will enable your client to learn the types of securities the fund buys to meet its objectives. Common types of mutual funds fall within three broad categories:

- stock funds
- bond funds
- money market funds

Funds may consist of domestic or foreign securities or some combination. They can hold taxable as well as tax-free securities. Their risk factors can appeal to clients with risk tolerances ranging from conservative to very aggressive.

Each mutual fund will contain a brief explanation within its prospectus of its basic investment objectives. Clients should choose mutual funds that are consistent with their personal risk tolerance and those that will enable them to achieve long-term investment goals relevant to retirement.

Taxation of Distributions

Income that corporations realize is taxed before the stockholders receive their dividends. Dividends are then taxable to the stockholders as individuals.

Mutual fund distributions to shareholders avoid this double taxation. Although mutual funds are usually corporations, they are not taxed as corporations. As regulated investment companies, they enjoy an exemption on net investment income and realized gains as long as they comply with applicable rules set forth by the Internal Revenue Service.

A mutual fund is like a pipeline. Dividend income and gains from securities flow through the pipeline to the fund's shareholders.

The chief requirement is that a mutual fund company pass along substantially all of its net investment income and gains to its shareholders. Thus, a mutual fund is like a pipeline. Dividend income and gains from various securities flow through the pipeline to the fund's shareholders. For tax purposes, the shareholder is required to report all distributions in the year received, whether the distributions are in cash or in additional shares. The income distributions are then subject to ordinary income tax.

Transfers within a Fund Family

exchange privilege

Most mutual fund families allow investors to transfer from one fund to another with no charge or transaction fees. This *exchange privilege* feature is often a good selling point for a prospect or client who wants to try a fund but would like the flexibility to be able to manage the investments without penalty if he or she is dissatisfied.

Although this is a valuable feature and a good selling point, such transfers may create a taxable event. For tax purposes, the funds have been redeemed and then reinvested. Any gain that is realized on the funds being transferred is taxable when the transfer is made. Although the fund imposes no charge or penalty, the tax implications of such transfers may be significant.

A Word of Caution

You must make it clear that the future value of an investment is not guaranteed.

You must exercise considerable restraint when discussing potential fund performance with clients. As an advisor, you are not permitted to illustrate or project future values of a mutual fund. Although you may discuss funds' historical performance, you must make it clear that past performance is not a guarantee of future success. You must also make it clear that the future value of an investment is not guaranteed.

Mutual Funds and Retirement Planning

An Investment Company Institute survey confirmed the common assumption that mutual fund accumulation plan holders most frequently have retirement in mind. Investors' top objectives are ranked in this order:

- retirement needs: 74.7 percent
- education of children: 35.4 percent
- estate building: 28.6 percent

The total exceeds 100 percent because many people have more than one objective. For example, an individual may establish an accumulation plan for education costs and intend to continue the plan as a source of retirement dollars. Furthermore, when several generations of mutual fund investors were asked about their views on various desired financial goals, they categorically listed retirement as their primary goal. (See table 5-3.)

TABLE 5-3
Primary Financial Goal for Mutual Fund Investing (by Percentage)

Financial Goal	Generation X (Age 40 or Younger)	Baby Boomers (Ages 41–60)	Silent Generation (Ages 61 or Older)
Retirement	66%	78%	63%
Education	17	12	3
Other (for example, emergencies, estate building)	17	10	35

Annuities

annuity

An *annuity* is a series of periodic payments that begin at a specific date and continue throughout a fixed period or for the duration of a designated life or lives. One unique feature of a life-contingent annuity contract that other investments or accumulation vehicles do not have is that it provides a stream of income that the annuitant—the person receiving the benefits—cannot outlive. Whereas life insurance protects against the risk of premature death, an annuity can protect against the risk of living too long.

Two Basic Types of Annuities

As solutions to the problem of providing retirement income, annuities are issued and sold in two forms:

- immediate annuity
- deferred annuity

immediate annuity

Immediate Annuity. An *immediate annuity* typically guarantees that payments, which begin within 1 year of purchase, will continue for the rest of the annuitant's life, no matter how long that is, or for a specified period of time. Immediate annuities are generally purchased by someone who pays one large single premium in exchange for a stream of income that is payable to him or her for a specified period of time. They can also be purchased by first remitting a series of smaller periodic premiums into another vehicle, called a deferred annuity, and then annuitizing or converting it into an immediate annuity at some time in the future.

deferred annuity

Deferred Annuity. Premiums paid into a fixed-interest *deferred annuity* are left to accumulate, rather than be received immediately as income, and to grow into a larger sum of money over the course of many years. The insurer then reinvests the premiums and credits the annuity contract with a specified interest rate. The invested premiums plus the contract's growth create the fund from which future immediate annuity distribution payments can be made.

To purchase a deferred annuity, owners must periodically make payments into it, or they can buy the annuity with a lump sum from some other source of capital. By purchasing a deferred annuity, your clients can enjoy the advantages of tax-deferred growth on their earnings until they are withdrawn. These funds accumulate on an income-tax-deferred basis, which means that the owner does not pay any income tax on the growth of these funds until withdrawals are taken from the annuity. This feature enhances its long-term growth. The concept has been referred to as triple benefits. That is, deferred annuities provide their owners with interest on their principal investment, compounding interest (interest on the interest previously accrued), and current income tax savings.

> A deferred annuity provides triple benefits: interest on the principal investment, compounding interest, and current income tax savings.

How Annuities Work

An annuity contract has two distinct phases:

- accumulation phase
- distribution or annuitization phase

We will consider the characteristics of both phases below.

accumulation phase

Accumulation Phase. The *accumulation phase* is the period of time from the purchase of an annuity until the annuity owner decides to begin to receive benefit payments from the annuity. It is during this time that the annuity builds up or accumulates the funds that will provide the future benefits.

As mentioned previously, the interest credited to an annuity is income tax deferred, which means it is not taxed each year to the holder of the annuity. There are no federal or state income taxes on the money building in an annuity contract until money is withdrawn.

Before we discuss the ways payments can be made during the distribution phase, let us consider the concepts of partial and full surrenders that are available in deferred annuities.

Partial Surrender. After the first year, almost all deferred annuity contracts permit the owner to withdraw up to 10 percent of the accumulated funds each year without imposing company surrender charges. Some contracts limit the frequency with which partial surrenders may be made, and some require that a minimum amount be left in the annuity after the partial surrender. Surrender charges usually gradually diminish and no longer apply after an annuity has been in force between 5 and 10 years.

Full Surrender. A deferred annuity may be surrendered in full at any time prior to the distribution phase. In addition to the federal income tax that will be due on the interest that was previously tax deferred, contract surrender charges and income tax penalty taxes may be applicable. After a full surrender, the annuity contract is no longer in force. Be alert to the restrictions that apply to withdrawals after annuitization begins.

Annuity owners who make partial or full surrenders of their deferred annuity contracts should be aware that a withdrawal of funds from the annuity before the owner reaches age 59 1/2 is subject to a 10 percent IRS penalty and is treated on a last-in first-out basis for tax purposes. Thus, the amounts paid out of a deferred annuity are considered to come from interest first. Therefore, until the surrendered amount exceeds the interest accumulated in the annuity, the surrendered amount is fully taxable. Under IRS rules, a 10 percent premature distribution penalty tax may be applicable if the owner is under the age of 59 1/2.

distribution phase

Distribution Phase. The *distribution phase* begins with the payment of the first benefit amount from the annuity to the annuity owner or other designated annuitant. This is sometimes referred to as the payout phase. There are a variety of payout options for distributing the principal and earnings in an annuity. These annuity payout options include payments that can be made for a fixed period or fixed amount without regard to the annuitant's life expectancy. However, immediate annuities that make guaranteed individual or joint payments to retirees and/or their spouses for their respective lifetimes are much more appropriate. There are a variety of recommended payout options that are consistent with retired clients' need for guaranteed streams of income.

Income Tax Considerations

When it is annuitized, an annuity payout is a distribution of both the annuitant's original payments and the tax-deferred accrued interest; the entire payment is not income. Some of each payment is a return of a portion of the cost basis, while some is considered to be a distribution of earnings.

> The portion of each annuity payment that is a return of cost basis and "excluded" from taxation under the annuity exclusion ratio depends on the type of immediate annuity purchased.

A portion of each annuity payment is taxable as ordinary income to the recipient. The portion of each payment that is a return of cost basis and "excluded" from taxation under the annuity exclusion ratio depends on the type of immediate annuity purchased. Basically, for a straight life immediate annuity payable for the annuitant's life only with no beneficiary, the annuity exclusion ratio is the total cost basis of the contract, divided by the total amount of expected payments to the annuitant's life expectancy. The percentage derived from dividing these two figures will determine the portion of each annuity payment that is tax free upon distribution.

Example: If George contributed $100,000 of premiums into a straight life immediate annuity on an after-tax basis and at age 70 took a distribution in the form of an immediate annuity that pays $10,000 a year for 15 years to his life expectancy, then two-thirds (66.67 percent) of each payment would represent a tax-free return of cost basis:

$$\frac{\text{Cost basis (after-tax) contributions}}{\text{Total payments to life expectancy}} =$$

$$\frac{\$100,000}{\$150,000} = 66.67\%$$

Note: Under current tax law, if the annuitant lives beyond his or her life expectancy, from that age forward, every dollar of annuity payment becomes taxable income.

How Annuity Funds Are Invested

Deferred annuity premium dollars may be invested in several ways. Fixed-interest deferred annuities offer the most guarantees. Equity-indexed and variable annuities offer the potential for greater growth. Clients need to be aware of these options so that they can make appropriate product choices.

fixed-interest deferred annuity

Fixed-Interest Deferred Annuity. In a *fixed-interest deferred annuity,* the term "fixed" refers to the interest rate paid by the issuing insurance company on the funds paid into the annuity. In a fixed-interest deferred annuity contract, the insurance company invests the owner's money. The company guarantees the owner's principal and credits the account with a set interest rate that is usually guaranteed not to change, regardless of what the market does for a certain period that ranges from 1 month to 10 or more years, depending on the contract. Thus, the insurance company assumes the investment risk. At the end of that period, the company can raise or lower the interest rate (called the current rate), based on the company's own investment goals. All fixed-interest deferred annuity contracts, however, include a minimum guaranteed rate of interest, usually 2 to 3 percent for the life of the contract.

The amount of the benefit paid out during the distribution phase is fixed. If the annuitant chooses a life annuity option, the amount of the check he or she receives each month will be the same without any investment decisions or risk.

The downside of a fixed-interest deferred annuity is that, over time, such an approach may fall behind the cumulative effect of inflation.

equity-indexed annuity

Equity-Indexed Annuity. An *equity-indexed annuity* is so named because the amount of interest earned is linked to changes in some type of securities index. The most commonly used index is the Standard & Poor's 500 Index (S&P 500). In addition to the potential for growth from the link to an index, principal and earnings are locked in and guaranteed not to drop below a certain specified level, regardless of potential securities market declines. Thus, an equity-indexed annuity gives its owners the opportunity to participate in the growth of the stock market without completely giving up the guarantee of principal and a minimum interest rate, similar to that offered by a fixed-interest deferred annuity.

> Clients in their late 50s, early 60s, and those who intend to work beyond retirement may find an equity-indexed annuity to be well suited to their needs.

Equity-indexed annuities are desirable for prospects and clients who do not want to put money into a product where there is risk of loss but do want to take advantage of the potential gains to be made in the stock market. Clients in their late 50s, early 60s, and those who intend to work beyond retirement may find an equity-indexed annuity to be particularly well suited to their needs as they look for a place to accumulate funds over time to build their retirement nest egg.

variable deferred annuity

Variable Deferred Annuity. In a *variable deferred annuity*, the owner receives varying rates of interest or capital growth on the annuity funds, depending on the investment options chosen. Typically, a variable deferred annuity has two investment accounts:

- separate account
- general account

separate account

Separate Account. The separate account is what makes a variable deferred annuity different from a fixed-interest deferred annuity. It is called a separate account because the money within it is segregated from the assets contained in the general account assets of the insurance company. The assets in the separate account are invested and managed by professional portfolio managers in a way similar to a mutual fund. In a variable deferred annuity, the policyowner's investment purchases accumulation units or shares in one or more of the company's separate accounts.

The separate account is made up of several subaccounts that offer a variety of investment options to the contract owner. The owner can switch among the various investment options in the separate account free of current income taxation, sometimes as often as daily, either for no charge or for a small transaction fee. Account values fluctuate, depending on the performance of the underlying investments.

general account

General Account. The general account of an insurance company is the repository for all of its assets. Within the general account, the company segregates a fixed or guaranteed account that complements the variable annuity separate accounts. The fixed account is usually structured like a traditional fixed-interest deferred annuity, often with multiple-year interest rate guarantees from 1 to 10 years, as well as a guarantee of principal. The contract owner has the right to transfer funds from the general account to the separate account and *vice versa.*

When your clients purchase a variable annuity, they determine which portion of their premium payments, usually on a percentage basis, will be allocated to the general account and each of the subaccounts of the separate account. Once these percentages are determined, they remain in effect until the contract owner notifies the insurance company that he or she wishes to change the allocation. This means that the owner has control over the allocation of premiums into and assets within the chosen investments, but it also means that the owner assumes the investment risk to the extent that he or she chooses to invest funds in the separate account.

Distributions from Variable Deferred Annuities. When it is time to begin the distribution phase of the variable deferred annuity, the contract owner must decide which portion of the payment he or she wishes to receive from the separate account and which from the general account. Funds annuitized from the general account produce a guaranteed income that will not change from period to period. Funds annuitized from the separate account produce an income that changes from period to period based on the performance of the subaccount in which the funds are placed.

Regulation of Variable Annuities. Because of the separate accounts, variable annuities are considered securities under federal law. This means that anyone who sells variable annuities must have a life insurance license and be registered with the NASD. It is also necessary to obtain state licensing powers or authorization to sell variable annuities within each jurisdiction where business is transacted. In addition, any potential buyer of a variable annuity must be given a prospectus. The advisor must also take steps to determine that a variable annuity is a suitable product choice for the purchaser. Suitability involves assessing a potential investor's investment objectives, time horizon, and risk tolerance.

> **Until the client has a solid financial plan that adequately addresses insurance and risk management needs, variable investment products may not be appropriate.**

Advisor's Responsibility. As with all other investment products, it is the financial advisor's duty to ascertain the suitability of the product for the prospect or client. Variable annuities are not suitable for everyone. Unless your client has adequately invested in other long-term, more secure products, you should help him or her understand the value of more conservative investments with minimum guarantees. Until the client has a solid financial plan that adequately addresses insurance and risk management needs, variable investment products may not be appropriate to purchase. You have an obligation to help your prospects and clients see the value and risk of each kind of investment product.

Life Insurance

Life insurance can provide a source of cash that may be used to generate retirement income; the cash accumulation is tax deferred. It is therefore an especially attractive vehicle for people who have both a need for death benefits and a need to accumulate funds for retirement.

Life insurance policies also offer some financial flexibility. Accumulated funds can be available through policy loans or partial surrenders, usually without tax penalty. Likewise, only the gain—the amount of money over and above that paid as premium—is taxable at withdrawal, but only after the entire cost basis (premiums paid into the policy) has been withdrawn.

In addition to tax-deferred growth and liquidity, life insurance offers some other inherent advantages, which we will discuss briefly, for individuals who are planning for retirement:

- freedom from management responsibility
- safety of principal
- return of investment

Freedom from Management Responsibility. Whole life and universal life insurance policyowners do not need investment skills to manage the accumulation component of traditional life insurance products. The insurer assumes the management function, including the task of reinvesting income and capital gains.

With variable life insurance products, policyowners assume some management responsibility through the selection of investment accounts within the policy. They also accept the investment risk for the cash value accumulation because it depends on the success of the underlying investment funds.

Safety of Principal. With whole life insurance policies, the guaranteed cash values and the return on investment are contingent on the insurance company's financial acumen. The same is true for universal life policies. With universal life policies, the insurer guarantees the safety of principal and a stated minimum return on investment. Success beyond the minimum guarantee is contingent on the insurer's financial success.

The safety-of-principal issue is different in variable policies. Buyers of variable policies are attracted by the opportunity for greater returns offered by the separate investment accounts. Because the policyowner, not the insurance company, assumes the responsibility for directing the investments, the risk of loss of principal is shifted from the insurer to the policyowner.

Return of Investment. The measurement of the return achieved on the cash value element of a whole life policy is complicated, and the return itself is often characterized as too conservative. The trade-off is that some of the values are guaranteed. You and your clients need to keep this feature in mind, as well as the fact that the primary purpose of life insurance is the insurance element, not the investment component.

Universal life policies were developed to respond to the criticisms of low returns and the inflexibility of traditional whole life insurance contracts. By unbundling the various components of life insurance—insurance cost, administrative cost, and investment return—companies were able to show policyowners the rate of return being applied to their accumulated cash values while guaranteeing certain minimum rates.

The return on investment in a variable life or variable universal life policy depends fully on the earnings of the underlying investment accounts that the policyowner selected. Unlike the guaranteed values of a whole life or universal life contract, there is no guarantee for the investment accounts in variable life insurance policies.

Life Insurance in Retirement Planning. The primary role of life insurance is to provide money for beneficiaries when the insured dies. The reason that money is needed, the amounts necessary to meet the insured's goals, and how the money is distributed are all secondary to this main purpose. Early death can leave a surviving family adrift with unfulfilled dreams and expectations if care has not been taken to meet the needs of those who are left behind.

Life insurance protects loved ones from the hardships created when an insured dies too soon. Most people, however, will live to retirement age and want to have enough income to continue to live comfortably when they are no longer wage earners. At retirement, without the income earned from working, most retirees will be dependent on the money they have set aside to supplement their Social Security benefits and any employer-sponsored retirement plans they have.

Although retirement planning is complicated and usually cannot be done on a single-need basis, permanent life insurance used to protect a family can also provide additional income at retirement if the insured lives. Furthermore, with the use of the disability waiver-of-premium rider in a whole life insurance policy, the coverage will remain in effect if the insured is disabled and otherwise cannot pay the premium. Using life insurance to help your prospects and clients solve the problems of dying too soon can also help them avoid some of the financial problems associated with living too long.

> **Using life insurance to help your prospects and clients solve the problems of dying too soon can also help them avoid some of the financial problems associated with living too long.**

Variable Life Insurance Products

Variable life insurance products have an underlying structure that resembles variable deferred annuities in that they are funded by separate accounts that are similar to mutual fund accounts. Variable life insurance products differ from variable deferred annuities, however, in that their primary function is to provide financial protection against the possibility of premature death. The major consideration for purchasing a variable life insurance product should be its protection, not its cash accumulation. This is especially true because the variable nature of the product and its flexibility can, in fact, reduce the amount of protection it provides.

An understanding of the separate accounts that underlie a variable life or variable universal life insurance policy and their investment possibilities is important because the separate account value has a direct bearing on cash surrender value, account withdrawals, loan value, and death benefits. The prospectus details the mechanics and administrative procedures affecting each.

Flexible Premiums

A variable universal life insurance policy has an applicable minimum premium based on the policy's initial face amount. The policyowner has flexibility in choosing the frequency and amounts of premium payments, as long as certain limits are maintained. This planned premium or minimum periodic payment is intended to produce the minimum values necessary to keep the policy in force for the policyowner's lifetime.

It is necessary to approach the issue of flexible premiums very carefully because discontinuance of premium payments can exhaust the net cash surrender value of the policy and its separate accounts and cause the policy to lapse. Investment performance directly affects policy continuation when minimum premium schedules are not maintained.

Death Benefits

With a variable universal life insurance policy, the death benefit paid to the policy beneficiary is equal to the policy's initial face amount plus any additional policy features such as the accidental death benefit. The prospectus clearly details the methods to calculate the exact death benefit. Typically, the policy offers a choice of either a fixed death benefit equal to the initial face amount or a variable death benefit that fluctuates with the investment performance of the separate investment accounts.

Withdrawals from the Policy

Usually, after the first policy year, a policyowner may request withdrawals from the policy's net surrender value. Withdrawals are subject to the terms and conditions of the policy. The prospectus outlines any withdrawal charges, potential time delays and denials, the effects of partial withdrawals on the death benefit and net surrender values, and tax regulations.

Borrowing from the Policy

A policyowner may borrow up to approximately 90 percent of the policy's net cash surrender value using the policy as security for the loan. When a policyowner borrows, the amount of the loan is set aside in the policy's general or fixed-interest account and continues to earn interest, usually at a rate below the rate charged for the loan. Generally, the interest rate charged for the loan is 1 percent above the interest rate earned in the general account. Although loan interest rate spreads are not guaranteed, the declared rate earned on the loan amount is usually set or guaranteed at about 5 percent, and the loan interest has typically been 6 percent.

Deductions and Charges against Premiums

Applicable charges for taxes, administration, and insurance are deducted from premiums, and the remaining net premium is invested as directed in the separate investment accounts.

The cost of insurance is determined by multiplying the net amount at risk at the beginning of a policy month by the monthly cost of insurance applicable at that time. The net amount at risk is the difference between the current death benefit and the amount in the policyowner's separate account.

The applicable monthly cost of insurance is based on the insurer's current monthly insurance rates. Most prospectuses state that current rates are subject to change. Rates can never be greater, however, than the guaranteed maximum rates set forth in the policy.

Variable Insurance Company Products

In recent years, there has been a proliferation of variable life insurance and variable annuity products. Their popularity speaks to the increasing sophistication of consumers and the remarkable success of equity products over several decades.

However, variable financial products have risks that fixed products do not have, and it is your job to guide your prospects and clients to the products that are most suitable for their needs. You must educate your prospects and clients about both the positive and negative aspects of all the financial products available to them.

> **Variable financial products have risks that fixed products do not, and it is your job to guide prospects and clients to the products that are most suitable for their needs.**

Stocks and Bonds

Stocks and bonds are the underlying investment vehicles of most investment products. They are the basis for financial products like variable life insurance and variable universal life insurance, variable annuities, and mutual funds. For this reason, it is important to have a basic understanding of stocks and bonds.

Corporate Perspective

When a corporation needs to raise funds to use for working capital beyond its general revenue, it has essentially three alternatives. It can

- tender a new issue of stock
- issue bonds
- request a loan from a commercial bank

stock

A share of *stock* is a share of ownership in the corporation that issues it. As part owner of the company, a stockholder is entitled to share in the profits of the company but is generally free from any additional liability beyond his or her investment of the stock's purchase price.

bond

While ownership of stock represents partial ownership of a corporation, a *bond* represents a loan of money to a corporation. In return for loaning corporations money, bondholders expect to receive regular interest payments.

Bank loans are typically used to meet short-term corporate funding needs. Stocks and bonds are more common sources of long-term financing. When a corporation needs to raise capital, the decision to issue stocks or bonds for long-term financing is part of the company's overall capital structure planning.

In determining the best mix of stocks and bonds, management recognizes that fixed interest payments to bondholders during profitable years allow any increase in earnings to be reinvested in the firm in the form of retained earnings, or paid to stockholders in the form of dividends. Companies with stable or increasing cash flow may see bonds as the best way to raise capital.

On the other hand, bondholders must be paid even if the corporation has low or negative earnings. To live up to this expectation, the corporation has to anticipate sufficient revenues to pay the interest obligation and still meet all other operating obligations. For this reason, firms with volatile cash flows tend to rely more heavily on stock issues.

Because stock represents ownership in a company, issuing new stock dilutes ownership. When new stock is issued, corporate profits must be spread among more shareholders. Profits, however, are not guaranteed. Unlike the interest due on bonds, the corporation is under no obligation to pay dividends, so issuing new stock can raise capital without placing a financial obligation on the corporation.

The Individual Perspective

Individuals who purchase stocks and bonds expect a positive return on their investments. As a part owner of the company, a stockholder may receive income from his or her investment in two forms:

- dividends
- profits from selling the stock at a price higher than he or she paid

Corporate Bonds

corporate bond

A *corporate bond* is, in effect, a promissory note given to an investor in exchange for a loan to the corporation. As such, it pays interest to the bondholder, usually in the form of coupon payments and generally on a semiannual basis. The amount of interest paid is determined by the nominal (or coupon) rate and the bond's par value. Par value is the principal that will be paid back at the bond's maturity date.

> The market price of a bond and its par value are not always the same.

The market price of a bond and its par value are not always the same. Bonds often sell at a discount (below their par value) or for a premium (above their par value). The market price depends on expected yield of the bond. Yield, in turn, depends on these two factors:

- coupon interest payments
- difference between the price at which an investor can sell a bond and what the investor paid for it

Although yield is important to any investor, the risk associated with a given stock or bond is equally important.

Example: If the par value of a bond is $1,000 and the coupon rate is 9 percent, the annual interest payments will total $90 (9% x $1,000). If interest payments are made semiannually, the bondholder will receive $45 every 6 months.

Bond interest payments are fixed. They do not change even as the general economy rises or falls.

Municipal Bonds

municipal bond

A *municipal bond* represents the debt of a state, city, county, public utility authority, or other political subdivision. Interest on general-purpose obligations of this government unit issued to finance operations is generally tax exempt.

General-obligation bonds are backed by the full taxing power of the government entity that issued them. General-obligation bonds typically are less risky than revenue bonds because revenue bonds are backed only by the income from a specific government project like a utility plant, hospital, or toll road.

Government units may also issue a wide variety of private-purpose bonds, known as industrial development bonds (IDBs). IDBs are used to build commercial facilities—such as manufacturing plants or office buildings—that are then leased to a company that the municipality wishes to attract. Interest paid on IDBs is not tax exempt.

Although tax-exempt bonds are backed by government entities, they are not free of default risk. Public defaults are rare, but they do occur. For example in 1983, $225 billion in bonds was rendered nearly worthless by the default of Washington Public Power Supply System.

Municipal bonds generally are issued only in relatively large denominations of $1,000 or more per bond. Clients who wish to make small periodic investments usually will not be attracted to these tax-exempt bonds. They can, however, invest in tax-exempt municipal bond mutual funds. Not only do these municipal bond funds reduce the minimum investment, but they also reduce the default risk to investors by providing a well-diversified portfolio of bonds from many different government units.

> Clients who wish to make small periodic investments usually will not be attracted to municipal bonds.

Federal Obligations

federal obligations

The federal government offers a number of investment opportunities. Most of these opportunities, called *federal obligations*, are guaranteed by the government, which eliminates the default risk that exists with corporate bonds.

Investors in government securities are still subject to interest rate and market risk factors, and because of the extra security provided by government backing, they may earn lower rates than those provided by corporate and municipal issues. Also note that, unlike municipal bonds, the earnings on federal government securities are generally not exempt from federal income taxes.

Treasury Bills. Treasury bills have short-term maturities of 13, 26, and 52 weeks and can be purchased through a bank or a broker. Auctioned by competitive bids, they are issued with minimum face amounts of $10,000 and sold on a discount basis with the face amount payable at maturity. Treasury bills are highly liquid, and the yields can fluctuate greatly.

Treasury Notes. Treasury notes are also available through banks and brokers. They are issued in terms of 2, 3, 5, and 10 years, and offered in multiples of $1,000. They pay interest on a semiannual basis at a fixed rate.

Treasury Bonds. Treasury bonds are long-term instruments with maturities from 10 to 30 years. Like Treasury notes, they pay fixed rates of interest. The sale of newly issued 30-year Treasury bonds was discontinued in 2001 but reinstated on August 15, 2005.

Agency Securities. Government-sponsored agencies are quasi-private organizations that are federally sponsored but privately owned and operated. These include the Federal Home Loan Bank, the Government National Mortgage Association, the Federal Farm Credit Bank, and the Federal National Mortgage Association.

These organizations all offer a variety of securities with various maturation periods. Some securities are sold at a discount; others pay fixed interest on a semiannual basis. One disadvantage of some of the issues is that they require a minimum investment of $25,000.

Savings Bonds. Series EE savings bonds have always been a reliable investment. These bonds are issued in small face amounts on a discounted basis. They earn fixed interest rates.

On April 4, 2005, the U.S. Treasury announced that EE bonds issued during May 2005 and later earn fixed interest rates. The fixed rate for bonds purchased in May 2005 through October 2005 was 3.5 percent. EE bonds earn interest for 30 years; the fixed rate applies during the first 20 years and will automatically be extended for 10 more years unless the Treasury announces different terms for the final 10-year period. Rates for new issues are announced each May 1 and November 1.

Investors can cash EE bonds any time after they are 1 year old, but there is a 3-month interest penalty for cashing them less than 5 years from their issue date. The United States Treasury guarantees that an EE bond issued in May 2005 or later will at least double in value at its 20-year original maturity. If the fixed rate fails to double a bond's value by 20 years, the U.S. Treasury will make a one-time adjustment to make up the difference.

Series EE bonds and the related Series HH bonds provide federal tax deferral on accrued interest and are exempt from state and local income taxes. Savings bonds also provide some special tax advantages if they are used for educational purposes (as discussed in chapter 4).

Treasury I Bonds. These bonds are relatively new federal savings bonds that provides a return that rises and falls with inflation. I bonds, which are issued at face value in amounts of $50 to $10,000, can be purchased from banks and credit unions. They earn interest for up to 30 years. The interest is added to a bond monthly, and it is paid when the bond is redeemed. The owner forfeits 3 months' interest if the bond is redeemed in the first 5 years; these bonds cannot be redeemed within the first 12 months. Tax reporting is the same as for EE bonds, which allows the owner either to report the interest earned each year as income or to defer federal income tax until the bond is redeemed.

Interest on an I bond is determined by two rates. One rate that is set by the Treasury Department remains constant for the life of the bond. The second rate is a variable inflation rate announced each May and November to reflect the changes in the consumer price index (CPI). If deflation occurs, a decline in the CPI will not reduce the redemption value of the bond, even if the deflation rate exceeds the fixed base rate.

As with eligible series EE bonds, investors can exclude all or part of the interest on I bonds from income as long as the proceeds are used to pay for tuition and fees at eligible postsecondary educational institutions.

Barriers to Investing

Although there are tools and strategies to help investors make fairly good decisions, investing—especially in stocks and bonds—is not for everyone.

If you see that any or all of this may require a good amount of capital, and be time consuming and confusing, then you have gotten the point. Although tools and strategies exist to help the investor make fairly good decisions, you should suspect, if you did not already know, that investing—especially in stocks and bonds—is not for everyone.

Even if your prospects and clients have a high tolerance for risk and their financial objectives require higher rates of return, it may be easier for them to talk about the theory of investing than to invest directly in stocks and bonds. You may find that many potential investors face one or more of the following problems:

- They cannot afford to buy stocks and bonds.
- They lack liquidity.
- They are unable to diversify adequately.
- They do not have enough knowledge or experience to make appropriate choices.

Insurance Planning Applications

The concept of risk has applications for insurance planning as well as investment planning. Frequently, a potential prospect for life or disability income insurance will believe that he or she does not need additional protection because of the projected growth of an investment portfolio.

> **Death and disability may not strike conveniently when an investment portfolio is at its maximum value.**

There are numerous factors that can easily cause a significant drop in the market value of investment assets. Unfortunately, death and disability may not strike conveniently when an investment portfolio is at its maximum value. If death occurs when the stock market or bond market is down, the surviving family may suffer significant and unanticipated financial hardship. This misfortune can be avoided if your prospects and clients maintain sufficient life and disability income insurance coverage.

Furthermore, a financial plan that includes a satisfactory life and disability income insurance program places your clients in a better position to pursue the potentially higher returns associated with riskier investments. Without adequate life and disability income insurance coverage, a concerned client may be forced to take other steps to guard against the financial hazards of default, market, and interest rate risk.

Example: Arlene maintains excessive liquid balances in low-yielding savings accounts and non-interest-bearing checking accounts. These defensive actions are likely to reduce the overall return on her total portfolio of assets. The cost of the reduced return may well exceed the cost of an effective insurance program.

Life and disability income insurance continue to be the most cost-effective mechanisms to meet the cash or income needs associated with the uncertain timing of death or disability. A thorough insurance program is the true foundation of a well-balanced financial plan.

The Advisor's Role

To be successful in working with your prospects and clients, you must help them not only to select the best accumulation product, but also to determine the product that is best for them based on their needs and risk tolerance.

There are tens of thousands of prospects who need to plan and save for retirement but who are not saving at all or not saving enough to meet their retirement income needs. The majority of them do not have the resources to actively trade stocks and bonds, to maintain balanced portfolios, and to avoid unnecessary risk. But many prospects have money that they can invest on a regular basis.

Mutual funds and variable deferred annuities are ideal products for many of these individuals. If you are a registered representative, you can offer your prospects and clients a variety of accumulation products. By thoroughly understanding the products you can sell, you will be in the best position to assist your prospects and clients in meeting their retirement needs. ◊

CHAPTER FIVE REVIEW

Key Terms and Concepts are explained in the Glossary. Answers to the Review Questions and Self-Test Questions are found in the back of the book in the Answers to Questions section.

Key Terms

suitability	back-end load
risk tolerance	no-load fund
systematic risk	12b-1 fee
unsystematic risk	prospectus
diversification	exchange privilege
asset allocation	annuity
rebalancing	immediate annuity
reallocation of assets	deferred annuity
dollar cost averaging	accumulation phase
mutual fund	distribution phase
investment company	fixed-interest deferred
open-end company	annuity
fund manager/management	equity-indexed annuity
company	variable deferred annuity
custodian	separate account
transfer agent	general account
underwriter	stock
net asset value	bond
bid price	corporate bond
asked price	municipal bond
sales charge	federal obligations
front-end load	

Review Questions

5-1. Identify the six criteria that an investor can use to choose between various savings, investment, and insurance products.

5-2. Identify and briefly describe the four categories of saving and investment vehicles.

5-3. Exlain the following concepts:
   a. suitability
   b. risk tolerance

5-4. Explain the difference between systematic and unsystematic risk, and give examples of each.

5-5. Define the portfolio management technique of diversification, and list three ways diversification can be accomplished.

5-6. Explain the technique of asset allocation, and identify the three primary factors on which successful asset allocation depends.

5-7. Describe the investment strategy of dollar cost averaging.

5-8. Explain the potential income tax consequences of mutual fund distributions.

5-9. Explain the tax consequences of transferring from one fund to another within a family of mutual funds.

5-10. Differentiate between an immediate annuity and a deferred annuity.

5-11. Identify and briefly describe the three types of deferred annuity products.

5-12. List five advantages of using life insurance as a source of funds for retirement planning.

5-13. Briefly explain the difference between a stock and a bond.

Self-Test Questions

Instructions: Read chapter 5 first, then answer the following questions to test your knowledge. There are 10 questions; circle the correct answer, then check your answers with the answer key in the back of the book.

5-1. Asset allocation is a portfolio management tool that allows investors to do which of the following?

   (A) Match investments to a specified index.
   (B) Time all purchases and sales to maximize market changes.
   (C) Wait out market ups and downs, thus avoiding high transaction costs.
   (D) Spread risk across different types of investments in a planned and predetermined way.

5-2. When an advisor assesses whether or not a specific investment is appropriate for a particular prospect based on his or her financial objective(s), which of the following is he or she determining about that product?

(A) marketability
(B) suitability
(C) safety
(D) risk

5-3. Which of the following statements concerning investing is correct?

(A) Risk and return are independent of each other.
(B) Liquidity is generally not important to investors.
(C) The higher the risk, the greater the potential return.
(D) Risk is the only factor that investors should consider.

5-4. Which of the following statements concerning tax-deferred savings vehicles is correct?

(A) Permanent life insurance, deferred annuities, and U.S. savings bonds are tax-deferred financial products.
(B) Taxes on accumulations are deferred until age 59 1/2.
(C) Money may be withdrawn from tax-deferred savings vehicles without penalty any time it is needed.
(D) They are always purchased with pretax dollars.

5-5. Which of the following statements concerning a prospectus is (are) correct?

I. It provides official projections of the investment's future value.
II. It gives potential investors information about an investment.

(A) I only
(B) II only
(C) Both I and II
(D) Neither I nor II

5-6. Which of the following statements concerning the payout from a variable deferred annuity is (are) correct?

I. Funds annuitized from the general account produce a guaranteed income that will not change from period to period.
II. Funds annuitized from the separate account produce an income that changes from period to period based on the performance of the subaccount in which the funds are placed.

(A)   I only
(B)   II only
(C)   Both I and II
(D)   Neither I nor II

5-7.   Which of the following terms is another term for the contingent deferred sales charge?

I.   back-end load
II.   12b-1 charge

(A)   I only
(B)   II only
(C)   Both I and II
(D)   Neither I nor II

5-8.   All the following statements concerning characteristics of variable deferred annuities are correct EXCEPT:

(A)   Variable deferred annuities are not suitable for all prospects.
(B)   The separate account is integrated with the assets contained in the general account assets of the insurance company.
(C)   Because of the separate accounts, variable deferred annuities are considered securities under federal law.
(D)   The separate account is made up of several subaccounts that offer a variety of investment options to the contract owner.

5-9.   All the following are common sources of funds that a corporation can use for working capital beyond its general revenue EXCEPT

(A)   obtaining a loan from a commercial bank
(B)   issuing bonds
(C)   tendering a new issue of stock.
(D)   selling its assets

5-10. A prospectus must be provided when selling all of the following products EXCEPT

(A)   variable annuity
(B)   mutual fund
(C)   universal life insurance policy
(D)   variable universal life insurance policy

6

Tax-Advantaged Retirement Plans

Learning Objectives

An understanding of the material in this chapter should enable the student to

6-1. Identify the basic types of qualified retirement plans.

6-2. List the advantages of saving in a qualified plan.

6-3. Describe the differences between qualified and nonqualified plans.

6-4. Explain the effect of salary reduction on income taxes and the impact of tax deferral on the accumulation of money.

6-5. Explain the benefit of stock option plans.

6-6. Explain how 403(b) plans (tax-deferred annuities) work.

6-7. Explain the applications of nonqualified deferred-compensation plans.

6-8. Describe Sec. 457 plans, and explain how they work.

6-9. Explain how to avoid the IRS early withdrawal penalty by using an IRA rollover.

6-10. Explain the basic eligibility rules for IRAs, Roth IRAs, and rollover IRAs, and the rules on the taxation of distributions.

Chapter Outline

QUALIFIED PLANS

This section of the chapter introduces qualified plans. It explains the plans' concept and gives an overview of the types of plans available, as well as the legal requirements and tax aspects that apply to qualified plans in general. Understanding the basics of qualified plans will enable you to discuss them intelligently during your initial conversations with prospects. In addition, it may enhance your ability to give advice when installing other employer-sponsored tax-advantaged retirement plans.

Concept of Qualified Plans

tax-advantaged retirement plan

The federal government encourages the private financing of a working individual's retirement by granting favorable tax treatment to retirement plans that meet certain legal requirements. In general, we refer to all retirement plans that provide favorable tax treatment by meeting the stipulated legal requirements as *tax-advantaged retirement plans*. These plans include individual retirement plans such as the traditional and Roth IRAs. In addition, they include employer-sponsored retirement plans, which encompass qualified plans, the focus of this section; SEPs (simplified employee pensions); SIMPLEs (savings incentive match plans for employees); and 403(b) plans (also known as tax-sheltered annuities or TSAs). Employer-sponsored plans must meet certain requirements that are designed to prevent abuse by employers who might otherwise use the tax breaks to finance only their own retirement.

qualified plan

A *qualified plan* is an employer-sponsored retirement plan that meets the legal requirements specified in Sec. 401(a) of the Internal Revenue Code and thus "qualifies" for favorable tax treatment. These plans include the following:

- defined-benefit pension plans
- cash-balance pension plans
- money-purchase pension plans
- target-benefit pension plans
- profit-sharing plans
- 401(k) plans
- stock bonus plans
- ESOPs (employee stock ownership plans)
- HR 10 (Keogh) plans

The favorable tax treatment affects all aspects of the plan—the contributions to the plan, the growth of the plan's assets, and the distributions from the plan. In exchange for these tax advantages, the plan must meet certain legal requirements. For example:

- The plan must cover a significant number of employees—not just the business owner and/or key employees—and it must meet IRS non-discrimination requirements.
- The plan must have a vesting schedule that gives employees a portion of the benefits if they should terminate from the business before full retirement age.
- The plan must require that assets be contributed in such a way that the employer no longer owns the assets. These assets can be used only to pay retirement benefits. Thus, they are safe from the employer's creditors.

The legal requirements and the tax aspects of qualified plans are discussed in more detail later in this section.

Employer-sponsored plans such as SEPs, SIMPLEs, and 403(b) plans are not considered qualified plans. Although these tax-advantaged retirement plans share many similarities, they are not subject to Sec. 401(a) of the Internal Revenue Code. These plans are discussed later in this chapter.

The Qualified Plan Advantage

Individuals are assisted in their retirement planning by the government and, in many cases, by their employers.

The tax policy reflects the government's concern for the financial security of older retired workers. To encourage people to plan and save for their nonworking years, the government provides tax incentives to those who establish retirement savings plans. Retirement plans that qualify under the standards established in the tax code receive favorable tax treatment as discussed below.

Employer plans also play an important role in retirement planning, but the amount of responsibility employers assume differs significantly. Even though the cost of an employer-sponsored retirement plan is tax deductible to the employer, some employers provide no retirement benefits, while others have very generous programs. The success of these programs should not be taken for granted. All too frequently, workers do not understand the programs and do not fund them adequately. Likewise, these same employees often ignore the individual opportunities they have to ensure their own financial security at retirement.

> **Even though the cost of an employer-sponsored retirement plan is tax deductible to the employer, some employers provide no retirement benefits, while others have very generous programs.**

Saving for retirement through a tax-qualified plan gives individuals at least two key advantages over other forms of savings plans:

- Contributions made to a qualified plan are made with pretax dollars. A $1,000 contribution made to a qualified plan by someone in the 28 percent tax bracket defers $280 in federal income taxes. The net current outlay to the taxpayer is only $720. Although the full amount is taxable when it is withdrawn, in effect the government is letting the taxpayer use the $280 to earn interest until he or she retires.
- Contributions and the earnings on preretirement contributions accumulate on a tax-deferred basis. They grow without creating additional taxation until they are withdrawn. Again, it is as if the government is allowing the taxpayer to use the money interest free.

The biggest disadvantage of a qualified plan compared to an after-tax savings plan is that any withdrawal made from a qualified plan is generally 100 percent taxable as ordinary income to the taxpayer. An IRS 10 percent penalty tax under IRC Sec. 72(t) applies to withdrawals and distributions made by an individual prior to age 59 1/2. Major exceptions to this rule, however, are distributions

- made on or after the participant is aged 59 1/2
- made to a beneficiary or the individual's estate on or after the death of the individual
- attributable to the individual's disability
- made to an employee after separation from service during or after the year he or she reaches age 55
- made because of a levy under Sec. 6331 on the qualified retirement plan

- made for medical care but only to the extent allowable as a medical expense deduction for amounts paid during the taxable year for medical care
- made under a qualified domestic relations order (QDRO)
- that are part of a series of substantially equal periodic payments made for the life or life expectancy of the individual or the joint lives or joint life expectancy of the individual and his or her designated beneficiary

On the positive side, the purpose of the tax penalty, which is generally 10 percent of the amount withdrawn, is to discourage using funds set aside for retirement for current needs. To the extent that the penalty serves as a deterrent to withdrawing savings that will help build retirement security, it is not really a disadvantage.

Categories of Qualified Plans

Qualified plans can be categorized by the choices that employers must make when implementing them. Table 6-1 illustrates the choices and sets the stage for the discussion that follows.

TABLE 6-1 Categories of Qualified Plans		
	Pension Plan	**Profit-Sharing Plan**
Defined benefit plan	Defined-benefit pension plan Cash-balance pension plan	N/A
Defined-contribution plan	Money purchase pension plan Target-benefit pension plan	Profit-sharing plan 401(k) Stock bonus ESOP

The first choice is whether to select a defined-benefit plan or a defined-contribution plan. The selection is important because different rules apply to each category of plan. Therefore, every qualified plan must be one or the other.

Defined-Benefit Plan

defined-benefit plan

A *defined-benefit plan* promises the employee a specified benefit at retirement based on a formula. The employer is required to contribute an amount necessary to ensure it can pay the promised benefit at retirement age. The defined-benefit plan provides a predetermined benefit but at a variable cost to the business. In general, it has the characteristics described below.

Contributions Are Determined by an Actuary. An actuary determines the annual contributions to the defined-benefit plan. The following factors affect the amount of the employer's annual contribution:

- current salary level of each participating employee
- projected future increases in salary level
- earnings rate of plan assets
- estimates, if any, on the number of participating employees who will die or leave before receiving benefits
- expected life span of retirees who will be receiving pension benefits

Plan Must Be Funded Adequately. Because the retirement income amount is a fixed promise, the employer legally must fund the plan in order to pay the projected amount. If the earnings rate of the plan assets is less than expected, the employer must contribute more money.

If the employer suffers financial trouble and the plan does not have sufficient assets to pay the promised benefits, the Pension Benefit Guaranty Corporation (PBGC), a quasi-governmental agency, may provide some assistance. Most employers with defined-benefit plans are required to pay the PBGC a modest premium based on the number of participants in the plan.

Benefits Are Limited. Internal Revenue Code Sec. 415 places a limit on the annual benefit allowed. The defined-benefit plan maximum equals the lesser of 100 percent of the participant's highest 3-year average compensation or $175,000 (2006 amount, indexed for inflation) payable at age 65.

Defined-Contribution Plan

defined-contribution plan

In contrast to a defined-benefit plan, a *defined-contribution* plan specifies the amount that will be allocated to the participating employee's individual account. The amount of the benefit at retirement is composed of the contributions and the investment growth of the account, which means that it is affected by market volatility. The PBGC does not act as a guarantor of the retirement benefit. The defined-contribution plan provides a variable benefit (depending on the investment growth of the account) but at a predetermined cost to the business. In general, it has the characteristics described below.

Individual Accounts Are Established. For defined-contribution plans, individual accounts established for each plan participant are credited with contributions and earnings. In contrast, a defined-benefit plan tracks benefit accruals for each individual participant but does not allocate the monies to separate accounts.

An Actuary Is Not Required. Because defined-contribution plans are not required to accrue a minimum benefit, they do not require an actuary; nor do they require a total valuation of the plan assets each year. Thus, they tend to have lower administrative expenses than defined-benefit plans.

Contributions Are Limited. Contributions, or annual additions, to a defined-contribution plan can be made by (1) the business (2) reallocated forfeitures (the account value of those who terminated from the business before they were fully vested), or (3) the employee (when applicable). Sec. 415 limits the annual additions to a participant's account to the lesser of 100 percent of the participant's compensation or $44,000 (2006 amount, indexed for inflation).

In addition, the maximum amount of employee compensation that can be used to calculate employer contributions is $220,000 (2006 amount, indexed for inflation).

Example:	If the defined-contribution plan stipulates that the amount of the contribution will be 10 percent of compensation, and Mel earns $250,000, then only $22,000 ($220,000 x 10%) can be contributed to Mel's account.

Table 6-2 provides a quick comparison of defined-benefit and defined-contribution plans.

TABLE 6-2
Defined Benefit-Plans versus Defined-Contribution Plans

Defined-Benefit Plans	Defined-Contribution Plans
The employee's benefit is defined.	The business's contribution is defined.
Benefit amounts are restricted.	Contribution amounts are restricted.
Costs are unpredictable.	Costs are predictable.
The business bears the investment risk.	The employee bears the investment risk.
Their complexity makes them difficult to understand.	Their relative simplicity makes them easy to understand.
Administration is expensive.	Administration is less expensive than for defined-benefit plans.
The PBGC oversees and insures most plans.	The PBGC has no role.

Pension Plan or Profit-Sharing Plan

If a defined-contribution plan is selected, the employer must choose between a pension plan and a profit-sharing plan. A defined-contribution plan must be categorized as either a pension plan or a profit-sharing plan. (Note that defined-benefit plans are always pension plans, never profit-sharing plans.)

pension plan

> The sole purpose of a pension plan is to provide retirement income. Participants cannot withdraw funds from the plan during their employment.

Pension Plan. A *pension plan* is a qualified plan that requires the employer to create a definite, ongoing commitment to fund it. This usually means that the employer makes an annual contribution to the plan. There is little or no relief for the employer who encounters a bad cash flow situation for 1 or several years. The employer must make the pension contribution on time, as specified in the plan document.

In addition, the sole purpose of a pension plan is to provide retirement income. Thus, pension plans cannot allow in-service distributions. In other words, participants are unable to withdraw funds from a pension plan during their employment.

Finally, a pension plan is restricted in the amount of company stock in which it can invest. Pension plans can invest only 10 percent of plan assets in employer stock.

profit-sharing plan

Profit-Sharing Plan. Unlike a pension plan, a *profit-sharing plan* does not require an employer to maintain any specified level of annual contributions. The employer is permitted to determine how much to contribute each year. Therefore, an employer may elect to make no contribution for 1 year, or even for several years.

That does not mean there is no commitment—there is. All qualified plans are required to be permanent, which means that the employer adopting the plan must intend to continue the plan for some period of time and not use it merely to make a one-time contribution for 1 year. A profit-sharing plan for which contributions are not made for many years might be challenged on the grounds that it does not meet the permanency test, resulting in expensive tax consequences.

> The purpose of a profit-sharing plan is to share profits on a tax-deferred basis. Therefore, it may allow in-service distributions.

Also, the purpose of a profit-sharing plan is to share profits on a tax-deferred basis. Therefore, these types of plans may be written to allow in-service distributions.

Furthermore, in contrast to the pension plan, the profit-sharing plan generally has no restrictions on the amount of company stock in which it can invest. Restrictions are encountered only if the employee is required to purchase employer stock.

Types of Qualified Plans

Now that you understand the different categories of qualified plans, let's look at the different types of plans, using the following groupings:

- defined-benefit pension plans
- defined-contribution pension plans
- defined-contribution profit-sharing plans

Each grouping is a combination of the two different categorizations previously discussed. For example, defined-benefit pension plans are plans that are defined-benefit plans and pension plans. Therefore, they generally meet the criteria of both categories.

We will briefly discuss HR-10 (Keogh) plans at the end of this section.

Defined-Benefit Pension Plan Grouping

The defined-benefit pension plan grouping includes the defined-benefit pension plan (it is both a grouping and a type of plan) and the cash-balance pension plan.

Defined-Benefit Pension Plan. The defined-benefit pension plan is referred to by the formula it uses to calculate the retirement benefit. Formulas are typically based on final average earnings, years of service, or a combination of the two. The formulas are often designed with a maximum replacement income or income percentage.

cash-balance pension plan

Cash-Balance Pension Plan. The *cash-balance pension plan* is a hybrid plan. It is a defined-benefit plan that utilizes the defined-contribution plan feature of individual accounts to report accrued benefits to employees. Instead of reporting an employee's benefit as a projected payout at full retirement age, the cash-balance pension plan reports the employee's individual account balance, which is the sum of the contributions and interest. In reality, there are no individual accounts. The accrued benefits do belong to the employee, however, if he or she terminates from the company and is fully vested.

Figure 6-1 illustrates the difference between the traditional defined-benefit plan and the cash-balance pension plan.

> Cash-balance pension plans favor younger employees who may change jobs a few times during their careers.

Cash-balance pension plan benefits accrue much more evenly throughout an employee's career than benefits for a traditional defined-benefit pension plan do. Therefore, the plans favor younger employees who may change jobs a few times during their careers. This aspect becomes a problem only when an employer converts from a traditional defined-benefit pension plan. The conversion tends to hurt older, longer-term employees, and it has been the center of court battles since the 1990s.

Defined-Contribution Pension Plan Grouping

The defined-contribution pension plan grouping includes the money-purchase pension plan and the target-benefit pension plan.

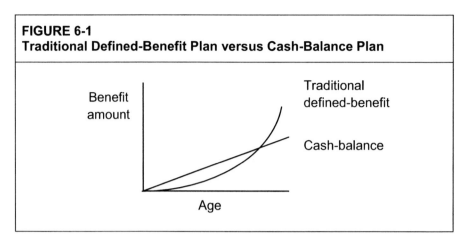

FIGURE 6-1
Traditional Defined-Benefit Plan versus Cash-Balance Plan

money-purchase plan

Money-Purchase Pension Plan. The most basic form of the defined-contribution plan is the *money-purchase plan*. With a money-purchase plan, the business contributes a percentage of compensation, ranging typically between 3 and 12 percent, into an individual account for each participating employee. The benefit is the value of the individual account at retirement age, which is the sum of the contributions and any investment gain (or loss).

target-benefit pension plan

Target-Benefit Pension Plan. The *target-benefit pension plan* is a hybrid plan like the cash-balance pension plan. It uses a defined-benefit formula to calculate the "target benefit" for each employee. Then, an actuary uses the target benefit to calculate the level of annual contribution that is needed to achieve it.

From this point forward, the target-benefit pension plan operates as a defined-contribution plan. Contributions and investment gain are credited to individual accounts for each employee. The contribution amount changes only when new participants are added to the plan and when existing plan participants' compensation increases. No adjustments are made if the plan is doing better or worse than expected. Thus, the employees could do better or worse than the projected benefit amount.

Defined-Contribution Profit-Sharing Plan Grouping

The last grouping is the defined-contribution profit-sharing plans, which include profit-sharing plans, 401(k) plans, stock bonus plans, and ESOPs (employee stock ownership plans).

Profit-Sharing Plan. A profit-sharing plan is both a category and a type of plan. Profit-sharing plans provide flexibility, allowing employers to make annual contributions as they see fit. The amount of an annual contribution is often a reflection of the profitability of the business, thus linking the employees' financial gain to the employer's profitability. However, an employer can make contributions even if the business has not made a profit.

Once the employer has determined how much of an annual contribution to make, the contribution is allocated among the participants according to a formula that is clearly stated in the plan document. Traditionally, the allocation was usually stated as a percentage of compensation. A flat percentage is a simple way to ensure that the plan meets nondiscrimination tests. However, the use of newer methods, such as cross-testing and integration with Social Security, are growing more popular because they allow contributions to be skewed to favor older employees, who typically are the owners of the business.

401(k) plan

cash or deferred arrangement (CODA)

401(k) Plan. A *401(k) plan* is a profit-sharing plan or stock bonus plan (stock bonus plans are discussed later) that includes the option known as *cash or deferred arrangement (CODA)*. The CODA option enables employees annually to elect to receive a portion of their compensation in cash or to have that portion paid into the plan on a tax-deferred basis. CODA changes the complexion of the profit-sharing or stock bonus plan, creating more flexibility. But CODA comes with some strings attached. There are maximum salary deferral, vesting, and in-service withdrawal rules. There is also a special non-discrimination test.

Flexibility of 401(k) Plans. Because of CODA, 401(k) plans expand the contribution options available to traditional profit-sharing plans and stock bonus plans. One of the most appealing options is the stand-alone 401(k) plan, which is fully funded by salary deferrals. This option enables small businesses that cannot afford to fund a pension or profit-sharing plan to offer a retirement plan as a voluntary benefit.

A second option is the 401(k) matching contribution, in which an employer matches a percentage of the contributions that participants make. For example, a business could match 50 percent of the participants' salary deferrals up to 6 percent of their salary to provide a financial incentive to employees to save for their retirement.

Also, the 401(k) plan can utilize the traditional profit-sharing feature. If the plan includes this option, contributions are made for eligible participants even if they have not made any salary deferral contributions. (Note that 401(k) plans can allow for both profit-sharing and matching contributions.)

Finally, most 401(k) plans allow participants to direct the investment of at least the salary deferral portion of their contributions. The reason is that employees perceive the salary deferrals as their money and want the right to manage it.

maximum salary deferral amount

Maximum Salary Deferral Amount. In addition to the Sec. 415 limits that apply to the annual additions of all defined-contribution plans (the lesser of 100 percent of an employee's salary or $44,000 in 2006, as indexed for inflation), 401(k) plans are subject to a maximum salary deferral amount.

The maximum salary deferral amount is the annual maximum that a plan participant can contribute to the 401(k) plan. In 2006, the maximum amount is $15,000. After 2006, the maximum salary deferral amount will be adjusted for inflation in increments of $500.

Participants aged 50 and older are eligible to defer an additional $5,000 to their 401(k) plans over and above the maximum salary deferral amount. This extra amount is known as a *catch-up contribution*.

catch-up contribution

The maximum salary deferral amount applies to the total salary deferrals for all 401(k) plans, 403(b) plans, and SIMPLEs in which an employee participates.

> **Maximum salary deferral amount in 2006 for 401(k) participants:**
>
> Under age 50—
> $15,000
> Age 50 and older—
> $20,000

Example:	Pat, aged 40, works for two employers. Employer A sponsors a 401(k) plan, and Employer B has a SIMPLE. The maximum salary deferral applies to the combined amounts of Pat's salary deferrals at both employers.

vesting

Vesting Schedule. Vesting is the right to a benefit that is not contingent upon continued employment with the company. Generally, an employer may specify a vesting schedule for a profit-sharing or stock bonus plan. However, because the 401(k) plan is funded by employee salary deferrals, any contributions attributed to salary deferrals are 100 percent vested immediately. Profit-sharing contributions can be subject to a normal vesting schedule. However, the vesting schedules for matching contributions are subject to accelerated vesting rules that usually apply to top-heavy plans. (Vesting requirements applicable to qualified plans are discussed later in this chapter.)

> **Withdrawals from a 401(k) plan are allowed only if the participant is at least 59 1/2 or has incurred a financial hardship.**

In-Service Withdrawals. A 401(k) plan has more stringent rules for in-service withdrawals than a regular profit-sharing plan does. Withdrawals from 401(k) plans are allowed only if the participant has attained at least age 59 1/2 or has incurred a financial hardship. Examples of financial hardship are circumstances related to medical expenses, the purchase of a principal house for the participant, and postsecondary education tuition for a participant and/or his or her dependents.

Special Nondiscrimination Test. In addition to the nondiscrimination tests that all qualified plans must satisfy, 401(k) plans are subject to the actual deferral percentage (ADP) test. The purpose of this test is to force employers to design plans that encourage the participation of lower-paid employees. The ADP test ties the amount of salary that higher-paid employees can defer to the amount that lower-paid employees actually do defer.

Stock Bonus Plan. A stock bonus plan is a profit-sharing plan that is designed primarily to distribute employer stock and securities. It has the following characteristics:

- It is available only to corporations.
- It provides a market for employer stock and can be a method to finance the growth of a business.
- The appreciation of the stock is not taxable until it is sold.

Stock bonus plans have declined in popularity due to the emergence of the ESOP.

ESOP. An ESOP enjoys the same advantages as a stock bonus plan. In addition, the ESOP has the feature of being able to borrow to make contributions to the plan. When an ESOP uses this feature, it is referred to as a leveraged ESOP. The ESOP borrows money from the lender and uses the borrowed funds to purchase employer stock. As a tradeoff, ESOPs have more restrictions than stock bonus plans.

The main goals of the ESOP are to enable employees to obtain an ownership interest in the business, create a market for employer stock, and increase the business's cash flow through leveraging.

HR-10 (Keogh) Plans

At one time, plans for partnerships and the self-employed were governed by separate statutory provisions, and the plans were referred to as Keogh plans. Today, all types of businesses choose from among the same group of qualified plans. Currently, a sole proprietor does not establish a Keogh plan; he or she establishes a profit-sharing, defined-benefit, or other plan from the array of tax-advantaged retirement plans. And, except as described below, the rules for sole proprietorships and partnerships are entirely the same as for corporate entities, and the same considerations regarding plan choice and design apply.

However, one recent and major change is that loans from a Keogh plan are now permitted for S corporation shareholders, partners, and sole proprietors. Prior to 2002, a loan was not permitted from a qualified plan to an owner-employee and certain relatives.

Another significant distinction between Keogh plans and corporate plans involves how contributions are calculated.

> Corporate contribution limits are based on salary. Keogh contributions are based on net earnings.

Basis of Contributions. Corporate contribution limits are based on salary. Keogh contributions are based on net earnings, not salary. This creates some complications because net earnings can be calculated only after taking into account all allowable business deductions. Because one of the deductions is the Keogh contribution, the amount of net earnings and the amount of the deduction depend on each other.

This means that a sole proprietor or partner with a profit-sharing plan or money-purchase pension plan can contribute only 20 percent of compensation, not 25 percent of compensation as with a corporate plan. Further complicating matters is the fact that self-employed individuals receive a deduction for income tax purposes equal to one-half of their Social Security self-employment tax on their federal tax return. In addition, when calculating the contribution, the maximum compensation that can be used is $220,000 (as indexed in 2006).

Legal Requirements

This section takes a brief look at the more important legal requirements that apply to qualified plans. Among the basic requirements, the plan must

- be written and communicated to employees
- be established for the exclusive benefit of the employees
- contain certain coverage and participation provisions
- meet nondiscrimination rules
- meet contribution and benefit requirements
- include a vesting provision
- contain provisions regarding distributions

Written and Communicated to Employees

There is no such thing as an "informal qualified plan." A qualified plan must be written.

There is no such thing as an "informal qualified plan." A qualified plan must be written. It must contain specific provisions, some of which are distinct to the type of qualified plan. Furthermore, the plan must be communicated to eligible employees. Thus, employees must know about the plan in order for those rights to have any meaning.

Exclusive Benefit of the Employees

The plan must be established for the exclusive benefit of the employees. Therefore, the plan must prohibit the use of plan assets for purposes other than uses that benefit the employees. One of the implications of this is that plan assets generally should not revert back to the employer. In other words, the plan sponsor must not have any ownership interests, which effectively keeps the plan assets safe from seizure by creditors.

Coverage and Participation Requirements

Qualified plans must meet certain coverage and participation requirements that ensure the plans cover a broad spectrum of employees.

highly compensated employee (HCE)

Coverage Requirements. The purpose of coverage requirements is to ensure that the plans are not used exclusively to provide a tax shelter for the income of *highly compensated employees (HCE)*. For the purposes of qualified plans, an HCE generally includes (1) individuals who are 5 percent owners during the current or previous year and (2) individuals who earn at least $100,000 (the limit in 2006) in the preceding year.

If the qualified plan does not include all employees, then it must meet certain additional requirements as specified in the tax law.

Participation Requirements. Employers have only a few options in determining when an employee can begin to participate in a qualified plan. Generally, they can limit participation based on an employee's age and years of service. There are two basic rules:

- the 21-and-1 rule. The employee must be at least 21 years of age and have been employed for at least 1 year.
- the 2-year/100 percent rule. The employee must be at least 21 years of age and have been employed for at least 2 years. Once the employee has met the 2-year minimum, he or she is 100 percent vested.

In determining years of service, an employee has worked 1 year of service if he or she has worked at least 1,000 hours during a 12-month period.

Nondiscrimination Rules

All qualified plans must be designed so they do not discriminate in favor of HCEs with regard to the

- allocation of benefits and contributions
- availability of benefits, rights, and features the plan provides
- effect of plan amendments and plan terminations

> **A qualified plan can meet the benefits and contributions requirement by design or by annual testing. A safe harbor design meets the requirement automatically.**

Allocation of Benefits and Contributions. A plan satisfies the benefits and contributions requirement if either the contributions or benefits are nondiscriminatory. There are two ways to meet this requirement: by design or by annual testing. If a plan is designed to certain specifications, it automatically meets this requirement and no annual testing is required. Such a design is often referred to as a safe harbor. If the plan's design does not meet these specifications, it needs to satisfy a general test on an annual basis.

Cross-Testing. Generally, defined-contribution plans and defined-benefit plans are tested for the benefits and contribution requirements using general tests designed for each type of plan. However, the IRS does allow the testing of defined-contribution plans on the basis of benefits, and of defined-benefit plans on the basis of contributions. This method, known as cross-testing, typically favors older employees and is a popular option for profit-sharing plans.

Integration with Social Security. Nondiscrimination requirements allow qualified plans to integrate their benefits with Social Security. That is, an employer can use modestly higher percentages (within specified limits) for HCEs than for non-HCEs when determining the contributions to a defined-contribution plan or the benefit amounts from a defined-benefit plan. The higher percentages are allowed as a means of minimizing the effect of reverse discrimination inherent in Social Security.

Reverse discrimination exists because an employer pays the Social Security tax of 6.2 percent only on taxable wages up to an amount known as the taxable wage base ($94,200 in 2006). Thus, employees who earn more than the taxable wage base receive less in contributions and the resulting benefits in terms of percentage of compensation than those who earn less.

Example:	Harry and Sally work at ABC Corporation and earn $100,000 and $200,000, respectively. ABC pays $5,840 ($94,200 x 6.2%) in Social Security taxes for both employees. (Recall that the taxable wage base is $94,200.) As a percentage of compensation, ABC contributes a little less than 6 percent of compensation for Harry and 3 percent of compensation for Sally.

Availability of Benefits, Rights, and Features. The benefits, rights, and features the plan provides must be available in a nondiscriminatory manner. For example catch-up contributions are not discriminatory as long as the option is made available to all participants aged 50 and older.

Effect of Plan Amendments and Terminations. A plan cannot create a discriminatory effect toward HCEs in the manner in which any changes to or termination of the plan is handled.

Contribution and Benefit Requirements

Contributions and benefits are regulated by law. The contribution limits for defined-contribution plans and the benefit limits for defined-benefit plans have already been examined. In addition to these limits, there are rules that govern employer deductions (these are discussed shortly) as well as miscellaneous rules such as the stipulation that unisex rates must be used in qualified plans.

Vesting Requirements

The law requires a qualified plan to include a vesting provision for employer contributions. A vesting provision is usually stated in the form of a table that stipulates the amount of accrued benefit (from employer contributions) that is "earned" for each year of service with the employer.

top-heavy plan

Under the law, there are minimum vesting standards to protect employees who change jobs. In addition, there are accelerated vesting standards that apply to top-heavy plans and the matching employer contributions of 401(k) plans. A *top-heavy plan* is a plan in which a disproportionate percentage of the plan's assets are allocated to key employees. In oversimplified terms, a plan is top heavy if over 60 percent of aggregate account balances are for key employees.

> Under cliff vesting, a participant has vested rights to 100 percent of employer-provided benefits after 5 years of service.

Minimum Vesting Standards. The law spells out the minimum vesting standard for qualified plans. A plan must satisfy one of two vesting schedules—either a 5-year cliff vesting or a 7-year graded vesting schedule. Under cliff vesting, a plan participant has vested rights to 100 percent of employer-provided benefits after 5 years of service, but none before then. The 7-year graded vesting schedule is shown in table 6-3.

TABLE 6-3
7-Year Graded Vesting Schedule

Years of Service Completed	Minimum Required Vested Portion of Benefits
1	0%
2	0%
3	20%
4	40%
5	60%
6	80%
7	100%

Accelerated Vesting Rules. Minimum vesting standards are accelerated for top-heavy plans and for the employer-matching contribution feature of 401(k) plans. In these two situations, a 3-year cliff vesting schedule (participant is 0 percent vested until the third year in which he or she is 100 percent vested) or a 6-year graded vesting schedule applies (see table 6-4).

Distribution Requirements

Qualified plans are required to contain a number of provisions with regard to distributions. There are rules that cover when distributions must start, what forms they may take, maximum distribution amounts, and minimum distribution amounts.

Tax Aspects

The tax aspects of qualified plans are rather involved and intricate. We will summarize a few of the major aspects below.

TABLE 6-4
6-Year Graded Vesting Schedule

Years of Service Completed	Minimum Required Vested Portion of Benefits
1	0%
2	20%
3	40%
4	60%
5	80%
6	100%

Employer

Taxation of Contributions. The contributions for both defined-benefit and defined-contribution plans are tax deductible.

Taxation of Benefits. There are no tax implications to the employer for plan benefits.

Employee

For the employee, contributions are typically not taxable and distributions are generally taxable.

Taxation of Contributions. Employer contributions generally are not taxable. The one exception is when life insurance is included in the plan. Employee contributions (through salary deferrals) under a 401(k) plan are not includible as income for federal income tax purposes. However, they are subject to Social Security and Medicare (FICA) and federal unemployment (FUTA) taxes.

Taxation of Distributions. Usually, none of the monies in a qualified plan have been taxed; therefore, the full distribution is taxable. In addition, there are penalties for early withdrawals and for failing to follow required minimum distribution (RMD) rules (discussed more fully later in this text). ◊

OTHER TAX-ADVANTAGED RETIREMENT PLANS

Qualified plans can be overwhelming for the small business owner—so overwhelming that he or she may decide not to do anything to assist employees with their retirement planning. Thus, the federal government has

The government has created tax-advantaged employer-sponsored plans that share many of the features and benefits of qualified plans but without some of the administrative hassles.

created tax-advantaged employer-sponsored retirement plans that share many of the same features and benefits of qualified plans but without some of the administrative hassles.

In this section, we will provide an overview of other tax-advantaged employer-sponsored retirement plans. These plans are not qualified plans, but they have many of the features and benefits, especially regarding distributions. The types of tax advantaged retirement plans include

- SEPs
- SIMPLEs
- 403(b) plans

We will briefly review the concept, legal requirements, tax aspects, and planning considerations for each type of plan.

(Traditional IRAs—individual retirement annuities and accounts—and Roth IRAs are tax-advantaged retirement plans for individuals. These plans will be discussed later in this chapter.)

SEP

SEP (simplified employee pension)

The first of the tax-advantaged plans is the *SEP* (*simplified employee pension*).

Concept of the SEP

The SEP is a tax-advantaged retirement plan that operates like a profit-sharing plan. Each year, the small business owner determines whether to make a contribution to the plan. The contributions are allocated as written in the plan document. Employees are not able to contribute to the plan.

The SEP is funded by individual retirement accounts or annuities (IRAs) that are set up for each employee. These IRAs are often referred to as SEP IRAs.

The SEP's simpler documentation and reporting translate into reduced administrative tasks and expenses.

As its name implies, the SEP's documentation and reporting requirements are much simpler than their qualified plan counterparts. The fewer requirements translate into reduced administrative tasks and expenses.

Legal Requirements

Coverage Requirements. If an employer adopts a SEP, contributions must be made on behalf of each employee who has

- attained age 21
- been employed with that employer for at least 3 of the past 5 years
- received at least $450 in compensation from that employer for the year. This amount is subject to annual adjustment for inflation.

Allocation Formula. The allocation formula must be either a level percentage of compensation (for example, 5 percent of compensation) or integrated with Social Security. The latter formula provides slightly higher contributions to more highly compensated employees. Integration with Social Security is the only exception to the level percentage of compensation. Note that only the first $220,000 (in 2006) of a participant's compensation can be considered for the purpose of calculating the amount allocated to his or her account.

Maximum Allocation Limits. The maximum allocation limits are the same as those for defined-contribution plans. The maximum amount that can be allocated to each participant's account is the lesser of 100 percent of compensation or $44,000 (indexed for 2006).

Investment Restrictions. Because the SEP is funded by an IRA, it inherits some of the limitations of the IRA. The most prominent of these limitations is the one that prohibits investments in life insurance and collectibles. In addition, loans are prohibited.

Vesting Requirements. All contributions to a SEP must be 100 percent vested. In this respect, the vesting requirements of qualified plans are more advantageous to the employer.

In-Service Withdrawals. Participants are able to withdraw from their individual accounts at any time (although a tax penalty may apply). That provision is not available to pension plans and may or may not be included in profit-sharing plans.

Tax Aspects

Tax Treatment of Employer Contributions. Employer contributions to a SEP are treated in the same way as they are for defined-contribution plans. Contributions are tax deductible to the employer, with a maximum deductible contribution of 25 percent of compensation of all eligible participants. The maximum compensation that can be considered for any one employee is $220,000 (in 2006, as adjusted for inflation). Likewise, the contributions are not includible as income to the employee for federal income tax purposes.

In addition, contributions can be made for a particular tax year up to when the employer's tax return is filed, including extensions.

Tax Treatment of Distributions. Distributions are treated as ordinary income. In addition, the 10 percent penalty for early withdrawal applies. SEP IRA distributions can be rolled over to other IRAs.

SIMPLE

The *SIMPLE (savings incentive match plan for employees)* was first made available on January 1, 1997.

Concept of the SIMPLE

The SIMPLE replaced a variation of the SEP, known as the SARSEP (salary reduction simplified employee pension). The SARSEP, which resembles a 401(k) plan, enabled employees to contribute via salary reduction. SARSEPs that existed before December 31, 1996, are grandfathered and still operate under the old rules. All new plans of this variety are under the new rules of the SIMPLE.

The SIMPLE works as follows: Like a SEP, contributions by the employer are made to an IRA established for each participating employee (the SIMPLE IRA). In addition, the employee can make contributions through salary deferral. SIMPLEs are relatively easy to adopt and administer.

Legal Requirements

**An employer cannot
maintain a SIMPLE
at the same time it
maintains a qualified
plan, 403(b) plan,
or SEP.**

Eligible Employers. Only employers with 100 or fewer eligible employees in the preceding year may establish a new SIMPLE. If the employer grows beyond the 100-employee limit, the law provides an additional 2-year grace period in which the employer may sponsor the plan. Also, an employer cannot maintain a SIMPLE at the same time it maintains a qualified plan, 403(b) plan, or SEP.

Coverage Requirements. The plan must cover all eligible employees. An employee is eligible if he or she

- has earned $5,000 in any 2 previous years
- is expected to earn $5,000 in the current year

Allocation Formula. The employer is required to make a contribution based on either of the following:

- a dollar-for-dollar matching contribution on all employee contributions up to 3 percent of an employee's compensation (the IRC 401(a) limit of $220,000 does not apply). A lower percentage greater than 1 percent may be contributed in no more than 2 out of 5 years.
- a contribution equal to 2 percent of an eligible participant's compensation (up to the IRC 401(a) limit of $220,000), regardless of whether or not the employee contributes to the plan

Maximum Contribution Limits. The maximum amount that can be contributed is the maximum salary deferral amount ($10,000 for 2006) plus the 3 percent matching contribution. Because the matching contribution is dollar-for-dollar, the maximum amount that can be contributed on behalf of any one person is two times the maximum salary deferral amount.

Maximum Salary Deferral Amount. The maximum amount an employee under age 50 can contribute annually through salary deferrals is $10,000 (in 2006). The amount must also be coordinated with any salary deferrals associated with a qualified plan, 403(b) plan, or SIMPLE with other employers.

Furthermore, employees aged 50 and older can make an additional catch-up contribution. In 2006, the catch-up contribution is $2,500, increasing by $500 inflation-adjusted increments in future years.

> **Maximum salary deferral amount in 2006 for SIMPLE plan participants:**
>
> **Under age 50—$10,000**
> **Age 50 and older—$12,500**

Investment Restrictions. Because the SIMPLE is funded by an IRA, it inherits some of the limitations of the IRA. The most prominent of these limitations prohibits investments in life insurance and collectibles. Loans are also prohibited.

Vesting Requirements. All contributions to a SIMPLE must be 100 percent vested. Thus, the vesting requirements of qualified plans are more advantageous to the employer.

In-Service Withdrawals. Participants are able to withdraw from their individual accounts at any time (although a tax penalty may apply). That provision is not available to pension plans, and it may or may not be included in profit-sharing plans.

Nondiscrimination Testing. Unlike other salary deferral plans (the old SARSEP and 401(k) plans), the SIMPLE is not subject to nondiscrimination testing. Thus, highly compensated employees are not limited in the amount of salary they can defer by the amount that non-HCEs actually defer.

Tax Aspects

Tax Treatment of Employer Contributions. Employer contributions to a SIMPLE are tax deductible to the employer. Likewise, the contributions are not includible as income to the employee for federal income tax purposes.

Tax Treatment of Employee Contributions. Employee contributions are excluded as income but are subject to FICA and FUTA taxes.

Tax Treatment of Distributions. Distributions are treated as ordinary income. In addition, a penalty for early withdrawal applies. However, unlike other IRAs, premature distributions during the first 2 years of a SIMPLE IRA carry a penalty tax of 25 percent.

Rollovers can be made from a SIMPLE IRA to other IRAs. However, the SIMPLE IRA must be at least 2 years old.

Planning Considerations

SEP versus a SIMPLE. Both a SEP and a SIMPLE can potentially be low-cost plans. Although the SIMPLE does allow employee contributions, this is probably not the determining factor for selecting it. More than likely, the decision between a SIMPLE and other plans will be the amount of money that can be contributed on behalf of the owner-employee(s) in relationship to the amount of total outlay.

> **The decision between a SIMPLE and other plans will likely be the amount that can be contributed on behalf of the owner-employee(s) in relationship to the total outlay.**

Example: Bob moonlights and would like to use his unincorporated side business to start a retirement plan. He earns $25,000 from this business. Under a SEP, the maximum contribution would be $5,000: 20% (because Bob is self-employed) x $25,000. Under a SIMPLE, on the other hand, the maximum contribution would be $10,750: $10,000 in salary deferrals + $750 (3% x $25,000) in matching contributions.

SIMPLE versus 401(k) Plan. The SIMPLE gives the small business employer (100 employees or fewer) an excellent alternative to the 401(k) plan.

In general, a small business employer should consider a SIMPLE if the employer is looking for a low-cost plan with few administrative requirements. In addition, the SIMPLE is a solution for the employer whose HCEs would be greatly limited in their ability to defer salary in a 401(k) plan because of nondiscrimination rules.

> **In a 401(k) plan, both profit-sharing and matching contributions can be made in the same year.**

On the other hand, a 401(k) plan is more appropriate if the employer wants to skew contributions to older and more highly paid employees. Furthermore, a 401(k) plan allows for both profit-sharing and matching contributions to be made in the same year. It also allows the employer to vary the amount of employer contributions from year to year, and it can offer a loan provision. Finally, provided all nondiscrimination requirements are met, the 401(k) plan has higher maximum aggregate contribution limits—the lesser of 100 percent of compensation or $44,000.

403(b) Plan

403(b) plan

The *403(b) plan*, also known as a tax-deferred annuity (TDA) or tax-sheltered annuity (TSA), is a special tax-advantaged plan that serves a specific market: nonprofit organizations. Many nonprofit organizations operate on a tight budget. If they have a retirement plan in place, it may provide only a nominal level of benefits. A 403(b) plan can enable the organization to offer an attractive benefit with minimal additional outlay.

Concept of the 403(b) Plan

The 403(b) plan is named after the section in the Internal Revenue Code that governs it. It is available only to certain tax-exempt organizations and public school systems. Amounts contributed to a 403(b) plan are excluded from the participant's income and grow tax deferred until withdrawn at retirement.

The 403(b) plan operates like a profit-sharing plan. Individual accounts are created for each participant. Contributions can come solely from the employer, solely from the employee, or from a combination of both.

Legal Requirements

Eligible Employers. The 403(b) plan must be purchased by an eligible employer. An eligible employer is either a 501(c)(3) organization or a public school system. A *501(c)(3) organization* is a "corporation, and any community chest, fund or foundation, organized and operated exclusively for religious, charitable, scientific, testing for public safety, literary, or educational purposes, or to foster national or international amateur sports, or for the prevention of cruelty to children or animals."[1]

501(c)(3) organization

Documentation. The plan may or may not be subject to ERISA. When an employer makes contributions to the plan, it is typically subject to ERISA and thus the plan must be in writing. However, it is wise for all plans to be in writing.

Employer Contributions. The options for employer contributions are the same as they are in a 401(k) plan. An employer may elect to match an employee's salary deferral contributions or make nonelective contributions.

Maximum Contribution Limits. As in the 401(k) plan, Sec. 415 contribution limits apply to the 403(b) plan. The total amount contributed to a participant's account in the form of employer and/or employee contributions cannot exceed the lesser of 100 percent of compensation or $44,000 (the amount for 2006), which will be adjusted for inflation. Note that Sec. 415 limits do not apply to catch-up contributions allowed for employees aged 50 or older.

Maximum Salary Deferral Amount. Although the employer must establish the 403(b) plan, contributions can be made by the employer, the employee, or both. An employee contributes to a 403(b) plan through a salary deferral agreement. The employer must remit the premium; the employee cannot make direct payments to the insurer or custodian and gain the tax advantages. The employee, however, is the owner of the tax-sheltered annuity, which must be nonforfeitable and nontransferable.

If the 403(b) plan is funded only through salary deferrals, the plan is not subject to ERISA, making it an extremely simple plan to operate.

The 403(b) plan salary deferrals are subject to the same dollar limits that apply to 401(k) plans—that is, $15,000 for employees under age 50 and $20,000 for employees aged 50 or older because they are entitled to make an additional $5,000 contribution. Both limits are subject to future increases to adjust for inflation. (Note that the total of all salary deferrals from all 403(b) plans, 401(k) plans, SARSEPs, and SIMPLEs for which the employee is considered to be a participant cannot exceed this limit.)

In addition, a special catch-up election may apply to plan participants who have completed at least 15 years of service with certain employers, such as an educational organization, hospital, church, and so forth. Under this special catch-up election, an employee may be able to defer up to an additional $3,000.

Maximum salary deferral amount in 2006 for 403(b) plan participants:

Under age 50—$15,000

Age 50 and older—$20,000

Funding Vehicles. The contributions to 403(b) plans may be made to only certain types of funding vehicles, including

- annuities (group or individual, fixed or variable)
- life insurance contracts (if they follow the incidental life insurance protection rules that apply to other qualified plans)
- mutual funds

Unlike qualified plans, 403(b) plans are prohibited from investing directly in stocks, bonds, and money instruments.

Vesting. An employee is 100 percent vested in the contributions made through salary deferral. However, an employer's share of contributions can be subject to a vesting schedule. If a vesting schedule applies, it generally must comply with the vesting standards imposed by ERISA. Usually, 403(b) plans do not have vesting requirements.

Distributions. Typically, rules that govern distributions from qualified plans also govern distributions from 403(b) plans. Thus, generally, plans may offer

- in-service withdrawals
- a loan provision

Nondiscrimination Rules. As with qualified plans, nondiscrimination rules generally apply to 403(b) plans.

Plans that allow employees to contribute through salary deferral usually must allow all employees to make salary deferrals. Employees can be required to meet an annual minimum contribution of $200.

Plans in which employers make contributions typically must comply with nondiscrimination rules that apply to qualified plans. For example, the plan must not discriminate in favor of HCEs in regard to contributions or benefits.

As always, there are exceptions. For example, churches do not have to adhere to either of the above nondiscrimination rules.

Tax Aspects

Tax Treatment of Employer Contributions. Employer contributions are generally not considered taxable income to the plan participant.

Roth 403(b) Contribution Program. Effective in 2006, 403(b) plans will be allowed to offer a qualified Roth contribution program, which is basically a Roth account for elective deferrals. Essentially, members of participating plans will be able to designate all or a portion of the elective deferrals as Roth contributions. The Roth contributions will be included in the participant's gross income in the year the contribution is made and then be held in a separate account with separate record keeping.

Tax Treatment of Employee Contributions. Employee contributions are typically excluded from current income. They are, however, generally subject to FICA and FUTA taxes.

Tax Treatment of Distributions. Distributions are taxed as ordinary income and are usually subject to the 10 percent penalty tax for early withdrawal.

Revenue Ruling 90-24. Revenue Ruling 90-24 provides that a plan-to-plan amount directly transferred from a former employer's tax-sheltered annuity that is subject to early distribution restrictions is not treated as a distribution if the transferred amount continues to be subject to the early distribution restrictions under the existing employer's plan. This represents a significant sales opportunity in the preretiree market for direct transfers of existing assets in these tax-favored plans.

Salary Agreement. Employees of an eligible employer that adopts a 403(b) plan may enter into a salary reduction agreement to lower salary or defer a salary increase. The agreement specifies the dollar amount or percentage of salary reduction. The employer will contribute the reduced or deferred salary to the 403(b) plan.

Using a percentage of salary has the advantage of automatically adjusting the contribution if an employee's salary changes during the year.

Marketing to Employees

There is a large, yet essentially untapped, market for 403(b) plans. Changing demographics mean that the market for 403(b) plans should continue to grow. The TDA market can be exciting and lucrative. There are several advantages to working in this market:

- Frequently, 403(b) plans are presented at employee group meetings. Numerous sales may result from a single presentation.
- Whether a presentation results in a TDA sale or not, you have a chance to sell other products to meet the employee's personal needs.
- The employer, not the employee, must remit premiums that are payroll deducted.
- Because contributions are paid by the employer on behalf of the employee primarily through a salary reduction agreement, there is excellent persistency.
- Premiums of $4,000 per year or more per employee are common.
- Each year, employees can increase their contribution as their salaries increase.
- The tax advantages often motivate employees to participate in 403(b) plans.

Summary

The SEP and the SIMPLE are products you may find useful when you talk to small business owners about retirement plans. Many unincorporated

> There is a large, yet essentially untapped, market for 403(b) plans. And changing demographics mean that the market should continue to grow.

Prospecting Tool: IRS Publication 78

Because every 501(c)(3) organization must register with the IRS, the information stored in an IRS database is available to the public. You can search the database by name, city, or state. That means you can identify all of the 501(c)(3) organizations in any city. The following steps explain how to access this information (unfortunately, the link is too complex to write here):

1. Go to www.irs.gov.
2. Click on "Charities & Non-Profits" in the table of contents area.
3. Locate the "Related Topics" area (you may have to page down) and click on "More Topics."
4. Click on "Search for Charities."
5. Read the instructions and click on "Search Now."

If you have problems with the above instructions, instead of following steps 2 through 5, type in "Publication 78" in the search field, and you can find the information that way.

businesses do not incorporate because they want simplicity. Therefore, the ease of a plan like a SEP or SIMPLE could be ideal, especially when the only other straightforward alternatives are a traditional or Roth IRA.

The 403(b) plan is a specialized product. It can be an excellent tool if you do a lot of work with nonprofit organizations and/or educational institutions.

Selling/Planning Opportunities

Employer-sponsored qualified retirement plans and other tax-advantaged retirement plans are a tax-favored way for employers and employees to facilitate an employee's financial security in his or her retirement years. As a financial advisor interested in your prospects' and clients' plans for their futures, you must help them to recognize the employer-sponsored retirement benefits they have and understand how to maximize those benefits.

As part of the planning process, you must help prospects and clients project the retirement income benefits they will receive. You can often accomplish this by reviewing their plan statements; in doing so, you may discover other sales opportunities.

Adequate life and disability income insurance protection is especially important in families in which there is a significant discrepancy between the husband's and wife's funds in their respective retirement plans. If both spouses are depending on one or both retirement plans to provide retirement income, there is a need to protect the plan with insurance. Asking the right questions can prompt your prospects or clients to reexamine their own situation.

Example: "(Prospect), if you were to die before you are ready to retire, what will happen to your (spouse's) retirement income?"

Or

"(Prospect), if you were to become disabled before you are ready to retire, what will happen to your (and spouse's, if applicable) retirement income?"

Both life and disability income insurance products play a significant role in clients' retirement planning. Even the best plan will not meet a family's retirement needs if contributions stop as the result of death or disability. Adequate life insurance planning can protect the survivors' lifestyle immediately and guarantee a comfortable retirement. Adequate disability income coverage is also important in protecting the assets already accumulated should disability strike.

Permanent life insurance, structured as part of retirement planning, can also be used to enhance retirement income. The cash values accumulated

> Even the best retirement plan will not meet a family's needs if contributions stop as a result of death or disability.

during the period that protection is necessary can be used to supplement other sources of retirement income if the need for death benefit protection diminishes in retirement. ◊

NONQUALIFIED RETIREMENT PLANS

nonqualified retirement plan

A *nonqualified retirement plan* is a plan that provides benefits to an employee or group of employees, including the business owner, but does not receive the tax benefits that federal regulations offer because it does not meet ERISA requirements.

Typically, nonqualified plans are known as deferred-compensation plans. A deferred-compensation plan is an agreement between an employer and an employee to set aside current compensation for payment in the future. In other words, instead of being paid today, the employee will be paid in the future.

In this section we will present an overview of three of the most popular types of nonqualified retirement plans:

- nonqualified deferred-compensation plans
- stock option plans
- IRC Sec. 457 plans

Nonqualified Deferred-Compensation Plans

Like their qualified retirement plan counterparts, nonqualified deferred-compensation plans are employer-sponsored plans that enable employees (typically owners and key employees of a C corporation) to defer taxation, usually until they retire. There are, however, important differences that you should understand. It is also important to understand the requirements that a nonqualified deferred-compensation plan must meet to defer taxation.

These plans are more common among mid-sized to large C corporations. They have very limited use in S corporations, partnerships, and other forms of business that are not tax-paying entities. It follows that nonqualified deferred-compensation plans will probably not be a common sale for the advisor who is new to the employee benefits market. Thus, the purpose of this section is to provide a general overview of the different types of nonqualified deferred-compensation plans, summarize their tax aspects, and look at the associated planning considerations.

Nonqualified versus Qualified

Remember that nonqualified deferred-compensation plans do not meet the ERISA requirements for qualified plans. As a result, they are not eligible for the same favorable tax treatment. Remember also that qualified retirement plans enable the employee to defer taxation and the employer to take a current tax deduction. Nonqualified deferred-compensation plans follow the normal tax law—an employer deduction occurs in the same year the employee is taxed on the benefit.

In spite of the lack of preferential tax treatment, nonqualified deferred-compensation plans do have some advantages over their qualified retirement plan counterparts. Nonqualified deferred-compensation plans

- do not usually have to comply with all of the burdensome requirements of ERISA
- give employers greater flexibility in selecting whom to cover
- offer employers greater flexibility in designing vesting requirements
- enable employers to protect themselves from an employee's post-employment activity that could potentially create competition
- allow owners and key employees to supplement their retirement income from qualified plans, which is limited by the current tax laws

Unfunded versus Funded

unfunded

An *unfunded* plan for tax purposes means that the employee's contractual right to the payment of deferred benefits in the future is unsecured. In other words, the funds from which benefits will be paid are not transferred to an account for the exclusive and irrevocable benefit of the plan participants. Thus, these funds are subject to the claims of the employer's general creditors. In contrast, a *funded* plan is one for which the funds have been placed out of the reach of the employer's general creditors, as is the case in an irrevocable trust.

funded

In addition to tax implications, whether or not a plan is funded or unfunded affects what ERISA requirements it must meet. A funded plan is required to meet most of ERISA's requirements, whereas an unfunded plan is not. In other words, a funded plan must follow many more of the ERISA requirements that qualified plans must follow.

> A funded nonqualified deferred-compensation plan is required to meet most of ERISA's requirements; an unfunded plan is not.

Generally, a plan that is unfunded for tax purposes is unfunded for ERISA purposes.

Types of Plans

We will briefly discuss three basic types of nonqualified deferred-compensation plans:

- SERPs
- salary reduction plans
- death-benefit-only plans

SERP (supplemental executive retirement plan)

SERP. The *SERP (supplemental executive retirement plan)*—also referred to as salary continuation plan—is a nonqualified deferred-compensation plan in which the employer agrees to continue the employee's salary at retirement, death, and sometimes disability. The employer funds the plan as an additional benefit, not as a true deferral of an employee's income.

SERPs can be structured to address different concerns. For example, they can enable an employer to cut back on qualified retirement plan costs and still meet the needs of owners and key employees. In addition, they can be used to restore the benefits lost by owners and key employees because of the limits imposed by the Internal Revenue Code on qualified retirement plans. Finally, SERPs can give owners and key employees a higher percentage of benefits than the rank-and-file employees receive.

SERPs generally have lengthy vesting requirements in order to meet the retention objective.

salary reduction plan

Salary Reduction Plan. In the *salary reduction plan*, the employer and the employee agree either to reduce the employee's salary or to defer a future bonus in order to postpone receipt and taxation to a future tax year. Thus, the cost of the plan is borne solely by the employee's deferral of compensation that he or she would otherwise have received in cash.

In addition, the employer generally provides an investment return on the deferred amount based on a fixed interest rate, an index, or the actual investment return if the deferrals are invested. If the deferrals are invested, the employee may have some ability to direct the investments. For the tax to be deferred, however, there are some limitations that must be followed.

Why should an employee consider deferring his or her income? There are at least two good reasons. First, by deferring current income, the employee can obtain additional retirement income that would significantly exceed what he or she might be able to obtain by investing the net after-tax salary. Second, insurance-funded plans can give the employee significant current death and/or disability benefits without any current income tax obligation.

Death-Benefit-Only (DBO) Plan. The death-benefit-only plan, as its name suggests, provides a death benefit to the participant's heirs and has no living benefits. The payment of benefits may be either a lump sum or installments. The DBO plan is typically used in estate planning situations.

Stock Option Plans

Today, executive compensation is tied more and more to performance.

stock option plan

In today's world, executive compensation is tied more and more to performance. It is common for salary to represent only a fraction of an executive's overall compensation; the balance is made up of cash bonuses, deferred compensation, and stock options. A *stock option plan* gives the employee the right to purchase shares of stock in the future at a predetermined price. Stock options are attractive to both the employee and the employer.

Example: Jim Smith is the executive vice president of sales for ToolCo, Inc., a publicly traded company. Jim's compensation is made up of a base salary of $150,000, cash bonuses for hitting quarterly sales goals, participation in the company-sponsored profit-sharing and 401(k) plans, and stock options.

     The stock option plan grants Jim the option to buy 2,000 shares of ToolCo beginning in 5 years. The share price is currently $20 and is expected to rise in price by an average of 8 percent annually over this period. In 5 years, 2,000 shares of ToolCo will be worth about $59,000, but Jim will pay only $40,000 for them. The benefit to Jim is $19,000. The company's out-of-pocket outlay is zero.

Nonqualified Stock Option Plans

The most commonly encountered stock option is the nonqualified stock option (NSO) plan. An important consideration with NSOs is their income taxation. The income taxation of NSOs is best understood by considering the likely tax consequences on the occurrence of the three major events in an NSO's life: grant, exercise, and disposition.

The general rule is that the executive is not taxed at the granting of an NSO. Upon exercise, assuming there are no transfer restrictions on the stock, the executive is taxed on the difference between the fair market value of the shares at the time of exercise and the option price. This is known as the spread. The spread is taxed at ordinary income tax rates. When the executive ultimately disposes of the stock acquired through exercise of the option, he or she is taxed at capital gains rates on the difference between the sales price and his or her stock adjusted taxable basis. Adjusted taxable basis is the amount included in income on exercise of the option plus the amount paid to exercise the option.

Example: Returning to the example above, Jim incurs no income tax when ToolCo grants him the right to purchase 2,000 shares at $20 per share. If he exercises the option when the stock is worth $59,000, however, he must include the spread of $19,000 as ordinary income. If, a few years later, Jim sells the stock acquired under the option for $80,000, he will pay capital gains taxes of $21,000—the difference between the sales price and the sum of the exercise price ($40,000) and the amount included in income at the time of the exercise ($19,000), which is the adjusted taxable basis of $59,000.

Incentive Stock Option (ISO) Plans

Another form of stock option is the incentive stock option plan. ISOs were introduced into the tax law in 1981 to provide additional tax benefits for stock options.

ISOs are not available to major shareholders of the employer. Unlike NSOs, which are unregulated under the tax law, there are restrictions on the dollar amount of ISOs that may be exercised in a year. In addition, holding periods are imposed on both options granted and stock acquired in exercising an ISO. Provided all of the requirements are met, ISOs generally do not produce ordinary income recognition at the grant date or exercise date. Instead, all the potential income is treated as capital gain and not recognized until the underlying stock is disposed of. The option's spread, however, which is the excess of the fair market value of the stock when the option is exercised over the presumably lower option price, is generally subject to the alternative minimum tax liability.

Example: Susie Q. Bickle is granted an ISO to purchase 100 shares at $5 per share. She is not taxed at grant. When the stock is valued at $10 per share, she exercises the option. However, the $1,000 paid for the stock becomes her adjusted taxable basis. Again, she is not taxed at exercise.

Instead, she is taxed when she disposes of the stock. If she sells the stock within 1 year of the grant date or within 2 years of the exercise date, she will pay ordinary income tax to the extent that the sales price is greater than the adjusted taxable basis. Therefore, if she sells the stock within 2 years of the exercise date for $1,700, her $700 gain is taxed as ordinary income. If she sells the stock 5 years after the exercise date, her $700 gain is taxed at the capital gains tax rate.

Selling/Planning Opportunities

Stock options present you with two life insurance sales opportunities. First, if the executive dies and stock options are unexercised, the executive's estate may require cash to take advantage of the benefit of the options. Second, an executive's estate will need liquidity to pay estate taxes associated with inclusion of options in the estate and income taxes attributable to estate beneficiaries' exercise of the options. Life insurance in the executive's irrevocable life insurance trust is the perfect solution to meet both of these liquidity needs.

Qualified and nonqualified plans are not mutually exclusive. The two can exist together, giving the employer the opportunity to offer all employees a qualified plan and to make additional resources available for selected key people in the organization.

Sec. 457 Plans

A specialized application of deferred compensation is a Sec. 457 plan. Sec. 457 of the Internal Revenue Code permits a state or political subdivision of a state, rural electric cooperatives, and nonprofit organizations to establish nonqualified deferred-compensation plans for their employees. These are referred to as 457 plans or Sec. 457 plans.

These plans permit employees to reduce their salaries by a fixed-dollar monthly contribution. If the plan is an eligible deferred-compensation plan, employees are not taxed on amounts deferred and earnings on these amounts until they are paid or made available to the employee or a beneficiary.

To be eligible, the plan must be

- established and maintained by a state, subdivision, agency or instrumentality, political subdivision of a state, or tax-exempt organization
- available to individuals or independent contractors performing service for the employer
- applicable to future earnings only
- based on an agreement between employer and participant

The plan must not permit payments until separation from service or the occurrence of an unforeseeable emergency. Deferred amounts remain assets of the employer subject to the general claims of creditors.

Some of the features of a 457 plan are the following:

- For maximum elective deferrals, the same applicable dollar amounts that apply to 403(b) and 401(k) plans apply to 457 plans as a result of the Economic Growth and Tax Relief Reconciliation Act (EGTRRA) 2001.
- The same applicable dollar amounts for eligible employees over age 50 that pertain to catch-up contributions to 403(b) plans and 401(k) plans apply to 457 plans, also as a result of EGTRRA 2001.
- A special catch-up provision allows employee-participants who are in 457 plans and within 3 years of retirement to contribute twice the otherwise applicable dollar amount.

- Employees who participate in a 457 plan and simultaneously contribute to a 403(b), 401(k), or other defined-contribution plan are permitted to make contributions up to the applicable deferral limits for each plan.
- Deferred amounts in plans sponsored by governmental employers must be held in a trust for the exclusive benefit of the plan participants.
- Deferred amounts in plans sponsored by nongovernmental employers are considered unfunded and remain the property of the employer and subject to the claims of general creditors.
- Rollovers of non-tax-exempt organizations' plan assets to and from government-sponsored 457 plans and 403(b) plans, other 457 plans, and IRAs are permitted, subject to the liberalized direct transfer and rollover provisions of EGTRRA 2001.
- Under present law, eligible 457 plans are generally subject to the same required minimum distribution rules as other qualified plans.
- Deferral amounts can be invested in the same way as in any other deferred-compensation arrangement.

Investment vehicles include life insurance, annuities, and mutual funds. Some states do not permit the use of life insurance in 457 plans.

Finally, amounts deferred under Sec.457 are generally subject to Social Security and federal unemployment taxes at retirement if the employee's rights to these amounts are no longer subject to a substantial risk of forfeiture under the plan agreement. ◊

PLANNING WITH IRAs AND IRA ROLLOVERS

Traditional IRA

Individual retirement accounts (IRAs) have been available since 1974. Over the years, tax law changes have both improved and restricted IRAs' appeal. IRAs are individual accounts usually offered through banks, mutual funds, and insurance companies. Current tax law retains the traditional IRA tax advantages for many taxpayers and provides additional opportunities for many others. A *traditional IRA*, in which contributions are made on a tax-deductible basis and qualifying distributions are taxed, is subject to most of the qualified plan rules. You will recognize many of them as you read this section.

traditional IRA

> Virtually anyone who wishes to do so may establish a traditional IRA.

Virtually any individual who wishes to do so may establish a traditional IRA. However, the individual must have

- compensation (either earned income of an employee or self-employed person, or alimony)

- not attained age 70 1/2 during the taxable year for which the contribution is made

Contribution Limits

Under current rules, an individual can contribute the lesser of the respective annual IRA contribution limits listed below, or 100 percent of compensation (on a non-catch-up basis). In 2006, contributions are generally the lesser of 100 percent of earned income or $4,000. In addition, a catch-up contribution of $1,000 is permitted in 2006 for those workers over 50 years old.

Sec. 408 also provides that a person can make an IRA contribution on behalf of his or her spouse if that spouse does not have the required amount of earned income to fund his or her own IRA. Contributions to a *spousal IRA*—an IRA for a nonworking spouse—can be up to $4,000 (2006 amount) in any given year.

spousal IRA

Example: In 2006, a married couple who are both under 50 years old may make a total of $8,000 in IRA contributions as long as the contributing spouse earns compensation of $8,000 or more. The contributions must be split between two IRAs, but neither one of them can exceed the individually specified annual IRA contribution limit. The couple must file a joint income tax return. The IRA policy must be established in the name of the nonworking spouse with that spouse as the owner.

Table 6-5 lists scheduled increases in contribution limits for both traditional and Roth IRAs as they were amended under EGTRRA 2001.

In addition, according to rules established under EGTRRA, individuals who are aged 50 or older may increase their contributions over the regular

TABLE 6-5 IRA Contribution Limits			
Year	General Limit	Catch-up for Individuals Over Age 50	Total for Individuals Over Age 50
2006	$4,000	$1,000	$5,000
2007	4,000	1,000	5,000
2008	5,000	1,000	6,000

limits shown in table 6-5 by the $1,000 IRA catch-up limits in year 2006 and later. The IRA catch-up limits will be indexed for inflation in $500 increments after 2006 as the need arises.

Contributions can be made in any year a taxpayer receives compensation. Federal income tax deductions are permitted for contributions that a wage earner makes into a traditional IRA, subject to the restrictions discussed below for those who are active participants in qualified plans. However, contributions cannot be made into a traditional IRA for tax years in which the individual is aged 70 1/2 or older.

Current law defines several classes of wage earners eligible for some tax benefits for IRA participation as follows:

- Individuals not covered by a qualified retirement plan, regardless of income, may contribute to a traditional IRA subject to the rules above.

- Individuals who are active participants (described below) in a retirement plan at work but who have an adjusted gross income above certain income thresholds may or may not be allowed to deduct their contributions, depending on the amount of income earned.

adjusted gross income (AGI)

active participant

Active Participant Defined. Tax deductibility of traditional IRA contributions depends on a person's adjusted gross income and whether he or she is an active participant in a qualified retirement plan. *Adjusted gross income (AGI)* is gross income minus all allowable above-the-line deductions. An *active participant* is an individual who makes voluntary contributions to or for whom employer contributions are made or accrued benefits exist within a qualified corporate, Keogh, pension, profit-sharing, stock bonus, or annuity plan, or in a simplified employee pension, a 403(b) tax-sheltered annuity, SIMPLE IRA, or government plan.

The deduction for contributions made to an individual or spousal traditional IRA may be reduced or eliminated if the individual or spouse is an active participant. The deduction for contributions will be phased out for active participants with AGI that exceeds the applicable dollar amounts shown in table 6-6.

Example: Husband and wife John and Mary are both aged 45. They have earned income in 2006 that results in AGI before their IRA deduction of $90,000—$40,000 for John and $50,000 for Mary. John is not an active participant in any qualified retirement plan, but Mary is. Can John make a deductible IRA contribution since his AGI is less than $50,000 and he is not an active participant in a qualified plan? Can Mary also make a deductible contribution?

TABLE 6-6
Deduction Phaseout

Filing Status	For Taxable Years Beginning In	The Applicable Dollar Amount Is	No Tax Deduction If AGI Is
Single or head of household	2006 and thereafter	$50,000	$60,000 or more
Married filing jointly*	2006 2007 and thereafter	$75,000 $80,000	$85,000 or more $100,000 or more
* When both spouses are active participants *or* when only one is an active participant			

The answer for John is yes; for Mary, it is no. John can deduct his contribution because he is not an active participant in a qualified plan. Mary is the active participant, so she cannot deduct her IRA contribution because the couple's AGI is $90,000 ($5,000 over the limit in 2006).

For joint filers, this restriction applies only to the joint filer who is the active participant in the plan. The joint filer who is not an active participant in a qualified plan will not have his or her IRA deductibility phased out until combined AGI exceeds $150,000.

Note: Adjusted gross income as used to determine eligibility for an IRA deduction is calculated before the deduction. That is, *modified adjusted gross income (MAGI)* is generally equal to the total income on an individual's Form 1040, minus adjustments to income other than for IRA deductions. Also, deductions from gross income taken for certain items, such as student loan interest, or exclusions from income, such as interest on U.S. Series EE savings bonds used to pay college tuition, must be added back to adjusted gross income to determine MAGI.

Taxpayers who are ineligible for a deduction can still contribute as much as $4,000 to an IRA (in 2006), and the earnings will not be taxable until they are withdrawn. Based on this aspect and depending on an individual's investment objectives, it may be advisable to contribute to a nondeductible IRA to reap the advantages of tax-deferred earnings.

modified adjusted gross income (MAGI)

Taxpayers who are ineligible for a deduction for their IRA contribution can still put in as much as $4,000 to an IRA (in 2006), and the earnings will not be taxable until they are withdrawn.

Investments Available

IRA contributions may be invested in the following:

- deferred annuities
- mutual funds

- trusts or custodial accounts of banks or certain other financial institutions
- special gold and silver coins issued by the U.S. government

Deferred annuities can be fixed or variable, and they can be single premium or annual premium. However, the deferred annuity cannot have a required minimum annual premium and it must be nontransferable.

Exclusions. Vehicles that are prohibited from use for the purpose of IRA contributions are

- life insurance policies
- collectibles such as stamp collections

Retirement Savings Credit

A temporary, nonrefundable credit for elective deferrals and for contributions to a traditional or Roth IRA is available to certain low-to-moderate-income taxpayers for taxable years beginning 2002 through 2006. The credit is allowed against the sum of the regular tax and the alternative minimum tax (minus certain other credits), and it is in addition to any other deduction or exclusion that would otherwise apply. The credit is limited to the "applicable percentage" of "qualified retirement savings contributions" up to $2,000. The applicable percentage is shown in table 6-7.

TABLE 6-7
Adjusted Gross Income

Joint Return		Head of Household		All Other Cases		Applicable Percentage
Over	Not Over	Over	Not Over	Over	Not Over	
$ 0	$30,000	$ 0	$22,500	$ 0	$15,000	50%
30,000	32,500	22,500	24,375	15,000	16,250	20
32,500	50,000	24,375	37,500	16,250	25,000	10
50,000	—	37,500	—	25,000	—	0

Qualified retirement savings contributions are the total of IRA contributions, elective deferrals to Sec. 401(k) plans, Sec. 403(b) tax-sheltered annuities, SARSEPs, SIMPLE IRAs, and Sec. 457 governmental plans for the taxable year, less any distributions during a "testing period." The testing period for such plans that are includible in income is the 2 prior years and the current taxable year up to the due date (including extensions) for filing the federal income tax return for the current taxable year. Dependents, workers under age 18, and full-time students are ineligible for this credit.

Example: John and Jane have an adjusted gross income of $31,000 for 2006. They each contribute $2,000 to a traditional IRA, neither participates in an employer-provided retirement plan, and neither received any distributions during the testing period. Not only can John and Jane each deduct their $2,000 contribution, but they can also each claim a credit of $400 (20% x $2,000) on their federal income tax return for 2006.

Distribution of Benefits

Generally, an individual may begin to withdraw benefits from a traditional IRA as early as age 59 1/2 and must begin withdrawing them by April 1 of the year after the year in which he or she reaches age 70 1/2, whether or not he or she has retired.

required minimum distributions (RMDs)

The IRS mandates *required minimum distributions (RMDs)* that must be made based on life expectancy. If withdrawals do not take place or if too little is withdrawn, there is a 50 percent penalty tax applied to the amount by which the withdrawal falls short of the required minimum distribution amount.

> **If IRA withdrawals do not take place or if too little is withdrawn, there is a 50 percent penalty tax on the amount by which the withdrawal falls short.**

Premature distributions from an IRA, which are taken before age 59 1/2, are subject to normal taxation plus a penalty tax equal to 10 percent of the amount of the distribution. This penalty does not apply to distributions that are

- made to a beneficiary or the individual's estate due to the death of the individual
- the result of the individual's disability
- part of a series of periodic payments based on the life expectancy of the individual or joint life expectancy of the individual and a beneficiary
- funds withdrawn for educational expenses
- funds withdrawn for first-time home purchases up to $10,000
- medical expenses
- used to pay health insurance premiums for the unemployed
- used to pay an IRS levy on an IRA

Taxation of Benefits

Generally, distributions from a traditional IRA are fully taxable as received. However, only part of the distribution attributable to nondeductible contributions is taxable and part is not. If cash is taken from the account in a lump sum, an amount equal to the nondeductible contributions is recovered

It may be a good idea for your clients to keep their deductible and nondeductible contributions in separate IRA accounts.

income tax free and the balance is taxable. If the withdrawal is in the form of an annuity, part of each payment is taxable while the part representing nondeductible contributions is tax free.

It may be a good idea for future tracking and accounting purposes for your clients to keep their deductible and nondeductible contributions in separate IRA accounts.

Roth IRA

Roth IRA

The Taxpayer Relief Act (TRA) of 1997 introduced the *Roth IRA*, which is a retirement planning alternative to the traditional IRA. To be eligible for the Roth IRA, individuals must have earned income, and unlike the traditional IRA, they can make contributions to these plans beyond the age of 70 1/2. In contrast to contributions to a traditional IRA, all contributions to a Roth IRA are non-tax deductible. Nondeductible contributions to a Roth IRA in 2006 generally may not exceed the lesser of $4,000 or 100 percent of earned income, reduced by those contributions made to a traditional IRA. The contribution amount is phased out for joint filers with modified adjusted gross income between $150,000 and $160,000, and for single filers with adjusted gross income between $95,000 and $110,000. With a Roth IRA, not only does the taxpayer escape taxation of earnings and growth during the accumulation period, but retirement distributions are also designed to be income tax free.

Because contributions to Roth IRAs are made with after-tax dollars, distribution penalties and restrictions are less burdensome than with traditional IRAs. Generally, contributions to Roth IRAs can be withdrawn any time free of income taxation. (However, with traditional IRAs that have been converted to Roth IRAs, if withdrawals are made within 5 years of the conversion, a 10 percent penalty will apply only to converted funds withdrawn.) All contributions and earnings accrue income tax free during the accumulation period.

qualified distribution

Qualified distributions of earnings are also income tax free. A *qualified distribution* is any distribution made after the Roth IRA is established, provided the distribution satisfies two tests:

- The distribution must be made after the end of the 5-year period beginning with the first day of the first taxable year for which any Roth IRA contribution was made.
- One of the following must be met:
  - The individual is 59 1/2 or older when the distribution is made.
  - The individual has become totally and permanently disabled.
  - The distribution is used to pay up to $10,000 of qualifying first-time home-buyer expenses.
  - The beneficiary is receiving distributions following the death of the account owner.

Withdrawals of earnings from Roth IRAs are subject to income tax but no penalty if they are used to pay for

- a life annuity
- educational expenses
- medical expenses
- health insurance for the unemployed

All other withdrawals of earnings are subject to income tax plus a 10 percent penalty.

The required minimum distribution rules referred to earlier in this chapter and discussed in greater detail elsewhere in this text, do not apply to Roth IRAs. In other words, owners of Roth IRAs do not have to begin making withdrawals from them at age 70 1/2. Also, the same 5-year holding period rules for receiving fully income-tax-free distributions that applied to the account owner during life will apply to the beneficiary of a Roth IRA after the account owner's death. Distributions received by the Roth IRA beneficiary after the end of the 5-year holding period are completely income tax free as well, and any distributions that are a recovery of the deceased's Roth IRA contributions are always income tax free. Thus, the proceeds from a Roth IRA can totally escape income taxation when passed on to heirs.

If the beneficiary is the spouse, distributions can be delayed even further until the death of the spouse. After that, distributions can be made over the expected lifetime of the beneficiary or beneficiaries. This makes the Roth IRA a good way to pass on unused wealth income tax free to the next generation.

Furthermore, as mentioned above, unlike with traditional IRAs, workers can continue to make contributions to a Roth IRA beyond age 70 1/2, provided they continue to earn wages.

Another feature of the Roth IRA is that the tax-free source of income gives the participant more flexibility in how and when to liquidate other taxable assets during retirement. The income-tax-free funds in a Roth IRA can be used in retirement to

- minimize taxable withdrawals from traditional IRAs or qualified plans
- minimize taxable income to stay in a lower tax bracket
- provide a source of income that will not increase the portion of Social Security benefits that are taxed (as earnings from CDs or even tax-free bonds do)
- fund life insurance premiums for estate planning purposes
- provide liquidity for estate taxes
- minimize liquidation of other taxable investments, such as stocks and mutual funds, which currently receive a step-up in cost basis if left intact to heirs

There are downsides to Roth IRAs—for example, there is income taxation and a penalty on funds that are withdrawn too soon after being deposited or before 59 1/2 years of age. However, restrictions on liquidity are a relatively small price to pay for freedom from income taxation.

Conversion to a Roth IRA

Another issue that arises with the Roth IRA is conversion of a traditional IRA to a Roth IRA. Individuals can convert their traditional IRA to a Roth IRA, pay the income tax, and reap the income-tax-free benefit of the Roth IRA on future earnings and growth. Remember, however, that distributions made from a traditional IRA as a conversion to a Roth IRA are subject to income tax, but they are usually not subject to the 10 percent IRS penalty for early withdrawals for individuals under age 59 1/2 years old.

Although the introduction of Roth IRAs into the tax law complicates the retirement planning process, you can provide added value to your prospects and clients by helping them understand their choices so that they can make informed decisions.

Distributions from a traditional IRA as a conversion to a Roth IRA are subject to income tax but usually not subject to the IRS 10 percent early withdrawal penalty.

Qualified Roth Contribution Program

A new provision in EGTRRA that took effect January 1, 2006, will permit 401(k) and 403(b) plans to offer a "qualified Roth contribution program," which is basically a Roth account with elective deferrals. The same limits on elective deferrals ($15,000 in 2006) and on the after-age-50 catch-up ($5,000 in 2006) that apply to 401(k) and 403(b) plans will be permitted for employee-designated Roth contributions in lieu of all or a portion of elective deferrals that the employee is otherwise eligible to make. The Roth contributions are included in the employee's income in the year they are made, and they must be held in a separate account with separate record keeping. Earnings allocable to Roth contributions remain in the separate account and grow income tax free.

A designated Roth contribution account is subject to the same minimum distribution requirements of other qualified plans. However, rollovers can be made to another Roth account or a Roth IRA. Funds in an individual Roth IRA are not subject to minimum distribution requirements. A "qualified distribution" from a designated Roth contribution account, like those from an individual Roth IRA, will not be includable in the participant's gross income. The requirements for a qualified distribution are nearly identical to those for a Roth IRA, except that no exception is permitted for first-time home purchases.

Traditional IRA versus Roth IRA

The obvious question posed by the introduction of the Roth IRA is, which is better—the Roth IRA or the traditional IRA? As the following example illustrates, the Roth IRA is the preferred choice, assuming an individual can afford the cash flow sufficient to forgo the current income tax deduction.

| *Example:* | Roy has $2,000 to invest toward his retirement. In a 15 percent marginal income tax bracket, the current after-tax outlay for a Roth IRA is $2,000, compared to $1,700 for a traditional IRA. |

	Traditional IRA	Roth IRA
IRA contribution	$2,000	$2,000
Less tax savings	(300)	0
After-tax outlay	$1,700	$2,000

Assume that the contribution grows at 10 percent in either the traditional or Roth IRA. Also assume that the tax savings of $300 associated with the traditional IRA grows at a pretax rate of 10 percent but at an after-tax rate of only 8.5 percent. In 20 years when Roy retires, he is slightly better off with the Roth IRA (as long as his marginal income tax bracket does not increase).

	Traditional IRA	Roth IRA
Account balance	$13,455	$13,455
Plus accumulated tax savings	1,534	0
Total accumulations	$14,989	$13,455
Less tax on distribution	(2,018)	0
Net for living expenses	$12,970	$13,455

The Roth IRA maximizes Roy's after-tax return. Earnings and growth are not merely income tax deferred as with the traditional IRA; they are entirely income tax free.

Rollovers and Direct Transfers

Perhaps one of the greatest sources of funds that are deposited into IRAs is distributions from qualified plans. Certain kinds of distributions from qualified plans, tax-deferred annuities, and individual traditional IRAs can be rolled over to a traditional IRA. A *rollover* is a transfer of funds from one IRA or qualified plan to the individual who reinvests it in a second IRA or qualified plan.[2] (However, funds cannot be transferred from an employer-sponsored qualified plan directly into a Roth IRA; they must go into a traditional IRA first.) When

rollover

the provisions of the Internal Revenue Code and regulations are followed, these distributions will not be treated as currently taxable income.

Also, there is no dollar or percentage-of-compensation limit on the amount that can be rolled over. Nevertheless, the IRA rollover is generally subject to the same required minimum distribution rules as non-rollover IRAs.

How the transfer of funds is handled is extremely important. Under previous regulations, an individual could receive a lump-sum payment from an employer-sponsored qualified retirement plan and redeposit it into another IRA within 60 days. This is no longer the case. Under current regulations, the qualified plan custodian of the funds being rolled over is required to withhold 20 percent of the total amount as federal tax unless the transaction is a *direct transfer*—that is, a rollover directly from the custodian of one qualified plan to the custodian of an IRA or other qualified plan. This means that the participant will receive only 80 percent of the funds.

direct transfer

To complete the rollover transaction successfully, the participant must redeposit 100 percent of the amount being rolled over. In other words, he or she must provide the withheld 20 percent from other funds. The participant is then reimbursed as part of the normal federal income tax filing and refund procedure.

Example: Steve wants to take a $100,000 distribution from his 401(k) plan and roll it into a traditional IRA. Out of a $100,000 distribution, Steve will receive only $80,000 ($100,000 minus the $20,000 sent to the IRS). To complete the rollover, he must come up with an additional $20,000. If the deposit is only $80,000, the $20,000 will be considered a taxable distribution. If Steve is under age 59 1/2, the undeposited amount will be subject to the 10 percent penalty tax for early distributions.

To avoid this situation, your prospects and clients should not take a qualified plan distribution with the intention of redepositing it at a later time. Help them make sure that the transaction is properly conducted directly between the two account custodians.

Also, note that a rollover of money from an existing IRA into a new IRA does not require any withholding of a portion of the funds.

Basically, there are four situations in which an income-tax-free rollover might be desirable:

- active IRA rolled over into another active IRA. This type of rollover gives individuals a degree of flexibility in changing from one investment to another.

- IRA transferred into tax-sheltered annuity, Sec. 403(b) plan, Sec. 457 plan, or other qualified employer-sponsored defined-contribution plan (under rules established under EGTRRA 2001)
- active IRA rolled over to freeze the present account. This type of rollover can be desirable if the participant is no longer eligible to deduct IRA payments.
- employer's qualified plan rolled over to an IRA when there is a lump-sum distribution because of early retirement, termination of employment, or termination of the qualified plan

This fourth situation—a lump-sum distribution from an employer's plan—may give you a significant opportunity to assist your prospects and clients. For instance, a distribution may come at a time when your client is faced with other difficult decisions and is suddenly confronted with a large sum of money that needs to be invested quickly. The first step in helping your client is to make sure he or she understands the 20 percent withholding rule discussed earlier.

Next, you have to make your client aware of the advantages of directly transferring the funds into an IRA. Some of the most apparent advantages involve issues of flexibility and control of the funds. For example, funds in a transferred IRA account within a commercial family of mutual funds enable the owner to make future additional IRA deposits into it. Former employer-controlled plans will remain frozen. Also, if a partial distribution of funds is needed, the client can take it from his or her personally owned IRA but not from the former employer's plan. The IRA owner may be able to move the money into a personally selected family of funds with more investment options than what his or her former employer may provide.

Income Taxes on the Distribution

Income taxes are not due until the individual begins to take withdrawals from the IRA rollover or at age 70 1/2, if later. Income from an IRA rollover investment is not taxed as it is earned. It is taxable only when withdrawals begin.

Premature Distribution Penalty

Unless a qualified plan distribution is deposited into an IRA rollover account, it will be subject to ordinary income taxation and a 10 percent penalty if the individual is under age 59 1/2 (age 55 if also separated from service). ◊

CONCLUSION

The federal government has encouraged employers to participate in funding their employees' retirement plans by creating inherent tax advantages for qualified plans. These tax advantages, combined with the fact that employees consider retirement plans to be a very important employee benefit, make a working knowledge of retirement plans a must for the advisor who wants to succeed in the retirement planning marketplace.

Furthermore, encouraging individuals to take advantage of the tax-favored features of contributions to employer-sponsored and individual retirement plans, and helping them effectively manage rollovers and distributions from these plans, can enhance your client's financial security during retirement. ◊

CHAPTER SIX REVIEW

Key Terms and Concepts are explained in the Glossary. Answers to the Review Questions and Self-Test Questions are found in the back of the book in the Answers to Questions section.

Key Terms

tax-advantaged retirement plan
qualified plan
defined-benefit plan
defined-contribution plan
pension plan
profit-sharing plan
cash-balance pension plan
money-purchase plan
target-benefit pension plan
401(k) plan
cash or deferred arrangement
  (CODA)
maximum salary deferral amount
catch-up contribution
vesting
highly compensated employee
  (HCE)
top-heavy plan
SEP (simplified employee pension)
SIMPLE (savings incentive match
  plan for employees)

403(b) plan
501(c)(3) organization
nonqualified retirement plan
unfunded
funded
SERP (supplemental executive
  retirement plan)
salary reduction plan
stock option plan
traditional IRA
spousal IRA
adjusted gross income (AGI)
active participant
modified adjusted gross income
  (MAGI)
required minimum distributions
  (RMDs)
Roth IRA
qualified distribution
rollover
direct transfer

Review Questions

6-1. Explain how qualified plans differ from other tax-advantaged retirement plans.

6-2. Identify the major difference between a defined-benefit plan and a defined-contribution plan.

6-3. Summarize the major differences between a pension plan and a profit-sharing plan.

6-4. Explain why a 401(k) plan is called a cash or deferred arrangement (CODA).

6-5. Assuming a 55-year-old worker earns $35,000, determine the maximum that he or she can contribute (through salary deferrals) to his or her 401(k) plan in 2006.

6-6. Identify the two minimum vesting standards applicable to most qualified plans from which an employer can choose.

6-7. Explain the main difference between a SEP and a SIMPLE plan.

6-8. Briefly describe how a 403(b) plan works, and list the types of organizations that can sponsor them.

6-9. Briefly describe the three basic types of nonqualified deferred-compensation plans.

6-10. Explain when contributions made into a traditional IRA are deductible for workers who are active participants in qualified plans.

6-11. Explain the circumstances under which distributions from traditional IRAs are taxable and subject to or free from the IRS 10 percent penalty for early withdrawals.

6-12. Describe how a Roth IRA differs from a traditional IRA.

6-13. Explain the differences between an IRA rollover and a direct transfer.

Self-Test Questions

Instructions: Read chapter 6 first, then answer the following questions to test your knowledge. There are 10 questions; circle the correct answer, then check your answers with the answer key in the back of the book.

6-1. Which of the following plans is always subject to a maximum salary deferral amount?

(A) SIMPLE
(B) SEP
(C) cash-balance pension plan
(D) stock bonus plan

6-2.   Which of the following plans can base an employee's retirement benefit on final average earnings, years of service, or a combination of the two?

(A)   profit-sharing plan
(B)   401(k) plan
(C)   defined-benefit pension plan
(D)   money-purchase plan

6-3.   A client can contribute $4,000 (in 2006) on behalf of his or her nonworking spouse plus $4,000 to his or her own IRA as long as which of the following circumstances exists?

(A)   The nonworking spouse has $4,000 of unearned income.
(B)   The contributing spouse has $8,000 of earned income.
(C)   The contributing spouse is the owner of the spousal IRA.
(D)   The nonworking spouse is an active participant in a pension plan.

6-4.   Which of the following statements concerning contributions to traditional IRAs is (are) correct?

I.   Individuals can make regular (non-catch-up) contributions up to 100 percent of earned income with a cap of $4,000 (in 2006).
II.   Contributions can be made beyond age 70 1/2 as long as the IRA owner is still receiving earned income.

(A)   I only
(B)   II only
(C)   Both I and II
(D)   Neither I nor II

6-5.   Which of the following qualified plans can be categorized as a defined-contribution pension plan?

I.   cash-balance plan
II.   stock bonus plan

(A)   I only
(B)   II only
(C)   Both I and II
(D)   Neither I nor II

6-6. Which of the following statements concerning the legal requirements of a qualified plan is (are) correct?

    I.   The plan must be written and communicated to employees.
    II.   The plan must be established for the exclusive benefit of the employees.

    (A) I only
    (B) II only
    (C) Both I and II
    (D) Neither I nor II

6-7. Which of the following statements concerning pension plans is (are) correct?

    I.   They do not require an employer to maintain any specified level of annual contributions.
    II.   Their sole purpose is to provide retirement income.

    (A) I only
    (B) II only
    (C) Both I and II
    (D) Neither I nor II

6-8. All the following statements concerning nonqualified retirement plans are correct EXCEPT:

    (A) They usually are required to comply with all of the burdensome requirements of ERISA.
    (B) They give employers greater flexibility in selecting whom to cover.
    (C) They provide employers with greater flexibility in designing vesting requirements.
    (D) They enable owners and key employees to supplement their retirement income from qualified plans, which is limited by the current tax laws.

6-9. All the following statements concerning SIMPLEs are correct EXCEPT:

    (A) They replaced SARSEPs.
    (B) Employees are 100 percent vested in contributions to SIMPLEs.
    (C) SIMPLEs are not subject to nondiscrimination testing.
    (D) In-service withdrawals are not permitted.

6-10.   A distribution from a profit-sharing plan is eligible to be invested in a roll-over IRA for all of the following reasons EXCEPT

    (A)   death of the participant
    (B)   termination of the participant's employment
    (C)   retirement of the participant
    (D)   withdrawal due to illness

NOTES

1.   Internal Revenue Code, Sec. 501(c)(3).
2.   The term *rollover* generally refers to a transfer of funds from either an employer-sponsored qualified retirement plan or an existing IRA to the individual who then reinvests them in another IRA account. This rollover procedure can create a significant tax problem when the funds originate from a qualified retirement plan. The preferred method of moving funds from a qualified retirement plan to an IRA is by a direct transfer from one custodian to another.

Wealth Management and Distribution Strategies for Retirees

Learning Objectives

An understanding of the material in this chapter should enable the student to

---

7-1.   Identify reasons for and against taking early retirement.

7-2.   Explain the effect that early retirement has on Social Security benefits and company-sponsored retirement plans.

7-3.   Identify selling/planning opportunities available with early retirees.

7-4.   Explain the role of Social Security retirement benefits in retirees' asset distribution planning.

7-5.   Explain the role of qualified plan and IRA required minimum distribution rules in asset distribution planning at retirement.

7-6.   Identify important issues to consider when working with retiring employees.

7-7.   Compare and contrast preretirement and postretirement investment strategies.

7-8.   Explain the role of life insurance in asset distribution planning at retirement.

7-9.   Identify the steps involved in developing effective retirement planning solutions.

Chapter Outline

PLANNING CONSIDERATIONS AT EARLY RETIREMENT

> Many advisors automatically pencil in age 65 as the starting date for retirement despite the fact that the average retirement age is 62.

early retirement

The Early Retirement Trend

Many advisors automatically pencil in age 65 as the starting date for retirement despite the fact that the average retirement age in the United States is 62. In fact, according to one Life Insurance Marketing and Research Association (LIMRA) survey, roughly 80 percent of people in large companies with pension plans retired before they reached age 65. Another important statistic: 51 percent of all 64-year-olds are retired. These statistics point to a growing trend among workers today—*early retirement*.

Factors That Affect the Early Retirement Decision

There are a number of reasons that workers are retiring earlier. Some individuals have worked hard and planned carefully so that they could accumulate the financial resources necessary to stop working and pursue more relaxed, enjoyable lifestyles. Others, perhaps facing reorganization, downsizing, and restructuring in the workplace, find themselves considering early retirement options offered by their employers.

Reasons for Early Retirement

Some individuals approach retirement planning as financial independence planning. For these people, the retirement age assumption equates with their goal for financial independence. For example, these individuals approach planning by asking, "What percentage of my salary do I need to save to retire at age 55?" It is generally easy to adjust computer models and worksheets to fit these individuals' needs. (It is often difficult, however, for most people to acquire the needed savings by such an early age!)

In addition to retiring early for financial independence, many individuals look at the issue of health to help make the early retirement decision. Some want to retire early while they are still in good health. In many instances, they have perceived health issues—that is, they may fear that future bad health may prevent them from accomplishing their retirement objectives. Others are forced to retire early because of actual health issues—for example, a diabetic client who retires early to pursue a 10-mile-a-day walking regimen to keep his blood sugar low. And in many cases, a client is forced to retire early because of caregiving health issues—for example, the poor health of his or her spouse (or sometimes a parent).

golden handshake

Another reason for early retirement is corporate downsizing. In some companies, retirement packages known as golden handshakes are offered to cut payroll costs attributable to older employees. A *golden handshake* is an incentive offer by an employer made to an employee or group of employees to encourage early retirement. Incentives typically include lump-sum payments based on service with the firm, funding for retiree health care, and/or other monetary inducements. In a recent Charles D. Spencer & Associates Survey of 71 large companies, 32 percent of early retirements during the tested year were the result of golden handshakes. No matter what the company's motivation, advisors must face the fact that some people are being shown the door (pushed out?) earlier and earlier when economic conditions change and the need arises for the business to reduce its workforce.

> A recent survey of 71 large companies showed that 32 percent of early retirements were the result of golden handshakes.

Other reasons that an employee may prefer retirement prior to age 65 include the following:

- retirement of the spouse. In many cases, one spouse's retirement at full retirement age may prompt the younger spouse's early retirement. One study showed that the profile of the individual most likely to retire early was a married person whose spouse was retired.
- death of the spouse. Statistics show that another group likely to retire early is widows, perhaps because they received death benefits and other inheritances from their partners.
- inability to meet physical requirements of the job. Laborers and manual workers, for example, often retire early, perhaps because of the physically demanding nature of their work.

- problems in the workplace. Some people retire early because their jobs have grown intolerable. A recent change in the company may make the job environment a difficult one. For example, the problem may be "I can't work with that person" or "I feel the company just doesn't care about quality anymore, and I can't work that way."
- willingness to compromise financial goals. Some individuals, even though they have not yet achieved the goal of financial independence, are ready to trade a lower standard of living for freedom from employment.
- health and pension incentives. The structure of the employer's health and pension plan may encourage early retirement. For example, an individual with retiree health coverage at age 62 and a pension that provides 60 percent of salary may perceive that he or she is working for 40 cents on a dollar.

> **According to a recent survey, 45 percent of current retirees retired earlier than they had planned.**

Finally, it is important to note that a recent Retirement Confidence Survey, sponsored by the Employee Benefit Research Institute and the Principal Financial Group, revealed that 45 percent of current retirees retired earlier than they had planned. Reasons most frequently cited for earlier than planned retirement are

- health problems or disability (40 percent)
- downsizing or closure (14 percent)
- family reasons (14 percent)
- other work-related reasons (12 percent)

Because these reasons typically arise unexpectedly, few of these retirees had enough time to prepare adequately. They simply did not know when they would retire.

Reasons against Early Retirement

Despite the trend toward early retirement, advisors must be ready to point out the downside of retiring too early. Factors include the following:

full retirement age (FRA)

- Social Security *full retirement age (FRA)* is slated to increase from 65 to 67 for some baby boomers and over 65 but before age 67 for others (see chapter 2). Clients affected by this change should be aware that the early retirement benefit will also be reduced. Typically, it had been 80 percent of the client's primary insurance amount (PIA). For individuals with an FRA of 67, the reduced benefit will drop to 70 percent of the client's PIA.
- Early retirement may decrease the amount of Social Security benefits paid. In other words, Social Security benefits will be reduced if the

35 years of averaged indexed monthly earnings (used to calculate the Social Security PIA) include some low- or zero-earning years.

- The impact of early retirement on pension benefits can be devastating. In a final-average-salary defined-benefit plan, the pension is lowered because the peak earning years are curtailed. (In other words, had the worker stayed on the job, the pension would have been higher because it would have been based on higher earnings.) The same holds true for the account balance in a defined-contribution plan.

- Pensions are often adjusted downward to reflect the longer payout that comes with early retirement.

- Early retirement means increased exposure to inflation.

- It may not be feasible to retire early because of the necessity to pay off fixed long-term liabilities such as a mortgage and college tuition for the kids. Many baby boomers had children later in life, which exacerbates this problem.

- Retiring early may mean the loss of health insurance. In one study, only 46 percent of large companies provided some form of health coverage for early retirees. What's more, continuation of health insurance coverage under COBRA lasts only 18 months for retirement.

Considering an Early Retirement Offer

Planning for early retirement, whether as the result of a retirement offer from the employer or as the result of successful planning, needs to take into account all of the considerations given to retirement at the employee's FRA. In addition, regardless of the reason for early retirement, some special factors must be evaluated.

Early retirement offers can be extremely attractive, providing a generous range of benefits, including cash severance settlements, enhanced pensions, postretirement medical expense and life insurance, financial or retirement planning services, and even job and outplacement counseling for those who want to find new jobs.

Employees cannot be forced to accept an early retirement offer. But the alternative may be that the company eliminates their jobs or reassigns them to other positions.

A company is not required to offer early retirement, and there is no required form for an early retirement offer. Nevertheless, more and more companies are using early retirement incentive offers as a cost-effective way to reduce their work forces. Each offer has to be considered in its own right. Under federal law, an employee cannot be forced to accept an early retirement offer. Employees do have to keep in mind, however, that the alternative may be for the company to elect to eliminate their jobs or reassign them to other positions, perhaps at a lower level and reduced wages.

The choice can be very difficult, especially for people who have not planned to retire for another 5 or 10 years. And often the determination has to be made within 60 to 90 days of the offer. During this time, the employee must resolve a number of questions, including the following:

- Will the available benefits be enough to support the worker and his or her family?
- Will there be enough to provide for the family until Social Security retirement benefits are available?
- Will the needed ancillary benefits, such as health insurance, be available?

None of these questions is easy to answer, and the answers depend on the early retirement package that the company offers.

Comparing Pre- and Postretirement Income

The first step in evaluating an early retirement offer is to analyze the financial difference between working and retiring. The worker must compare current salary minus expenses directly related to employment to the amount that will be available in the retirement package. Costs directly related to employment include such expenses as commuting costs, clothing expenses, and parking fees.

The comparison must also include a consideration of taxes. Retirement pension payments are subject to income taxes but not to Social Security (FICA) taxes. Making the comparison will show the difference between how much net income the employee will realize by working and how much will be available by taking the early retirement offer. If the difference is small, early retirement may be an attractive option.

> **The first step in evaluating an early retirement offer is to analyze the financial difference between working and retiring.**

Example: Paul is considering early retirement. He is 62, married, and has worked as an operations specialist for a large pharmaceutical manufacturer for 25 years. He currently earns $50,000 per year. He has a defined-benefit pension plan that will provide him with a fixed reduced benefit of $18,000 per year for the rest of his life. His Social Security retirement benefit is $19,000 this year, and it is scheduled to increase with the rate of inflation as measured by the consumer price index (CPI). His wife is 3 years younger than he is, and she is working. Paul can obtain health insurance through her employer for about the same as he pays now through his employer. This will bring him to age 65 when he can qualify for Medicare.

Based on the facts in Paul's case, retirement may be the better option for him than continuing to work. This would be especially true if he had other activities he wanted to pursue such as volunteer work, a new part-time self employment endeavor, and spending more time with his grandchildren.

Comparison between Working and Retiring		
	Continuing to Work	Retiring Early
Gross income	$50,000	$37,000
Federal income tax	-$5,270	$3,320
State income tax—3%	-$1,500	-0-
FICA tax	-$3,825	-0-
Annual costs associated with working (lunches, transportation, clothing)	-$4,000	-0-
Net income	$35,405	$33,680

Social Security. The full retirement age for Social Security benefits for people born in 1941 is 65 years and 8 months. It is increasing to age 67 for those born after 1959. The youngest age for which early retirement benefits can be received under the Social Security retirement benefit rules will remain at 62, despite the increase in the Social Security FRA.

Is it better to begin collecting benefits at age 62 or to wait until full retirement age? There is no way to say for sure. The answer depends in part on how long benefits are received once they begin. In other words, it depends on when the retiree dies. It is possible, however, to calculate the hypothetical cross-over point—or *breakeven age*—to which a retiree must survive to make delaying the decision to begin receiving Social Security benefits the better option. A calculation using an assumed inflation rate for future Social Security benefits and an assumed interest (discount) rate at which money can safely accumulate will determine the real inflation-adjusted interest rate. For example, a 62 year-old will reach the breakeven point if he or she lives to age 80 years and 8 months, assuming a constant 3 percent annual inflation rate for benefits. (See table 7-1.) There is also a breakeven analysis available on the Social Security website at www.ssa.gov.

Generally, the longer a worker waits to start collecting monthly retirement benefits from Social Security, the higher the amount. Covered workers can begin drawing Social Security benefits when they reach age 62, but the monthly benefit is permanently reduced. For a worker whose FRA is 66, the reduction in Social Security retirement benefits is 25 percent at age 62, 20 percent at age 63, 13.33 percent at age 64, and 6.67 percent at age 65. However, it is generally recommended that a person take the reduced benefit if he or she does not intend to work past age 62.

In 2006, a single worker who retires prior to full retirement age (as mentioned above, 65 years and 8 months for those born in 1941) can earn up

Is it better to begin collecting Social Security retirement benefits at age 62 or to wait until full retirement age? There is no way to say for sure.

breakeven age

Generally, the longer a worker waits to start collecting monthly retirement benefits from Social Security, the higher the amount.

TABLE 7-1
Breakeven Life Expectancy for Early Social Security Benefits[1]

Age Early Benefits Begin	Real (Inflation-Adjusted) Discount Rate[2]				
	0%	1%	2%	3%	4%
62	77.00	78.00	79.02	80.08	82.08
63	78.00	79.01	80.05	82.01	84.03
64	79.00	80.02	81.07	83.05	85.11

1. The breakeven life expectancies are expressed in a format of years and months. For example, 79.02 is age 79 years and 2 months. An age 65 full retirement age is assumed.
2. The real (inflation-adjusted) discount rate is derived by the following formula: Real discount rate = (nominal discount rate − inflation rate) ÷ (1 + inflation rate). For planning purposes, subtracting the assumed growth rate of Social Security benefits from the nominal discount rate is sufficient.

---

to $12,480 annually without a reduction in Social Security retirement benefits. If the worker earns more than this amount, Social Security benefits are reduced $1 for each $2 above the $12,480 limit. In the year the worker reaches full retirement age, there is a limit on annual earnings of $33,240 (in 2006) only for those months' earnings before the worker reaches his or her FRA. If the worker exceeds the $33,240 limit during 2006 before reaching FRA, Social Security benefits are reduced by $1 for each $3 of earnings. There is no limit whatsoever on earnings beyond full retirement age.

Example: If a worker who collects Social Security early retirement benefits reaches age 65 years and 8 months on November 1, 2006, and earned $38,240 from January through October and an additional $5,000 in November through December, only the $5,000 of excess wages the worker earned before November 1 would cause a reduction of $1 of Social Security benefits for each $3 earned.

Unearned income does not affect the reduction of Social Security retirement benefits, but as we will explain later in this chapter, it may affect the amount of federal income tax that an individual must pay on those benefits.

Company Pension Plan

Individuals who are covered under a company-sponsored early retirement plan need to consider certain factors.

Defined-Benefit Plans. Defined-benefit plan formulas calculate a retiree's monthly pension based on a single life annuity at age 65. If an individual retires early, he or she will have fewer years with the company, be younger, will probably have a lower final or average salary, and may face penalties for retiring early.

These factors are usually part of calculating pension benefits. Generally, benefits under defined-benefit plans are determined as a percentage of final pay multiplied by the number of years with the company. For instance, an individual's annual retirement benefit may be 1.5 percent of average or final annual pay multiplied by the number of years of service. Thus, workers with 30 years of service may be entitled to 45 percent of their final average pay.

The way that early retirement benefits are calculated can penalize an individual. The company may reduce benefits for each year the individual's retirement date is earlier than the full-benefit retirement date. For example, the plan may call for a 0.25 percent reduction per month for early retirement. In this case, if the employee elects to retire at age 62—36 months early—the reduction in benefits will be 9 percent.

Early retirement can have another negative impact on benefits. Because plans are based on average earnings—either a career average or a final average—retiring early removes a number of high-earning years from the final calculation. Although the impact may be small, it is worth considering for the client who is making an early retirement decision.

On the other hand, the company plan may encourage early retirement by limiting the maximum monthly benefit. For instance, the plan may state that a maximum benefit is reached when an employee has been with the company for 30 years and has attained age 55. In this case, therefore, a worker will accrue no increases in pension payments beyond these age and service limits. A person who retires at age 55, however, has fewer years of saving before retirement begins and more years of spending after retirement commences, compared to a person who retires at age 65.

Sometimes incentives are offered to encourage longer-term employees to retire in order to reduce a company's total work force. One component of an early retirement offer may be an enhanced adjustment to the company's pension formula. If years of service are part of the retirement formula, the company may offer to add to the number of years of actual service to calculate the pension benefit. The company may also adjust the employee's age to make it meet the age required to receive full pension benefits. The company may even offer some combination of adding years of service and adjusting age so that preretirees may receive higher pension payments for the rest of their lives if they retire early, compared to waiting a few years.

Example: To encourage long-time employees to retire early, a company may make a temporary offer to all employees over age 50 to add 5 years to their age and 5 years to their number of years of employment for the purpose of calculating their pension retirement benefits. Thus, a 57 year-old employee with 25 years of service to the company would be considered to be aged 62 and have 30 years of service for pension payment purposes.

> **For those planning to retire early, it is important to have other financial resources to draw on to offset the negative impact of inflation.**

Finally, because most pension plans do not provide cost-of-living increases, the retiree will receive the amount that is calculated at his or her retirement date for as long as he or she lives. Early retirees may receive reduced benefits over a longer period of time, but the longer period of time may result in inflation's having a greater impact as the purchasing power of the benefits erodes. For those planning to retire early, it is important to have other financial resources to draw on to offset the negative impact of inflation.

Defined-Contribution Plans. Generally, in a defined-contribution plan, pension payments begin at retirement and are paid monthly over the employee's life. At early retirement, some defined-benefit pension plans allow an employee to take benefits in a lump sum. Lump-sum distributions are more common in defined-contribution plans or 401(k) plans.

Defined-contribution plans do not present the same problems at early retirement as defined-benefit plans. For individuals covered under defined-contribution plans, the downside of early retirement is that leaving work early reduces the number of years that contributions are made.

But the retiree still controls the amounts accumulated in his or her accounts and will have to make the decisions about investing and distributing them. With a lump-sum distribution, your prospects and clients have the flexibility to choose how their money is invested and how and when to pay income taxes. Perhaps the biggest disadvantage of taking a lump-sum distribution is that there is a 10 percent early withdrawal penalty if an individual is younger than age 59 1/2. Without proper tax planning, your client can be hit with a sizable tax bill.

Important note: Withdrawals from defined-contribution plans in which a worker was a participant immediately prior to retiring are exempt from the 10 percent early withdrawal penalty beginning at age 55.

To avoid the early withdrawal penalty, your younger clients can transfer qualified plan funds to a traditional IRA intended for future distributions.

Money in the traditional IRA will continue to grow on a tax-deferred basis and be taxed as ordinary income when it is withdrawn. Whether or not it is better for an individual to pay taxes on a lump-sum distribution or to roll it into a traditional IRA and defer taxes depends on the individual's situation and needs.

Once the money is in the traditional IRA, your client can choose whether to withdraw income or principal or both. From age 59 1/2 to age 70 1/2, your client can withdraw any amount at any time without incurring the IRS early withdrawal penalty, although the withdrawals are subject to ordinary income taxation. When your client reaches age 70 1/2, the IRS requires him or her to begin taking minimum distributions.

Severance Pay

severance pay

Many early retirement offers include a cash incentive as *severance pay*. This can be a flat amount offered to all employees across the board or an amount based on years of service. Often, severance packages are based on a formula, but with an overall cap on the severance amount payable such as 1 year's salary.

Example: A formula that offers 2 weeks of salary for every year of service would potentially give a 30-year employee 60 weeks of salary for accepting the early retirement offer. However, because of the company's severance cap, the early retiree will be given only 1 year's salary, which is 8 weeks less compensation than the employee would have otherwise received.

Typically, severance pay is made in a lump sum and subject to both income and FICA taxes. This is, of course, no different than if the employee had earned the payment over the same period as salary, and it leaves the retiree with a sizable amount to invest.

Insurance Coverage

> In evaluating an early retirement option, the employee should consider the cost and availability of individual medical expense coverage.

The early retirement package may include an offer to continue medical coverage until the employee reaches age 65 and is eligible for Medicare, but this option is being offered less frequently. Medical expense insurance is a valuable benefit, and early retirees must be prepared to pay several thousand dollars a year to purchase it on their own. In evaluating an early retirement option, the employee should consider the cost and availability of individual medical expense coverage. If the employee's spouse is employed (as in Paul's case in the earlier example), coverage may be available for the employee as a dependent under that plan.

Another consideration is life insurance coverage provided by the employer. Many people depend on employer-provided life insurance that will gradually end—or be reduced drastically—if the employee retires. In making a decision on early retirement, the employee must consider the impact of losing these benefits and the cost of replacing them.

IRA Withdrawals in Early Retirement

A person's IRAs, including transfers, can also be an important part of an early retirement program, but the retiree has to be careful to avoid the IRS's 10 percent penalty tax on early withdrawals from traditional IRAs before he or she reaches age 59 1/2.

In order to avoid the 10 percent penalty tax, withdrawals as periodic payments must be for approximately equal amounts and made at least annually for 5 years or until the individual reaches age 59 1/2, whichever is longer. The amount of the periodic payments can be calculated in one of the three ways below, but once a method is selected, it cannot be changed:

- straight life expectancy. The balance of the account is divided by the individual's life expectancy or the combined life expectancy of the individual and his or her beneficiary.
- amortization. This method amortizes the account balance over the individual's life expectancy (or joint life expectancies, if applicable), using a reasonable interest rate.
- annuity. Similar to the amortization method, this method uses life insurance mortality tables rather than the table the IRS provides.

Selling/Planning Opportunities

A prospect's or client's early retirement gives you a number of opportunities to offer financial products and services, as discussed below.

Investment of Severance Pay Lump Sums

> The receipt of severance pay as the result of early retirement creates challenges for the retiree and opportunities for you.

The receipt of severance pay as the result of early retirement creates challenges for the retiree and opportunities for you, the financial advisor. The quandary for the retiree is to decide what to do with an unusually large sum of money. As mentioned previously, severance packages for long-time employees can be a significant amount of the employee's final year's earnings. After income taxes are paid, and possibly after some frivolous expenditures for such items as an extravagant cruise or pricey new car, most people become serious about investing the remaining money intelligently. These dollars are often an integral part of their retirement nest egg. This is where you can provide a value-added service.

Using some of the financial products and investment techniques discussed in chapter 5, you can help your client develop a well-rounded, diversified, tax-wise investment strategy that will increase the chances for capital appreciation or enhance retirement income, depending on the individual's needs. Explaining the advisability of a retirement plan that combines tax-deferred annuities and mutual funds in conjunction with a suitable asset-allocation strategy will help to allay your client's fear of squandering his or her severance pay. Do not underestimate the value of your expertise within this context.

IRA Rollover of Qualified Accounts Not Needed Immediately

Similar opportunities arise for early retirees regarding tax-qualified monies. Although most employers will allow terminated employees to leave their defined-contribution funds in the former employer's existing plan accounts, this option offers little flexibility or access to partial withdrawals for emergencies or even for education funding opportunities for grandchildren. Also, investment choices may be more restrictive than those you can provide by moving the money into a family of mutual funds available through your broker-dealer.

Furthermore, a direct transfer into a traditional IRA (sold by you) can also set the stage for a conversion of some or all of those funds into a Roth IRA, if that is your client's desire. (Remember, funds cannot be transferred from an employer-sponsored qualified plan directly into a Roth IRA; they must go into a traditional IRA first.) As the advisor of record on a newly established IRA account, you will receive copies of statements that go to your client. This will enable you to help your clients understand the status of their accounts, and it will put you in a position to give clients future asset-allocation advice, provided you are properly licensed to do so. Often, the lay public does not easily understand mutual fund statements and exchange privileges.

Health Insurance Coverage

Early retirees may need you to guide them through the many managed care versus personal choice options available today.

Most retiring employees will qualify for an 18-month extension of their employer's health coverage under COBRA provisions. However, this is not free coverage. As a matter of fact, it may be more expensive and less desirable than the quality comprehensive medical expense insurance that you can provide to them. Many retirees are anxious about their medical expense insurance options after retiring and before age 65 when they qualify for Medicare. Early retirees may need you to guide them through the many managed care versus personal choice options available on today's medical expense insurance landscape. They will appreciate your efforts to help them find affordable and reliable coverage. If you do not sell medical expense insurance, perhaps you can refer clients to a reputable advisor who does. This enables you to be an additional resource to your clients and to strengthen the all-important client-advisor relationship.

Another pressing concern for most retirees is their need for long-term care insurance. People do not have to be in their 70s to buy this critical coverage—it is more affordable if purchased at younger ages, and a person's insurability is likely to be more favorable as well. If your client has recently separated from the service of a long-time employer, the client is likely to be evaluating all of his or her personal financial issues. This would be a great time to initiate a discussion of long-term care insurance.

Life Insurance Coverage

At the cessation of employment, individuals face the loss (or drastic reduction) of a large block of life insurance coverage—namely their group life insurance. For many workers, this insurance represents several times their annual salary. Retirees will have 31 days from the termination of their employment during which they can convert this group term insurance to permanent coverage. This is a valuable option for someone who is uninsurable or has serious health problems. However, the cost to convert group life insurance to individual permanent life insurance is based on a flat rate that is usually much higher than the cost of life insurance that a well-qualified healthy person could otherwise purchase from you. Also, if the retiree wants to buy term insurance, he or she cannot do so under the group conversion option. This gives you the opportunity to explain the permanent life insurance options and product flexibility available to them.

Another selling/planning opportunity is the pension maximization concept, discussed in the next section of this chapter, for individuals who are not retiring early. Although they may not even consider taking these payments for 5, 10, or more years after early retirement from a business where they were long-time employees, many companies require retirees to decide at termination of employment whether pension payments will be based on single or joint life expectancies. If your client is insurable at early retirement—and it makes economic sense to do so—the client can purchase some type of life insurance today that will permit him or her to take the higher maximum single life pension payout tomorrow. This life insurance coverage will provide sufficient dollars to a named beneficiary that would have been paid under the joint-survivor pension option.

Summary

As you can see, there are many ways to solidify your relationship with retiring clients by providing valuable and affordable life insurance coverage to protect their families, and other financial products to protect their assets. These are just a few of the selling/planning opportunities available in marketing to early retirees.

Preretirees are being bombarded with invitations to personal planning seminars offered by their employers or senior citizen associations, not to mention seminars advertised through periodicals, community centers, and direct mail. So remember this: If you don't ask retirees and early retirees about the concepts and products mentioned above, someone else surely will. ◊

LIFETIME ASSET DISTRIBUTION PLANNING

> **The decision to retire is not about reaching a certain age.**

The decision to retire is not about reaching a certain age. In the simplest terms, most people retire when they can economically and emotionally afford to do so. The decision to retire does not and should not mean that your clients stop planning. The economic decisions they make at retirement are important because they affect both their incomes and their nonfinancial choices. As you would expect, the determination to retire brings a new set of planning challenges.

Because most retirement income usually comes from three sources—Social Security, employer-sponsored qualified retirement plans, and personal savings—it is not surprising that a person's decision to retire often coincides with his or her eligibility for Social Security or qualified plan benefits. The law and regulations govern eligibility for Social Security benefits and distributions from qualified plans.

For example, a person may withdraw money from a qualified retirement plan at age 59 1/2 without penalty, but he or she is not eligible for full retirement benefits under Social Security until the full retirement age. As we stated earlier, full retirement age for a person born in 1941 is 65 years and 8 months (2006). Thus, a person who wants to retire at 60 can do so as long he or she does not need Social Security retirement benefits to replace the income lost from not working.

One of the challenges your clients face at retirement is to budget their assets and resources effectively to replace the income they give up when they leave their jobs or their businesses. At retirement, individuals may be limited to living on whatever assets they have accumulated.

The decisions they must make involve long-term planning for events that they cannot predict. To be successful, they must balance the use of government, previous employment, and personal resources in a way that will give them the greatest security.

Planning often revolves around timing distributions to maximize benefits. If your prospects and clients are well prepared for retirement financially, they will be able to take advantage of some timing opportunities. In the previous section, we discussed early retirement issues. In this section, we will discuss the timing issues at full retirement age and later.

Social Security

As explained earlier, Social Security FRA will gradually increase. For persons born after 1959, the full retirement age will be 67. At the full retirement age, covered workers can collect the full retirement benefit. In Social Security terminology, the benefit that is payable at FRA is the primary insurance amount. (You may wish to refer back to the section on Social Security benefits in chapter 2 for a quick review of how Social Security works and the benefits that are provided at retirement.)

If workers wait to collect their Social Security benefits until after their full retirement age, they earn delayed retirement credits that increase their benefits. The amount of the increase is expressed as an annual percentage and based on the worker's year of birth. Table 7-2 shows the percentage increase for workers born after 1933.

TABLE 7-2
Increases in Social Security Benefits for Delayed Retirement

Year of Birth	Yearly Rate of Increase	Rate of Increase
1933–1934	5.5%	11/24 of 1%
1935–1936	6.0%	1/2 of 1%
1937–1938	6.5%	13/24 of 1%
1939–1940	7.0%	7/12 of 1%
1941–1942	7.5%	5/8 of 1%
1943 or later	8.0%	2/3 of 1%

Note: If the date of birth is January 1, refer to the rate of increase for the previous year.

Important point: If a worker decides to delay retirement, he or she should sign up for Medicare at age 65. In some circumstances, medical insurance costs more if applying for it is delayed.

Source: Social Security Web site (www.ssa.gov)

How It Works

The increase in benefits for a worker who retires after FRA is calculated to be actuarially equivalent to the full retirement benefit. In other words, the value of the benefit a worker who retires late receives is equivalent to the benefit a worker who retires at FRA receives if both live an average life expectancy. In simple terms, the worker does not gain more benefits by delaying them. Neither does the worker lose benefits.

> The value of the benefit a worker who retires late receives is equivalent to the benefit a worker who retires at FRA receives if both live an average life expectancy.

Whether your client should delay collecting Social Security benefits depends on his or her individual situation. Two questions may help assess your client's needs:

- Does the client need Social Security retirement benefits to meet income needs at the full retirement age?
- If your client continues to work after retirement, will the client need a larger Social Security retirement benefit when he or she is fully retired?

Some advisors believe that it is better for workers to begin to collect Social Security benefits as early as age 62 if they are no longer working or are earning no more than the Social Security retirement earnings limit ($12,480 in 2006). However, a growing number of people continue to work in retirement. The effect of working after Social Security payments begin, as we explained earlier, is that there may be a reduction of $1 in benefits for every $2 in earnings above the earnings limit between age 62 and the worker's FRA.

Tax on Benefits

Generally, Social Security benefits are received tax free for federal income tax purposes, but they can be taxed for senior retirees with high incomes. The amount of a senior client's Social Security retirement benefits that is subject to income tax depends on whether the person is receiving income from sources in addition to Social Security. To determine if any of your client's benefits are income taxable, begin by totaling the following items:

- the client's adjusted gross income
- one-half the client's Social Security benefits
- tax-exempt interest such as interest on municipal bonds
- exclusions such as tax-free foreign earned income and foreign housing

The next step is to compare, using a formula as shown below, the total income from these sources to two different thresholds to calculate the portion of Social Security benefits that will be taxable. The thresholds for determining the potential income taxation of Social Security retirement benefits are shown in the table 7-3.

TABLE 7-3		
Thresholds for Taxation of Social Security Retirement Benefits		
Single Filers		**Married Filing Jointly**
$25,000	Taxation of up to 50% of Social Security benefits	$32,000
$34,000	Taxation of up to 85% of Social Security benefits	$44,000

Using an example, table 7-4 illustrates how to apply these income thresholds to calculate taxable Social Security retirement benefits.

Although decisions about retirement should not be based solely on the impact of income taxes, it is imperative to consider the tax ramifications.

TABLE 7-4
Calculating Your Taxable Social Security Benefit Amount

	Example	Your Figures
1. Social Security benefit amount	$12,500	_____
2. Adjusted gross income (excluding Social Security)	36,000	_____
3. Tax-exempt interest (and other excluded income)	6,000	_____
4. One-half of Social Security benefits (from line 1)	6,250	_____
5. Sum of lines 2, 3, and 4 to get provisional income	48,250	_____
6. Threshold amounts: $32,000 (married); $25,000 (single)	32,000	_____
7. Result of subtracting line 6 from line 5	16,250	_____
8. 50% of line 7	8,125	_____
9. Lesser of lines 4 and 8	6,250	_____
10. Enter $6,000 (married); $4,500 (single)	6,000	_____
11. Lesser of lines 9 and 10	6,000	_____
12. 85% of (line 5 minus $44,000 if married) 85% of (line 5 minus $34,000 if single)	3,613	_____
13. Sum of lines 11 and 12	9,613	_____
14. 85% of Social Security benefits (line 1)	10,625	_____
15. Lesser of lines 13 or 14 = taxable benefits	9,613	_____

> **Retirees who wish to reduce the amount of their Social Security benefits subject to income tax can do so by lowering the amount of their income that exceeds the taxation threshold amount.**

When planning, it is necessary to examine all the alternatives. The best choice may be the one that minimizes the retiree's income taxes.

Retirees who wish to reduce the amount of their Social Security benefits subject to income tax can do so by lowering the amount of their income that exceeds the taxation threshold amount. One way to accomplish this is to replace taxable retirement income with tax-free Roth IRA income. Another way is to transfer money from financial products that generate interest or dividends that are currently income taxable (such as CDs) into tax-deferred products (such as deferred annuities).

Inflation

Unlike most other retirement benefits, Social Security benefits are indexed for inflation with an automatic cost-of-living adjustment (COLA). The amount received increases each year based on the economy as measured by the CPI. This means that benefits will not lose buying power over the retirement period.

What is important to remember in retirement planning is that the Social Security benefit amount you are working with today will increase as inflation increases.

Applying for Social Security Retirement Benefits

Your prospects and clients should apply for Social Security retirement benefits about 3 months before they expect to receive them. They can apply at any Social Security office, call Social Security's toll-free number (800-772-1213), or visit its Web site at www.ssa.gov to obtain information about how or where to apply.

Social Security administrators will need some or all of the following from the applicant:

- Social Security number
- birth certificate
- W-2 forms or tax forms
- checking or savings account information for direct deposit
- military discharge papers, if applicable
- divorce documents, if applicable

If a spouse is applying on the worker's work record, Social Security administrators will need the following:

- spouse's birth certificate
- spouse's Social Security number
- copy of the couple's marriage certificate

Distributions from Qualified Retirement Plans

Social Security is a retirement resource that is available to almost all working Americans. Many workers also have retirement plans provided through their employers. The nature and scope of these plans have changed over the years, moving away from those that clearly define the benefits to which a retiree is entitled to those that provide a way for the employee, alone or with contributions from the employer, to accumulate retirement funds.

At retirement, there are two key decisions people must make about their qualified retirement plans:

- when to begin receiving distributions from the plan
- which distribution option best accomplishes individual retirement goals

Defined-Benefit Plans

Defined-benefit plans guarantee a fixed monthly income at retirement. The amount is set by a formula based on salary levels and years of service. The company is obligated to pay benefits even if the plan investments perform poorly. The investment responsibility rests with the employer.

Three elements determine the size of the monthly benefit a retiree receives:

- average salary. The average salary is generally calculated in one of two ways: averaging the worker's salary over his or her entire career with the company, or averaging the final 3 or 5 years of the last 10 years before retirement. The career-average method tends to yield lower payment amounts. The final-average plan pays higher amounts because it emphasizes the worker's final years with the company, usually a time when salary is at its highest.
- years of service. The years of service are the number of years the worker has been employed by the company.
- plan factor or formula. This factor or formula is determined by the plan itself.

Many plans build a Social Security offset into their benefit formula, meaning that employer-paid defined benefits may be reduced depending on how much monthly Social Security retirement benefits the retired worker receives. This is one way that the employer can recoup a portion of its share of the Social Security taxes paid on its workers' behalf.

Unlike Social Security, most pension plans do not provide cost-of-living increases. This means that the retiree receives the same amount for as long as he or she is retired, with inflation eroding its purchasing power. With longer life expectancies, this erosion of purchasing power can become a significant problem in the later stages of retirement.

> Unlike Social Security, most pension plans do not provide cost-of-living increases.

Defined-Contribution Plans

Defined-contribution plans, including profit-sharing plans, employee thrift plans, money purchase plans, stock bonus plans, and employee stock ownership plans, allocate resources to the individual employee's retirement account. This shifts the investment risk from the company to the individual, although in some plans—money purchase plans—the employer controls how the funds are invested.

Under defined-contribution plans, the employee is not guaranteed a fixed amount at retirement. Instead, the employee receives the value of the account at retirement and has to determine how the amount will be allocated. With these plans, the retiree will have to decide how to invest his or her retirement nest egg and when and how to make withdrawals.

Lump Sum or Annuity Payout Options. A choice that many retirees will have to make is whether to receive their retirement benefits in a *lump sum payout* or as an *annuity payout*. The choices available depend on the particular plan and the requirements of law.

lump-sum payout

annuity payout

Traditional tax-qualified retirement plans offer annuity payouts, and some provide a lump-sum option; 401(k) plans offer a lump-sum option but may allow the retiree to keep money in the plan to be paid out over time. One advantage of the annuity option is that it is guaranteed. The retiree does not have to worry about managing the investments and cannot outlive the stream of payments the annuity provides.

Lump-sum payments, on the other hand, offer more flexibility. With a lump-sum payment, the retiree may receive a favorable tax rate, or he or she can defer taxes by rolling the distribution into a traditional IRA. The lump-sum distribution gives the retiree control of investment decisions and, unlike the annuity option, provides funds that can be passed on to children and other heirs.

Another factor to consider: A prerequisite for tax-qualified retirement plans is that benefits be paid as a qualified joint and survivor annuity unless waived by the participant's spouse. This provision protects the spouse from alienation of a participant's retirement benefit. Unless the spouse consents to waive it, he or she is guaranteed a survivor benefit.

Deciding between an annuity and a lump-sum option can be a difficult choice, and it may present an opportunity to suggest that part of a lump-sum distribution be used to purchase an immediate annuity and the remainder transferred into an IRA for future distribution. The annuity will provide a lifelong income, while the IRA will maintain the future distribution flexibility and tax-deferred growth potential of the invested portion.

Annuity Choices. If the retiree selects the annuity option (or purchases an annuity), the retiree still has choices to make. He or she can elect to take a single life annuity, provided the spouse consents, or a joint and survivor annuity.

> **If the retiree outlives his or her spouse, the single life option is the better choice. But if there is a spouse who also depends on the retirement income, the joint and survivor option is generally better.**

The single life option pays the largest available monthly benefit. It continues as long as the retiree lives and then stops when the retiree dies. Retrospectively, if the retiree outlives his or her spouse, this is the better choice. But if there is a spouse who also depends on the retirement income, the joint and survivor option is generally better.

The joint and survivor annuity offers another benefit if the company or pension plan provides for the payment of retirees' medical expense insurance. If the single life annuity option is selected, the spouse's medical expense insurance coverage might end with the retiree's death. In a joint and survivor annuity, the coverage usually continues for the surviving spouse.

In a joint and survivor annuity, the initial amount of the monthly benefit payable to the retiree is reduced. The amount of the initial reduction depends on the amount of survivor benefit the spouse will receive when the retiree dies. Typically, there are two or more levels of benefits to select. In a 50 percent joint and survivor annuity, the spouse receives one-half of the initial benefit the retiree receives. In a 100 percent joint and survivor annuity, the retiree's initial benefit is reduced even more, but the surviving spouse continues to receive the same dollar amount when the retiree dies.

Example: Shawn is 65 years old and about to retire. His wife, Terry, is aged 62. He has the choice of the following monthly payout options from his pension plan:

Options	While Living	After Death
1. Single life annuity	$2,000	$0
2. Joint and 50 percent survivor annuity	$1,500	$750
3. Joint and 100 percent survivor annuity	$1,000	$1,000

Selling/Planning Opportunity—Pension Maximization. Given the facts in the example above, there is a beneficial way for Shawn to take the higher single life annuity and still provide the desired survivorship income for Terry if he dies first. The lost pension income for Shawn between option 1 and options 2 or 3 represents the premium cost of what is, in effect, life insurance protection equivalent to the value of the income stream that will subsequently be paid to Terry at Shawn's death. Furthermore, if Shawn dies first, there is no reversion back to the higher single life payout option.

Another choice for Shawn is the pension maximization strategy. It works this way:

- Shawn chooses a single life annuity for $2,000 per month rather than either the joint and 50 percent or joint and 100 percent survivor annuity. Pension payments do not continue to Terry at Shawn's death. The election of the single life option will require written and notarized permission of the employee's spouse.
- Life insurance is then purchased on Shawn, naming Terry as the beneficiary and their children (or other people to whom Shawn wants to leave money) as contingent beneficiaries. The life insurance face amount is sufficient to safely generate enough monthly income to replace the income that would have been received with either of the joint annuity survivorship options.

As long as the cost of the life insurance is less per month than the amount of income that would have been lost from choosing either option 2 ($500 per month) or option 3 ($1,000 per month), this concept will benefit Shawn and Terry. The life insurance is specifically earmarked to replace the lost survivor payments Shawn forfeited when he selected the single life pension option.

Married senior retiring clients who are considering the election of a single life option need to keep the following in mind:

- The retiring employee must be insurable at affordable rates.
- This option is generally not appropriate if the retiree is in poor health due to high life insurance costs for rated individuals.
- This strategy is generally not appropriate if there is a concern about future household income remaining at levels that are adequate to pay premiums and keep the policy in force.
- This choice is not wise if the difference between the increased payout and the cost of the life insurance actually reduces the married couple's disposable income.
- An employee who wants a form of pension payout other than a joint and survivor annuity must get written consent to the alternative form of payment from his or her spouse because choosing another form of payment could leave the spouse with limited income after the employee's death.
- The surviving spouse will lose the benefit of pension COLAs, if any, payable under the joint and survivor annuity, and he or she may also lose access to retiree health benefits under the employer's plan.

In the example above, if Shawn and Terry die at the same time or if Shawn dies first, children or other contingent beneficiaries will receive the insurance death benefits. If Terry dies first and Shawn does not have any other beneficiaries, he can surrender the policy for its total cash value.

Ten-Year Averaging. For employees who reach age 50 before January 1, 1986 (born before 1936), special 10-year averaging rules may be applicable to lump-sum distributions from qualified plans. The rules are complex and require assistance from a qualified tax advisor. For the purpose of this discussion, suffice it to say that an employee may make the election to take 10-year tax averaging only once, and the election applies to all lump-sum distributions received in that year. (The Internal Revenue Code provisions allowing 5-year forward averaging of lump-sum distributions from qualified plans were repealed for tax years beginning after 1999.)

Required Minimum Distributions

Tax law provisions that affect the timing and amount of distributions from defined-contribution plans, as well as traditional IRAs, are called minimum distribution requirement rules. According to these rules, a 50 percent penalty tax is imposed if certain required minimum distributions (RMDs) are not made from a qualified plan (or traditional IRA) by the required beginning date. The rules say that participants must begin to receive distributions from qualified plans no later than April 1 of the year following that year in which the retiree reaches 70 1/2 years of age.

Example: If Lisa reaches age 70 1/2 during 2006, she may receive a minimum distribution for 2006 during calendar year 2006, or she may delay it until no later than April 1, 2007. If, however, she delays her 2006 distribution until early 2007, she will still also have to receive a minimum distribution for 2007 by December 31, 2007. Thus, if she does not take her first distribution during 2006 and waits until between January 1 and April 1, 2007, to do so, she will have to take two distributions in 2007—one by April 1 (2006's RMD), and another by December 31 (2007's RMD).

Distributions must be paid in either a lump-sum or a series of substantially equal periodic payments based on life expectancy. The RMD for most IRA owners and defined-contribution qualified retirement plans is usually based on a uniform table that reflects the participant's life expectancy. (See appendix D, "Required Minimum Distribution Tables.")

The only exception is when the IRA owner or qualified plan retiree has named a sole beneficiary whose spouse is more than 10 years younger. In this case, RMDs are based on the joint life expectancies of the participant and spouse.

The joint life payouts (see "Joint Life and Last Survivor Expectancy Table" in appendix D) are lower because of longer distribution periods than those provided by the "Uniform Lifetime Table" (see appendix D), which is based on a single life.

Selling/Planning Opportunity. For most individuals, the minimum distribution requirement is not considered a disadvantage. Most people will require at least minimum distributions from their employer-sponsored retirement plans if they are to enjoy the kind of retirement lifestyle they want.

On the other hand, for those relatively few affluent individuals with sufficient retirement resources outside of their employer-sponsored plans, the minimum distribution requirement forces them to lose the benefit of ongoing tax deferral on tax-qualified account balances. For these individuals, there are two benefits associated with ongoing tax deferral.

First, the amount that would have been paid in tax on a current distribution remains invested for the benefit of the participant. Second, the earnings on the qualified retirement plan benefit or traditional IRA, including the amount that would have been paid as income tax, continue to accumulate while avoiding current taxation on earnings and growth. However, everyone with money in either employer qualified retirement plans or traditional IRAs must begin to take distributions after age 70 1/2 or at retirement age, if later, where a covered worker remains employed.

In any event, individuals can avoid RMDs if they take distributions from employer-sponsored qualified retirement plans when separation from employment occurs. This is presumably at full retirement age or earlier for most retirees. If they take distributions at that time, the deferral approach likely to make the most sense is to name the spouse as primary beneficiary in a period-certain annuity distribution equal either to the participant's life expectancy or the joint and last survivor life expectancy of the participant and his or her spouse.

Example: Roy, a 65-year-old retiree, selects a 16-year period-certain annuity. This gives him a guaranteed income for life, but if his death occurs before his life expectancy of about age 81, then payments will continue to his wife for the remainder of the certain period.

Alternatively, Roy could take a lesser payout amount for a longer certain period equal to the life expectancy of his spouse (age 84). On balance, this approach provides the combination of a long deferral period and the greatest flexibility in the event Roy predeceases his spouse.

Furthermore, part of these qualified plan distributions could also be leveraged by directing them to the purchase of life insurance. This gives Roy the opportunity not only to defer receipt of undistributed plan account balances for as long as possible, but also to create tax-free wealth for the benefit of his heirs. Although he will be taxed on distributions from the qualified plan, his beneficiaries will receive the death proceeds of the life insurance Roy purchased income tax free. If ownership is properly arranged, the life insurance may also escape estate taxation.

Rolling the lump-sum qualified plan distribution into an IRA account will avoid current income tax and defer income tax on the growth and appreciation of the funds until RMDs must be taken.

IRA Rollovers. The other option for lump-sum distributions is the IRA rollover or direct transfer. Transferring the lump-sum qualified plan distribution into an IRA account will avoid current income tax and defer income tax on the growth and appreciation of the funds until RMDs must be taken. There is no dollar limit on the amount of money that can be contributed to a rollover IRA.

IRA Management

There are two ways a person can make an IRA rollover. The first is to receive the money from the retirement account and deposit it into the new account. This is risky and can lead to tax penalties.

As we discussed in chapter 6, the way to avoid this problem is to use the second rollover technique—the direct rollover or transfer. In a direct rollover, the retirement plan trustee sends the money directly to the IRA. In a direct rollover or transfer, no withholding is required.

Taxation of IRA Distributions. Withdrawals from traditional IRAs are treated as taxable ordinary income to the extent that they were never taxed previously. There is also a 10 percent penalty for withdrawing funds from a traditional IRA prior to reaching age 59 1/2 unless the withdrawal satisfies one of the eight exceptions noted in chapter 6. Distributions from a Roth IRA are generally considered to be income tax free to the extent of new contributions and qualified distributions, which are made from earnings in accounts that have been in existence for at least 5 years. ◊

WORKING WITH RETIRING EMPLOYEES

Working plays a central role in most people's lives. It provides more than salaries and benefits. A person's occupation fills his or her time and gives structure and meaning to life. Indeed, many people identify themselves in terms of their career.

Working outside of the home has a social dimension that goes beyond the status of job positions or titles. Few people want their jobs to be their entire social life. But none would deny that their work is part of it.

Many individuals go to the workplace where they are part of teams, departments, and divisions. Within the workplace society, they may identify themselves as members of one of these groups. On the other hand, some workers are independent of their workplace. For example, some financial advisors are independent contractors who may have offices without staff. For this type of worker, clients form the society in which they work.

Fortunately, many people enjoy their work. They find it challenging and stimulating, filled with opportunities to learn and grow and contribute. In return, they are paid and their salaries provide for their own well-being, as well as that of their families. In the process of working, most people gain a sense of self-worth.

Retirement—When Work Ends

Some people retire from work because they want to. Others do so involuntarily. Whether they want to retire or not, many of your prospects and clients may be somewhat anxious about the transition into retirement. Because of the value of their work, some clients may find it difficult to leave it.

For many people, retirement is disorienting. Even the process of planning for retirement may cause concern. There are at least three reasons why this may be true:

- Retirement means change—psychological, social, and financial change.
- Retirement moves individuals from the known and familiar to the unknown and unfamiliar.
- Retirement may evoke a sense of loss.

Changes Surrounding Retirement

> Retirement is not a sole event. It is a series of changes and transitions that move individuals into new lifestyles.

Retirement is not a sole event. It is a series of changes and transitions that move individuals into new lifestyles. It does not cause one single effect or a narrow range of effects. It effects change in every aspect of an individual's life.

Many of your prospects and clients start dealing with retirement issues years before they actually retire. Thus, some of them will be more prepared for the change than others. But when it comes time, few will be fully ready.

Psychological Changes. Most people resist change. Change is uncomfortable. But even though change is not easy, it offers opportunities. When change is imminent, however, it is often difficult to see the opportunities.

To many people, retirement implies inactivity, with no compensation and intangible outcomes. For some people, self-esteem and pride wane. For others, values, expertise, and relationships change. In 1975, sociologist Robert Atchley identified four phases of retirement, which can be summarized as follows:

- honeymoon. A state of euphoria occurs, with a testing of fantasies.
- disenchantment. There is boredom, depression, and a general let-down.
- reorientation. The person explores a more realistic and satisfactory lifestyle.
- stability. Activities become a more important part of the individual's daily life and routine.

> The more prepared an individual is for retirement, the less likely he or she is to become disenchanted.

Preparation and planning for change play an important role in the smooth, steady transition from one phase of an individual's life into another one. Most individuals are unable to prepare for retirement as completely as they would like. Yet the more prepared an individual is, the less likely he or she is to become disenchanted.

Social Change. Work is part of the socialization process. It gives individuals a reason to go out into the world each day and mix with other individuals of all ages and socioeconomic groups. Although your prospects and clients may look forward to a change of pace or more leisure in retirement, they are also likely to experience a series of social changes.

A person's social status may be indirectly tied to the work he or she does. People tend to associate with others who have similar interests and experiences. It is not uncommon for people to socialize with their work colleagues. At the very least, people often mix with others at similar levels of employment or in similar careers. For example, executives frequently play golf with other executives.

In retirement, the rules may change somewhat. The shared interest may no longer be work or career—it may be retirement. In the early retirement years, there may be little dramatic change in a person's social life. As the retiree's interests change, however, his or her social group may also change. Over time, a retired person's social status may become based on his or her health or financial situation.

> Having enough money is often the key to a secure retirement. In other words, retirement has a dollars-and-cents impact.

Financial Change. As their retirement dates approach, most of your prospects and clients are likely to have concerns over financial security during retirement. Their concerns may be exacerbated by media coverage of inflation, health care needs, and proposed Social Security legislative changes.

Although people work for many reasons, money is often the primary motivator. Achieving a happy retirement can be complicated. But having enough money is often the key to a secure retirement. In other words, retirement has a dollars-and-cents impact.

Although it may be obvious to you, some of your prospects and clients may not link the concepts of working, money, and retirement until it is time to retire. At that time, they may be in good health and working at their peak. When they stop working, their salaries stop. They must then depend on Social Security and the planning they have done to cover the 20 or more years they may spend in retirement.

Individuals who have planned and saved adequately may be concerned that they have not saved enough. Those who have not properly planned and adequately saved may feel that they have no choice but to continue working.

The Unfamiliar and Unknown

Even individuals who are financially prepared are sometimes anxious about retirement because they do not really know what to expect. In reality, your prospects and clients may have only limited control over what will change. But it is as unlikely that everything will change as it is that everything will stay the same. What most of your clients have in common is the knowledge that reality is often very different from their expectations.

Some of your prospects and clients have an idealized picture of retirement. They may visualize extended vacations, pleasant retirement communities, or days filled with the activities they could not pursue when they were busy working. Others have a very different concern about retirement. They fear that they may be alone and lonely, spending hours and days in boredom in the final stage of life.

A Sense of Loss

After long years of work, personal productivity, and growth, some of your prospects and clients may experience a sense of loss in retirement. They may feel they are losing their purpose, identity, and prestige. For this reason, some prefer to phase out of work.

Part-time work allows an individual to phase in retirement, but part-time work may not provide enough income to meet financial needs. There may also be penalties for working after Social Security benefits and pension payments begin if a retiree is under full retirement age.

In the past, retirement was often thought of as the end of an individual's productive years. In part, that notion was true. Average life expectancy in the 1940s, for example, was less than 70 years. No one thought of retiring before age 65, and most workers lived less than 5 years after retiring. Even though times were relatively harsher, planning for 5 years was comparatively simple.

Today, the average span of time spent in retirement has changed. Retiring at age 65 is no longer the norm, and most retirees can expect to live well beyond age 70. Planning is much more complex. If for no other reason, individuals must plan for retirement to be a much longer period of time.

Employer's Perspective

One of the reasons that retirement has changed is that the workplace has changed. Changing technologies and changing economies have caused employers to restructure their work forces. Companies try to cut costs by trimming what they consider to be excess workers and layers of management.

Companies continue to downsize and tend to rely on outsourcing—using more consultants and part-time or temporary workers as they ease out older and usually higher paid workers. To avoid layoffs, many employers encourage workers to leave voluntarily through retirement incentive programs. Your prospects and clients may not plan to retire early, but they may be surprised with the incentives contained in an early retirement offer.

Worker's Perspective

Corporate restructurings force many people to make changes. People who lose their jobs as the result of a restructuring have no choice but to find another job, work for themselves, or retire. Even individuals who survive a restructuring often choose to leave the employer. Retiring early, however, causes the total cost of funding retirement to rise sharply.

> An individual who works for four different employers for 10 years each will receive roughly half the pension of a person who works for the same employer for 40 years.

Today, people are changing jobs more often than they did in the past. But there are risks involved with changing jobs frequently. One consequence of changing jobs is that employees may have fewer opportunities to build stakes in traditional defined-benefit qualified retirement plans.

According to The *Wall Street Journal Guide to Understanding Personal Finance*, an individual who works for four different employers for 10 years each will receive roughly half the pension of a person who works for the same employer for 40 years. Today, many employees do not have the option of working for the same employer until retirement.

Working during Retirement

Whether there is a need to supplement income or a need to phase in retirement, some of your prospects and clients will continue to work during retirement. Some older workers who are financially unable to retire comfortably will be forced into second careers or self-employment. Others will see working during retirement as an opportunity.

For those who can work, there may be several options, including the following:

- working as an independent contractor for the old company or for a new one
- working part-time or seasonally
- being self-employed
- changing careers

Each option has advantages and disadvantages that the retiring employee must consider. In general, however, there is employment opportunity for retired workers. According to the U.S. Bureau of Labor Statistics, in 2004, of the nearly 25 million Americans who worked outside of their homes on a part-time basis, slightly more than 5 million were aged 55 or older.

Unless working during retirement is planned carefully, however, it may cause problems involving the reduction of Social Security retirement benefits or the income taxation of those benefits. In addition, not everyone who wants to work can work. Some people cannot find jobs. To some extent, there is a negative perception about older workers. Although federal and state laws prohibit age discrimination, some employers feel that older workers lack technical skills. Other employers are concerned that older workers will be absent more often because of chronic health problems.

The Advisor's Role

The retirement planning market has been evolving, increasing in size and longevity, and developing new needs for your financial products and services.

Baby boomers will begin to turn age 65 in the year 2011. If you have not had the opportunity to work with retiring employees, the chances are good that you soon will.

How will you respond to them when they ask for your financial advice and services? Your response depends, to some degree, on whether the retiring employee is a client or a prospect. If you are working with a client with whom you have an ongoing relationship, you will have the opportunity to reinforce and refine the planning you have already done.

A new prospect may be more of a challenge. Your first hurdle is to establish your credibility. This statement may seem simplistic. After all, you must establish credibility with all of your prospects or they will not become your clients. But think about what you have just read. You will be approaching a retiring prospect at a time when a great change is about to happen—a change that will affect the rest of the prospect's life.

In some measure, your success in establishing credibility depends on your prospects' perception of you. If you are young, your prospects may think that you do not have enough experience or knowledge. If you are more mature or near your retiring prospect's age, he or she may be concerned that you will have retired when your assistance is most needed.

Selling yourself as a viable financial advisor may mean turning adversity into advantage. For example, if you are a younger advisor, you may point out to retiring prospects that you will be working for them for years to come. On the other hand, if you are more mature, you may stress your experience, and focus on your ability to understand retirees' needs and empathize with them.

Whether you are working with your existing clients or new prospects who are retiring, there are some points to remember:

- Keep an open mind—be objective.
- Empathize but don't sympathize. Remember that your prospect is facing a major life event.
- Retirement affects your prospect's spouse as well as your prospect. Involve them both in the planning process.
- Get the facts about your prospect's financial situation.
- Understand the prospect's feelings—listen carefully for concerns as well as hopes and dreams.
- Assess the prospect's situation carefully.
- Make recommendations that will help your prospect achieve his or her goals.
- Know when to seek the help of a more experienced or specialized advisor.

Also, do not forget to review your clients' insurance needs. There is no better time to review their life, medical expense, and long-term care insurance

---

Helpful Resources for Retirement Planning

The following resources may be helpful for you and your clients:

- The Social Security Administration has offices across the country. *Understanding Social Security and Retirement* is a booklet that is available upon request. You can also obtain information toll-free at 800-772-1213 or via the Internet at www.ssa.gov.
- The Centers for Medicare and Medicaid Services (CMS) is part of the Department of Health and Human Services. You can get information about Medicare, medigap, Medicaid, and other health-related issues. Call 1-410-786-3000 or visit the Web site at www.cms.hhs.gov.
- The Medicare Hotline is operated by the CMS. Call toll-free at 800-638-6833. For Medicare publications, call 800-633-4227 or 800-MEDICARE, or visit the Web site at www.Medicare.gov.
- The American Association of Retired Persons (AARP) is a consumer advocacy group offering printed material on retirement. Call toll-free at 800-424-3410, or visit the Web site at www.AARP.org.

---

protection needs than when your clients are facing change. You will want to make sure not only that adequate insurance coverage is in place, but also that beneficiary designations on life insurance and annuity policies are current. ◊

POSTRETIREMENT SAVING AND INVESTING STRATEGIES

> Retirement planning is a continual process. However, the planning perspective is usually different in the years before retirement from what it is after retirement occurs.

The decision to retire does not mean that people should stop planning. On the contrary, although the strategies employed after retirement may differ, they are no less important than those you suggest to your prospects and clients who are planning and saving prior to retirement. For your clients to achieve financial success in retirement, it has to be planned. Retirement planning is a continual process. However, the planning perspective is usually different in the years before retirement from what it is after retirement occurs.

Preretirement Mentality

In retirement planning, there are not only financial considerations but also dynamic psychosocial factors. When preretirees are younger and beginning their careers in their 20s and 30s, they tend to see retirement as a remote, elusive concept that they will probably have to deal with someday. These workers are much too busy climbing corporate ladders, establishing their own businesses, and starting their families to give the illusory concept of retirement too much thought or to allocate too many financial resources to it. They may begin investing in an IRA or contributing to a matching 401(k) program with their employer, often simply because their parents, friends, or a respected role model told them it was a good idea. When workers are very young, their investment strategies are often characterized by sporadic contributions, premature distributions for current expenditures or speculative financial opportunities, and portfolios of investments that display a very high risk tolerance due to the long time horizon before these workers will need their nest egg.

As people enter their 40s and 50s, however, retirement takes on a much higher priority. The picture of retirement begins to crystallize in their minds as the possibility of living to old age becomes more real to them. It is during this period of life (usually between ages 40 and 60 or 65) that workers are demographically classified as preretirees. There is a growing concern about their future well-being beyond their working years. Many people become obsessed with the need to accumulate enough money to maintain their lifestyle during their retirement years. Accordingly, they begin to devote greater resources to their qualified and nonqualified retirement plans, despite their contemporary financial obligations such as education funding for their children, long-term care funding for their parents, and their own personal living expenses. Their sense of urgency regarding retirement funding is typically at its peak during these middle years.

> As people enter their 40s and 50s, the picture of retirement begins to crystallize as the possibility of living to old age becomes more real.

preretirement mentality

This *preretirement mentality* is driven by the need to ensure a comfortable and financially secure retirement. Financial planning goals are geared toward amassing a large sum of money in an effort to allay the increasing fear of financial destitution in old age. However, preretirees have the advantage of having time on their side. They can, therefore, recover from potentially bad investment decisions due to overaggressive risk taking. They show less concern about stock market downturns and have a more risk-tolerant investment attitude because of the luxury of longer time horizons.

Their mind-set is in sharp contrast to the postretirement mentality discussed below. Postretirement investment objectives have to be much more carefully balanced and monitored in order not to subject retirees to undue risk.

Postretirement Financial Concerns

> The major concern in postretirement is not how full the retirement moneybag has become but rather that the bag never becomes empty.

Not all of your prospects will be comfortable with their financial outlook during retirement. The major concern in postretirement is not how full the retirement moneybag has become but rather that the bag never becomes empty. This paradigm shift often arises from the insecurity about becoming poor. This fear, like many others, may have little rational basis. Nonetheless, after 40 working years of conditioning to be thrifty and to put something away for tomorrow, it is difficult to overcome this tendency during retirement. Some retirees, no matter how much money they have accumulated for retirement, are concerned that they cannot properly enjoy it for fear of exhausting the funds before they die. Retirees may deprive themselves of modest luxuries and reasonable indulgences even if they can actually afford them. This concept can be referred to as the *postretirement mentality syndrome.* This may explain why some retirees whom we might consider well-to-do take part-time jobs to bolster their incomes. Although you can attempt to

postretirement mentality syndrome

alleviate clients' feelings of financial insecurity during retirement, you must also be sensitive to their reality.

Running Out of Money

You may also encounter retired people who have simply not planned as well as they should have and are looking for ways to protect their limited resources. Prospects or clients who feel they are running out of money may be overly anxious about downturns in the stock market. Even small stock market fluctuations may cause them to worry about maintaining their lifestyle.

The best advice you can offer is not to panic. Although they may not be able to maintain their current lifestyles, they still have Social Security; it has been the financial safety net since its inception. Even though future Social Security is increasingly perceived to be potentially less reliable than it once was, it is generally believed that it will continue to be there for baby boomers, albeit with possibly lower benefits than their predecessors have enjoyed. Therefore, careful planning is essential. A person who is running out of money cannot afford to make mistakes.

Planning Considerations and Strategies

Options for Retired Homeowners

Retirees should not overlook the planning opportunities inherent in home ownership. For retired homeowners who are running out of money, there are at least five other strategies to consider:

- selling the home
- trading down to a smaller home
- refinancing a home mortgage at a more favorable interest rate
- taking a home-equity loan
- obtaining a reverse mortgage

The advantage of any of these strategies is that homeowners can free up some of the equity in their homes and allocate the money to income.

A disadvantage of selling or trading down is that it is disruptive. It may be difficult for an older client who has lived in the same home for many years to think of selling and moving. Another disadvantage of selling a home is that it does not completely solve the problem. The retiree still needs a place to live. A disadvantage of trading down to a smaller home is that there are commissions to be paid on the home that is sold and closing costs to be paid on the new home. In addition, tax may be due on any gain from the sale of a high-priced home.

There may be some merit to the idea of refinancing an existing mortgage if the interest rate can be reduced to free up enough additional monthly cash flow to make it worthwhile. This would assume that your retired client has a mortgage on the house, and that the interest rate is higher than what he or she could obtain currently. It would also make sense for the client to stay in the house long enough after the refinancing to recover the closing costs associated with refinancing.

Although home equity loans and reverse mortgages allow retirees to remain in their homes, these strategies have some disadvantages. Home-equity loans must be repaid. Although the loan proceeds can be used as income, the repayments are an expense against the income. There is also a limitation on the amount of home-equity loan interest that can be deducted for income tax purposes.

With a reverse mortgage, nothing has to be repaid until the homeowner moves out of the home or dies. The home is the only security for the loan. The amount owed is the loan balance or the value of the home, whichever is less. A disadvantage of a reverse mortgage is that there are sizable transaction costs.

Balancing Investment Return with Safety of Principal

Retirees and those nearing retirement should strive to protect themselves against downturns in the financial markets. A good planning strategy balances the desire for investment return with the need for security of principal. There are a number of ways to achieve balance, including portfolio diversification, tax planning, and holding bonds and CDs with varying maturity dates.

Portfolio Diversification. Portfolio diversification among market sectors and across types of investment products, such as stocks, bonds, and fixed-interest-rate vehicles, can minimize market risk for your clients. By maintaining a diversified investment portfolio, an investor can achieve a greater overall return in the long run, as opposed to having all his or her funds in a single financial vehicle such as a passbook savings account. Some fixed-rate funds are fine; bonds or bond mutual funds usually offer a higher rate of return or income in exchange for some additional risk. Equity funds or stocks are even riskier, but they offer the potential for growth or appreciation of principal.

Tax Planning. Another strategy that allows your clients to achieve balance is to allocate savings and investments in both tax-advantaged plans and fully taxable vehicles. This approach balances the impact of taxation during the accumulation years and at retirement. For example, many of your younger prospects and clients may be participating in qualified retirement plans and purchasing nonqualified mutual funds. Taxes are deferred on contributions to qualified retirement plans until funds are withdrawn, but taxes are due each year on the nonqualified mutual fund dividend earnings. On the other hand, withdrawals from Roth IRAs or life insurance cash values, if engineered properly, can totally escape income taxation during retirement years.

Varying Maturity Dates. It is a good idea to vary maturity dates on bonds and CDs. This strategy keeps some money available that is not subject to early withdrawal penalties. When purchasing bonds, for example, your prospects and clients might consider 5-, 7-, and 10-year maturities. The disadvantage to purchasing longer-term vehicles is that they are most vulnerable to inflation risk. If your client purchases a long-term bond at a low rate and bond rates begin to increase, he or she is locked into the low rate or may have to take a loss on the sale of the bond. Mixing maturity periods reduces this risk.

The same line of thinking applies to certificates of deposit. Although CDs with longer terms pay higher rates of interest, they are subject to inflation risk. Short-term CDs pay less interest, but the trade-off is that they mature more frequently, which makes them more liquid. When investing in CDs, it is wise to mix maturity terms to take advantage of higher rates of interest on some of the CDs while making part of the CD portfolio more frequently renewable, thus avoiding early surrender penalties. Your clients may want to consider combining CDs with 6-month, 1-year, and 3- to 5-year maturities.

Addressing Client Concerns about Market Downturns

Retirees and people approaching retirement need to feel confident that they can withstand extended stock market downturns before they are willing to take risks. It may take retirees or preretirees longer than your younger clients to recover from downturns in the stock market. This is because older clients may no longer be contributing to their retirement nest eggs, which would allow them to use dollar cost averaging as an investment strategy. Instead, they may be living on interest and dividends from their accumulations or even depleting some of their principal.

> **Even your most confident clients will tend to worry when they see downturns in the stock market.**

Even your most confident clients will tend to worry when they see downturns in the stock market. They may call you for advice when they see unfavorable fluctuations. The most practical advice, of course, is, "Don't panic. Downturns are a natural event in the stock market."

It is generally recognized that people become more cautious as they age. Traditionally, prospects and clients have been advised to approach investing conservatively as they near retirement. Years of bull markets, especially in the mid- to late 1990s, however, encouraged some older people to be more aggressive in their investments. Some advisors suggest that older investors put their money in a wide range of investments, including such vehicles as aggressive growth funds and technology stocks. However, in the aftermath of the 3-year stock market downturn beginning in April 2000 and the recession of 2001–2002, conventional investing wisdom has once again dominated investing strategies, especially for retirees.

If a concerned client calls you during a market downturn, you may want to schedule an appointment to review his or her investing and saving strategies. Concern over market downturns may indicate that your client is growing less

tolerant to risk and is worried that his or her savings or investment v
too risky. You and your client should give careful consideration to r
retirement assets to investment sectors and vehicles that will accommodate the
client's changing investment objectives.

Use of Annuities

Annuity products offer advantages that make them attractive financial
vehicles for more conservative investors. Immediate annuities can help alleviate the retiree's fear of running out of money. Immediate-annuity buyers
generally purchase them for one obvious financial reason: to provide
guaranteed income in retirement.

Besides income tax deferral, one advantage of deferred annuities is their
potential for guaranteed income at annuitization that cannot be outlived.
Another advantage is the death benefit—a feature that is often undersold,
especially with deferred annuities. Even with variable deferred annuities, the
inherent guarantees are what make an annuity an insurance product, rather
than a pure investment vehicle.

Basically, the fixed-interest, indexed, or variable deferred annuity death
benefit almost always pays survivors no less than the money invested in the
contract during the annuity's accumulation phase, less any money withdrawn
prior to death.

Example: If Sam places $100,000 in a variable deferred annuity
and dies some years later before annuitizing the
contract, his survivors will receive $100,000 even if
the stock market has tumbled and the value in the
contract is less than his original deposit.

The annuity death benefit varies from company to company. It is
important for you to understand any limitations that your company's
products place on this benefit. For example, your company's contract may
state that the guaranteed annuity death benefit expires when the annuity
holder reaches age 75 or 80.

Keep in mind that the annuity death benefit is a feature that is in force
during the accumulation phase of the annuity. Once the annuity holder begins
to receive payments from the annuity in the form of settlement options, the
lump-sum death benefit no longer applies.

Role of Life Insurance in Retirement Planning

Life insurance protects against the financial effects caused by death.
Adequate life insurance completes and enhances any financial plan because it

removes some uncertainty about the future. In effect, life insurance provides a contingency plan by performing several postretirement strategic functions.

Retirement Insurance. During the accumulation years, life insurance proceeds can be used to replace income, make mortgage payments, and educate children. Also, beneficiaries can use life insurance to ensure that the projected retirement nest egg that a worker aspires to accumulate will be available for the family during his or her retirement years, even if he or she becomes disabled or dies.

Asset Insurance. The need for life insurance does not go away when your clients retire. Rather, adequate life insurance should be an important part of any postretirement plan for many of the same reasons that it is important during the accumulation years. Adequate life insurance in place during retirement can free retirees to consume and enjoy (without guilt or remorse) more of those liquid assets that they might otherwise have been reluctant or unwilling to spend because the assets were earmarked as a financial legacy for their heirs. In other words, life insurance purchased before retirement is the most cost-effective method to provide legacy dollars for heirs and to enhance retirees' enjoyment of their own retirement assets by permitting them to spend down more of their nest egg without inadvertently disinheriting any heirs.

> **Adequate life insurance should be a part of any postretirement plan for many of the same reasons that it is important during the accumulation years.**

Supplemental Life Insurance Retirement Proceeds (SLIRP). Permanent life insurance that was purchased at younger ages and consistently paid for can provide a source of tax-free withdrawals of cash values (or dividends) up to the policy's cost basis. This is because of the first-in first-out method to determine income taxation. These withdrawals can provide valuable supplemental income to enhance a retiree's lifestyle.

Furthermore, in some situations, it may make sense not only to withdraw the cash values free of income taxation up to the policy's cost basis, but also to borrow carefully from funds remaining in the policy once the cost basis is exhausted. Loans withdrawn from policies that are not modified endowment contracts can be taken on an income-tax-free basis. Many universal life insurance policies sold today provide that after they have been in force for 10 or 15 years, the interest rate credited to outstanding loans equals the interest rate charged for the loan. This "interest-free spread" on outstanding loans makes these universal life insurance contracts ideal for applying the SLIRP concept to them as a retirement income supplement to pension and Social Security income.

Important note: It is essential to exercise extreme caution when taking loans from whole life insurance policies to supplement retirement income. First of all, the death benefit will be reduced. Second, the cash values may become exhausted because of compounding interest on outstanding loans that probably will not be paid back. Also, in whole life insurance policies with variable loan interest rates, it is impossible to predict the impact of future loans on the policy's net death benefit as interest rates fluctuate. Furthermore, if the policy exhausts itself of cash values and lapses before the owner-insured dies, all outstanding loan proceeds that are considered to be a reduction in cost basis could trigger a large unwanted taxable income event. It is prudent to check with your company regarding the use of this strategy and to ensure that your clients receive proper disclosure of the tax laws and risks relevant to this procedure.

Life Insurance Settlement Options. It is a well-known fact that the proceeds from life insurance can be used to replace incomes when one spouse dies, to make mortgage payments, to educate children or grandchildren, and to pay final death and estate tax expenses.

However, one of the most overlooked features of life insurance is that it gives the policyowner or the beneficiary the flexibility to elect when and how proceeds will be paid. The choice of how to use the proceeds can be made by the policyowner during lifetime, or the policyowner can leave the choice to the beneficiary.

life insurance settlement options

Generally, the following *life insurance settlement options* are available:

- Proceeds can be paid as a lump sum to a designated beneficiary.
- Policy proceeds can be left with the insurance company to earn interest.
- Proceeds can be paid in installments for a fixed period of time.
- Proceeds can be paid in installments of a specified fixed amount until the proceeds are exhausted.
- Policy proceeds can be paid in installments that are guaranteed to last for the life of the beneficiary.

Do not take these options for granted. They have significant implications for the planning process. Planning implies making assumptions about future events. But there is no certainty that anything will work as planned. Life insurance settlement options add flexibility to your clients' retirement plans. They allow for choices to be made when clients' needs change.

lump-sum option

Lump-Sum Option. According to the American Council of Life Insurance, most life insurance proceeds are paid to family members under the lump-sum option. One obvious reason to select this option is to satisfy the need for a large amount of money to cover final expenses or pay off a mortgage.

Some beneficiaries do not need all of the proceeds at one time but believe they can manage and invest the money better themselves. They may be able to earn a higher rate of interest than the insurance company is paying, or they may feel they have greater control if the proceeds are distributed. In either of these situations, you have an opportunity to suggest the purchase of annuities or mutual funds.

Other beneficiaries have little or no experience managing money, or they have little or no desire to do it. For these beneficiaries, leaving the proceeds at interest or selecting one of the installment options may be appropriate.

interest option

> Leaving policy proceeds with the insurance company at interest is the simplest and most flexible settlement option.

Interest Option. Leaving policy proceeds with the insurance company at interest is the simplest and most flexible settlement option. The insurance company pays interest on the proceeds that remain intact. The beneficiary may be given varying degrees of control over the disposition of the proceeds—from no control to full control. Usually, insurers pay interest to the beneficiary at least annually. The interest may be used as part of the beneficiary's income.

Choosing the interest option postpones the distribution of proceeds. Many companies will allow proceeds to be left under the interest option for the life of the primary beneficiary or for 30 years, whichever is longer. At some point, however, proceeds must be paid under one of the liquidating options.

The interest option allows you and your client to consider many applications during the planning process. For example, a policyowner may select this option to provide income for his or her beneficiary. Or beneficiaries may select this option until they determine how they want the proceeds to be distributed. In the interim, the beneficiary receives interest payments that may be used to supplement his or her other income.

fixed-period option

Fixed-Period Option. The fixed-period option is appropriate for a beneficiary who needs income over a specified period of time, such as 10 or 15 years.

Proceeds are liquidated at a uniform rate over the specified number of years. The amount of each annual payment is the present value of annual payments due at the beginning of the year. Because the period is fixed, any variations, such as dividend accumulations, paid-up additions, or outstanding loans, increase or decrease the amount of the payments.

fixed-amount option

Fixed-Amount Option. If the beneficiary's need is for temporary but adequate income without regard to how long the payments last, the fixed-amount option is appropriate. In simplest terms, the amount selected is paid until the proceeds are exhausted.

Mathematically, this option is similar to the fixed-period option. That is, it is based on the present value of annual payments made at the beginning of the year. What differs is that the amount of the payment is known and the length of time that payments will be made must be calculated. Under this option, the payment amount is fixed. Any interest or earnings variations lengthen or shorten the time over which the payments will be made.

life income options

Life Income Options. Life income options protect the beneficiary against the possibility of outliving his or her income. The proceeds are liquidated over the life of the beneficiary.

As you might expect, these options are the least flexible. The annuity concept is applied to the proceeds to calculate the benefit. There are many variations, just as there are many variations in immediate annuities. In addition, payments may be based on one, two, or more lives. Benefits depend on the age and gender of the beneficiary or beneficiaries. Once payments begin, no changes can be made.

The Advisor's Role. Many advisors mention the settlement options but fail to explain how they work or what a valuable and flexible planning tool they are. As you and your clients plan for retirement and review their life insurance needs, you may want to spend a little more time explaining the settlement options so that clients can see how their life insurance continues to be a valuable asset during their retirement years. ◊

RETIREMENT PLANNING PROCESS REVISITED

Planning for a successful retirement requires making appropriate decisions before and during retirement. The first step in effective decision making is analyzing needs and evaluating options that will meet the needs. You can help your clients at retirement just as you would during the years they were saving and planning for retirement.

As we discussed in chapter 3, a thorough fact finding interview will help you learn how much income your prospect will need during retirement and how long it must last. During the fact finding interview, you can assess risk tolerance and review risk management strategies. Your review should include determining if adequate life and disability income insurance is in force. Without a firm foundation on which to stand, any retirement plan could be rendered useless.

> **Without a firm foundation on which to stand, any retirement plan could be rendered useless.**

During the fact finding interview, you should also determine what your prospects want to pass on to their heirs. Retirement planning naturally leads to estate planning, which is discussed in chapter 8. The assets that are not consumed during retirement may be left to heirs.

Many of the choices that individuals face at retirement are confusing. This is where you can be of real service. By explaining their options, you can help your prospects and clients make informed decisions. But your role may go beyond simply explaining options. Integrating the timing of the distribution of assets at retirement with the need to conserve enough of them to live on requires an understanding of your prospects' and clients' retirement goals as well as the financial resources available to them. Asset distribution planning during retirement will have a direct effect on an individual's wealth transfer plans after death.

Preparing for Your Presentation

Once you have gathered all the information you need, you must analyze it, develop your recommendations, and present them in a way that makes sense for your prospects. Developing recommendations requires you to draw on your knowledge of insurance, retirement, and estate planning. It may also require the involvement of other members of the professional team of advisors. If you are working with a team, as you often will be, you will develop recommendations jointly. If you are new to the retirement planning market, you may want to enlist the help of an experienced advisor, a member of your management team, or someone from your home office's advanced underwriting department to discuss the case with you.

Steps to Develop Retirement Planning Solutions

This seven-step procedure will help you organize the material you have gathered about the prospect:

- List and value assets and cash flow.
- Identify goals and objectives.
- Prioritize the goals and objectives.
- Assess the current retirement plan.
- Outline recommendations.
- Compare the current and recommended plan.
- Develop an implementation plan.

List and Value Assets and Cash Flow. From the information you gathered in the fact finding process, list all the prospect's assets. Divide the assets into categories. Compare them to existing liabilities to arrive at a picture of the prospect's current net worth. Use the income statement to evaluate potential cash flow management opportunities. This will help you identify budgetary changes that may be advantageous for your prospect and can be used for proposed retirement planning recommendations.

Identify Goals and Objectives. For the retirement plan to be meaningful, it has to incorporate the prospect's goals and objectives. In other words, what did your client say he or she wishes to achieve in the retirement planning process? To help your prospect focus on these goals objectives, it can be useful to arrange them into the following categories:

- investment management
- retirement income
- income tax planning strategies
- asset distribution strategies
- retirement plan administration

Prioritize the Goals and Objectives. After you identify your prospect's goals and objectives in the fact finding interview, have the prospect rank them by order of importance. Then list your ideas for potential solutions to each one.

Assess the Current Retirement Plan. Once you have ident
assets, listed and prioritized the major goals and objectives, and d
ideas for potential solutions, you need to assess the prospect's ......
retirement plan that you determined during the fact finding process. You will
want to include the impact of Social Security and qualified plan benefits, in
addition to any other savings, investment, and insurance resources to
determine where the current plan falls short. This step may pinpoint the need
for additional investment and insurance products to close the prospect's
potential retirement income gap.

The computer software your company provides or that is available
through private vendors can perform the complicated projections that
calculate and quantify specific shortfalls, often with printouts of the results to
show where additional investments or insurance products are needed, and
how they may fit into the prospect's retirement plan. Often, these programs
include financial product sales illustrations to support the recommendations
you make. These illustrations, of course, become part of your presentation.

The basic presentation, however, should be simple and to the point,
focusing on the prospect's objectives and moving through a logical sequence
from the recommendations to plan implementation.

Outline Recommendations. Based on the differences between the prospect's current plan and his or her future retirement planning goals and
objectives, summarize your recommendations. A single recommendation will
often deal with more than one objective. Writing a will, for example, addresses
distribution, administration, and asset management objectives, just as purchasing additional life insurance addresses both retirement income and tax planning
strategies.

Compare the Current and Recommended Plan. After you have developed
your recommendations, you should re-compute your projections and incorporate them into the plan. This will show your prospect the impact of your
recommendations and how they can help achieve the prospect's objectives.

Develop an Implementation Plan. The final step in determining retirement
plan solutions is to develop an action plan for the implementation of your
recommendations now and in the future. The plan should outline all the steps
needed to implement the plan, identify the people who need to be involved,
ascertain who is responsible for each component of the plan's implementation,
and determine a time line for accomplishing each step.

Delivering Your Presentation

No matter how well you have prepared or how good your recommendations are, presenting them to your prospect is still the critical element. Even

Advisors sometimes
make the mistake
of believing that the
mere logic of their
recommendations will
motivate the prospect
to act.

good recommendations will not sell themselves, and advisors sometimes make the mistake of believing that the mere logic of their recommendations will motivate the prospect to act. This is not the case. At some point in the process, you will have to encourage the prospect to take action by asking him or her to purchase the financial products necessary to implement the plan.

It is a mistake, too, to think that the presentation is an education in the legal and tax implications of retirement planning. This is also not the primary goal. Like any other sale, the retirement planning sale must focus on the features and benefits of the recommendations. This is especially true when life insurance is one of the recommendations.

A retirement planning presentation is no different from any other sales presentation you make. Although it is based on investment concepts, tax savings, and insurance products, it is the benefits they provide to the prospect that make the sale. Focus your presentation on the emotional and monetary benefits the plan offers your prospects and their families. When you recommend the purchase of a financial product, remember that the prospect's trust in you as a financial advisor is paramount.

Retirement planning presentations that get prospects to say "yes" focus on their prioritized needs and communicate effectively how the recommendations benefit them by meeting those needs. You must translate recommendations into tangible benefits.

Make Your Recommendations

Having set the stage, you are now ready to present your recommendations. Including them as part of your written presentation gives you an outline to follow as you discuss each recommendation with the prospect. Ideally, there should be a recommended solution for each of the prospect's objectives.

Begin with recommendations that are the easiest to implement. This entails the prospect's taking action in incremental steps, which are more palatable to most people, and it facilitates the prospect's acceptance of you in the context of a client-advisor relationship.

Outline the Implementation Plan

Persuading a prospect
to accept your
recommendations
and commit to
taking the first steps
in a comprehensive
retirement plan is
the primary goal of
the presentation.

Finally, the implementation plan offers a means to review your recommendations while giving the prospect the steps necessary to act on those recommendations. The plan should identify who is responsible for implementing each step and establish a deadline for its completion.

As with any sales interview, you want to present your plan in a way that will make the prospect accept your recommendations and follow through with the proposed plan. Persuading a prospect to accept your recommendations and commit to taking the first steps of a comprehensive retirement plan is the primary goal of the presentation.

Periodic Review

To continue to help your clients achieve their retirement goals, you should periodically review their retirement plans and evaluate the progress of their savings, investment, and risk management strategies. No one strategy fits every need. By assessing your clients' needs and risk tolerance regularly, you can determine if the strategies clients have chosen match the financial goals they have set at their stage of life.

If your client's needs and goals have not changed, it may not be essential to reallocate investments and savings vehicles. If your client's goals have changed, however, it may be necessary to reposition assets to accomplish the new goals. Repositioning assets may mean that your client needs to rebalance the allocation of existing assets and future savings and investment contributions.

There may be costs involved in repositioning assets. The costs of investing—the sales and transaction charges—should be weighed against any potential gain that clients can realize and against their risk tolerance.

Periodically, your clients may wish to rid themselves of speculative investments. Clients who have become more cautious about their savings and investment objectives may want to consider selling some of the riskier individual stock shares they own but keeping their professionally managed, diversified mutual funds. These clients may want to forego undo risks that are not necessary to achieve their goals. ◊

CHAPTER SEVEN REVIEW

Key Terms and Concepts are explained in the Glossary. Answers to the Review Questions and Self-Test Questions are found in the back of the book in the Answers to Questions section.

Key Terms and Concepts

early retirement	postretirement mentality
golden handshake	syndrome
full retirement age (FRA)	life insurance settlement options
breakeven age	lump-sum option
severance pay	interest option
lump-sum payout	fixed-period option
annuity payout	fixed-amount option
preretirement mentality	life income options

Review Questions

7-1. List the reasons a person may have for deciding to retire early.

7-2. List the reasons a person may have against retiring early.

7-3. Explain why an employer might offer an employee an incentive to retire early.

7-4. Identify the factors involved in an employee's decision whether or not to accept an early retirement offer.

7-5. If a 62-year-old client decides to work until age 70, determine how much he could earn from his employment in 2006 without affecting Social Security benefits
   a. between age 62 and full retirement age of 65 years 8 months
   b. in the year he reaches full retirement age, assuming he was born in September
   c. after the year he reaches full retirement age until he reaches age 70

7-6. Briefly describe how Social Security benefits may be subject to income taxation for single and married recipients.

7-7. Describe the effect that early retirement may have on the size of the monthly benefit paid to a retiree under a defined-benefit and a defined contribution retirement plan.

7-8. Explain the two ways that an individual can make an IRA rollover, and discuss the advantages and disadvantages of each.

7-9. Briefly describe the emotional repercussions that individuals may experience when dealing with the reality of retirement.

7-10. Describe the important differences between the preretirement and postretirement mentality.

7-11. Identify several strategies and planning considerations that the advisor can use with retirees who fear they are running out of money during retirement.

7-12. Describe four ways that life insurance can be used in the context of retirement planning.

7-13. List the seven steps in developing retirement planning solutions.

Self-Test Questions

Instructions: Read chapter 7 first, then answer the following questions to test your knowledge. There are 10 questions; circle the correct answer, then check your answers with the answer key in the back of the book.

7-1. If a 63-year-old works after Social Security retirement payments begin and he or she earns wages above an annually published limit, which of the following will happen to his or her early retirement benefits?

(A) They will be reduced $1 for each $2 earned in the year Social Security retirement payments begin.
(B) They will be fully taxable at the capital gains rate.
(C) They will automatically terminate at age 70.
(D) They will be reduced $1 for each $3 earned in the year Social Security retirement payments begin.

7-2. Under which of the following circumstances may an individual who retires before age 55 withdraw money from an IRA without tax penalty?

(A) Retirement is mandatory.
(B) A family member is totally and permanently disabled.
(C) Money is distributed to someone other than the IRA owner.
(D) Withdrawals are made as a series of substantially equal payments.

7-3. Which of the following describes the main concern in the postretirement mentality syndrome?

(A) desire to maintain a comfortable lifestyle
(B) possibility of requiring long-term care
(C) need for estate planning
(D) irrational fear of running out of money

7-4. Which of the following life insurance settlement options is the simplest and most flexible?

(A) interest option
(B) life income option
(C) fixed-period option
(D) fixed-amount option

7-5. Which of the following statements about early retirement offers is (are) correct?

I. Companies are required to offer severance pay.
II. Companies often use early retirement offers as a cost-effective way to reduce their work force.

(A) I only
(B) II only
(C) Both I and II
(D) Neither I nor II

7-6.   Which of the following statements concerning the effect that unearned income has on Social Security benefits is (are) correct?

 I.   It lowers the monthly benefit payable to a retiree.
 II.   It may cause the benefit to become partially income taxable.

 (A)   I only
 (B)   II only
 (C)   Both I and II
 (D)   Neither I nor II

7-7.   Which of the following statements regarding retirement is (are) correct?

 I.   Someone who works for multiple employers usually fares better at retirement than the employee who works for a single employer.
 II.   Retirement is accompanied by financial, psychological, and social changes.

 (A)   I only
 (B)   II only
 (C)   Both I and II
 (D)   Neither I nor II

7-8.   All the following statements concerning severance pay are correct EXCEPT:

 (A)   It is not subject to FICA tax.
 (B)   It is often based on years of service.
 (C)   It is subject to federal income taxation.
 (D)   It can be used as a cash incentive to retire early.

7-9.   All the following are frequently utilized selling/planning opportunities when working with early retirees EXCEPT

 (A)   investment of severance pay lump sums
 (B)   IRA rollovers of qualified account money
 (C)   purchase of immediate annuities
 (D)   purchase of life insurance coverage

7-10. All the following are strategies that homeowners can use to provide additional income at retirement EXCEPT

 (A)   obtaining a reverse mortgage
 (B)   acquiring a home-equity loan
 (C)   paying off the existing mortgage
 (D)   selling the home

8

Wealth Transfer Planning and Professionalism

Learning Objectives

An understanding of the material in this chapter should enable the student to

8-1. Explain how the life insurance beneficiary designations can help accomplish the policyowner's intent for payment of policy proceeds.

8-2. Describe five ways that property transfers to survivors at the death of the property owner.

8-3. Explain the uses of basic estate planning techniques.

8-4. Explain what is meant by income in respect of a decedent (IRD).

8-5. Describe state regulation of insurance products.

8-6. Describe the federal regulation of securities products.

8-7. Explain the role of ethics and professionalism in the financial advisor's selling/planning activities.

Chapter Outline

LIFE INSURANCE PROCEEDS

A common theme throughout this textbook is that life insurance is the underpinning that allows your prospects to plan for retirement. It is the foundation on which they can build future financial strength, the contingency plan that protects against the consequences of unknown or untimely events. It is life insurance that makes a retirement plan flexible. And life insurance often allows your prospects to effect plans beyond their lifetimes.

For your prospects to accomplish their retirement goals, they must plan. Arranging for life insurance proceeds to be paid as the policyowner wants them to be paid is an important part of wealth transfer planning.

Sometimes we take the power of life insurance for granted. In an environment filled with technology and compliance issues, we often overlook basic concepts. Forget about illustrations, types of policies, premiums, and processes for a moment. Concentrate on what life insurance is and what it does. In simplest terms: *Life insurance guarantees beneficiaries future dollars.* This is a powerful statement and an awesome guarantee. Think of the life insurance benefit checks that are delivered and the impact that the money can have on the lives of the beneficiaries.

In chapter 4, we discussed the role of life insurance in financial and retirement planning. Here, we will briefly explore the effect of this essential financial product on those who receive its proceeds—the beneficiaries.

Beneficiary Designations

For a premium that is relatively small when compared to the death benefit, your prospects can purchase a life insurance policy that will pay their beneficiaries if the insured dies while the policy is in force. A life insurance

beneficiary

policyowner has a number of rights, but the right to name and change the *beneficiary* of the death benefit may be the most important.

The ownership right may not vest with the beneficiary until the insured's death. In effect, the life insurance policy beneficiary owns the death benefit.

Early in the history of life insurance, it was the beneficiary who purchased and paid for life insurance. It was rare for the insured to buy coverage on his or her own life for the benefit of someone else. This third-party arrangement, still available today, best recognizes the ownership rights of the beneficiary.

As individuals began to purchase policies on their own lives, insurers recognized the rights of the policyowner-insured to name and change the beneficiary of the policy. Standard policy provisions acknowledge the rights of policyowners. With a few exceptions that we will discuss later in this chapter, policyowners may name and change beneficiaries at will.

Revocable Beneficiary

revocable beneficiary

Generally, if the policyowner reserves the right to change the beneficiary, the designation of beneficiary is said to be revocable and the beneficiary is known as a *revocable beneficiary*.

> A revocable beneficiary has no rights under the policy—only an expectation of future benefits.

A revocable beneficiary has no rights under the policy—only an expectation of future benefits. Ownership of the death benefit does not vest in the revocable beneficiary until the insured dies. Thus, the policyowner can take out loans, stop paying premiums, change dividend options, and assign or surrender the policy without a beneficiary's knowledge or consent.

Irrevocable Beneficiary

irrevocable beneficiary

A policyowner can make an *irrevocable beneficiary* designation if he or she wishes. If a policyowner makes an irrevocable beneficiary designation, the beneficiary's ownership rights are vested immediately. What this means is that the policyowner can no longer take out loans, stop paying premiums, change dividend options, change beneficiaries, or assign or surrender the policy without the knowledge and consent of the irrevocable beneficiary(ies).

Only two situations terminate an irrevocable beneficiary designation:

- If the irrevocable beneficiary dies before the insured, the policyowner has the right to name a new beneficiary. The new beneficiary may be revocable or irrevocable.
- If the policy is not in force when the insured dies, no benefits are payable.

Limitations on the Policyowner's Rights

Naming a beneficiary is a valuable policy right; therefore, it is important that the beneficiary designation be clear and current. When a death claim is filed, the insurer must pay the benefit to the named beneficiary in a timely manner in order to carry out its contractual obligations.

There are some limits on the rights of policyowners to name or change beneficiaries. Some limits are self-imposed; others are company required or statutory restrictions.

Insurable Interest

insurable interest

> To prevent the purchase of life insurance for speculative purposes, companies typically limit a policyowner's choice to beneficiaries who have an insurable interest in the insured.

An *insurable interest* exists when one person would potentially suffer an economic loss as a result of the death of another person. At the insurance policy's inception, insurance companies typically limit a policyowner's choice to beneficiaries who have an insurable interest in the life of the insured. The reason for this is to attempt to prevent someone from purchasing life insurance for speculative purposes.

Beneficiaries are required to have an insurable interest if an individual is purchasing insurance on the life of someone else. For example, one spouse may purchase insurance on the life of the other, naming a child as beneficiary. The child is said to have an insurable interest in his or her parent's life.

Minor Beneficiaries

Generally, contracts made by minors are voidable at the option of the minor. Because minors have very limited contractual capacity, it is not advisable to designate minors as beneficiaries.

Group Life Insurance

Typically, states place an additional restriction on group life insurance contracts. A group certificate holder cannot name the group policyholder as beneficiary. For example, an employee who is insured under a group contract cannot name his or her employer as beneficiary.

Community-Property States

In community-property states, each spouse owns an undivided interest in any property acquired during marriage unless the property is acquired by gift or inheritance. When insurance premiums are paid with community funds, each spouse has an interest in the policy. Community-property laws may restrict one spouse's right to name a beneficiary without the consent of the other spouse.

Effect of Divorce

In several states, divorce or annulment of a marriage has the effect of revoking a beneficiary designation.

Example:	Suppose a husband purchases life insurance on his own life and names his wife beneficiary. If they divorce, the beneficiary designation is revoked. If the husband wants his former wife to remain the beneficiary of his life insurance, he must reaffirm or rename her as beneficiary.

The statutes vary in the states with this provision. You should be aware that these provisions exist and stay alert to your clients' needs for policy service.

Naming a Beneficiary

On the insurance application, there is generally a section in which you write the names of the primary beneficiary and the contingent beneficiary. The primary beneficiary is the person who receives the death benefit. The contingent beneficiary receives the death benefit if the primary beneficiary is not living. The insurance company may have guidelines for naming a beneficiary, which you may wish to review. However, a few common guidelines are worth mentioning:

- A policyowner may name more than one primary beneficiary. If multiple primary beneficiaries are named, the death benefit is divided in the proportions specified by the policyowner.
- The beneficiary should be named or described well enough to be easily identified.
- Children may be designated as beneficiaries either by name or by class, depending on the policyowner's intent.

per capita

per stirpes

Most beneficiary designations are on a *per capita* basis. This means that they are generally named and only living beneficiaries share the death benefit equally. However, a policyowner may choose to make a *per stirpes* beneficiary designation. When a policyowner makes a per stirpes beneficiary designation, his or her intent is to have the death benefit divided among the living members of a class of beneficiaries and the children of deceased members.

Example:	A parent may designate her two children—Lucy and Jake—beneficiaries of her $200,000 life insurance policy. At the parent's death, Jake is living, but Lucy, who has two children, has predeceased

her mother. If the designation is per stirpes, Jake will be paid $100,000 and each of Lucy's children will receive $50,000. In other words, the benefit is divided among the members of a family branch— the policyowner's children. Because Lucy is not living, her share is divided equally among her living children.

Beneficiary designations should be reviewed regularly to be sure they reflect the policyowner's current needs and circumstances.

Beneficiary designations should be examined regularly to ensure that they reflect the policyowner's current needs and circumstances. You should review your clients' beneficiary designations as a part of their periodic insurance reviews.

Life Insurance Proceeds

As mentioned in chapter 5, few opportunities for your financial services are as natural and welcome as those tied to money received from death claims. Often, a beneficiary receives a large lump sum of money that is critical to maintaining the beneficiary's lifestyle, as is often the case with life insurance proceeds. The beneficiary must view these funds as an important resource for his or her future.

Assisting Beneficiaries

Assisting a client when a death occurs requires compassion and skill. As a financial advisor, you should give both insurance settlement options and alternative investments thoughtful consideration to determine the best possible choices to meet the beneficiary's long-term needs. If a person is already your client, you should have developed and maintained the trusting relationship necessary to make your counsel extremely valuable during the difficult time following the death of a loved one. ◊

ESTATE PLANNING CONSIDERATIONS

One part of helping your clients manage their financial affairs deals with asset distribution at death. Asset distribution is the way your clients transfer their wealth to their children, grandchildren, and other beneficiaries. Most people want to accomplish this with a minimum loss to the government in the form of federal estate and gift taxes and state death taxes.

The problems of asset distribution are directly related to prudent and successful financial planning over the client's lifetime. If assets are not accumulated and invested wisely, little or no estate will be available for distribution.

For many, the goal of leaving an estate is secondary to ensuring financial security in retirement. Many of your prospects and clients may feel that by planning their retirements well, they will not burden their children. They may want to enjoy security and independence during retirement and pass what is left on to their children.

Your clients' needs for estate planning and estate tax minimization may be a direct result of your helping them to achieve their financial goals. Without your assistance, many of them may commit major errors in estate planning. They may delay estate planning until they are relatively old, such as in their 70s.

By the time they act, they may discover that it is too late to take advantage of many of the most important and tax-efficient estate planning tools. By encouraging your clients to initiate estate planning earlier in their lives than they would otherwise be inclined to, such as in their 40s or 50s, you may help them dramatically reduce—or even eliminate estate taxes. More important, you may help them accomplish all of their estate planning goals effectively and efficiently.

> By encouraging your clients to initiate estate planning earlier rather than later, you may help them to reduce—or even eliminate—estate taxes.

How Property Passes at Death

Generally, when a person dies, the property he or she owns will be transferred to heirs in one or more of the following ways:

- by intestacy laws. Intestacy laws are state laws that contain detailed instructions on who will receive a decedent's property not transferred by a valid will. At death, a surviving spouse may get as little as a third of the estate, with the remainder going to the children.
- by will through probate. If there is a will, property included in its provisions passes under the terms of the will once it has been admitted to probate. Probate is the legal process of validating the will. If there is no will, property passes according to the state's laws of intestacy.
- by right of survivorship. A typical example of this method is a home owned jointly by a husband and wife. At the death of the first spouse, the survivor has full ownership of the property.
- by right of contract. The prime example of this is life insurance that is payable directly to a beneficiary. Government and pension benefits paid directly to eligible survivors are other examples.
- by trust. Revocable trusts created prior to death become irrevocable at death and pass property to the named beneficiaries. Irrevocable trusts containing assets that are transfers or gifts made during lifetime also specify how and to whom property is transferred at death.

Need for a Will

You may encounter prospects and clients who do not have a will. People may assume that their assets will automatically go to their surviving spouse

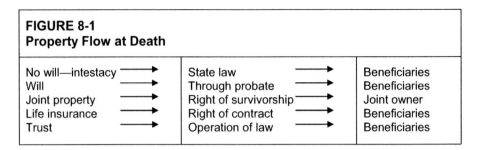

FIGURE 8-1
Property Flow at Death

No will—intestacy	→	State law	→	Beneficiaries
Will	→	Through probate	→	Beneficiaries
Joint property	→	Right of survivorship	→	Joint owner
Life insurance	→	Right of contract	→	Beneficiaries
Trust	→	Operation of law	→	Beneficiaries

People may assume that their assets will automatically go to their surviving spouse when they die. Unfortunately, this is often not the case.

when they die. Unfortunately, this is often not the case. When a person dies without a will, his or her assets are distributed according to the intestacy laws of his or her resident state. In other words, the laws of the state and not the wishes of the decedent will decide how assets are distributed.

This means, for example, that the surviving spouse may not get all the assets. Assets that are not jointly titled with right of survivorship are distributed according to state law, usually with a portion going to the surviving spouse and a portion distributed to any surviving children.

To make certain that your clients' assets are distributed according to their wishes, you should encourage them to create and maintain a valid will. The simplest form of estate planning uses a will to transfer property to heirs. Because both tax laws and the client's situation change, the will should be reviewed periodically to make sure it is up-to-date, continues to reflect the client's wishes, and maximizes any available tax benefits.

The following examples show the importance of keeping a will updated.

Example 1:   Suppose your client has a will written before 1981. There is a good chance that it does not take advantage of the unlimited marital deduction. Generally, an estate is allowed a deduction for the full value of all estate property that passes to the decedent's surviving spouse. This tax-advantaged provision was legislated after 1981. (The marital deduction is discussed more fully later in this chapter.)

Making sure that your client takes maximum advantage of the marital deduction is one reason to review and update a will.

Example 2:   Let's say your client wrote a will that left her shares of stock in the XYZ Company to her nephew. Since the will was written, the XYZ Company merged with the ABC Company, and your client received shares of ABC stock in exchange for her XYZ stock. Subsequently, she sold the ABC stock and used the money to purchase tax-free municipal bonds. In this case, the property that she intended to pass to her nephew no longer exists in her estate and therefore cannot be transferred to him. Her intent to provide him with a portion of her estate has been defeated.

Making sure that the client's will reflects any changes that have taken place in his or her assets is the second reason for reviewing and updating a will.

> **You should stress the importance of maintaining a properly executed will and help your clients understand the negative implications of failing to do so.**

Of course, you cannot prepare a will for your clients or provide them with any form of legal advice. Preparing a will requires the expertise of a licensed attorney. You can and should, however, stress the importance of maintaining a properly executed will and help your clients understand the negative implications of failing to do so. Ideally, you will work with the client's attorney as part of a total planning team that includes other professional advisors, such as the client's accountant and trust officer, to develop the best plan possible.

Federal Estate Tax

The federal estate tax is a tax imposed, at graduated rates, on the right to transfer property at death. The federal estate tax return (Form 706), if required, must be filed and the tax paid by the executor of a deceased person's estate within 9 months after the decedent's death. Time of payment may be extended for "reasonable cause."

Progressive Tax

The estate tax has graduated rates and therefore takes a proportionately bigger bite out of larger estates than it takes from smaller ones. This is known as a progressive tax. The federal income tax system works the same way.

Measured by Estate's Value

The estate tax is measured by the current value of property transferred at death. For purposes of this tax, the concept of "transfer" is much broader than you would generally expect. The starting place is the decedent's "gross estate," which encompasses all property and rights to property in which the decedent had an ownership interest at death.

Taxable Estate

When the value of a decedent's gross estate has been determined, a number of adjustments and deductions can be applied to determine the "taxable estate."

Tentative Tax

The taxable estate is multiplied by an appropriate rate (taken from the federal estate and gift tax rate table) to arrive at a tentative estate tax.

Final Tax

Any available credits are subtracted from the tentative tax to arrive at the final estate tax. The basic calculation is as follows:

> Gross estate
> − <u>Statutory deductions</u> (marital deduction, charitable gifts, debts, funeral
>   expenses, state death taxes)
> = Taxable estate
> x <u>Tax rate</u>
> = Tentative tax
> − Miscellaneous credits
> − <u>Applicable credit amount</u> (explained later in the chapter; see table 8-2)
> = NET TAX DUE

What Is Included in the Gross Estate

What makes up the gross estate? For practical purposes, it is everything the decedent owned in any way on the date of death. More specifically, it includes but is not limited to, the following categories of property:

- probate estate
- jointly owned property
- transfers with retained interests
- gifts in contemplation of death
- pension plans, IRAs, and annuities
- life insurance

Probate Estate. This is all property that passes by will or under the laws of descent and distribution. Usually, the probate estate is all the property the decedent owned outright in his or her own name only, and not jointly with any other person.

Jointly Owned Property. Many prospects mistakenly believe that jointly owned property is not subject to estate taxes. The gross estate includes a decedent's interest in jointly owned property. In the case of a husband and wife who own property as tenants by the entireties, each is treated as owning one-half of the property. The value of other jointly owned interests may depend on the nature of the joint ownership or the relative ages of the joint owners. In any event, a prospect cannot avoid estate tax by placing property in joint names.

> **Many prospects mistakenly believe that jointly owned property is not subject to estate taxes.**

Transfers with Retained Interests. One way to avoid estate tax on the value of something is to get rid of that something. Often this is done by gift. If the gift is made fully and irrevocably, with no strings attached, it works. Occasionally, however, an individual will make a transfer of property and retain certain rights or powers regarding the transfer. Congress has declared that keeping such rights or powers to the gift is equivalent to keeping the gift itself. Therefore, for estate tax purposes, such transfers are not considered gifts.

Gifts in Contemplation of Death. Certain gifts made within 3 years of death are brought back into the gross estate for purposes of computing the tax if there are any retained or reversionary interests or any right to amend, alter, revoke, or terminate the gift. This means that the transfer (gift) was incomplete, because a grantor must relinquish irrevocably all power and control over the property. Strings are attached, which requires inclusion of the gift in the grantor's estate.

Pension Plans, IRAs, and Annuities. Along with other tax-advantaged retirement fund proceeds, pension plans, IRAs, and annuities are included in the gross estate.

Life Insurance. Generally, life insurance proceeds on the life of the decedent are included in the gross estate if one of the following is true:

- The decedent had any incidents of ownership in the insurance contract.
- The proceeds are payable to or for the benefit of the estate.
- The decedent owned the policy and transferred ownership within 3 years of death.

Valuation of the Estate Property

The law requires that an estate be valued at its fair market value on the date of death or at the alternative valuation date 6 months later.

Fair Market Value. Fair market value is the price which a willing buyer and a willing seller would agree to, neither being under any compulsion to buy or to sell, and both having reasonable knowledge of all relevant facts.

Estate owners are sometimes lulled into a false sense of security. They think they have no estate tax problem because they believe their estate is too small to be taxed. They overlook inflation in the value of the assets. They overlook any appreciation in the value of the assets. They believe that the value of the property for tax purposes is the amount at which they bought the property, but this is not correct. The value for tax purposes is the current fair market value at date of death or on the alternate valuation date of 6 months

> **Estate owners may think they have no estate tax problem because they believe their estate is too small to be taxed.**

after death. One of your functions as a financial advisor is to clarify the prospect's misunderstandings about valuation of assets and to explain the likelihood of estate taxation. This knowledge can encourage the prospect to take the necessary estate planning steps.

Statutory Deductions

After the gross estate has been established and valued, certain deductions are allowed to reduce the estate that will be subject to taxation. The allowable deductions fall into the following categories:

- death costs
- administrative expenses
- debts
- charitable requests
- marital deduction
- state death tax deduction

Death Costs. The decedent's estate is entitled to a deduction for the costs of the decedent's funeral and for the expenses associated with the decedent's last illness. This may include doctor's fees, hospital charges, medication, and similar costs.

Administrative Expenses. The estate is also allowed a deduction for the costs of administering the estate. As a rule of thumb, many estate planners use a figure of 5 percent to 8 percent of the estate's value as the approximate cost (executor and lawyer) of administering the estate. This includes court costs, executor's commissions and fees, legal fees, appraisal fees, accounting fees, and certain other costs, claims, and obligations.

Debts. Unpaid mortgages and other indebtedness on estate property are deductible from the taxable estate.

Charitable Bequests. The estate is allowed a deduction for the full value of estate property that is left to qualifying charities. Generally, these are the same charities for which a deduction is allowable for federal income tax purposes. There is no limit on the amount or percentage of the gross estate that can qualify for the charitable deduction. Usually, in order to qualify for the charitable deduction, a gift or bequest to charity must transfer to the charity full and immediate ownership. Exceptions do exist, however, for certain "split interest" bequests. Allowable split interests are charitable remainder trusts, charitable lead trusts, and pooled-income funds.

Marital Deduction. The most significant estate tax deduction, in terms of total dollars, is the marital deduction. Generally, an estate is allowed a deduction for the full value of all estate property that passes to the decedent's surviving spouse. This deduction is available only if the surviving spouse is a U.S. citizen.

Under current law, the full value of all property passing to the surviving spouse qualifies for the marital deduction. In fact, it is referred to as the "unlimited marital deduction." (This is discussed in greater detail later in this chapter.)

For married couples, although the estate tax might not be imposed until both spouses have died, it will be imposed eventually. The greatest impact will be on well-to-do single people, including widows, widowers, divorcees, and people who have never married. For them, the estate tax cannot be postponed.

State Death Tax Deduction. There is also a deduction for state death taxes. A number of states impose an estate tax, much like the federal estate tax. The personal representative of the deceased has the principal burden of making sure that the state death tax is paid. Like the federal tax, it is usually calculated using graduated rate tables, but at lower rates. State estate taxes are frequently payable even if no federal estate taxes are due.

A number of other states impose an inheritance tax. Unlike the estate tax (which is taxed to the estate), an inheritance tax is imposed on the person who receives the inheritance. The tax is determined from rate tables published by the state. Inheritance taxes often have different rates for different recipients, depending on the nature of the kinship (spouse, parent, sibling, and so on) between the recipient and the decedent.

The Economic Growth and Tax Relief Reconciliation Act (EGTRRA) in 2001 eliminated what was the previous state death tax credit in the year 2004. For years 2005 through 2009, the state death tax credit has been replaced with a deduction for state death taxes. In 2010, the credit will be abolished, along with the repeal of the estate tax. If the sunset provision of EGTRRA is allowed to transpire, the full state death tax credit will be reinstated in 2011 as it existed prior to EGTRRA.

Tentative Tax

After all appropriate deductions have been made, the remaining balance is the taxable estate. Initially, a tentative tax is calculated on this amount, determined as shown in table 8-1.

Estate Tax Credits

After the tentative tax has been calculated, all available credits are subtracted. The balance remaining after these credits is the net estate tax due.

TABLE 8-1
Federal Gift and Estate Tax Rate Schedule: 2006 through 2009

If the amount with respect to which the tentative tax is to be computed is. . .	The tentative tax is. . .
Not over $10,000	18% of such amount
Over $10,000 but not over $20,000	$1,800, plus 20% of excess of such amount over $10,000
Over $20,000 but not over $40,000	$3,800, plus 22% of excess of such amount over $20,000
Over $40,000 but not over $60,000	$8,200, plus 24% of excess of such amount over $40,000
Over $60,000 but not over $80,000	$13,000, plus 26% of excess of such amount over $60,000
Over $80,000 but not over $100,000	$18,200, plus 28% of excess of such amount over $80,000
Over $100,000 but not over $150,000	$23,800, plus 30% of excess of such amount over 100,000
Over $150,000 but not over $250,000	$38,800, plus 32% of excess of such amount over 150,000
Over $250,000 but not over $500,000	$70,800, plus 34% of excess of such amount over 250,000
Over $500,000 but not over $750,000	$155,800, plus 37% of excess of such amount over 500,000
Over $750,000 but not over $1,000,000	$248,300, plus 39% of excess of such amount over 750,000
Over $1,000,000 but not over $1,250,000	$345,800, plus 41% of excess of such amount over 1,000,000
Over $1,250,000 but not over $1,500,000	$448,300, plus 43% of excess of such amount over $1,250,000
Over $1,500,000 but not over $2,000,000	$555,800, plus 45% of excess of such amount over $1,500,000
Over $2,000,000	$780,800, plus 46% of excess of such amount over $2,000,000
For 2007 through 2009: Eliminate the over $2,000,000 bracket; highest bracket becomes over $1,500,000	$555,800, plus $45% of excess of such amount over $1,500,000

The law provides several credits. The principal credits are the applicable credit amount, gift tax credit, credit for estate taxes on earlier transfers, and credit for foreign death taxes paid.

Basic Estate Tax Calculation

The following two provisions of estate taxation are important to understand if you are to help your prospects and clients plan for the distribution of their accumulated assets at death:

- applicable credit amount
- unlimited marital deduction

Estate and Gift Tax Applicable Credit Amount

applicable credit amount

The estate and gift taxes are offset by a credit referred to as the *applicable credit amount*. This cumulative credit is applicable for both federal estate and gift taxes due on taxable transfers. In other words, whatever amount of the applicable credit amount someone uses during his or her lifetime against gift taxes will reduce the amount of the total remaining credit that can be applied against estate taxes after death.

After the passage of EGTRRA 2001, the applicable credit amount remained the same ($1 million) for both gift and estate tax purposes in 2002 and 2003 only. Starting in 2004, the credit increases in step-rate fashion for estate tax purposes, while for gift tax purposes it remains at the 2002 and 2003 level through 2009. During 2002 and 2003, a donor was able to exhaust the total credit while making gifts, leaving nothing to offset estate taxes at death. However, starting in 2004, the credit became larger for estate tax purposes than for gift tax purposes. The applicable credit amount is $780,800 in year 2006, which exempts $2 million from taxation. It is now impossible for a donor to fully exhaust the applicable credit amount by making lifetime gifts. Even if the amount of the credit allocated to satisfying gift tax liability is fully used, a certain amount of the credit will remain for use against estate taxes. (See tables 8-2 and 8-3.)

Unlimited Marital Deduction

unlimited marital deduction

In 1981, the laws on estate taxes were modified to permit a 100 percent deduction—the marital deduction—for all property transferred between husband and wife. This *unlimited marital deduction* means that an unlimited estate can be passed to a surviving spouse with no estate tax.

The unlimited marital deduction may lead many of your clients to believe that estate planning is not a critical part of their overall financial planning. This perception is far from the truth. In fact, from a planning perspective, it is

---

TABLE 8-2
Federal Estate Tax Law after EGTRRA

EGTRRA 2001 increased the exemption equivalents from 2002 through 2009. In 2010, the estate tax is repealed for 1 year, but it is scheduled to be reinstated in 2011 as it existed prior to EGTRRA.

For Decedents Dying During	Top Estate Tax Rate	Applicable Credit Amount	Exemption Equivalent
2002	50%	$345,800	$1,000,000
2003	49%	$345,800	$1,000,000
2004	48%	$555,800	$1,500,000
2005	47%	$555,800	$1,500,000
2006	46%	$780,800	$2,000,000
2007	45%	$780,800	$2,000,000
2008	45%	$780,800	$2,000,000
2009	45%	$1,455,800	$3,500,000
2010	Repealed	N/A	N/A
2011	55%	$345,800	$1,000,000*

* The "sunset" provision of EGTRRA 2001 causes a reversion to pre-2002 tax rates.

TABLE 8-3
Federal Gift Tax Law after EGTRRA

Calendar Year	Top Gift Tax Rate*	Applicable Credit Amount	Gift Tax Lifetime Transfer Exemption
2002	50%	$345,800	$1,000,000
2003	49%	$345,800	$1,000,000
2004	48%	$345,800	$1,000,000
2005	47%	$345,800	$1,000,000
2006	46%	$345,800	$1,000,000
2007	45%	$345,800	$1,000,000
2008	45%	$345,800	$1,000,000
2009	45%	$345,800	$1,000,000
2010	35%	$345,800	$1,000,000
2011	55%**	$345,800	$1,000,000

* The applicable credit and exclusion amounts for gratuitous lifetime transfers (that is, gifts) are fixed at the 2002 levels of $345,800 and $1 million, respectively, for gifts in 2004 through 2009. The top gift tax bracket and exclusion amounts for gifts reduces to 35% and $1 million, respectively, in 2010.

**The "sunset" provision of EGTRRA 2001 causes a reversion to pre-2002 tax rates.

potentially disastrous. Even if your client intends to leave all of his or her estate to a spouse, what will happen when the spouse dies? At that point, there is no marital deduction and the entire estate is exposed to taxation.

Complacency based on the fact that part of an estate is not subject to taxation is also ill-founded. Although accumulating a taxable estate may seem to be an unrealistic goal to many of your young or middle-aged clients, even modest real growth in assets and the inflation of real property values may combine to generate an estate well in excess of the exemption equivalent.

Note that when calculating the tax, you cannot just reduce the estate by the amount of the applicable credit amount. Because the estate tax is a progressive tax, the credit, in effect, comes off the top taxable dollars. Therefore, the tax must be calculated first and then the credit applied.

> **Even modest growth in assets and the inflation of real property values may combine to generate an estate well in excess of the exemption equivalent.**

Example: Chris and Pat Brown were both aged 45 in 1976. Their financial statement included the major assets and liabilities shown below.

The corporate interest that is included in the Browns' statement is a family business. Pat's father and mother owned the remaining stock in the firm. At the urging of their financial advisor, Chris and Pat attempted to project the value of their potential estate. As they looked ahead 20 years to their

Brown Family Retirement Estate		
Assets Age 45	**(1976)**	**Age 65 (1996)**
Home	$ 50,000	$ 193,484
Savings	$ 10,000	$ 26,533
Stocks/mutual funds	$ 20,000	$ 53,066
Business—50%	$100,000	$ 386,966
Retirement accounts	$ 45,000	$ 456,858
TOTAL ASSETS	$225,000	$1,116,907
Liabilities		
Mortgage	$ 40,000	0
NET WORTH	$185,000	$1,116,907
Parent's share of business		$ 386,966
NET WORTH AT RETIREMENT		$1,503,873

retirement at age 65, they realized that when Pat's father and mother died, Chris and Pat would control the business.

For planning purposes, they estimated that the value of the business would increase by 7 percent each year through real growth and inflation. They also anticipated that their house would appreciate by 7 percent annually. By retirement, they would have paid off the mortgage.

They took a conservative view of their savings and investments, projecting that they would increase by only 5 percent each year with no additions to the accounts. They projected that additions to their retirement accounts of $5,000 a year would appreciate at a rate of 8 percent annually between 1976 and the time they retired in 1996.

By the time the Browns reached age 65, their estate had grown to $1,503,873. Fortunately, by then, their combined exemption equivalents equaled $1.2 million. With proper planning, had they both died then, their estate tax would have been relatively negligible ($89,117). However, even though estate tax legislation increased both the applicable credit amount and exemption equivalents, the picture changed dramatically a few years down the road.

Pat and Chris did not die at age 65. (In fact, their life expectancies were to beyond age 75 and 80, respectively.) However, for illustration's sake, let's assume that they both died in 2006. If the

Browns' estate continued to grow at a rate of 7 percent per year in the 10 years from their age 65 to age 75, the total gross estate would have grown to over $2.95 million. Given that Pat and Chris had similar ages and life expectancies, they could take very little comfort from the fact that they were eligible for a 100 percent marital deduction or the applicable credit amount. When the Browns passed their assets to their children, under current tax provisions, they will incur an estate tax liability.

If one of the Browns died first and left everything to the surviving spouse without taking advantage of any of the available estate planning tools, the estate tax bill when the surviving spouse dies in 2006 would look like this.

Estate Tax Bill at Second Death: Year 2006	
Gross estate	$2,958,346
Less:	
Funeral expenses	$ 10,000
Debt	0
Executor expenses	88,752
Adjusted gross estate	$2,859,594
Less:	
Marital deduction	0
Charitable deductions	0
Taxable estate	$2,859,594
Tentative tax (before credit)	$1,176,213
Applicable credit amount	$ 780,800
Federal estate taxes due	$ 395,413

Of course, increases in the applicable credit amount that became effective after 2003 will ease the tax bite, if not eliminate it entirely, thanks to EGTRRA. However, what if EGTRRA is allowed to sunset (expire)? Whether this is likely is a controversial issue among financial advisors. No one has a crystal ball to accurately predict the future of federal estate tax legislation. There is a schedule of projected changes in the applicable credit amount, and planning is essential. You must help your clients see the impact of their assets' compound growth potential, as well as future scheduled or unscheduled changes in relevant estate tax laws that may affect the assets they pass down to their heirs. If you do your retirement planning job well and urge your clients to invest systematically, their potential estate tax problems will grow as well.

You are faced with a dilemma. Doing an excellent job of assisting your clients accumulate wealth will enhance the growth of their taxable estate, which will mean increased taxation.

So you are faced with a dilemma: Doing an excellent job of assisting your clients accumulate wealth will enhance the growth of their taxable estate, which will mean increased taxation. Therefore, you must motivate your clients to take early actions to minimize their estate tax liability and to prepare for paying estate taxes using the most cost-efficient means possible. The preferred method for doing that is to encourage clients to provide liquidity for the payment of estate taxes and other estate settlement costs using the discounted dollars that are available only from the purchase of life insurance.

Estate Planning Techniques

The basic techniques for achieving estate and gift tax reduction can be summarized as follows:

- Create tax-exempt wealth.
- Purchase estate-tax-free life insurance.
- Divide the estate.
- Discount the estate tax obligation.
- Eliminate the estate taxes.
- Freeze the estate.
- Incur estate tax at the first death.

Given that most of these procedures involve complex tax laws, their actual implementation typically requires input from all members of the financial planning team. You, however, can be a catalyst for action. Therefore, you must be able to recognize situations where one or more of these techniques will benefit your client. You then need to encourage the appropriate professional advisors to review the techniques as they apply to each client's specific needs and tax status.

Because estate planning issues are complicated, it is a good idea for inexperienced financial advisors to seek the help of those who are experienced in estate planning cases. Sharing a case with an experienced advisor gives you the opportunity to develop your skills without jeopardizing the client's financial situation.

Create Tax-Exempt Wealth

Most financial advisors are well aware of the role of life insurance in estate creation. Life insurance is unique among financial assets because, with proper planning, it can be structured to be fully exempt from federal estate taxation as well as federal income taxes. You should stress this characteristic of life insurance because most prospects are unaware of its significant tax advantages.

Purchase Estate-Tax-Free Life Insurance

Life insurance can be excluded from the insured's estate if the insured retains no incidents of ownership. This can be done as follows:

- The policy is owned by and payable to an owner-beneficiary other than the insured.
- The policy is owned by and payable to an irrevocable trust.

The first possibility, an owner-beneficiary other than the insured, has the immediate advantage of providing liquidity for estate settlement costs. With a separate owner and beneficiary, neither the value of the life insurance nor its proceeds are part of the estate. Therefore, they will not cause additional administrative expenses and are not subject to estate claims.

The second method is to have an irrevocable trust apply for and unconditionally own insurance on the insured's life. Once again, the trust can be created so that a source of cash exists to settle the estate. When the trust is properly arranged, the insurance death proceeds are not subject either to federal estate or state death taxes. It is important that the policy be owned by a trustee and that the insured have no incidents of ownership. In addition, the trustee must not be obligated to make insurance proceeds available for estate liabilities.

Divide the Estate

One common way to divide a client's estate is by direct or indirect gifts using trusts. Both types of gifts can help clients save estate and income taxes.

Under the Taxpayer Relief Act of 1997 (TRA 1997), the annual gift tax exclusion is indexed for inflation. Thus, a donor can make gifts of up to $12,000 (2006 indexed amount) per recipient and escape gift taxes. The gift tax exclusion is doubled to $24,000 (2006) if the donor's spouse consents to split the gift. For example, a couple with three children can give each of their children $24,000 each year without incurring a gift tax, for a total estate reduction of $72,000 annually.

Here is another use of the $12,000 gift exclusion that some clients may find attractive, especially those concerned with college education funding. Grandparents can make gifts that will pay the premium for a life insurance policy on a grandchild's life. Although overfunding the life insurance policy will result in making it a modified endowment contract, grandparents can create a fund to be used for their grandchild's college costs while reducing the grandparents' estates. The taxes and penalties paid when the child uses the funds for education may be significantly less than the tax on money left in the estate.

Although many of your clients will be hesitant to give away assets that generate income during their retirement years, owners of closely held businesses can transfer significant portions of their ownership to their children without impairing their ability to control the business or to enjoy its profits. By giving a minority business interest to a child, your client can retain management control, yet gradually transfer the stock ownership. This type of transfer is especially prudent for clients whose children ultimately will run the company.

Another tool for dividing the estate is the credit-shelter or bypass trust. The credit shelter trust is used to maximize all of the estate tax credits available to the client. The credit shelter trust is an effective estate tax reduction tool because it makes use of two of the estate planning provisions we have already mentioned: the applicable credit amount and the unlimited marital deduction. To see how the credit shelter trust works, let's look at two ways Bob and Carol King can plan the transfer of their estate.

> **The credit shelter trust is an effective estate tax reduction tool because it makes use of both the applicable credit amount and the unlimited marital deduction to maximize estate tax credits.**

Example 1:

Bob and Carol have an estate worth $2.5 million. Like many couples, they own almost everything jointly with right of survivorship. Carol understood the value of the marital deduction, and therefore she left everything to her husband, Bob, in her will, knowing that the marital deduction would exempt the full value of her estate from estate taxation. On his death, all assets could be left to their children.

Assuming Carol dies in 2006, her situation is as follows:

Carol's adjusted gross estate	$2,500,000
Less: marital deduction	2,500,000
Taxable estate	0
Estate tax	0

Carol dies happy, knowing she had reduced her taxable estate to zero and saved her family all those taxes. But at what cost to them? Carol's husband, Bob, now has a $2.5 million estate that by his will goes to their children.

Being a careful spender, Bob manages to leave the full $2.5 million intact. But now, at his death there is no surviving spouse and no marital deduction. The full amount is subject to estate taxes, with only his applicable credit amount to offset the taxes.

Assuming Bob dies in 2006, here is his situation:

Bob's adjusted gross estate	$2,500,000
Less: marital deduction	0
Taxable estate	$2,500,000
Tentative tax	$1,010,800
Less: applicable credit amount	780,800
Estate tax is	$ 230,000

Consider the results of this first example. Upon Carol's death in 2006, she left everything to Bob, using the unlimited marital deduction. When Bob dies in 2006, he has no marital deduction. Thus, the total federal estate tax due following Bob's death is $230,000. With the right planning, the couple could have entirely eliminated the $230,000 of federal estate tax, passing that amount to their children instead. Our second example shows how this can be accomplished.

Example 2:   Suppose that at Carol's death in 2006, she leaves only $500,000 to go directly to Bob, instead of the full $2.5 million. Carol's will facilitated the transfer of $2 million into a credit shelter trust at her death, and all income from the trust was to be paid to Bob during his lifetime. At Bob's subsequent death in 2006, the trust terminates, and the $2 million from the trust goes to the children.

     The $500,000 that Carol leaves outright to Bob also goes to the children under Bob's will. At Bob's death, his estate receives no marital deduction, leaving a taxable estate of $500,000. The tentative tax on Bob's estate will be $155,800, but after applying his applicable credit amount, the tax will be reduced to zero. Consequently, Bob's estate will not have to pay any federal estate taxes.

Compare the Results. In the first example, Bob's estate owes $230,000 in estate taxes. This tax burden is completely eliminated under the second example, which uses a credit shelter trust to take full advantage of Carol's applicable credit amount. In the second example, the Kings' children receive the full $2.5 million, while in the first scenario they receive only $2,270,000. The second example provides an additional $230,000 to the children.

The result of overqualifying the marital deduction in the first example is that Carol's applicable credit amount is wasted at her death in 2006. In the second example, both Carol and Bob can take full advantage of their respective applicable credit amounts, thereby reducing estate taxes by $230,000.

Discount the Estate Tax Obligation

As you can see in the second example above, even when you assist your clients in using available estate planning techniques, there may still be significant amounts of estate tax due. This estate tax obligation requires cash within 9 months of death. Nonliquid assets in the estate usually experience substantial reductions in value if they must be sold quickly to pay estate taxes. Paying estate taxes on an installment basis, while sometimes possible, is generally distasteful and expensive because of interest charges.

> The premium for a life insurance policy represents only a small fraction of the death proceeds it can provide to the estate at the insured's death.

A sound financial plan will identify a client's potential estate tax obligation, monitor increases in this obligation that are tied to rising estate values, and help the client prepare to meet the potential estate tax obligation with dollars obtained at a discount. To this end, life insurance is a unique and valuable financial asset. The premium for a life insurance policy represents only a small fraction of the death proceeds it can provide to the estate at the insured's death. Moreover, properly arranged ownership of life insurance need not compound the estate tax burden.

Often, the greater need for liquidity to pay estate taxes occurs when the second spouse dies. Life insurance is a vehicle to provide the necessary cash. One approach is to use individual life insurance policies to insure both spouses' lives in an amount sufficient to meet projected expenses. A second approach is to use a joint life insurance policy that provides an adequate death benefit at the first death. A third approach is to use a joint life insurance policy that pays the face amount when the second insured, rather than the first one, dies. Another option, offered by some companies as a rider on individual life insurance policies, permits the beneficiary to buy life insurance without evidence of insurability on his or her life when the insured person dies.

Eliminate the Estate Taxes

Charitable gifts are an effective means of eliminating or reducing the size of an estate. Rather than making charitable gifts at death, some clients make significant distributions during their lifetimes.

> Lifetime giving need not preclude your clients from continuing to enjoy the financial benefits of their assets.

Lifetime giving need not preclude your clients from continuing to enjoy the financial benefits of their assets. There are a number of creative techniques that enable a client to give away assets to a charity while continuing to receive the income those assets generate. Many of these arrangements involve the charity's purchase of an immediate annuity to guarantee the donor ongoing income without exposing the charity to the risk that the donor will live too long.

Sometimes a client will want to leave assets to a charitable organization but does not want to disinherit his or her heirs. Life insurance is the financial product that can provide dollars to replace the value of the assets transferred to a charity. By purchasing life insurance with the heirs as the owner and beneficiary, the client provides an equivalently valued inheritance that can pass outside the estate while the estate assets go to the favored charity.

Finally, do not overlook the possibility of providing new life insurance coverage for a client with the client's favorite charity as the beneficiary. This is a way that even clients with modest resources and estates can make significant charitable contributions.

Freeze the Estate

A private annuity allows your client to transfer assets to children or other beneficiaries on an estate-tax-free basis and, in exchange, receive a lifetime income.

Example :	Your client, aged 65, can transfer property worth $500,000 to her child and receive a life annuity of at least $50,000 each year. Assuming this is an arm's-length transaction, there is no gift tax liability. IRS life expectancy tables must be used to determine the value subject to income taxation.
	A portion of this annual income is subject to income tax, but the property, now owned by the child, is not included in your client's estate. If we assume that the property appreciates in value at 10 percent a year and the client dies at age 75 (10 years after the transfer), the value of the property at the time of your client's death is $1,250,000. In effect, this technique has stopped estate growth, thus freezing the estate tax obligation. Your client transfers $1,250,000 to the next generation without gift or estate tax consequences.

Incur Estate Tax at the First Death

Sometimes, there may be an incentive to incur estate taxes at the first spouse's death, rather than using the unlimited marital deduction. Let's look at the example of Jack and Mary's case.

Example :

Together, Jack and Mary have an estate valued at $3 million. Jack dies in 2006, leaving everything to Mary. Under the unlimited marital deduction, no estate tax is due. When Mary dies in 2007, however, the tentative tax on her $3 million estate is $1,230,800. After applying the applicable credit amount of $780,800, the estate tax is $450,000. That leaves $2,550,000 for transfer to her heirs.

Jack's total estate at his death in 2006 $3,000,000

Mary's total estate at her death in 2007 $3,000,000

Tentative tax on her estate	$1,230,800	
Applicable credit amount	−780,800	
Total estate tax payable	$ 450,000	
		(450,000)

Net amount distributed to heirs $2,550,000

What if they had divided their estate equally and when Jack died in 2006, incurred tax on his $1.5 million estate? The tentative tax on a $1.5 million estate in 2006 is $555,800. When the applicable credit amount of $555,800 is subtracted, the tax is $0.

Jack's total estate at his death in 2006 $1,500,000

Tentative tax on his estate	$555,800	
Applicable credit amount	−555,000	
Total estate tax payable	$ 0	
		0

Net amount distributed to heirs $1,500,000

When Mary dies in 2007, the tax on her $1.5 million estate after applying the credit is the same $0. The total tax paid by dividing their estates is $0 instead of $450,000. That leaves a total transfer to their heirs of $3,000,000, which is an increase of $450,000! (Of course, this assumption is oversimplified for the purpose of illustrating the potential savings that result from incurring estate taxes on fewer dollars in lower brackets.)

One way to achieve the kind of savings in the example above is to use two trusts to split the estate. Here is how the two trusts work: At the first death, one-half the estate passes directly to the spouse or to an A trust. (A and B trusts are common terminology in the estate planning field.) The A trust qualifies for the marital deduction, and its assets are not taxed until the second spouse's death. The balance of the estate passes to their nonspousal heirs in a B trust in a way that is taxed.

> **To maximize the effectiveness of A and B trusts, assets most likely to appreciate should be transferred to the already taxed B trust.**

To maximize the effectiveness of this technique, assets most likely to appreciate significantly in value should be transferred to the already taxed B trust. This helps decrease the growth of the value of the A trust, further reducing exposure to estate taxation.

There may be nontax reasons to use this technique. For example, if an estate owner has children by a previous marriage, it may be appropriate to have at least some part of the estate transferred to a qualified terminable interest property trust, commonly known as a QTIP trust, for the benefit of the children of the former marriage. In addition, the estate owner may prefer that, should the surviving spouse remarry, children of a future marriage not share in the estate.

Trusts

Retirees and individuals who are nearing retirement are likely to have substantial income and wealth and are therefore likely to have a greater need for establishing trusts. We have discussed some trust arrangements and the tax advantages that can be derived from them. Essentially, a *trust* is an arrangement in which a person or entity holds legal title to property and manages it for the benefit of another person or group of people.

trust

Trust Terminology

grantor
corpus
trustee

The person who creates the trust is known as the *grantor*. The property held in trust is known as the *corpus* or principal. The person or entity holding legal title to the property is known as the *trustee*, and the person or group for whose benefit the property is being held are the beneficiaries.

The way a trust works is fairly simple. A trustee holds property for the benefit of another person. This arrangement separates the legal interest from the beneficial interest. Typically, this might involve ownership of property by the trustee (the legal interest), with income from the property being given to the beneficiary (beneficial interest).

Trusts are managed according to instructions stipulated by the grantor in the trust agreement. If the grantor retains the right to terminate or change the trust, regaining the corpus, the trust is a revocable trust. If the grantor has no right to terminate or change the trust, it is said to be irrevocable.

inter vivos trust

testamentary trust

A trust that becomes operative during the lifetime of the grantor is known as an *inter vivos trust* or living trust, while one created by the terms of the grantor's will is called a *testamentary trust.*

Contingent Testamentary Trust

Although there are many kinds of trusts, one of the most common is the contingent testamentary trust for the benefit of minor children.

It is unwise and impractical to bequeath substantial amounts of property to minor children. A prudent client uses his or her will to create a contingent trust to receive assets for a minor beneficiary. When the child reaches the age specified in the trust, his or her share of the trust assets are distributed.

Another approach is to hold the entire estate in trust until the youngest child attains majority or until some other predetermined event such as completing his or her education. At that time, the trust is terminated and the respective shares of trust assets are distributed to the children. This can be especially useful when there is a considerable difference between the ages or educational status of the children.

Revocable Life Insurance Trust

The typical revocable life insurance trust is an inter vivos or living trust. The purpose of a revocable life insurance trust is to receive the proceeds of insurance policies on the grantor's life.

Usually, the trust is unfunded during the life of the grantor, who owns and pays for the life insurance that names the trust as beneficiary. At the grantor's death, the trustee collects the life insurance proceeds and uses them for the benefit of the trust beneficiaries as directed by the trust agreement.

Revocable life insurance trusts provide protection for the beneficiaries from others and from themselves. The trustee's management and control assure the safety of the trust proceeds and prevent the beneficiary from using the proceeds unwisely. The terms of the trust ensure that the trustee will complete the grantor's wishes even though the grantor is no longer living.

> One use of a revocable life insurance trust is to make sure that resources exist to pay estate closing costs and taxes.

Another use of revocable life insurance trusts is to make sure that resources exist to pay estate closing costs and taxes. If life insurance proceeds are paid to a named beneficiary, there is no guarantee that they will be made available to the estate for closing purposes. Channeling the proceeds into the hands of the trustee assures that the funds will be used as intended.

Crummey Trust

The Crummey trust is an irrevocable trust designed to accept gifts that will qualify for the annual gift tax exclusion. To qualify as gifts, the contributions must provide a present interest to the beneficiaries. That means that the recipient must have an unrestricted, immediate right to use the gift.

This condition creates a dilemma. How can a trust be arranged so that the money is available for the beneficiary's future needs and, at the same time, allow the beneficiary the unrestricted immediate right to remove the gift from the trust? To solve this problem, a Crummey trust gives the beneficiary the unrestricted right to withdraw money from the trust but limits the right in two ways:

- It limits the withdrawal period. For example, the withdrawal period can be limited to the 30 days following the annual deposit to the trust. If no withdrawal is made during a 30-day period following the contribution, the contribution cannot be withdrawn later.
- It limits the maximum amount that can be withdrawn each year. For example, the withdrawal may be limited to the amount of the current year's contribution.

> **The advantages of the Crummey trust may be worth the risk, especially when the beneficiaries understand the trust's purpose.**

A disadvantage of the Crummey trust is that the beneficiary can exercise the withdrawal right, thus removing contributions and defeating the purpose of the trust. The advantages may be worth the risk, however, especially when beneficiaries understand the trust's purpose.

Irrevocable Life Insurance Trust. The irrevocable life insurance trust is a variation of the Crummey trust. The irrevocable life insurance trust is established for the sole purpose of owning a life insurance policy or policies.

The trust applies for and owns the policies on the life of the grantor, and it receives the death benefit when the grantor dies. The grantor makes annual gifts to the trust to fund the policies, and the Crummey provisions are followed. The contributions to the trust that are to be used to pay the life insurance premiums thereby reduce the size of the estate, and the proceeds of the insurance are kept out of the insured's estate.

Income in Respect of a Decedent

> **income in respect of a decedent (IRD)**

Income that a decedent earned prior to death but another person received following the decedent's death is referred to as *income in respect of a decedent (IRD)*. In general, the present value of survivor benefits payable to a third-party beneficiary under employer-sponsored tax-qualified pension plans and lump sums from profit-sharing plans, SEPs, SIMPLEs, traditional IRAs, and non-qualified deferred-compensation plans in which the decedent had no cost basis are all considered to be IRD.

IRD is includible in the decedent's gross estate and potentially subject to estate taxation. These survivor benefits are also includible in the decedent beneficiary's income and subject to income taxation.

You may be thinking that it is unfair that an asset, such as a retirement income benefit, is subject to *both* income and estate taxation. Keep in mind, however, that much of what we characterize as wealth results from the accumulation of after-tax dollars. The concept underlying taxation of IRD simply assures that because it would have been subject to income tax had the decedent lived, it should not avoid income taxation merely because the decedent died.

Example :

Suppose that a retiree has $500,000 of qualified plan assets at death in addition to an already taxable estate of $2,500,000. Let's first focus on the estate tax consequences of the $500,000 of qualified plan assets being paid to a nonspouse beneficiary.

Estate Tax Comparison for Death in 2006

	Without IRD	With IRD
Taxable estate	$2,500,000	$2,500,000
Plus: qualified plan	0	500,000
Total taxable estate	$2,500,000	$3,000,000
Tentative estate tax	$1,010,800	$1,240,800
Less: applicable credit	780,800	780,800
Net estate tax due	$ 230,000	$ 460,000

Difference: $460,000 – $230,000 = $230,000*

* This difference is an allowable itemized deduction that the recipient(s) of this IRD may deduct on line 27 of federal income tax form Schedule A as a miscellaneous itemized deduction.

The additional $500,000 of assets from a qualified plan will cause an additional $230,000 of estate tax to be due for a death occurring in 2006. However, the beneficiary is allowed an income tax deduction equal to the amount of estate tax attributable to the IRD, as long as both income and estate taxes are paid in the same tax year. This is determined by computing the amount of federal estate taxes including IRD and comparing it with the amount of tax due excluding the IRD. The difference in estate tax payable ($230,000) is the amount of the allowable income tax deduction, which is shown below.

Income Tax Ramifications of Qualified Plan IRD
for Year 2006

	Potential Income Tax	Actual Income Tax Payable
Qualified plan proceeds	$500,000	$500,000
Less: deduction for estate tax paid	– 0	–230,000
Income tax due on	$500,000	$270,000
Income tax payable*	$148,250	$ 69,082

> *Difference in income taxes payable due to the deduction of estate taxes paid on qualified plan proceeds attributable to IRD is $79,168 ($148,250 – $69,082). (For simplicity purposes, this example assumes that the beneficiary has no other income in 2006 and files his or her tax return as married filing jointly.)*

Now, if we isolate the $500,000 of qualified plan assets in this case and total the combined estate tax and income tax attributable to those assets and paid in one year in a lump sum by the deceased retiree's heirs, we see that nearly 60 percent of those dollars go to taxation.

Total Taxes Paid on Lump-Sum Proceeds
Received from a Qualified Plan Distribution
as Income in Respect of a Decedent

Qualified plan proceeds		$500,000
Less: estate tax paid	$–230,000	
Income tax paid	– 69,082	
Total taxes paid		$299,082
Taxes paid as a percentage of total ($299,082 ÷ $500,000)		59.82%

Planning Considerations for Retirement Assets

A key to planning for retirement assets that are contractual and constitute IRD is to coordinate these assets with the prospect's overall estate planning objectives. This can be accomplished by coordinating life insurance ben-

> **One rule of thumb:
> If heirs are likely
> to require pension,
> profit-sharing, or
> nonqualified deferred-
> compensation benefits
> to meet living expenses,
> survivor benefits should
> be paid directly to them.**

eficiary designations with careful drafting of the retirement planning client's will and trust(s).

One rule of thumb is that if heirs are likely to require pension, profit-sharing, or nonqualified deferred-compensation benefits to meet living expenses following the death of the deceased estate owner, the survivor benefits should be paid directly to them. To mitigate the potential impact of IRD taxation, life insurance coverage that is owned by the heirs or a trust of which the heirs are the beneficiaries, and that is approximately equal to the amount of the projected estate shrinkage caused by the IRD, could be purchased on the life of the owner of the tax-qualified funds while living. If the heirs are not likely to depend on qualified plan benefits to meet living expenses, deferring distribution of qualified monies for as long as possible can be an excellent tax planning strategy.

One technique to achieve tax deferral for the decedent's spouse is the spousal IRA. In general, the surviving spouse may roll over a lump-sum survivor benefit from a tax-qualified plan to a spousal IRA and avoid current income tax on the distribution. No distributions are required until he or she reaches age 70 1/2. Thereafter, minimum distributions equal to a fraction of the remaining account balance must be made annually. However, deferral is achieved by delaying the start date for distributions for as long as allowable (the surviving spouse's age 70 1/2) and through minimizing distributions as much as possible.

Another planning alternative is the payment of qualified plan benefits to a trust for the benefit of a surviving spouse or for other beneficiaries. Although the lump-sum payment will be includible in trust income, the remaining proceeds are eligible for professional money management. Also, a trust may protect the assets from the claims of beneficiaries' creditors and provide the trustee with considerable flexibility in distributions of income and principal. ◊

ETHICS AND PROFESSIONALISM FOR THE FINANCIAL ADVISOR

Your career carries with it a tremendous responsibility. As a financial advisor, you approach others, both friends and strangers, and ask them for the opportunity to help them plan for their future financial security. You ask them to accept your advice and trust your recommendations. In doing so, you have an absolute obligation to maintain the highest ethical standards of professional behavior.

You assume responsibility for helping prospects and clients meet their financial needs. It is this responsibility, combined with your training, specialized knowledge in areas of financial planning that are often difficult for prospects and clients to understand, and the promise of continued service that raises your selling/planning activities to the level of career professional.

In today's financial services marketplace, there is a tremendous emphasis on ethical business practices and legal compliance issues. Ethical behavior in all business dealings is the responsibility of every professional advisor. What must you do to live up to this responsibility?

Certainly, an advisor must comply with

- state regulations for the sale of all insurance products
- federal regulations for the sale of securities and registered products
- company policies and procedures for all marketing activities

In fulfilling your responsibility to your prospects and clients and conducting yourself as a professional advisor, you must comply with all applicable laws and regulations. Compliance means following the laws and regulations, including company rules that apply to the sale of all financial products.

These are the minimum standards. State and federal laws regulate the insurance and securities industries to protect consumers from unfair sales practices. Financial services companies' rules are developed to make certain that the company and its advisors meet state and federal requirements. They are also designed to make sure that the company has complete and accurate information on which to base its marketing, sales, underwriting, and claims activities and decisions.

> **Professionalism and ethical conduct demand more than mere compliance with laws and regulations.**

Professionalism and ethical conduct demand more than mere compliance with laws and regulations. Nevertheless, following these regulations and rules is the first step in professional conduct.

State Regulation

Traditionally, insurance companies and insurance policies have been regulated primarily at the state, not the federal, level. Each of the states has established its own department of insurance to regulate the insurance activities conducted within the particular state. In addition to the state insurance department, the legislative bodies of each state set policy for the regulation of insurance. Each state legislature passes laws to guide the insurance company's activities and products.

The state regulation of insurance companies has several key functions:

- insurance company licensing
- producer licensing
- product regulation
- market conduct
- financial regulation
- consumer services

State insurance departments regulate the financial aspects of insurance companies. Therefore, states must be concerned with their insurers' financial solvency. They want assurance that the insurance companies have enough money invested to cover their policyowners. Making sure their insurance companies stay solvent to pay claims is of primary importance to state regulators.

There is also state regulation of market conduct. State insurance departments supervise the sales and marketing practices of both insurance companies and advisors. The goal is to make sure consumers are treated fairly. In fact, each state insurance department's number one priority is the protection of its insurance consumers.

> Each state insurance department's number one priority is the protection of its insurance consumers.

Licensing

Insurance Companies. To be able to sell insurance products in a particular state, the insurance company that offers the products must first be licensed by the state department of insurance. The insurance company must apply for a license and meet the specific requirements of the particular state.

The insurance company must file all the products it sells with the state insurance department. Some states require a mere informational filing, depending on the type of product. Other states require that the insurance company receive an official stamp of approval by the insurance department before the insurer can offer its products for sale.

Advisors. The advisor who is selling insurance products must also be licensed in the particular state. Typically, the basic life/health insurance license allows its holder to sell most life insurance, health insurance, and fixed-annuity products. Usually, the state requires that the advisor be licensed in the state where the application is written. This may or may not be the policyowner's state of residence.

Advisors may be licensed in more than one state to sell insurance products. Generally, an advisor will carry a resident license in his or her home state and have additional nonresident licenses in other states.

The advisor must also obtain an appointment from one or more companies. This appointment is what allows the advisor to sell a particular insurance company's products. During the appointment process, the insurance company will verify the existence of the advisor's insurance license and will most likely perform both financial and criminal background checks. If an advisor sells for several insurance companies, he or she will have several appointments.

Variable life insurance, variable annuities, and other investment or equity-based products, however, are generally not covered by the basic life/health insurance license. These products require special licenses and Registration with the *National Association of Securities Dealers (NASD)*. The NASD is a self-regulatory organization. It was established under authority granted by

> **National Association of Securities Dealers (NASD)**

Your Financial Services Practice: Unauthorized Entities

Regulation of insurance products and services varies from state to stare. In Florida, for example, regulations prohibit doing business with an unauthorized insurance entity. An unauthorized entity is an insurance company that has not gained approval to place insurance in the jurisdiction where it or a producer wants to sell insurance. These carriers are unlicensed and prohibited from doing business in that state. In most cases where these carriers have operated, they have characterized themselves as one of several types that are exempt from state regulation. It is the financial advisor's responsibility to exercise due diligence to make sure the carriers for whom they are selling are approved by the department of insurance in that state.

---

the Securities Exchange Act of 1934 to provide voluntary self-regulation of broker/dealers under the oversight of the Securities and Exchange Commission (SEC). Depending on the state regulations, separate state licenses may also be necessary.

Although state laws that regulate insurance company and advisor licensing vary, the state commissioners work together through the National Association of Insurance Commissioners (NAIC) to identify the issues of greatest importance to consumers and to set legislative standards through model legislation. Because of their work, there is general agreement on some practices in insurance sales. For example, all but two states—California and Florida—forbid rebating or the practice of sharing or returning part of the premium to a client as an inducement to purchase a policy.

Misrepresentation

All states are concerned with the misrepresentation of insurance products and benefits. Presenting an insurance policy as a savings plan, cash accumulation fund, educational savings plan, individual retirement plan, or any other similar savings device without making it clear that the underlying product is life insurance constitutes misrepresentation and is illegal. Suggesting that an insurance policy has certain features, benefits, values, or guarantees that are not specifically guaranteed in the written contract is, likewise, misrepresentation. So is a failure to reveal limitations or exclusions of coverage.

Illustrations

Allowing a prospect's misconceptions about benefits, or fostering them through the sales presentation, is a serious form of misrepresentation.

One concern over misrepresentation comes from the use of illustrations in the sales process. If they are not explained carefully, the prospect can easily be misled into believing that the policy promises significantly greater benefits than those guaranteed in the contract. Allowing misconceptions about benefits, or fostering them through the sales presentation, is a serious form of misrepresentation.

Most states subscribe to model legislation by the NAIC that describes procedures for the proper use of illustrations in the sales process. A complete illustration should explain clearly which values are guaranteed and which are not. The advisor should make sure that the prospect reads and understands the limitations of any projections that are made. He or she should give the prospect a full illustration, including all footnotes and explanatory pages, and review it with the prospect.

Replacement

Another major area that concerns the states is the unjustified replacement of existing policies in order to sell new policies. Unwarranted replacements can threaten the policyowner's benefits, damage the insurer's underwriting practices, and impugn the advisor's integrity.

There are circumstances when an insurance policy replacement is desirable. A variety of contractual enhancements that have emerged in the last few years for certain insurance products, along with the advent of a new life insurance mortality table, may warrant a review of an individual's existing coverage. It is extremely important, however, to adhere to state regulation procedures for providing comparative information on the existing and proposed insurance products. Furthermore, the advisor should never encourage a prospective insured to cease existing coverage until a new insurance policy has passed through underwriting and been satisfactorily issued and put into force.

Advice

States are also concerned with what advisors call themselves and the kinds of advice they give their prospects and clients. Advisors who call themselves financial planners or financial consultants may be breaking state laws unless they have obtained special licenses. In many states, financial advisors, planners, and consultants are considered separate professional groups, requiring specific licenses.

Even in routine contacts, an insurance or financial advisor's discussions with a prospect or client may touch on legal or tax matters. Giving a client or prospect specific legal or tax advice can be construed as practicing law without a proper license, and that is illegal. Although discussing legal or tax matters with clients in very general terms is allowed, you cannot give specific advice in these areas. When specific advice is requested, recommend that your prospects and clients consult an attorney or tax advisor.

> Giving a client or prospect specific legal or tax advice can be construed as practicing law without a proper license, and that is illegal.

Federal Regulation

Although the states are the primary regulators of the insurance industry, the main responsibility for regulation of securities products rests clearly with the federal government. Securities products include the variable life and variable annuity products many insurance companies now offer. Without the proper registration, an advisor is not allowed to discuss equity-based investment products with a prospective buyer.

To sell these products, you must be properly registered with the National Association of Securities Dealers. The NASD has the power to require and monitor compliance with standardized rules of fair practice for the industry. NASD regulatory responsibilities include registration and testing of securities professionals, review of members' advertising and sales literature, and services such as arbitration of investor disputes. Registered representatives must provide the NASD with personal information, including prior employment and any history of securities-related disciplinary action.

> The NASD has the power to require and monitor compliance with standardized rules of fair practice for the industry.

Selling Variable Annuities, Mutual Funds, and Other Variable Securities Products

To sell variable annuities, mutual funds, and other securities products, you must be registered with the NASD and successfully complete either the NASD Series 6 or Series 7 examination.

An NASD registration will not be issued until the you are affiliated with a broker/dealer. Most large life insurance companies have broker/dealer subsidiaries and thus make sponsorship and broker/dealer affiliation easy for their advisors. For independent advisors, there are broker/dealers who stand ready to establish an affiliate relationship.

Special licensing by the state or states in which you intend to sell variable life and annuity products and mutual funds is also required. For the advisor to obtain state licensing, most states require the successful completion of the Uniform Securities Agent State Law Examination; this is the Series 63 examination offered by the NASD. Other states may require different examinations and different licensing requirements.

Selling Stocks, Bonds, and Options

An advisor who wants to engage in the sale of individual stocks, bonds, and options must obtain a general securities license. This is the license held by registered representatives at brokerage firms. The examination required for this license, the Series 7, is more rigorous than the Series 6 examination. Passing the Series 7 examination qualifies an advisor for the solicitation, purchase, and/or sale of all securities products, including corporate securities, municipal securities, options, direct-participation programs, investment company products, and variable contracts.

The Series 7 examination cannot be taken without the sponsorship of a broker/ dealer, and continuing affiliation with a broker/dealer is required to maintain the Series 7 registration.

Registered Investment Advisor (RIA)

registered investment
advisor (RIA)

The Investment Advisers Act of 1940 defines an investment advisor as any person who, for compensation, engages in the business of advising others as to the value of securities or the advisability of acquiring or disposing of securities. Most persons who fall within the act's definition of an investment advisor and who make use of the mails or any instrumentality of interstate commerce are required to register with the SEC as a *registered investment advisor (RIA)*.

Merely dealing with a security does not, by itself, make someone an investment advisor. In the 1980s, the SEC issued three tests to determine whether or not individuals must register as an investment advisor. If all three tests are answered in the affirmative, registration is required unless specifically excluded or exempted. If any of the tests is answered in the negative, there is no need to become a registered investment advisor. According to the SEC's three tests, the individual or entity must

- give advice or analysis concerning securities (security advice test)
- be engaged in the business of advising others regarding securities (security business test)
- be in receipt of compensation (compensation test)

The SEC does not guarantee the competence or investment abilities of any individuals who register under the act; it merely seeks to provide a mechanism for discouraging unethical behavior.

It is important to remember that the purpose of the SEC in devising the three tests is to protect clients from fraud and other abusive situations. The SEC does not guarantee the competence or investment abilities of any individuals who register under the act; it merely seeks to provide a mechanism for discouraging unethical behavior, principally via full disclosure to clients.

Although the SEC does not require investment advisors who seek registration to successfully complete a qualifying exam, the individual advisor and advisory firm must follow strict rules for registration, record keeping, and compliance. Many states do require successful completion of a qualifying exam before registration as an investment advisor.

Financial Planners

There are no special federal licensing or registration requirements for financial planners. The services of most financial planners generally include analyzing their clients' financial situations, setting achievable financial goals, and developing and implementing sound financial plans. The development of a plan may include recommendations of securities to be purchased or sold, and a fee may be charged for the plan. Generally, if the financial planner meets the three tests cited above, the individuals involved with developing the plan must be registered as registered investment advisors with the SEC.

Many states have implemented legislation for persons calling themselves financial planners or those charging a fee for financial advice. The legislation requires licensing of those who hold themselves out as financial planners.

Other states are considering legislation. Contact your State Division of Securities for information on your state's licensing requirements.

You will need to know if your state allows you to charge a fee for planning and to collect commissions for products sold on the same case. This is illegal in some states. If you have any questions concerning your requirements, contact your broker/dealer and clarify your position immediately.

Affiliation with a Broker/Dealer

Most large life insurance companies now have broker/dealer subsidiaries with which their advisors become affiliated. Independent agencies generally become licensed as broker/dealers or initiate affiliations with existing broker/dealers as either satellite offices or branch offices, but this may involve more responsibility, expense, and licensing than is necessary for most advisors.

The regulations for marketing securities products are extensive. The company must approve all advertising materials, including letters that mention the sale or availability of securities products, as well as any sales literature. Even stationery and business cards that the registered representatives use must meet certain standards.

Failure to follow any of the rules can lead to the loss of licensing, significant fines and penalties, and a suspension of a company's right to do business. A failure to follow the proper procedures can be a very costly mistake.

As discussed in chapter 5, before securities products can be sold, the law requires that potential buyers be given information about the product in a form known as a prospectus. As with the other materials associated with the sale of securities, the prospectus must follow certain formats and guidelines.

Company Rules and Procedures

Financial services company rules are developed to make certain that the company and its advisors meet all state and federal regulations. They are also designed to make sure that the company has complete and accurate information on which to base the issuance of suitable financial products to its customers.

As a financial advisor who sells financial products, you function as an agent of the company you represent.

As a financial advisor who sells financial products, you function as an agent of the company you represent. In its simplest terms, an agent represents the company with a limited right to speak for the company he or she represents. What you say and do as an agent may be binding on the company. Clearly, investment and insurance companies must take due care to protect themselves from the possible misbehavior of those representing them.

Company rules also have a value to advisors. They are designed to help advisors make sure that they meet all applicable legal requirements. Keep in mind that most financial products are legal contracts between the owner and the financial services company. If the contract is not carefully and properly executed, it could lead to serious legal complications for the owner, the company, and the advisor. A company's rules are designed to ensure that all legal requirements have been met.

This is the major reason that insurers require that the company's home office approve in advance all sales materials an advisor uses. It is a simple way for the insurer to make certain that its products and benefits are not being presented in a manner that goes against federal or state regulations.

Ethical Considerations

Suitability

Your professional obligation to prospects is to help them determine and carry out the best solutions to meet their retirement planning needs. In identifying the need for financial products that address prospects' concerns, helping prospects understand how certain products meet those concerns, and implementing solutions to prospects' retirement planning needs, you have fulfilled your professional obligation.

With such financial products as life, disability income, and long-term care insurance, if the prospect has medical or other problems that cause the company to offer a different policy from the one he or she applied for or a policy at a higher premium, your responsibility is to help the prospect decide if the rated policy meets his or her needs and is the best solution to the problems it is meant to cover. If, for some reason, a prospect is not insurable, you are not at fault and have not failed in your professional duty. Your obligation to both the prospect and to the company you represent is to give the most accurate and complete information possible. Only then can the company decide if it is willing to offer a policy and at what premium. Your duty to the company to provide factual information supersedes your responsibility to obtain coverage for the prospect.

The need to provide complete and accurate information about a prospect goes beyond the need to protect an insurance company from inadvertently accepting extra risk. Failure to provide complete and accurate information, negligence in recording information provided by the prospect, or intentional misrepresentation of facts by the advisor or the prospect can void the insurance contract, leaving the prospect unprotected without his or her knowledge.

If a claim is contested or denied, both the advisor and the company may be held accountable for the misinformation. If the client is responsible, his or her family may suffer. If the advisor is responsible, he or she can be held personally liable. The risk to all parties involved is substantial.

> **Your duty to the company to provide factual information supersedes your responsibility to obtain coverage for the prospect.**

Compliance and Ethics

The conflict that may arise between the prospect's need for an insurance or investment product and the financial services company's underwriting rules or issuing standards spans both compliance and ethics. You may encounter

You may encounter situations when fair business practices, legal requirements, and company rules seem to conflict with your best efforts. How the conflict is resolved is a matter of ethics.

situations when fair business practices, legal requirements, and company rules seem to conflict with your best efforts. How the apparent conflict is resolved is a matter of ethics, and it goes beyond compliance with the law.

Burke A. Christensen, JD, CLU, former vice president and general counsel of the American Society of CLU & ChFC, wrote the following in an article for the *Journal of Financial Service Professionals* (formerly the *Journal of the American Society of CLU & ChFC*):

> . . . remember that there is sometimes a gap between what is legal and what is ethical. According to Potter Stewart, retired justice of the United States Supreme Court, that gap represents "the difference between what you have a right to do, and what is the right thing to do." To infuse your character with ethics, you must not be content to merely comply with the law. . . .

Another way to say it is that ethical behavior is doing the right thing. It is doing what is right and putting the prospect's best interests before your own. It is maintaining the highest possible standard of behavior in all your business dealings. It is continuing to develop your skills so you can provide the best possible service to those with whom you work. It is representing the industry, its companies, and its advisors, in the best possible light.

Professional Code of Conduct and Ethics

professional ethics

Professional ethics can be defined as behaving according to the principles of right and wrong—a code of ethics—that are accepted by the profession. By adopting and practicing a professional code of ethics, you will achieve the high standard of professionalism that a career in financial services demands. The codes of ethics of The American College and the National Association of Insurance and Financial Advisors (NAIFA) are standards of professional behavior to which you should constantly adhere. (See figures 8-2 and 8-3.)

Being a Professional

professionalism

Professionalism

To be successful as a financial advisor, you must be a professional. You must have the technical knowledge necessary to provide meaningful support and accurate advice to your prospects and clients. As a competent financial services professional, you must be fully aware of the legal and tax ramifications of the recommendations you make. You must also be able to outline the positive and negative implications of the various investment and insurance options available so that your prospects and clients can make informed purchasing decisions. You therefore must have a thorough understanding of your products, the problems that your prospects and clients face, and the solutions your products can provide.

FIGURE 8-2
The American College Code of Ethics

To underscore the importance of ethical standards for Huebner School designations, the Board of Trustees of The American College adopted a Code of Ethics in 1984. Embodied in the Code is the Professional Pledge and eight Canons.

The Professional Pledge and the Canons

The Pledge to which all Huebner School designees subscribe is as follows:

> *In all my professional relationships, I pledge myself to the following rule of ethical conduct: I shall, in light of all conditions surrounding those I serve, which I shall make every conscientious effort to ascertain and understand, render that service which, in the same circumstances, I would apply to myself.*

The eight Canons are:

I. Conduct yourself at all times with honor and dignity.
II. Avoid practices that would bring dishonor upon your profession or The American College.
III. Publicize your achievement in ways that enhance the integrity of your profession.
IV. Continue your studies throughout your working life so as to maintain a high level of professional competence.
V. Do your utmost to attain a distinguished record of professional service.
VI. Support the established institutions and organizations concerned with the integrity of your profession.
VII. Participate in building your profession by encouraging and providing appropriate assistance to qualified persons pursuing professional studies.
VIII. Comply with all laws and regulations, particularly as they relate to professional and business activities.

> To be a professional, you need to be client-centered. That means you have to put your clients' interests before your own.

Client Focus. To be a professional, you also need to be client-centered. This means you have to put your clients' interests before your own. In financial, estate, and retirement planning, your job goes beyond simply making a financial product sale. Your professional responsibility is to help your prospects and clients identify and implement all the steps that will help them accomplish their financial planning goals.

Legal Requirements. Professionalism requires you to meet the legal and ethical standards of the insurance and financial services industry. You must, for example, be licensed to discuss the products you sell in all jurisdictions in which you work. As mentioned earlier, unless you are a licensed attorney, it is illegal for you to give legal advice. It is also illegal for you to give tax advice when acting in the role of insurance advisor. Although you can discuss legal and tax considerations in general terms, you cannot provide specific legal or tax advice, or draft legal documents.

FIGURE 8-3
The National Association of Insurance and Financial Advisors (NAIFA) Code of Ethics

PREAMBLE: Those engaged in life underwriting occupy the unique position of liaison between the purchasers and the suppliers of life and health insurance and closely related financial products. Inherent in this role is the combination of professional duty to the client and to the company, as well. Ethical balance is required to avoid any conflict between these two obligations. Therefore,

I Believe It To Be My Responsibility

To hold my profession in high esteem and strive to enhance its prestige.

To fulfill the needs of my clients to the best of my ability.

To maintain my clients' confidences.

To render exemplary service to my clients and their beneficiaries.

To adhere to professional standards of conduct in helping my clients to protect insurable obligations and attain their financial security objectives.

To present accurately and honestly all facts essential to my clients' decisions.

To perfect my skills and increase my knowledge through continuing education.

To conduct my business in such a way that my example might help raise the professional standards of life underwriting.

To keep informed with respect to applicable laws and regulations and to observe them in the practice of my profession.

To cooperate with others whose services are constructively related to meeting the needs of my clients.

Adopted April 1986
NAIFA Board of Trustees

Professional Responsibility

Financial advisors have an obligation to think of themselves and conduct themselves as professionals. The public expects professional advice, and the courts see financial advisors as professionals. Financial advisors advertise themselves as having the special skills needed to provide investment guidance to clients and to protect their property and human life values. This advertising brings a higher legal standard of performance to the advisor's work.

If an advisor mentions an investment program for college or retirement funding purposes, or suggests the purchase of life or disability income insurance coverage for an individual's financial security, and the client is not interested, has the advisor fulfilled his or her professional responsibility? Isn't it your responsibility as a professional advisor to clearly explain the need for suitable investment or insurance products to your clients? Part of your professional responsibility is to encourage your prospects and clients to take actions they can reasonably afford that will enhance their financial security and that of their families. To do this, you need to educate them about the consequences of action or inaction so that they can make informed financial and retirement planning decisions.

> **There is a tremendous need for retirement planning, but with the need comes an opportunity for abuse.**

There is a tremendous need for retirement planning, but with the need comes an opportunity for abuse. Be aware that many of the people you will be approaching are skeptical of you because they have been the victims of abuse, they know someone who has been a victim, or they follow the media, which is filled with stories of scams and fraud.

We all must accept responsibility for solving these problems. For example, seniors have been the targets of investment swindles that robbed them of their life's savings. There has been overuse of living trusts, negligent replacement of life insurance policies, financial planners who have claimed specialty without expertise—to name just a few of the problems.

You have an important role to serve your prospects and clients in the best way you can. To accomplish this, you must educate them. A well-informed prospect is likely to make a good long-term client if your products and services provide solutions to his or her planning needs.

Professional Development through Education

> **To educate your prospects and clients, you must first educate yourself.**

To educate your prospects and clients, you must first educate yourself. Not only do you have to understand the basic concepts involved in financial planning, but you must also keep studying in order to learn advanced concepts. You must be prepared to address the exceptions and complications that are often part of the responsible planning process, as well as the routine situations that you most frequently encounter. You must stay abreast of new product innovations, legislative trends, and tax rulings that can affect your ability to provide the highest possible level of service.

By continually educating yourself, you will become a competent member of your clients' financial planning teams. Additional knowledge and skill development can result from pursuing the recognized professional designations of the financial services industry. The LUTCF, FSS, CLU, ChFC, and CFP designations, which are all earned in part by the successful completion of a qualified course of study, indicate your ongoing commitment to professionalism.

Membership and participation in the industry's professional organizations such as NAIFA and the Society of Financial Service Professionals, offer an opportunity for continuing education. You may also want to explore the various training and educational programs that are provided by insurance companies, universities, proprietary training organizations and other professional organizations. *Advisor Today* (the magazine of NAIFA), and *Life Insurance Selling* magazine are excellent sources of insurance news and sales ideas.

Formal programs can supplement your personal self-improvement regimen of daily and weekly readings in financial literature. For more information on additional training resources aimed at enhancing the skill and knowledge of the dedicated financial services professional, log on to The American College's website at www.theamericancollege.edu. ◊

A CONCLUDING THOUGHT

You have completed the last chapter of the *Foundations of Retirement Planning*. Now it is time to assimilate these concepts into your business endeavors. As you think of your business and focus on your future, remember that one day you will retire. At the very least, use what you have learned in this course to begin your own retirement plan. ◊

CHAPTER EIGHT REVIEW

Key terms and concepts are explained in the Glossary. Answers to the Review Questions and Self-Test Questions are found in the back of the book following the Glossary.

Key Terms

beneficiary	trustee
revocable beneficiary	inter vivos trust
irrevocable beneficiary	testamentary trust
insurable interest	income in respect of a decedent
per capita	(IRD)
per stirpes	National Association of Securities
applicable credit amount	Dealers (NASD)
unlimited marital deduction	registered investment advisor
trust	(RIA)
grantor	professional ethics
corpus	professionalism

Review Questions

8-1. Describe the two basic types of life insurance beneficiary designations

8-2. List the five ways property can be transferred at death.

8-3. Identify the four elements of a trust.

8-4. Define a trust and summarize how a trust works.

8-5. Briefly describe the federal estate tax.

8-6. List six categories of deductions that can be used to reduce the gross estate.

8-7. Identify four credits that can be used to reduce the tentative estate tax.

8-8. Briefly define the applicable credit amount and the unlimited marital deduction, and explain how each of these concepts can be used in estate planning.

8-9. Define income in respect of a decedent and briefly explain the effect it has on retirement plan assets.

8-10. Identify the major issues that state regulation of insurance companies and advisors address.

8-11. Identify the three tests used to determine if an advisor must register as a registered investment advisor.

8-12. Describe the role of the National Association of Securities Dealers in the regulation of financial advisors.

8-13. Explain what is meant by the apparent conflict between doing what is legal and doing what is ethical in dealing with prospects and clients.

Self-Test Questions

Instructions: Read chapter 8 first, then answer the following questions to test your knowledge. There are 10 questions; circle the correct answer, then check your answers with the answer key in the back of the book.

8-1. What is currently the maximum permissible amount of the estate tax marital deduction?

(A) $192,800
(B) $600,000
(C) $1,000,000
(D) unlimited amount

8-2. The person creating a trust is known as which of the following?

(A) grantor
(B) corpus
(C) trustee
(D) trust officer

8-3. Which of the following is the correct term for federal taxes that are imposed on the transfer of property at death?

    (A)   accumulated earnings tax
    (B)   inheritance taxes
    (C)   estate taxes
    (D)   income taxes

8-4. What is the applicable credit amount for federal estate tax in the years 2006, 2007, and 2008?

    (A) $345,800
    (B) $555,800
    (C) $780,800
    (D)   unlimited amount

8-5. Which of the following best describes an advisor's professional and ethical responsibility to prospects?

    (A)   to obtain the necessary coverage issued for the prospect
    (B)   to assist the prospect in presenting medical information in the most favorable light
    (C)   to help the prospect determine and carry out the best solutions available to meet his or her retirement planning needs
    (D)   to keep information received from the prospect in confidence from the home office

8-6. A financial advisor may be required to register as a registered investment advisor if which of the following is (are) answered in the affirmative?

    I.   Does the financial advisor provide advice or analysis about securities?
    II.   Is the financial advisor registered with the NASD to sell securities?

    (A)   I only
    (B)   II only
    (C)   Both I and II
    (D)   Neither I nor II

8-7. Which of the following situations concerning the change of an irrevocable beneficiary designation in a life insurance policy is (are) correct?

     I.   If the irrevocable beneficiary dies before the insured, the policyowner has the right to name a new beneficiary.

     II.   If the policyowner wants to change the irrevocable beneficiary, he or she has the contractual right do so without the beneficiary's consent.

    (A)   I only
    (B)   II only
    (C)   Both I and II
    (D)   Neither I nor II

8-8. All the following are the ways to transfer property at death EXCEPT by

    (A)   will
    (B)   gift
    (C)   right of survivorship
    (D)   right of contract

8-9. All the following are currently allowable credits that can be subtracted from the tentative estate tax to derive the net estate due EXCEPT

    (A)   the applicable credit amount
    (B)   credit for prior gifts
    (C)   the state death tax credit
    (D)   credit for foreign death taxes paid

8-10. All the following are basic techniques to achieve estate and gift tax reduction EXCEPT:

    (A)   Create tax-exempt wealth.
    (B)   Divide the estate.
    (C)   Discount the estate tax obligation.
    (D)   Incur estate tax at the second death.

Appendix A

Time-Value-of-Money Tables

TABLE A-1
Compound Interest
One Dollar Principal

Sum to which $1 will increase at compound interest rate

Year	3%	4%	5%	6%	7%	8%	9%	10%	11%	12%	13%	14%	15%
1	1.030	1,040	1.050	1.060	1.070	1.080	1.090	1.110	1.110	1.120	1.130	1.140	1.150
2	1.061	1.082	1.103	1,124	1.145	1.166	1.118	1.210	1.232	1.254	1.277	1.300	1.323
3	1.093	1.125	1.158	1,191	1.225	1.260	1.295	1.331	1.368	1.405	1.443	1.482	1.521
4	1.126	1.170	1.216	1,262	1.311	1.360	1.412	1.464	1.518	1.574	1.630	1.689	1.749
5	1.159	1.217	1.276	1.338	1.403	1.469	1.539	1.611	1.685	1.762	1.842	1.925	2.011
6	1.194	1.265	1.340	1.419	1.501	1.587	1.677	1.772	1.870	1.974	2.082	2.195	2.313
7	1.230	1.316	1.407	1.504	1.606	1.714	1.828	1.949	2.076	2.211	2.353	2.502	2.660
8	1.267	1.369	1.477	1.594	1.718	1.851	1.993	2.144	2.305	2.476	2.658	2.853	3.059
9	1.305	1.423	1.551	1.689	1.838	1.999	2.172	2.358	2.558	2.773	3.004	3.252	3.518
10	1.344	1.480	1.629	1.791	1.967	2.159	2.367	2.594	2.839	3.106	3.395	3.707	4.046
11	1.384	1.539	1.710	1.898	2.105	2.332	2.580	2.853	3.152	3.479	3.836	4.226	4.652
12	1.426	1.601	1.796	2.012	2.252	2.518	2.813	3.138	3.498	3.896	4.335	4.818	5.350
13	1.469	1.665	1.886	2.133	2.410	2.720	3.066	3.452	3.883	4.363	4.898	5.492	6.153
14	1.513	1.732	1.980	2.261	2.579	2.937	3.342	3.797	4.310	4.887	5.535	6.261	7.076
15	1.558	1.801	2.079	2.397	2.759	3.172	3.642	4.177	4.785	5.474	6.254	7.138	8.137
16	1.605	1.873	2.183	2.540	2.952	3.426	3.970	4.595	5.311	6.130	7.067	8.137	9.358
17	1.653	1.948	2.292	2.693	3.159	3.700	4.328	5.054	5.895	6.866	7.986	9.276	10.761
18	1.702	2.026	2.407	2.854	3.380	3.996	4.717	5.560	6.544	7.690	9.024	10.576	12.375
19	1.754	2.107	2.527	3.026	3.617	4.316	5.142	6.116	7.263	8.613	10.197	12.056	14.232
20	1.806	2.191	2.653	3.207	3.870	4.661	5.604	6.727\	8.062	9.646	11.523	13.743	16.367
21	1.860	2.279	2.786	3.400	4.141	5.034	6.109	7.400	8.949	10.804	13.021	15.668	18.822
22	1.916	2.370	2.925	3.604	4.430	5.437	6.659	8.140	9.934	12.100	14.714	17.861	21.645
23	1.974	2.465	3.072	3.820	4.741	5.871	7.258	8.954	11.026	13.552	16.627	20.362	24.891
24	2.033	2.563	3.225	4.049	5.072	6.341	7.911	9.850	12.239	15.179	18.788	23.212	28.625
25	2.094	2.666	3.388	4.292	5.427	6.848	8.623	10.835	13.585	17.000	21.231	26.462	32.919
26	2.157	2.772	3.556	4.549	5.807	7.396	9.399	11.918	15.080	19.040	23.991	30.167	37.857
27	2.221	2.883	3.733	4.822	6.214	7.988	10.245	13.110	16.739	21.325	27.109	34.390	43.535
28	2.288	2.999	3.920	5.112	6.649	8.627	11.167	14.421	18.580	23.884	30.633	39.204	50.066
29	2.357	3.119	4.116	5.418	7.114	9.317	12.172	15.863	20.624	26.750	34.616	44.693	57.575
30	2.427	3.243	4.322	5.743	7.612	10.063	13.268	17.449	22.892	29.960	39.116	50.950	66.212
31	2.500	3.373	4.538	6.088	8.145	10.868	14.462	19.194	25.410	33.555	44.201	58.083	76.144
32	2.575	3.508	4.765	6.453	8.715	11.737	15.763	21.114	28.206	37.582	49.947	66.215	87.565
33	2.652	3.648	5.003	6.841	9.325	12.676	17.182	23.225	31.308	42.092	56.440	75.485	100.700
34	2.732	3.794	5.253	7.251	9.978	13.690	18.728	25.548	34.752	47.143	63.777	86.053	115.805
35	2.814	3.946	5.516	7.686	10.677	14.785	20.414	28.102	38.575	52.800	72.069	98.100	133.176
36	2.898	4.104	5.792	8.147	11.424	15.968	22.251	30.913	42.818	59.136	81.437	111.834	153.152
37	2.985	4.268	6.081	8.636	12.224	17.246	24.254	34.004	47.528	66.232	92.024	127.491	176.125
38	3.075	4.439	6.385	9.154	13.079	18.625	26.437	37.404	52.756	74.180	103.987	145.340	202.543
39	3.167	4.616	6.705	9.704	13 995	20.115	28.816	41.145	58.559	83.081	117.506	165.687	232.925
40	3.262	4.801	7.040	10.286	14.975	21.725	31.409	45.529	65.001	93.051	132.782	188.884	267.864

TABLE A-2
Compound Interest
One Dollar Per Annum In Advance

Sum to which $1 per annum, deposited at the beginning of each year, will increase at compound interest rate

Year	3%	4%	5%	6%	7%	8%	9%	10%	11%	12%	13%	14%	15%
1	1.030	1.040	1.050	1.060	1.070	1.080	1.090	1.100	1.110	1.120	1.130	1.140	1.150
2	2.091	2.122	2.153	2.184	2.215	2.246	2.278	2.310	2.342	2.374	2.407	2.440	2.472
3	3.184	3.246	3.310	3.375	3.440	3.506	3.573	3.641	3.710	3.779	3.850	3.921	3.993
4	4.309	4.416	4.526	4.637	4.751	4.867	4.985	5.105	5.228	5.353	5.480	5.610	5.742
5	5.468	5.633	5.802	5.975	6.153	6.336	6.523	6.716	6.913	7.115	7.323	7.536	7.754
6	6.662	6.898	7.142	7.394	7.654	7.923	8.200	8.487	8.783	9.089	9.405	9.730	10.067
7	7.892	8.214	8.549	8.897	9.260	9.637	10.028	10.436	10.859	11.300	11.757	12.233	12.727
8	9.159	9.583	10.027	10.491	10.978	11.488	12.021	12.579	13.164	13.776	14.416	15.085	15.786
9	10.464	11.006	11.578	12.181	12.816	13.487	14.193	14.937	15.722	16.549	17.420	18.337	19.304
10	11.808	12.486	13.207	13.072	14.784	15.645	16.560	17.531	18.561	19.655	20.814	22.045	23.349
11	13.192	14.026	14.917	15.870	16.888	17.977	19.141	20.384	21.713	23.133	24.650	26.271	28.002
12	14.618	15.627	16.713	17.882	19.141	20.495	21.953	23.523	25.212	27.029	28.985	31.089	33.352
13	16.086	17.292	18.599	20.015	21.550	23.215	25.019	26.975	29.095	31.393	33.883	36.581	39.505
14	17.599	19.024	20.579	22.276	24.129	26.152	28.361	30.772	33.405	36.280	39.417	42.842	46.580
15	19.157	20.825	22.657	24.673	26.888	29.324	32.003	34.950	38.190	41.753	45.672	49.980	54.717
16	20.762	22.698	24.840	27.213	29.840	32.750	35.974	39.545	43.501	47.884	52.739	58.118	64.075
17	22.414	24.645	27.132	29.906	32.999	36.450	40.301	44.599	49.396	54.750	60.725	67.394	74.836
18	24.117	26.671	29.539	32.760	36.379	40.446	45.018	50.159	55.939	62.440	69.749	77.969	87.212
19	25.870	28.778	32.066	35.786	39.995	44.762	50.160	56.275	63.203	71.052	79.947	90.025	101.444
20	27.676	30.969	34.719	38.993	43.865	49.423	55.765	63.002	71.265	80.669	91.470	103.768	117.810
21	29.537	33.243	37.505	42.392	48.006	54.457	61.873	70.403	80.214	91.503	104.491	119.436	136.632
22	31.453	35.618	40.430	45.996	52.436	59.893	68.532	78.543	90.148	103.603	119.205	137.297	158.276
23	33.426	38.083	43.502	49.816	57.177	65.765	75.790	87.497	101.174	117.155	135.831	157.659	183.168
24	35.459	40.646	46.727	53.865	62.249	72.106	83.701	97.347	113.413	132.334	154.620	180.871	211.793
25	37.553	43.312	50.113	58.156	67.676	78.954	92.324	108.182	126.999	149.334	175.850	207.333	244.712
26	39.710	46.084	53.669	62.606	73.484	86.351	101.723	120.100	142.079	168.374	199.841	237.499	282.569
27	41.931	48.968	57.403	67.528	79.698	94.339	111.968	133.210	158.817	189.699	226.950	271.889	326.104
28	44.219	51.966	61.323	72.640	86.347	102.966	123.135	147.631	177.397	213.583	257.583	311.094	376.170
29	46.575	55.085	65.439	78.058	93.461	112.283	135.308	163.494	198.021	240.333	292.199	355.787	433.745
30	49.003	58.328	69.761	83.802	101.073	122.346	148.575	180.943	220.913	270.293	331.315	406.737	499.957
31	51.503	61.701	74.299	89.890	109.218	133.214	163.037	200.138	246.324	303.848	375.516	464.820	576.100
32	54.078	65.210	79.064	96.343	117.933	144.951	178.800	221.252	274.529	341.429	425.463	531.035	663.666
33	56.730	68.858	84.067	103.184	127.259	157.627	195.982	244.477	305.837	383.521	481.903	606.520	764.365
34	59.462	72.652	89.320	110.435	137.237	171.317	214.711	270.024	340.590	430.663	545.681	692.573	880.170
35	62.276	76.598	94.836	118.121	147.913	186.102	235.125	298.127	379.164	483.463	617.749	790.673	1013.346
36	65.174	80.702	100.628	126.268	159.337	202.070	257.376	329.039	421.982	542.599	699.187	902.507	1166.498
37	68.159	84.970	106.710	134.904	171.561	219.316	281.630	363.043	469.511	608.831	791.211	1029.998	1342.622
38	71.234	89.409	113.095	144.058	184.640	237.941	308.066	400.448	522.267	683.010	895.198	1175.338	1545.165
39	74.401	94.026	119.800	153.762	108.635	258.057	336.882	441.593	580.826	766.091	1012.704	1341.025	1778.090
40	77.663	98.827	126.840	164.048	213.610	279.781	368.292	486.852	645.827	859.142	1145.486	1529.909	2045.954

TABLE A-3
Compound Discount
One Dollar Principal

Present value of $1 to be received at the end of a specified number of years

Year	3%	4%	5%	6%	7%	8%	9%	10%	11%	12%	13%	14%	15%
1	.971	.962	.952	.943	.935	.926	.917	.909	.901	.893	.885	.877	.870
2	.943	.925	.907	.890	.873	.857	.842	.826	1.713	1.690	1.668	1.647	1.626
3	.915	.889	.864	.840	.816	.794	.772	.751	2.444	2.402	2.361	2.311	2.283
4	.888	.855	.823	.792	.763	.735	.708	.683	3.102	3.037	2.974	2.914	2.855
5	.863	.822	.784	.747	.713	.681	.650	.621	3.696	3.605	3.517	3.433	3.352
6	.837	.790	.746	.705	.666	.630	.596	.564	4.231	4.111	3.998	3.889	3.784
7	.813	.760	.711	.665	.623	.583	.547	.513	4.712	4.564	4.423	4.288	4.160
8	.789	.731	.677	.627	.582	.540	.502	.467	5.146	4.968	4.799	4.639	4.487
9	.766	.703	.645	.592	.544	.500	.460	.424	5.537	5.328	5.132	4.946	4.772
10	.744	.676	.614	.558	.508	.463	.422	.386	5.889	5.650	5.426	5.216	5.-19
11	.722	.650	.585	.527	.475	.429	.388	.350	6.207	5.938	5.687	5.453	5.234
12	.701	.625	.557	.497	.444	.397	.356	.319	6.492	6.194	5.918	5.660	5.421
13	.681	.601	.530	.469	.415	.368	.326	.290	6.750	6.424	6.122	5.842	5.583
14	.661	.577	.505	.442	.388	.340	.299	.263	6.982	6.628	6.302	6.002	5.724
15	.642	.555	.481	.417	.362	.315	.275	.239	7.191	6.811	6.462	6.142	5.847
16	.623	.534	.458	.394	.339	.292	.252	.218	7.379	6.974	6.604	6.265	5.954
17	.605	.513	.436	.371	.317	.270	.231	.198	7.549	7.120	6.729	6.373	6.047
18	.587	.494	.416	.350	.296	.250	.212	.180	7.702	7.250	6.840	6.467	6.128
19	.570	.475	.396	.331	.277	.232	.194	.164	7.839	7.366	6.938	6.550	6.198
20	.554	.456	.377	.312	.258	.215	.178	.149	7.963	7.469	7.025	6.623	6.259
21	.538	.439	.359	.294	.242	.199	.164	.135	8.075	7.562	7.102	6.687	6.312
22	.522	.422	.342	.278	.226	.184	.150	.123	8.176	7.645	7.170	6.743	6.359
23	.507	.406	.326	.262	.211	.170	.138	.112	8.266	7.718	7.230	6.792	6.399
24	.492	.390	.310	.247	.197	.158	.126	.102	8.348	7.784	7.283	6.835	6.434
25	.478	.375	.295	.233	.184	.146	.116	.092	8.422	6.843	7.330	6.873	6.464
26	.464	.361	.281	.220	.172	.135	.106	.084	8.488	7.896	7.372	6.906	6.491
27	.450	.347	.268	.207	.161	.125	.098	.076	8.548	7.943	7.409	6.935	6.514
28	.437	.333	.255	.196	.150	.116	.090	.069	8.602	7.984	7.441	6.961	6.534
29	.424	.321	.243	.185	.141	.107	.082	.063	8.650	8.022	7.470	6.983	6.551
30	.412	.308	.231	.174	.131	.099	.075	.057	8.694	8.055	7.496	7.003	6.566
31	.400	.296	.220	.164	.123	.092	.069	.052	8.733	8.085	7.518	7.020	6.579
32	.388	.285	.210	.155	.115	.085	.063	.047	8.769	8.112	7.538	7.035	6.591
33	.377	.274	.200	.146	.107	.079	.058	.043	8.801	8.135	7.556	7.048	6.600
34	.366	.264	.190	.138	.100	.073	.053	.039	8.829	8.157	7.572	7.060	6.609
35	.355	.253	.181	.130	.094	.068	.049	.036	8.855	8.176	7.586	7.070	6.617
36	.345	.244	.173	.123	.088	.063	.045	.032	8.879	8.192	7.598	7.079	6.623
37	.335	.234	.164	.116	.082	.058	.041	.029	8.900	8.208	7.609	7.087	6.629
38	.325	.225	.157	.109	.076	.054	.038	.027	8.919	8.221	7.618	7.094	6.634
39	.316	.217	.149	.103	.071	.050	.035	.024	8.936	8.233	7.627	7.100	6.638
40	.307	.208	.142	.097	.067	.046	.032	.022	8.951	8.244	7.634	7.105	6.642

TABLE A-4
Compound Discount
One Dollar Per Annum

Present value of periodic payments of $1 (payable at the end of each year)

Year	3%	4%	5%	6%	7%	8%	9%	10%	11%	12%	13%	14%	15%
1	.971	.962	.952	.943	.935	.926	.917	.909	.901	.893	.885	.877	.870
2	1.913	1.886	1.859	1.833	1.808	1.783	1.759	1.736	1.713	1.690	1.668	1.647	1.626
3	2.829	2.775	2.723	2.673	2.624	2.577	2.531	2.487	2.444	2.402	2.361	2.311	2.283
4	3.717	3.630	3.546	3.465	3.387	3.312	3.240	3.170	3.102	3.037	2.974	2.914	2.855
5	4.580	4.452	4.329	4.212	4.100	3.993	3.890	3.791	3.696	3.605	3.517	3.433	3.352
6	5.417	5.242	5.076	4.917	4.767	4.623	4.486	4.355	4.231	4.111	3.998	3.889	3.784
7	6.230	6.002	5.786	5.582	5.389	5.206	5.033	4.868	4.712	4.564	4.423	4.288	4.160
8	7.020	6.733	6.463	6.210	5.971	5.747	5.535	5.335	5.146	4.968	4.799	4.639	4.487
9	7.786	7.435	7.108	6.802	6.515	6.247	5.995	5.759	5.537	5.328	5.132	4.946	4.772
10	8.530	8.111	7.722	7.360	7.024	6.710	6.418	6.145	5.889	5.650	5.426	5.216	5.-19
11	9.253	8.760	8.306	7.887	7.499	7.139	6.805	6.495	6.207	5.938	5.687	5.453	5.234
12	9.954	9.385	8.863	8.384	7.943	7.536	7.161	6.814	6.492	6.194	5.918	5.660	5.421
13	10.635	9.986	9.394	8.853	8.358	7.904	7.487	7.103	6.750	6.424	6.122	5.842	5.583
14	11.296	10.563	9.899	9.295	8.745	8.244	7.786	7.367	6.982	6.628	6.302	6.002	5.724
15	11.938	11.118	10.380	9.712	9.108	8.559	8.061	7.606	7.191	6.811	6.462	6.142	5.847
16	12.561	11.652	10.838	10.106	9.447	8.851	8.313	7.824	7.379	6.974	6.604	6.265	5.954
17	13.166	12.166	11.274	10.477	9.763	9.122	8.544	8.022	7.549	7.120	6.729	6.373	6.047
18	13.754	12.659	11.690	10.828	10.059	9.372	8.756	8.201	7.702	7.250	6.840	6.467	6.128
19	14.324	13.134	12.085	11.158	10.336	9.604	8.950	8.365	7.839	7.366	6.938	6.550	6.198
20	14.877	13.590	12.462	11.470	10.594	9.818	9.129	8.514	7.963	7.469	7.025	6.623	6.259
21	15.415	14.029	12.821	11.764	10.836	10.017	9.292	8.649	8.075	7.562	7.102	6.687	6.312
22	15.937	14.451	13.163	12.042	11.061	10.201	9.442	8.772	8.176	6.645	7.170	6.743	6.359
23	16.444	14.857	13.489	12.303	11.272	10.371	9.580	8.883	8.266	7.718	7.230	6.792	6.399
24	16.936	15.247	13.799	12.550	11.469	10.529	9.707	8.985	8.348	7.784	7.283	6.835	6.434
25	17.413	15.622	14.094	12.783	11.654	10.675	9.823	9.077	8.422	6.843	7.330	6.873	6.464
26	17.877	15.983	14.375	13.003	11.826	10.810	9.929	9.161	8.488	7.896	7.372	6.906	6.491
27	18.327	16.330	14.643	13.211	11.987	10.935	10.027	9.237	8.548	7.943	7.409	6.935	6.514
28	18.764	16.663	14.898	13.406	12.137	11.051	10.116	9.307	8.602	7.984	7.441	6.961	6.534
29	19.188	16.984	15.141	13.591	12.278	11.158	10.198	9.370	8.650	8.022	7.470	6.983	6.551
30	19.600	17.292	15.372	13.765	12.409	11.258	10.274	9.427	8.694	8.055	7.496	7.003	6.566
31	20.000	17.588	15.593	13.929	12.532	11.350	10.343	9.479	8.733	8.085	7.518	7.020	6.579
32	20.389	17.874	15.803	14.084	12.647	11.435	10.406	9.526	8.769	8.112	7.538	7.035	6.591
33	20.768	18.148	16.003	14.230	12.754	11.514	10.464	9.569	8.801	8.135	7.556	7.048	6.600
34	21.132	18.411	16.193	14.368	12.854	11.587	10.518	9.609	8.829	8.157	7.572	7.060	6.609
35	21.487	18.665	16.374	14.498	12.948	11.655	10.567	9.644	8.855	8.176	7.586	7.070	6.617
36	21.832	18.908	16.547	14.621	13.035	11.717	10.612	9.677	8.879	8.192	7.598	7.079	6.623
37	22.167	19.143	16.711	14.737	13.117	11.775	10.653	9.706	8.900	8.208	7.609	7.087	6.629
38	22.492	19.368	16.868	14.846	13.193	11.829	10.691	9.733	8.919	8.221	7.618	7.094	6.634
39	22.808	19.584	17.017	14.949	13.265	11.879	10.726	9.757	8.936	8.233	7.627	7.100	6.638
40	23.115	19.793	17.159	15.045	13.332	11.925	10.757	9.779	8.951	8.244	7.634	7.105	6.642

Appendix B

Household Budget Summary

Household Budget Summary

Income

Personal expected income	$ _____
Spouse's expected income	$ _____

Total other expected income (list)

1. _____	$ _____
2. _____	$ _____
3. _____	$ _____

Total Expected Income $ _____

Expenses
Fixed Expenses

1. Food	$ _____
2. Home (mortgage, rent, taxes, repairs, utilities)	$ _____
3. Taxes (excluding taxes on principal home)	$ _____
4. Medical expenses (doctor, dentist, prescriptions)	$ _____
5. Clothing and cleaning (total of family)	$ _____
6. Transportation (gas, parking, maintenance, public transit, etc.)	$ _____
7. Debts (budgeted debt liquidation, revolving credit payments)	$ _____
8. Property and liability insurance (auto, homeowners, etc.)	$ _____
9. Life and individual health insurance (disability, long-term care, etc.)	$ _____
10. Current education/childcare expenses	$ _____

Discretionary Expenses

11. Vacations	$ _____
12. Home improvements and furnishings	$ _____
13. Entertainment and recreation	$ _____
14. Charity and gifts (church, donations, holidays, birthdays, etc.)	$ _____
15. Savings	$ _____
16. Investments	$ _____
17. Education fund	$ _____

18. Miscellaneous (list)

1. _____	$ _____
2. _____	$ _____
3. _____	$ _____

Total for Household Expenses $ _____

Anticipated Surplus or (Deficit) $ _____

Appendix C

Retirement Planning Fact Finder

Retirement Planning Fact Finder

Personal Data and Retirement Goals

Personal Data

Your Name _____   Your Spouse's Name _____

Social Security Number_____   Social Security Number _____

Date of Birth _____   Date of Birth _____

Home Address
Street _____

City _____   State _____ Zip _____

Home Phone _____   Your Business Phone _____

Your Cell Phone _____   Spouse's Cell Phone _____

Your Fax _____   Spouse's Fax _____

Your E-mail _____   Spouse's E-mail _____

Children

Name	Address	Age
_____	_____	_____
_____	_____	_____
_____	_____	_____

What are the names, addresses, and phone numbers of your professional and personal advisors?

Advisor	Name	Address	Phone
Attorney			
Insurance Advisor			
Securities Broker			
Accountant			
Banker / Trust Officer / Others			

Have you had any of the following documents prepared? If so, by whom and when?

Document		Prepared by	Date
Will	Yes / No	_____	_____
Living Will	Yes / No	_____	_____
Durable Power of Attorney	Yes / No	_____	_____
Health Care Power of Attorney	Yes / No	_____	_____
Revocable Living Trust	Yes / No	_____	_____
Irrevocable Trust	Yes / No	_____	_____
Financial Plan	Yes / No	_____	_____
Estate Plan	Yes / No	_____	_____

What other services have any of your professional advisors performed for you?

_____

1

Retirement Goals—Assumptions

1) Is your spouse to be included in this plan?   Yes   No

   *At what age do you (and your spouse) plan to retire?
   (When did you retire?)   You _____   Spouse _____

   How many years of retirement do you wish to plan for?   You _____   Spouse _____

2) Average inflation rate estimated over the span of this plan   _____%

3) Average compound interest rate assigned to all savings prior to retirement (optional)   _____%

4) Average compound interest rate assigned to all savings during retirement   _____%

5) Estimated average tax rate on taxable earnings prior to retirement   _____%

6) Estimated average tax rate on taxable earnings during retirement   _____%

Retirement Goals—Qualitative

*Where do you plan to live when you retire?

_____

What does retirement mean to you personally?

_____

*Do you expect to maintain your preretirement standard of living in retirement?   Yes   No

What types of recreational activities do your retirement plans involve?

_____

Will any of your children be involved in your retirement planning financial decisions?   Yes   No

*Indicates questions that are also found on the Personal Retirement Planning Review form.

QUANTITATIVE DATA

Financial Position Statement

Assets		Liabilities and Net Worth	
Cash, Near-Cash Equivalents	**Current Value**		**Current Value**
Checking accounts/cash		Charge accounts/credit cards	
Savings accounts		Family/personal/auto loans	
Money market funds		Margin/bank/life insurance loans	
Treasury bills		Income taxes (federal, state, local)	
Short-term CDs		Property taxes	
Savings bonds		Investment liabilities	
Other (specify)		Mortgage(s)	
Subtotal		Lease(s)	
Other Financial Assets		Child support	
Stock		Alimony	
Bonds, taxable		Other (specify)	
Bonds, tax exempt		Other (specify)	
Mutual funds		Other (specify)	
Other securities		**Total Liabilities**	$
Investment real estate			
Long-term CDs		**Net Worth (Total Assets Minus Total Liabilities)**	
Vested retirement benefits			$
Annuities (cash values)			
Life insurance cash values			
IRAs (Roth/traditional)			
Limited partnership units			
Interest(s) in trust(s)			
Value of business interest			
Other (specify)			
Other (specify)			
Other (specify)			
Subtotal			
Personal Assets			
Personal residence			
Seasonal residence			
Automobiles, other vehicles			
Household furnishings			
Boats			
Jewelry/furs			
Collections (art, coins, etc.)			
Other (specify)			
Subtotal			
Total Assets	$	**Total Liabilities Plus Net Worth**	$

3

Cash Flow Statement	
Annual Income	**Amount**
Wages, salary, bonus, etc.: Client	
Wages, salary, bonus, etc.: Spouse	
Business (self-employment) income	
Real estate rental	
Dividends—investments	
Dividends—close corporation stock	
Interest on bonds, taxable	
Interest on bonds, tax exempt	
Interest on savings accounts, CDs	
Interest on loans, notes, etc.	
Trust income	
Life insurance settlement options	
Annuities	
Child support/alimony	
Other sources (specify)	
Total Annual Income	$
Housing (mortgage/rent)	
Utilities and telephone	
Food, groceries, etc.	
Clothing and cleaning	
Federal income and Social Security taxes	
State and local income taxes	
Property taxes	
Transportation (auto/commuting)	
Medical/dental/drugs/health insurance	
Debt repayment	
House upkeep/repairs/maintenance	
Life, property, and liability insurance	
Child support/alimony	
Total Fixed Expenses	
Vacations/travel/etc.	
Recreation/entertainment	
Contributions/gifts	
Household furnishings	
Education fund	
Savings/investments	
Other (specify)	
Total Discretionary Expenses	
Total Annual Expenses	$
Net Cash Flow (Total Annual Income Minus Total Annual Expenses)	$

Using today's before-tax dollars, what percentage of total income is required during retirement?   _____%

(Multiply total income by percentage above)
Annual retirement income goal when you retire $_____

*Are you satisfied with the amount of money you currently have accumulated thus far?   Yes   No

*Are you currently saving and investing enough to reach your retirement goals?   Yes   No

*Do you feel you need to increase your savings?   Yes   No

(If yes) *By how much are you willing to increase your savings on a monthly basis? $_____

If you made additional investments or purchased additional financial products, what would your future objectives be in doing so?

---

*Are you concerned with reducing the taxes on your savings?   Yes   No

How do you feel about taking investment risks?

Do you consider yourself a successful investor?   Yes   No

Why or why not?

Do you have any funds on hand now that you might want to invest?   Yes   No

If yes, how much? $_____

Into what risk category(ies) would any additional financial products you purchase be included?

    High risk (aggressive)   _____%

    Moderate risk   _____%

    Balanced risk (some aggressive, some conservative)   _____%

    Conservative (little or no risk)   _____%

Do you worry about outliving or depleting the assets you've accumulated in your life's savings?   Yes   No

How much cash or pure liquid assets do you feel you should have available to you at all times? $_____

Have you purchased insurance coverage to protect against all other types of financial risks?   Yes   No

What kinds of insurance products do you own?

---

*Are you willing to consider purchasing additional financial products to help you reach your retirement goals?   Yes   No

Indicates questions that are also found on the Personal Retirement Planning Review form.

Retirement Income Sources

SUMMARY—INFLATION-INDEXED INCOME

Before and after retirement commences:

Category 1: Total Social Security Benefits in Today's Dollars
         (from page 7)   **(line 1-1)** $_____

After retirement income commences:

Total annual pension and taxable funded income
payments—indexed (from page 7)   (line 1-2) $_____

Total annual retirement income from current
investments—indexed (from page 8)   (line 1-3) $_____

Total projected income from all deposits and
earnings—indexed (from page 9)   (line 1-4) $_____

Total income from all distribution options—indexed
(from page 10)   (line 1-5) $_____

Net amount of additional funds/expenses per year—
indexed (from page 11)   (line 1-6) $_____

Category 2: Other Inflation-Indexed Income
         (Sum of lines 1-2 through 1-6)   **SOURCE 1** $_____

SUMMARY—FIXED INCOME

Total annual pension and taxable funded income
payments—fixed (from page 7)   SOURCE 2 $_____

Total annual retirement income from current
investments—fixed (from page 8)   SOURCE 3 $_____

Total projected income from all deposits and
earnings—fixed (from page 9)   SOURCE 4 $_____

Total income from all distribution options—fixed
(from page 10)   SOURCE 5 $_____

Net amount of additional funds/expenses per year—
fixed (from page 11)   SOURCE 6 $_____

Total Fixed Income   **(Total of SOURCES 2 + 3 + 4 + 5 + 6)** $_____

*To convert total fixed income into its inflation-adjusted equivalent income, divide total
fixed income by the average inflation rate factor during retirement.*

Total fixed income	÷	*Average inflation rate factor during retirement*	=	*Inflation-adjusted fixed income*
_____	÷	_____	=	$_____

ory 3: Total Inflation-Adjusted Fixed Income
                    (SOURCES 2 through 6 Adjusted for Inflation) $_____

1.   SOCIAL SECURITY BENEFITS
1)   Age you plan to start Social Security benefits   _____

2)   Estimated Social Security annual benefit $_____

3)   Age your spouse will start Social Security benefits   _____

4)   Spouse's estimated Social Security annual benefit $_____

Total Social Security Benefits in Today's Dollars (line 1-1) $_____

2.   PENSION AND OTHER FUNDED INCOME PAYMENTS
(Employer-funded pension, deferred-compensation, taxable trust income, etc.)

1)   Source _____

2)   Annual projected future retirement income from this source $_____

3)   Your age when these payments will start   _____

4)   Number of years benefits will be paid (use 0 if through lifetime) _____

5)   Check one: _____ Indexed starting now
                  _____ Indexed starting with first payment

Additional pension or taxable funded income

1)   Source _____

2)   Annual projected future retirement income from this source $_____

3)   Your age when these payments will start   _____

4)   Number of years benefits will be paid (use 0 if through lifetime) _____

5)   Check one: _____ Indexed starting now
                  _____ Indexed starting with first payment

(Please use additional sheets to list other income payment streams.)

Total Annual Pension and Funded Income Payments— Indexed (line 1-2) $_____

— Fixed SOURCE 2 $_____

3. CURRENT INVESTMENTS

Tax categories: taxable (T), tax free (TF), deductible tax deferred (TD), nondeductible tax deferred (ND), and Roth IRA (R)

Tax Category	Asset Class (Stocks, Bonds, Mutual Funds, CDs, Savings, etc.)	Current Value	Rate of Return	Future Value	Amount for Use in Retirement
_____	_____	$_____	____%	$_____	$_____
_____	_____	$_____	____%	$_____	$_____
_____	_____	$_____	____%	$_____	$_____
_____	_____	$_____	____%	$_____	$_____
_____	_____	$_____	____%	$_____	$_____
_____	_____	$_____	____%	$_____	$_____
_____	_____	$_____	____%	$_____	$_____
_____	_____	$_____	____%	$_____	$_____

Total Lump Sum of Capital from Investments for Use in Retirement $_____ +

+ This total may include tax-free income that will need to be converted to taxable equivalent amounts. See the bottom of page 11 for an example of how to convert tax-free income into taxable equivalent income.

How to Calculate the Fixed Income from Investments. Multiply the result from line above by the percentage of compound interest before taxes that this lump sum is expected to earn (i.e., if $100,000 earns 8%, then $100,000 x .08 = $8,000 annual fixed retirement income).

How to Calculate the Inflation-Indexed Income from Investments. Divide the sum above by the appropriate factor from table 4 (i.e., $100,000 ÷ by 13.23 = $7,558 of real income for 20 years at 8% interest and 3% inflation).

Total Annual Retirement Income from Investments — Indexed (line 1-3) $_____

— Fixed (SOURCE 3) $_____

8

4. **DEPOSITS and EARNINGS**
    The following five sections ask for annual savings and investments in the future. Targeted rates of return are assumed to be the average rates of return found in questions 3 or 4 of the Personal Data and Retirement Goals Section on page 2 of this form unless otherwise specified.

    Taxable Investments (e.g., stocks, bonds, mutual funds, money market, savings)
    1) Amount you plan to invest yearly in taxable assets   _____
    2) Percentage increase in these deposits each year   _____%
    3) Targeted annual rate of return prior to retirement   _____%
    4) Total projected lump-sum accumulation at retirement $_____

    Projected Income at Retirement $_____ +

    Tax-Free Investments (e.g., municipal bonds, tax-free mutual funds)
    1) Amount you plan to invest yearly in tax-free assets   _____
    2) Percentage increase in these deposits each year   _____%
    3) Targeted annual rate of return prior to retirement   _____%
    4) Total projected lump-sum accumulation at retirement $_____

    Projected Income at Retirement $_____ +

    Deductible Tax-Deferred Investments (e.g., traditional IRAs; 401(k), 403(b), and profit-sharing plans; Keoghs; SEPs)
    1) Annual tax-deferred contribution now planned   _____
    2) Percentage increase in tax-deferred deposits each year   _____%
    3) Targeted annual rate of return prior to retirement   _____%
    4) Total projected lump-sum accumulation at retirement $_____

    Projected Income at Retirement $_____

    Nondeductible Tax-Deferred Investments (after-tax dollars in annuities accumulating tax-deferred earnings)
    1) Total after-tax premium payments you will make each year   _____
    2) Percentage increase in these premiums each year   _____%
    3) Targeted annual rate of return prior to retirement   _____%
    4) Total projected lump-sum accumulation at retirement $_____

    Projected Income at Retirement $_____ +

    Roth IRA
    1) Amount you plan to invest yearly in tax-free assets   _____
    2) Percentage increase in premiums each year if IRS allows   _____%
    3) Targeted annual rate of return prior to retirement   _____%
    4) Total projected lump-sum accumulation at retirement $_____

    Projected Income at Retirement $_____ +

    + These totals may include tax-free income that will need to be converted to taxable equivalent amounts. See the bottom of page 11 for an example of how to convert tax-free income into taxable equivalent income.

    Total Projected Income from All Deposits and Earnings   — Indexed (line 1-4) $_____

    — Fixed (SOURCE 4)$_____

9

5. DISTRIBUTION OPTIONS

Alternatives on default selections for distributing portfolio funds when required during retirement

Calculation of Minimum Distributions

Client   _____Single-life calculation   _____ Joint-and-last-survivor calculation   _____ Other

Spouse   _____Single-life calculation   _____ Joint-and-last-survivor calculation   _____ Other

Annuity Payout Option for Deductible Tax-Deferred Assets

a) Annual distributions in the amount of $_____

b) Distributions will begin at your age   _____

c) Distributions will continue for ? years (Enter 0 for lifetime or until funds are depleted)   _____

Annuity Payout Option for Nondeductible Tax-Deferred Assets

a) Annual distributions in the amount of $_____ +

b) Distributions will begin at your age   _____

c) Distributions will continue for ? years (Enter 0 for lifetime or until funds are depleted)   _____

Insurance Products (private pensions, single-premium annuities)

Retirement benefits from insurance products should be listed here. Data entered should be taken only from an illustration prepared by the vendor of the insurance product.

Type of Product	Description	Cost Basis*	Start Age	Years**	Index	Annual Benefit
Life / annuity	_____	$_____	_____	_____	_____ %	$_____ +
Life / annuity	_____	$_____	_____	_____	_____ %	$_____ +
Life / annuity	_____	$_____	_____	_____	_____ %	$_____ +
Life / annuity	_____	$_____	_____	_____	_____ %	$_____ +

Total Income from Insurance Products $_____ +

 * Enter 0 if these benefits are tax-free draws from a life insurance policy.
** 0 years = lifetime

Total Income from All Distribution Options — Indexed (line 1-5) $_____

                                          — Fixed (SOURCE 5) $_____

+ These totals may include tax-free income that will need to be converted to taxable equivalent amounts. See the bottom of page 11 for an explanation of how to convert tax-free income into taxable equivalent income.

6.   INCOME AND EXPENSES IN ADDITION TO LIVING REQUIREMENTS

ADDITIONAL FUNDS EXPECTED (e.g., sale of house or business, inheritance, wages, rent, royalties, etc.)

Description	Tax Category	Start Age	Years	Amount per Year
_____	_____	_____	_____	$_____
_____	_____	_____	_____	$_____
_____	_____	_____	_____	$_____

ROTH IRA CONVERSIONS

Description	Tax Category	Start Age	Conversion Amount	Pay Taxes from Roth Savings	Net After Taxes	Tax-Free Amount per Year
_____	Roth IRA	_____	$_____	_____	$_____	$_____ +
_____	Roth IRA	_____	$_____	_____	$_____	$_____ +

+ These totals may include tax-free income that will need to be converted to taxable equivalent amounts. See the bottom of page 11 for an explanation of how to convert tax-free income into taxable equivalent income.

Total Additional Funds Expected per Year $_____

ADDITIONAL MAJOR EXPENSES (e.g., college education, major purchase, medical expenses, world cruise, etc.)

Description	Tax Category	Start Age	Years	Amount per Year
_____	_____	_____	_____	$_____
_____	_____	_____	_____	$_____
_____	_____	_____	_____	$_____

Total Major Expenses per Year in Retirement   – $_____

Net Additional Funds/Expenses per Year   **— Indexed (line 1-6)**   (+ or –) $_____

— Fixed (SOURCE 6)   (+ or –) $_____

Converting Annual Tax-Free Income into Its Taxable Equivalent Income Amount:

1. Obtain gross annual tax-free income from each respective income source—i.e., $1,000. Determine the taxable equivalent factor for tax-free income by applying the following formula: Tax-free income divided by (1 minus average tax rate %) = Taxable equivalent income factor:
$1,000/(1 − .15) = $1,000/.85 = 1.1765 (rounded to 1.18)

2. Multiply tax-free income from step 1 by the factor derived from formula above to obtain taxable equivalent income: $1,000 x 1.18 = $1,180

Calculations and Interest Tables

Retirement Income Calculation Worksheet

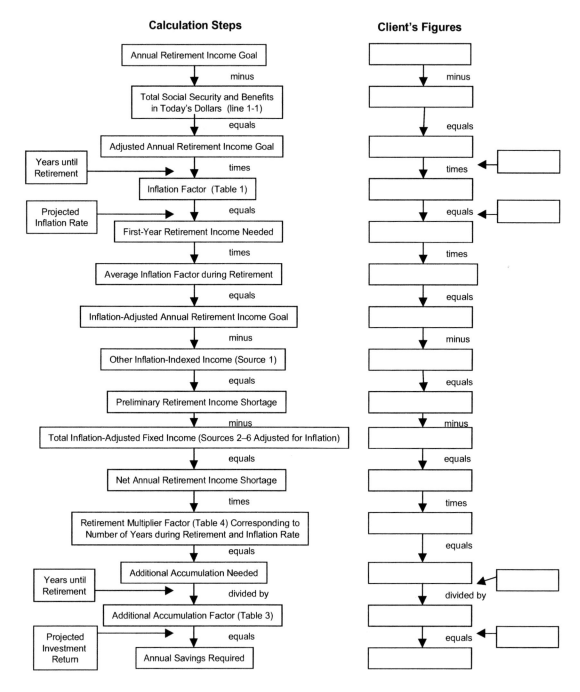

FACT FINDER TABLE 1
Inflation Factors (Compound Interest Factors for a Single Sum)
Where i = Inflation Rate and n = Number of Years until Retirement

i =	1%	2%	3%	4%	5%	6%	7%	8%	9%	10%
n =1	1.0100	1.0200	1.0300	1.0400	1.0500	1.0600	1.0700	1.0800	1.0900	1.1000
2	1.0201	1.0404	1.0609	1.0816	1.1025	1.1236	1.1449	1.1664	1.1881	1.2100
3	1.0303	1.0612	1.0927	1.1249	1.1576	1.1910	1.2250	1.2597	1.2950	1.3310
4	1.0406	1.0824	1.1255	1.1699	1.2155	1.2625	1.3108	1.3605	1.4116	1.4641
5	1.0510	1.1041	1.1593	1.2167	1.2763	1.3382	1.4026	1.4693	1.5386	1.6105
6	1.0615	1.1262	1.1941	1.2653	1.3401	1.4185	1.5007	1.5869	1.6771	1.7716
7	1.0721	1.1487	1.2299	1.3159	1.4071	1.5036	1.6058	1.7138	1.8280	1.9487
8	1.0829	1.1717	1.2668	1.3686	1.4775	1.5938	1.7182	1.8509	1.9926	2.1436
9	1.0937	1.1951	1.3048	1.4233	1.5513	1.6895	1.8385	1.9990	2.1719	2.3579
10	1.1046	1.2190	1.3439	1.4802	1.6289	1.7908	1.9672	2.1589	2.3674	2.5937
11	1.1157	1.2434	1.3842	1.5395	1.7103	1.8983	2.1049	2.3316	2.5804	2.8531
12	1.1268	1.2682	1.4258	1.6010	1.7959	2.0122	2.2522	2.5182	2.8127	3.1384
13	1.1381	1.2936	1.4685	1.6651	1.8856	2.1329	2.4098	2.7196	3.0658	3.4523
14	1.1495	1.3195	1.5126	1.7317	1.9799	2.2609	2.5785	2.9372	3.3417	3.7975
15	1.1610	1.3459	1.5580	1.8009	2.0789	2.3966	2.7590	3.1722	3.6425	4.1772
16	1.1726	1.3728	1.6047	1.8730	2.1829	2.5404	2.9522	3.4259	3.9703	4.5950
17	1.1843	1.4002	1.6528	1.9479	2.2920	2.6928	3.1588	3.7000	4.3276	5.0545
18	1.1961	1.4282	1.7024	2.0258	2.4066	2.8543	3.3799	3.9960	4.7171	5.5599
19	1.2081	1.4568	1.7535	2.1068	2.5270	3.0256	3.6165	4.3157	5.1417	6.1159
20	1.2202	1.4859	1.8061	2.1911	2.6533	3.2071	3.8697	4.6610	5.6044	6.7275
21	1.2324	1.5156	1.8603	2.2787	2.7860	3.3995	4.1406	5.0339	6.1088	7.4003
22	1.2447	1.5459	1.9161	2.3699	2.9253	3.6035	4.4304	5.4366	6.6586	8.1403
23	1.2572	1.5768	1.9736	2.4647	3.0715	3.8179	4.7405	5.8715	7.2579	8.9543
24	1.2697	1.6084	2.0328	2.5633	3.2251	4.0489	5.0724	6.3412	7.9111	9.8497
25	1.2824	1.6406	2.0938	2.6658	3.3864	4.2918	5.4275	6.8485	8.6231	10.8347

* Table values can be interpolated for partial years and/or inflation and investment return rates that are not represented in the tables.

FACT FINDER TABLE 2
Consumer Price Index
Average Inflation Rates; Most Recent Time Periods

3 years	1.9%
5 years	2.3%
10 years	2.4%
15 years	2.9%
20 years	3.1%
Prospect's Inflation Rate Assumption _____ %	

FACT FINDER TABLE 3
Annual Accumulation Factors: One Dollar per Year in Advance
Where R= Compound Interest Rate of Return and n= Number of Years until Retirement

R =	2%	3%	4%	5%	6%	7%	8%	9%	10%	11%	12%
Year											
n=1	1.020	1.030	1.040	1.050	1.060	1.070	1.080	1.090	1.100	1.110	1.120
2	2.060	2.091	2.122	2.153	2.184	2.215	2.246	2.278	2.310	2.342	2.374
3	3.122	3.184	3.246	3.310	3.375	3.440	3.506	3.573	3.641	3.710	3.779
4	4.204	4.309	4.416	4.526	4.637	4.751	4.867	4.985	5.105	5.228	5.353
5	5.308	5.468	5.633	5.802	5.975	6.153	6.336	6.523	6.716	6.913	7.115
6	6.434	6.662	6.898	7.142	7.394	7.654	7.923	8.200	8.487	8.783	9.089
7	7.583	7.892	8.214	8.549	8.897	9.260	9.637	10.028	10.436	10.859	11.300
8	8.755	9.159	9.583	10.027	10.491	10.978	11.488	12.021	12.579	13.164	13.776
9	9.950	10.464	11.006	11.578	12.181	12.816	13.487	14.193	14.937	15.722	16.549
10	11.169	11.808	12.486	13.207	13.972	14.784	15.645	16.560	17.531	18.561	19.655
11	12.412	13.192	14.026	14.917	15.870	16.888	17.977	19.141	20.384	21.713	23.133
12	13.680	14.618	15.627	16.713	17.882	19.141	20.495	21.953	23.523	25.212	27.029
13	14.974	16.086	17.292	18.599	20.015	21.550	23.215	25.019	26.975	29.095	31.393
14	16.293	17.599	19.024	20.579	22.276	24.129	26.152	28.361	30.772	33.405	36.280
15	17.639	19.157	20.825	22.657	24.673	26.888	29.324	32.003	34.950	38.190	41.753
16	19.012	20.762	22.698	24.840	27.213	29.840	32.750	35.974	39.545	43.501	47.884
17	20.412	22.414	24.645	27.132	29.906	32.999	36.450	40.301	44.599	49.396	54.750
18	21.841	24.117	26.671	29.539	32.760	36.379	40.446	45.018	50.159	55.939	62.440
19	23.297	25.870	28.778	32.066	35.786	39.995	44.762	50.160	56.275	63.203	71.052
20	24.783	27.676	30.969	34.719	38.993	43.865	49.423	55.765	63.002	71.265	80.699
21	26.299	29.537	33.248	37.505	42.392	48.006	54.457	61.873	70.403	80.214	91.503
22	27.845	31.453	35.618	40.430	45.996	52.436	59.893	68.532	78.543	90.148	103.603
23	29.422	33.426	38.083	43.502	49.816	57.177	65.765	75.790	87.497	101.174	117.155
24	31.030	35.459	40.646	46.727	53.865	62.249	72.106	83.701	97.347	113.413	132.334
25	32.671	37.553	43.312	50.113	58.156	67.676	78.954	92.324	108.182	126.999	149.334

* Table values can be interpolated for partial years and/or inflation and investment return rates that are not represented in the tables.

FACT FINDER TABLE 4
Retirement Income Multiplier/Divisor Factors
Compound Interest Rates

		Retirement Time Period—25 Years			
		4%	**6%**	**8%**	**10%**
	5%	28.11	22.36	18.20	15.12
	4%	25	20.08	16.49	13.82
I	**3%**	22.32	18.10	15	12.68
	2%	20	16.37	13.69	11.67
	1%	17.99	14.87	12.54	10.78
N		Retirement Time Period—20 Years			
F		**4%**	**6%**	**8%**	**10%**
	5%	21.94	18.31	15.51	13.32
L	**4%**	20	16.79	14.31	12.36
	3%	18.27	15.44	13.23	11.50
A	**2%**	16.74	14.22	12.26	10.71
	1%	15.36	13.13	11.39	10.01
T		Retirement Time Period—15 Years			
I		**4%**	**6%**	**8%**	**10%**
	5%	16.05	14.05	12.41	11.05
O	**4%**	15	13.17	11.67	10.43
	3%	13.99	12.36	10.99	9.85
N	**2%**	13.14	11.62	10.36	9.32
	1%	12.32	10.93	9.78	8.83
		Retirement Time Period—10 Years			
R		**4%**	**6%**	**8%**	**10%**
	5%	10.44	9.59	8.84	8.18
A	**4%**	10	9.19	8.49	7.87
	3%	9.58	8.82	8.15	7.57
T	**2%**	9.18	8.46	7.84	7.29
	1%	8.80	8.12	7.53	7.02
E		Retirement Time Period—5 Years			
		4%	**6%**	**8%**	**10%**
S	**5%**	5.10	4.91	4.73	4.57
	4%	5	4.81	4.64	4.48
	3%	4.90	4.72	4.56	4.40
	2%	4.81	4.64	4.47	4.32
	1%	4.72	4.55	4.39	4.25

15

Appendix D

Required Minimum Distribution Tables

Required Minimum Distribution (RMD) Tables

2002 Regulations

Effective with RMDs taken on or after January 1, 2003, the following tables must be used to determine the respective Single Life and Joint Life distribution periods according to the age or ages of the recipient(s).

Under IRS regulations that went into effect in 2002, distributions from a qualified plan or IRA can be calculated by dividing the account owner's balance by the applicable distribution period determined from the table below. For example, a 71-year-old with $100,000 in his or her account as of December 31 of the previous year would divide this balance by 26.5, to arrive at an RMD of $3,774.

Uniform Lifetime Table			
Age	**Distribution Period**	**Age**	**Distribution Period**
70	27.4	93	9.6
71	26.5	94	9.1
72	25.6	95	8.6
73	24.7	96	8.1
74	23.8	97	7.6
75	22.9	98	7.1
76	22.0	99	6.7
77	21.2	100	6.3
78	20.3	101	5.9
79	19.5	102	5.5
80	18.7	103	5.2
81	17.9	104	4.9
82	17.1	105	4.5
83	16.3	106	4.2
84	15.5	107	3.9
85	14.8	108	3.7
86	14.1	109	3.4
87	13.4	110	3.1
88	12.7	111	2.9
89	12.0	112	2.6
90	11.4	113	2.4
91	10.8	114	2.1
92	10.2	115+	1.9

Joint Life and Last Survivor Life Expectancy Table * Ages 70–77								
Ages	**70**	**71**	**72**	**73**	**74**	**75**	**76**	**77**
35	48.7	48.7	48.7	48.6	48.6	48.6	48.6	48.6
36	47.8	47.7	47.7	47.7	47.7	47.7	47.6	47.6
37	46.8	46.8	46.8	46.7	46.7	46.7	46.7	46.7
38	45.9	45.9	45.8	45.8	45.8	45.7	45.7	45.7
39	44.9	44.9	44.9	44.8	44.8	44.8	44.8	44.8
40	44.0	44.0	43.9	43.9	43.9	43.8	43.8	43.8
41	43.1	43.0	43.0	43.0	42.9	42.9	42.9	42.9
42	42.2	42.1	42.1	42.0	42.0	42.0	41.9	41.9
43	41.3	41.2	41.1	41.1	41.1	41.0	41.0	41.0
44	40.3	40.3	40.2	40.2	40.1	40.1	40.1	40.0
45	39.4	39.4	39.3	39.3	39.2	39.2	39.1	39.1
46	38.6	38.5	38.4	38.4	38.3	38.3	38.2	38.2
47	37.7	37.6	37.5	37.5	37.4	37.4	37.3	37.3
48	36.8	36.7	36.6	36.6	36.5	36.5	36.4	36.4
49	35.9	35.9	35.8	35.7	35.6	35.6	35.5	35.5
50	35.1	35.0	34.9	34.8	34.8	34.7	34.6	34.6
51	34.3	34.2	34.1	34.0	33.9	33.8	33.8	33.7
52	33.4	33.3	33.2	33.1	33.0	33.0	32.9	32.8
53	32.6	32.5	32.4	32.3	32.2	32.1	32.0	32.0
54	31.8	31.7	31.6	31.5	31.4	31.3	31.2	31.1
55	31.1	30.9	30.8	30.6	30.5	30.4	30.3	30.2
56	30.3	30.1	30.0	29.8	29.7	29.6	29.5	29.4
57	29.5	29.4	29.2	29.1	28.9	28.8	28.7	28.6
58	28.8	28.6	28.4	28.3	28.1	28.0	27.9	27.8
59	28.1	27.9	27.7	27.5	27.4	27.2	27.1	27.0
60		27.2	27.0	26.8	26.6	26.5	26.3	26.2
61			26.3	26.1	25.9	25.7	25.6	25.4
62				25.4	25.2	25.0	24.8	24.7
63					24.5	24.3	24.1	23.9
64						23.6	23.4	23.2
65							22.7	22.5
66								21.8

* Use the tables on these two pages to figure your required minimum distribution only if your spouse is your sole beneficiary and is more than 10 years younger than you. Find your age (as of your birthday for the year you are making the computation) on the horizontal line and your spousal beneficiary's age in the vertical column. For example, if you are age 74 and your spousal beneficiary is 63, the life expectancy factor is 24.5. If your age or your spouse's age is not shown here, refer to IRS Publication 590.

Joint Life and Last Survivor Expectancy Table Ages 78–85							
Ages	78	79	80	81	82	83	84	85
35	48.6	48.6	48.5	48.5	48.5	48.5	48.5	48.5
36	47.6	47.6	47.6	47.6	47.6	47.6	47.6	47.5
37	46.6	46.6	46.6	46.6	46.6	46.6	46.6	46.6
38	45.7	45.7	45.7	45.7	45.6	45.6	45.6	45.6
39	44.7	44.7	44.7	44.7	44.7	44.7	44.7	44.7
40	43.8	43.8	43.7	43.7	43.7	43.7	43.7	43.7
41	42.8	42.8	42.8	42.8	42.8	42.8	42.7	42.7
42	41.9	41.9	41.8	41.8	41.8	41.8	41.8	41.8
43	40.9	40.9	40.9	40.9	40.9	40.9	40.8	40.8
44	40.0	40.0	40.0	39.9	39.9	39.9	39.9	39.9
45	39.1	39.1	39.0	39.0	39.0	39.0	39.0	38.9
46	38.2	38.1	38.1	38.1	38.1	38.0	38.0	38.0
47	37.2	37.2	37.2	37.2	37.1	37.1	37.1	37.1
48	36.3	36.3	36.3	36.2	36.2	36.2	36.2	36.2
49	35.4	35.4	35.4	35.3	35.3	35.3	35.3	35.2
50	34.5	34.5	34.5	34.4	34.4	34.4	34.3	34.3
51	33.6	33.6	33.6	33.5	33.5	33.5	33.4	33.4
52	32.8	32.7	32.7	32.6	32.6	32.6	32.5	32.5
53	31.9	31.8	31.8	31.8	31.7	31.7	31.7	31.6
54	31.0	31.0	30.9	30.9	30.8	30.8	30.8	30.7
55	30.2	30.1	30.1	30.0	30.0	29.9	29.9	29.9
56	29.3	29.3	29.2	29.2	29.1	29.1	29.0	29.0
57	28.5	28.4	28.4	28.3	28.3	28.2	28.2	28.1
58	27.7	27.6	27.5	27.5	27.4	27.4	27.3	27.3
59	26.9	26.8	26.7	26.6	26.6	26.5	26.5	26.4
60	26.1	26.0	25.9	25.8	25.8	25.7	25.6	25.6
61	25.3	25.2	25.1	25.0	24.9	24.9	24.8	24.8
62	24.6	24.4	24.3	24.2	24.1	24.1	24.0	23.9
63	23.8	23.7	23.6	23.4	23.4	23.3	23.2	23.1
64	23.1	22.9	22.8	22.7	22.6	22.5	22.4	22.3
65	22.4	22.2	22.1	21.9	21.8	21.7	21.6	21.6
66	21.7	21.5	21.3	21.2	21.1	21.0	20.9	20.8
67	21.0	20.8	20.6	20.5	20.4	20.2	20.1	20.1
68		20.1	20.0	19.8	19.7	19.5	19.4	19.3
69			19.3	19.1	19.0	18.8	18.7	18.6
70				18.5	18.3	18.2	18.0	17.9
71					17.7	17.5	17.4	17.3
72						16.9	16.7	16.6
73							16.1	16.0
74								15.4

Glossary

12b-1 fee • named after the regulation that allows this type of fee, an asset-based sales charge assessed to cover a mutual fund's distribution services, which include any activity or expense intended to result in the sale of fund shares

401(k) plan • a defined-contribution profit-sharing plan that gives participants the option of reducing their taxable salary and contributing the salary reduction on a tax-deferred basis to an individual account for retirement purposes

403(b) plan • a tax-advantaged retirement plan similar to a 401(k) plan that is available to certain tax-exempt organizations and to public schools (also known as a tax-sheltered annuity, or TSA)

501(c)(3) organization • a corporation, and any community chest, fund or foundation, organized and operated exclusively for religious, charitable, scientific, testing for public safety, literary, or educational purposes, or to foster national or international amateur sports, or for the prevention of cruelty to children or animals

accumulation phase • the period of time from the purchase of a deferred annuity until the annuity owner decides to begin to receive payments. It is during this phase that the annuity builds up the funds that provide the future benefits.

active life expectancy • the number of years a person can expect to live without a disability

active listening • putting together a speaker's words and nonverbal behaviors to understand the essence of the communication being sent, to listen to the speaker from that individual's perspective, and to respond meaningfully to his or her messages

active participant • an individual who makes voluntary contributions to o r for whom employer contributions are made or accrued benefits exist within a qualified corporate, Keogh, pension, profit-sharing, or stock bonus plan, or in a simplified employee pension, a 403(b) plan, SIMPLE IRA, or government plan

activities of daily living (ADLs) • physical functions that are the basic and necessary tasks of everyday life and usually include eating, bathing, dressing, transferring from bed to chair, using the toilet, and maintaining continence

adjusted gross income (AGI) • gross income minus all allowable above-the-line deductions

ADLs • *See* activities of daily living.

after-tax income • income that remains after taxes have been paid (take-home pay)

AGI • *See* adjusted gross income.

annuity • a series of periodic payments that begin at a specific date and continue throughout a fixed period or for the duration of a designated life or lives

annuity payout • a qualified plan distribution option that represents annuitized installment payments

applicable credit amount • a credit to which the estate of every individual is entitled, which can be directly applied against the gift or estate tax

asset allocation • a portfolio management technique, which typically divides the investment portfolio among three broad asset categories (stocks, bonds, and cash equivalents) and specifies the percentage of total portfolio assets to be invested in each category

assisted-living facility care • continuing supervision and the availability of assistance on an unscheduled basis for elderly residents who, despite some degree of impairment, remain independent to a significant degree

asked price • the price that a consumer actually pays for a mutual fund share; the public offering price, including any applicable sales charges

back-end load • a sales charge imposed at the time a mutual fund is redeemed or when the investor withdraws funds from the account (also called a contingent deferred sales charge)

baby boom generation • individuals born from 1946 through 1964

balance sheet • *See* financial position statement.

beneficiary • the recipient of the death proceeds from a life insurance policy

bid price • the net asset value per share of the mutual fund; the redemption price for a share of the fund

bond • a loan of money to a corporation in return for which bondholders expect to receive regular interest payments

breakeven age • the hypothetical cross-over point to which a retiree must survive in order to make delaying the decision to begin receiving Social Security retirement benefits the better option than taking early retirement benefits

bridge job • a full- or part-time job that an individual holds while making the transition into retirement

budgeting • the process of creating and following an explicit plan for spending and investing resources

cash-balance pension plan • a defined-benefit plan that is designed to look like a defined-contribution plan in that the benefit grows based on contribution and investment credits. As a defined-benefit plan, it has some level of funding flexibility and is subject to minimum funding requirements.

cash flow analysis • the process of gathering data about an individual's cash flow situation, presenting the data in an organized format, and identifying strengths, weaknesses, and important patterns

cash flow management • the budgetary planning and control process

cash flow planning • the process of identifying courses of action that will help optimize cash flow

cash flow statement (income statement) • a statement that summarizes a client's financial activities over a specified period of time by comparing cash inflows and outflows and indicating whether the net cash flow for the period is positive or negative. The cash flow statement contains three basic classifications— income, expenses, and net cash flow—that are related in an equation, which states that income minus expenses equals net cash flow.

cash or deferred compensation arrangement (CODA) • a feature of a profit-sharing or stock bonus plan that allows participants to defer a portion of their compensation on a pretax basis

catch-up contribution • an additional contribution that participants aged 50 and older are eligible to make annually to their 401(k), 403(b), 457, SIMPLE, and IRA plans over and above the maximum annual salary deferral amount

center of influence (COI) • an influential person who knows an advisor favorably and agrees to introduce or recommend him or her to others

chronically ill person • a definition used in long-term care policies for someone who meets the criterion for benefit eligibility due either to a loss of functional capacity or a need for substantial supervision to protect the individual from threats to health and safety because of severe cognitive impairment

CODA • *See* cash or deferred compensation arrangement.

COI • *See* center of influence.

community care • LTC programs provided for individuals who are able to remain in the community, such as home health care, adult day care, a homemaker companion or home health aide, caregiver training, respite care, hospice care, and therapeutic devices

compound interest • the rate of interest computed by applying an interest rate to the sum of the original principal and the interest credited to it in previous periods

compounding • the process by which money today (present value) grows over time to a larger amount (future value)

consumer price index (CPI) • the index that measures the change in consumer purchasing power due to price inflation (deflation), as determined by a monthly survey of the U.S. Bureau of Labor Statistics (also referred to as the cost-of-living index)

contingent deferred sales charge • *See* back-end load.

corporate bond • a promissory note given by a corporation to an investor in exchange for a loan to the corporation. The bond pays interest to the bondholder, usually semiannually, in the form of coupon payments.

corpus • the property held in trust (also known as principal)

cost of living index • *See* consumer price index.

CPI • *See* consumer price index

currently insured • the term used to describe an individual who is eligible to receive some Social Security benefits because he or she has earned at least 6 credits in covered employment during the 13 quarters prior to death, eligibility for disability benefits, or eligibility for retirement

custodial care • assistance given to a person who has a limited ability to conduct his or her routine daily activities because of deficiencies in physical and/or cognitive functions. Persons without professional medical skills or training can usually provide custodial care.

custodian • an independent entity, usually a commercial bank named by the board of directors of a mutual fund that holds the mutual fund assets but has no voice in investment decisions

decision phase • the third stage of retirement planning, which coincides with the imminent event of retirement. During this phase, the advisor counsels clients on issues such as pension distributions, Social Security retirement benefits, and conversion of assets into retirement income.

deductive approach • an approach to the personal information-gathering process that starts with a thorough and lengthy fact finding form that broadly covers all the prospect's financial and retirement planning needs. The process requires quantifying those needs, prioritizing them, and then recommending that the prospect purchase the appropriate product or products that address the highest priority of need.

deferred annuity • an annuity in which premiums paid are left to accumulate and grow into a larger sum of money over the course of many years. The invested premiums plus the contract's growth create the fund from which future immediate annuity distribution payments can be made.

defined-benefit plan • a retirement plan that specifies the benefits that each employee receives at retirement. The employer is responsible for making contributions necessary to pay the promised benefit.

defined-contribution plan • a retirement plan in which the employer contributions are allocated to participants' accounts. The participant's benefit is based on the account balance, which consists of the employer's contributions and investment experience.

direct transfer • a rollover directly from the trustee of an IRA or qualified plan to another IRA or qualified plan

disability insured • the status of a person who is eligible for Social Security disability benefits. To qualify, a person must be fully insured and have a specified minimum amount of work under Social Security within a recent time period.

discounting • the process by which money due in the future (future value) is reduced over time to a smaller amount today (present value)

discovery agreement • a summary of a prospect's retirement planning goals, usually in writing, obtained at the conclusion of the fact-finding interview. The discovery agreement acknowledges that the advisor and prospect agree to work together to seek financial solutions to the prospect's retirement planning concerns.

distribution phase • the period of time during which annuity benefits are paid out (also known as the payout phase)

diversification • a portfolio management technique to minimize the impact of any one security, investment, or asset category on overall investment portfolio performance. It occurs when a portfolio is composed of several asset categories, each one of which is designed for investments with risk and return profiles that are dissimilar to the profiles of investments in other categories, so that a downward movement of investments in one asset category is offset by an upward movement of investments in another asset category.

dollar cost averaging • an investment strategy to level off the ups and downs in the market by investing the same amount of money in a financial vehicle at regular intervals, regardless of market performance. The result is that over time, the average cost for securities purchased is less than the average price paid for them. The key factors to successful dollar cost averaging are discipline and consistency.

early retirement • retirement before full retirement age

effective communication • the advisor's ability to explain financial products and services clearly, to listen carefully to what prospects and clients are saying, and to demonstrate a real interest in them as individuals

effective income tax rate • the tax rate determined by dividing the taxes actually paid into gross pretax income

equity-indexed annuity • annuity for which the amount of interest earned is linked to changes in some type of securities index. The most commonly used index is the Standard & Poor's 500 (S&P 500). In addition to the potential for growth from the link to an index, principal and earnings are guaranteed not to drop below a certain specified level, regardless of potential securities market declines.

exchange privilege • a feature that allows investors to transfer from one mutual fund to another without a charge or transaction fee

expense method approach • the method to estimate the retirement income requirement assumption based on the projected expenses a retiree will have during the first year of retirement. *See also* replacement-ratio approach.

facility care (nursing home) • a state-licensed facility that provides skilled, intermediate, and custodial care services. The care recipient's condition determines the combination and extent of services provided.

fact finder • an information-gathering form that a financial advisor and/or prospect needs to complete as part of the selling/planning process. It includes both quantitative and qualitative information about the prospect's current financial position and personal circumstances.

fair market value • the amount a willing buyer would pay a willing seller, neither being under any compulsion to buy and sell and both having reasonable knowledge of all relevant factors

federal obligations • investment opportunities offered and guaranteed by the federal government, thus eliminating the risk of default. Interest is subject to federal income tax.

financial assets • assets that consist of cash and cash equivalents (or liquid assets) and other financial (or investment) assets. Cash and cash equivalents are liquid in the sense that they are either already cash or can be converted into cash relatively quickly with little or no loss in value. Other financial assets represent a variety of assets with wide-ranging degrees of risk in which clients may invest in an effort to earn a return. *See also* nonfinancial assets.

financial position statement (balance sheet) • a statement that shows an individual's wealth at a certain point in time and reflects the results of his or her past financial activities. It covers three basic classifications: assets, liabilities, and net worth.

fixed-amount option • a qualified plan distribution option under which payment amounts are fixed and the amount selected is paid until the proceeds are exhausted. This option, like the fixed-period option, is based on the present value of annual payments made at the beginning of the year. The difference is that the amount of the payment is known and the length of time that payments will be made must be calculated. Any interest or earnings variations lengthen or shorten the time over which the payments will be made.

fixed-interest deferred annuity • an annuity in which payments are based on a set interest rate that is usually guaranteed not to change for a certain period of time, regardless of market performance

fixed-period option • a qualified plan distribution option under which proceeds are liquidated at a uniform rate over a specified number of years. The amount of each annual payment is the present value of annual payments due at the beginning of the year. Because the period is fixed, any variations, such as dividend accumulations, paid-up additions, or outstanding loans, increase or decrease the amount of the payments.

FRA • *See* full retirement age.

frailty phase • the final stage of retirement planning, which depends not on any specific age but on health issues, caregiving responsibilities for a spouse, or loss of mobility. Clients in this phase become more lonely and dependent on others.

front-end load • a sales charge included as part of the purchase price of the mutual fund at the time it is bought

full retirement age (FRA) • the age at which an individual is entitled to full retirement benefits from Social Security. In 2006, the FRA for a person born in 1941 is 65 and 8 months. Individuals born in 1960 and after will have a full retirement age of 67.

fully insured • the term used to describe an individual who is eligible to receive Social Security retirement benefits because he or she has 40 quarters of covered employment

fund distributor • *See* underwriter.

fund manager/management company • an entity hired by a mutual fund's board of directors to manage the day-to-day operation of the fund

fund sponsor • *See* underwriter.

funded • a type of retirement plan in which the funds have been placed out of the reach of the employer's general creditors, as is the case in an irrevocable trust

future value of a single sum (FVSS) • an amount determined by compounding a present value at a particular interest rate for a particular length of time

FVSS • *See* future value of a single sum.

general account • the repository for all of an insurance company's assets. Within the general account, the company segregates a fixed or guaranteed account that complements the variable annuity separate accounts. The contract owner has the right to transfer funds from the general account to the separate account and *vice versa*. *See also* separate account.

generation X • the population segment born from 1965 through 1985

goal prioritization • the process of ranking goals defined in goal setting according to their importance to the individual and his or her retirement plan

goal setting • the process of establishing clearly definable, measurable, achievable, and realistic financial and personal objectives toward which the financial advisor can target a client's efforts

golden handshake • additional benefit(s) paid to employees to encourage early retirement

grantor • the person or legal entity that creates a trust

gross income • all wages, salaries, commissions, alimony received, taxable pensions, IRA distributions, rents, royalties, the taxable portion of annuity payments, capital gains (or losses), dividend income, and net business income (for the self-employed), as well as many other items defined by the IRS. *See also* pretax income.

HCE • *See* highly compensated employee.

Health Insurance Portability and Accountability Act of 1996 (HIPAA) • federal legislation for the primary purpose of making medical insurance more available, particularly when an employed person changes jobs or becomes unemployed

highly compensated employee (HCE) • an individual who earned over the earnings limit in the preceding year. In 2006, that limit is $100,000. The employer can elect to limit this group to employees whose compensation puts them in the top 20 percent of payroll.

HIPAA • *See* Health Insurance Portability and Accountability Act of 1996.

holistic retirement planning • the planning approach that encompasses not only the client's financial goals and requirements but also his or her psychological and emotional needs

immediate annuity • an annuity that typically guarantees that payments, which begin within 1 year of purchase, will continue for the rest of the annuitant's life, no matter how long that is. Immediate annuities are usually purchased for one large single premium in exchange for a stream of income payable for a specified period of time. An immediate annuity can also be purchased by first remitting a series of smaller periodic premiums into a deferred annuity, and then annuitizing or converting it into an immediate annuity at some time in the future.

income in respect of a decedent (IRD) • income that was earned by a taxpayer but not actually or constructively received by the taxpayer's date of death

income requirement assumption • an estimate of the level of income a retiree needs to sustain the standard of living he or she enjoyed just prior to retirement throughout his or her retired life

income statement • *See* cash flow statement.

income tax credits • items that can be subtracted directly from the amount of income tax owed to determine the amount of income tax that must be paid

increased preparation and visualization phase • the second phase of retirement planning in which the client becomes more focused on his or her retirement plan by increasing savings and limiting spending. The advisor often suggests to clients in this phase that they save all raises earned during the 5 or 6 years prior to retirement to lock in spending habits and learn not to grow their lifestyle or budget.

inductive approach • the converse of the deductive approach to information gathering. This approach starts with a dominant or single need, then broadens into a comprehensive analysis of financial retirement planning needs during which several needs are identified and prioritized.

inflation • an economic condition created by too much demand for too few goods and services, as measured by various indices, the most widely known of which is the consumer price index

insurable interest • an interest in the subject matter of an insurance contract such that the holder of the interest can reasonably expect to lose, usually financially, from the occurrence of the insured event (such as the death of the insured) or to gain, usually financially, if the insured event does not occur

insurance planning and risk management • the analysis and consideration of the client's financial exposure because of the following factors: (1) mortality—survivor income and capital needs analysis, (2) morbidity—impact of ill health, (3) property—loss of value, (4) liability—legal exposure, and (5) business—loss due to business involvement

inter vivos trust • a trust that becomes operative during the grantor's lifetime (also known as a living trust)

interest option • the simplest and most flexible life insurance option, which entails leaving policy proceeds with the insurance company at interest, thus postponing their payment. The beneficiary may be given varying degrees of control over the disposition of the proceeds ranging from no control to full control.

intermediate care • medical care services that may be provided, or available perhaps 2 to 4 days per week. Intermediate care may be given in a nursing home, an intermediate-care unit of a nursing home, or at home.

investment company • a company that invests only in other companies. The company may be either a closed-end company or an open-end company.

IRD • *See* income in respect of a decedent.

irrevocable beneficiary • a beneficiary designation that the policyowner cannot change and under which the beneficiary's ownership rights in the policy are vested immediately. *See also* revocable beneficiary.

life income options • the least flexible of the life insurance options, under which proceeds are liquidated over the life of the beneficiary. Benefits depend on the age and gender of the beneficiary or beneficiaries. Once payments begin, no changes can be made.

life insurance settlement options • choices as to how life insurance proceeds will be paid. Generally, the following options are available: (1) paying proceeds as a lump sum to a designated beneficiary, (2) leaving proceeds with the insurance company to earn interest, (3) paying proceeds in installments for a fixed period of time, (4) distributing proceeds in installments of a specified fixed amount until they are exhausted, and (5) distributing proceeds in installments that are guaranteed for the life of the beneficiary.

life span • the maximum potential age of human beings

living trust • *See* inter vivos trust.

load • *See* sales charge.

long-term care (LTC) • the broad range of medical, custodial, social, and other care services to assist people who have an impaired ability to live independently for an extended period

long-term care insurance (LTCI) • any insurance policy designed to provide coverage for an extended period of time to persons who need nonacute care for their health needs, often in the form of personal care services

LTC • *See* long-term care.

LTCI • *See* long-term care insurance.

lump-sum option • a single distribution from a qualified plan that represents the participant's entire account balance (also known as lump-sum payment)

lump-sum payment • *See* lump-sum option.

MAGI • *See* modified adjusted gross income.

marginal income tax rate • the rate at which an individual's next dollar of income will be taxed

market segmentation • a marketing strategy that allows the advisor to customize his or her approach and presentation based on the common needs and characteristics of the prospects in the segmented market

maximum salary deferral amount • the annual maximum that a plan participant can contribute to a 401(k), 403(b), 457, or SIMPLE plan. In 2006, the maximum amount is $15,000 for 401(k), 403(b), and 457 plans and $10,000 for SIMPLE plans. After 2006, the maximum salary deferral amount will be adjusted for inflation in increments of $500.

maximum taxable wage base • an amount, indexed annually for inflation, above which Social Security taxes are not charged ($94,200 in 2006)

Medicaid • a federal/state program to provide medical expense benefits for certain classes of low-income individuals and families

Medicare • the health insurance program of the federal government available to persons who are aged 65 or older and to limited categories of persons who are under age 65

Medicare supplement insurance • insurance policies available to persons aged 65 or older under which benefits are provided for certain specific expenses not covered under Medicare

millennial generation • the population segment born between 1986 and the present

modified adjusted gross income (MAGI) • generally, the total income on an individual's Form 1040 tax return minus adjustments to income other than for IRA deductions

money-purchase plan • a defined-contribution plan that specifies a level of contribution (for example, 10 percent of salary) to each participant's account each year

municipal bond • a bond that represents the debt of a state, city, county, public utility authority, or other political subdivision. Interest is generally exempt from federal income tax.

mutual fund • open-end investment company, which pools investors' money and invests it according to fund objectives

NASD • *See* National Association of Securities Dealers.

National Association of Securities Dealers (NASD) • part of the self-regulatory structure established under the authority granted by the Securities Exchange Act of 1934 to provide voluntary self-regulation of broker/dealers under SEC oversight. The NASD has the power to require and monitor compliance with standardized rules of fair practice for the industry.

net asset value • the per-share market value of a mutual fund's portfolio. It equals the total net assets of the fund less any liabilities, divided by number of shares outstanding

net cash flow • the difference between income and expenses

networking • the mutual sharing of ideas and clients with other professionals whose work does not compete with the advisor's

no-load fund • a fund with neither a front-end nor back-end sales charge

nonfinancial (personal) assets • assets bought primarily for the creature comforts they provide. They include such things as the client's primary residence, his or her vehicles, and other tangible (personal) assets like clothes, household furnishings, antiques, and hobby equipment. *See also* financial assets.

nonqualified retirement plan • a plan that provides benefits to an employee or group of employees, including the business owner, but does not receive the tax benefits that federal regulations offer because it does not meet ERISA requirements. The three most popular types of nonqualified retirement plans are nonqualified deferred-compensation plans, stock option plans, and IRC Sec. 457 plans.

nursing home • *See* facility care.

OASDI • the old-age, survivors, and disability insurance program, commonly known as Social Security

open-end company • a mutual fund; any pooled portfolio of investments that stands ready to redeem or sell its shares at their net asset value (or net asset value plus load if the fund has a load)

payout phase • *See* distribution phase.

pension plan • a qualified plan that requires the employer to create a definite, ongoing commitment to fund it, usually by making an annual contribution. The sole purpose of a pension plan is to provide retirement income; in-service distributions are not allowed.

per capita • the distribution of life insurance policy proceeds in a manner that gives equal shares to all individuals who are beneficiaries

per stirpes • the distribution of life insurance policy proceeds in a manner that gives to a deceased person's issue or lineal descendants the share that the deceased would have taken had he or she survived

personal assets • *See* nonfinancial assets.

phased retirement • a reduction in an individual's hours worked and job commitments rather than his or her complete removal from the work force

PIA • *See* primary insurance amount.

postretirement mentality syndrome • the retiree's inability to enjoy the money he or she has accumulated for retirement because he or she fears exhausting the funds before he or she dies

preliminary discovery agreement • a trial close to which the prospect responds by expressing receptiveness and willingness to continue working with the financial advisor toward finding an individualized solution to the prospect's retirement planning needs, and thereby agrees to complete a comprehensive fact finder

preretirement mentality • a mind set driven by the need to ensure a comfortable and financially secure retirement. Financial planning goals are geared toward amassing a large sum of money to allay the fear of financial destitution in old age. Generally, this mentality is characterized by less concern about stock market downturns and a more risk-tolerant investment attitude.

present value of a single sum (PVSS) • an amount determined by discounting a future value at a particular interest rate for a particular length of time

pretax income • income that has not yet been subjected to income taxes. *See also* gross income.

primary insurance amount (PIA) • the amount of Social Security retirement benefits an individual is entitled to receive at full retirement age, based on a formula that is a function of the worker's average indexed monthly earnings

principal • *See* corpus.

pro forma • projected. A pro forma financial statement represents the advisor's best estimate of how the statement will look at a future point in time.

professional ethics • behavior according to the principles of right or wrong—a code of ethics—that are accepted by the profession. The American College and The National Association of Insurance and Financial Advisors codes of ethics set the standards of professional behavior for a financial advisor.

professionalism • the knowledge, conduct, responsibility, and client-focused attitude that characterize a professional financial advisor

profit-sharing plan • a defined-contribution plan structured to offer an employee participation in company profits that he or she may use for retirement purposes

prospectus • a document that gives possible investors information that will help them make an informed decision about a security's investment potential. It spells out in detail the financial position of the offering company, what the new funds will be used for, the qualifications of the corporate officers, risk factors, the nature of competition, and any other material information.

PVSS • *See* present value of a single sum.

qualified distribution • any distribution made after a Roth IRA is established, provided (1) the distribution is made after the end of the 5-year period beginning with the first day of the first taxable year for which any Roth IRA contribution was made, and (2) the individual is 59 1/2 or older when the distribution is made, he or she has become totally and permanently disabled, the distribution is used to pay up to $10,000 of qualifying first-time home buyer expenses, or the beneficiary is receiving distributions following the death of the account owner.

qualified LTC services • services that must be covered in a long-term care insurance policy deemed to be a tax-qualified insurance contract under HIPAA. Required services are necessary diagnostic, preventive, therapeutic, curing, treating, and rehabilitative services, as well as maintenance or personal care required by a chronically ill individual and called for by a plan of care prescribed by a licensed health care practitioner.

qualified LTCI contract • any long-term care insurance contract that meets the requirements of HIPAA for favorable tax treatment, or any long-term care insurance contract issued before January 1, 1997, that remains materially unchanged and met the long-term care requirements in the state where the policy was issued, even if it does not meet other HIPAA requirements (also known as a tax-qualified policy).

qualified plan • an employer-sponsored retirement plan that meets the legal requirements specified in Sec. 401(a) of the Internal Revenue Code and thus "qualifies" for favorable tax treatment. These plans include defined-benefit pension plans, cash-balance pension plans, money-purchase pension plans, target-benefit pension plans, profit-sharing plans, 401(k) plans, stock bonus plans, ESOPs, and HR 10 (Keogh) plans.

qualified prospect • an individual who needs and values the advisor's products and services, can afford to pay for them, is insurable, and can be approached favorably by the advisor

reallocation of assets • reapportioning the value accumulated in one asset to another asset to meet some other need

rebalancing • a portfolio management technique to maintain the original percentage balances of the assets that the investor had selected, using an asset-allocation investment strategy. A portfolio can become unbalanced over time because some asset categories will outperform others, throwing off the planned asset-allocation percentages. The portfolio can be brought back in line through rebalancing by selling assets that have appreciated and buying those that have fallen in price.

registered investment advisor (RIA) • an investment advisor who has registered with either the SEC or the appropriate state agency as an investment advisor

replacement-ratio approach • the method to estimate the income requirement assumption based on a percentage of the retiree's final salary. *See also* expense method approach.

required minimum distributions (RMDs) • the minimum payments participants must receive from defined-contribution plans or traditional IRAs by the required beginning date in either a lump sum or a series of substantially equal periodic payments based on life expectancy

retirement income gap • the difference between the amount of money an individual must accumulate to reach his or her retirement income goal and the amount he or she expects to have from all sources

retirement income needs • the total amount of savings that will generate the income required to allow an individual to sustain throughout retirement the standard of living he or she enjoyed just prior to retirement

retirement transition and lifestyle phase • the fourth stage of retirement planning, which follows immediately after retirement and is often characterized by a surge of increased spending on travel and other recreational pursuits. Clients in this phase become more asset rich and income poor.

revocable beneficiary • a beneficiary designation that the policyowner retains the right to change. A revocable beneficiary has no policy ownership rights, only an expectation of rights. *See also* irrevocable beneficiary.

RIA • *See* registered investment advisor.

risk tolerance • the degree to which an individual is willing to accept risk

RMDs • *See* required minimum distributions.

rollover • a tax-free transfer of funds from one IRA or qualified vehicle to another IRA or qualified vehicle

Roth IRA • an individual retirement account in which contributions are made on an after-tax basis and qualifying distributions are income tax free. *See also* traditional IRA.

Rule of 72 • a quick method to estimate how long it will take for an amount to double in value at various compound interest rates. In this method, the number 72 is divided by the applicable interest rate expressed as a whole number. The quotient is the approximate number of periods until the amount doubles.

salary continuation plan • *See* SERP.

salary reduction plan • a nonqualified retirement plan in which the employer and the employee agree either to reduce the employee's salary or to defer a future bonus in order to postpone receipt and taxation to a future tax year. The cost of the plan is borne solely by the employee's deferral of compensation that he or she would otherwise have received in cash; the employer generally provides an investment return on the deferred amount.

sales charge • a commission applied to mutual fund trades (also referred to as its load)

savings and incentive match plan for employees • *See* SIMPLE.

savings phase • the first phase of retirement planning, which starts as soon as possible after the client's career begins. Clients in this phase are concerned with other competing savings objectives such as buying a home and family-building expenses. The advisor's role is to motivate the client to save for retirement and to educate the client about the importance of starting to save early.

SEP (simplified employee pension) • a retirement plan that uses an individual retirement account (IRA) as the receptacle for contributions. A SEP is a simplified alternative to a profit-sharing or 401(k) plan.

separate account • a variable annuity investment account in which money is segregated from assets in the general account assets of the insurance company. *See also* general account.

SERP (supplemental executive retirement plan) • a nonqualified deferred-compensation plan in which the employer agrees to continue the employee's salary (as an additional benefit, not as a true deferral of an employee's income) at retirement, death, and sometimes disability (also known as salary continuation plan)

severance pay • a cash incentive to retire from the company. This incentive can be a flat amount offered to all employees across the board or an amount based on years of service.

silent generation • the population segment born prior to 1946

SIMPLE (savings incentive match plan for employees) • a simplified retirement plan that allows employees to save money for retirement on a pretax basis, with limited employer contributions

simple interest • the rate of interest computed by applying an interest rate only to the original principal sum

simplified employee pension • *See* SEP.

skilled-nursing care • medical care services performed by licensed medical professionals that may be provided or available 24 hours a day or on a daily basis. The most common setting for skilled care is in a nursing home classified as a skilled-nursing facility

social style • a predictable pattern of behavior that people display and that can be observed. The American population is evenly divided among four social styles: driver, expressive, amiable, and analytical. Appropriate responses to the characteristics of each social style indicate how an advisor can best establish rapport with a client who has that style.

specialized financial planning goals • goals that are subsets, and generally involve several, of the major planning areas and typically include planning for college education funding, divorce, terminal illness, nontraditional families, job or career change, job loss (including severance packages), dependent parents who need long-term care, other dependents with special needs, the purchase of a first home, and the purchase of a vacation or second home

spousal IRA • a traditional or Roth IRA for a nonworking spouse

step-up rate • the percentage of growth in an individual's annual allocation to savings

stock • a share of ownership in the company that issues it in return for which the stockholder is entitled to a share of the company's profits

stock option plan • a nonqualified retirement plan that gives the employee the right to purchase shares of the employer's stock in the future at a predetermined price

suitability • whether or not a specific investment is appropriate for a particular prospect or client

supplemental executive retirement plan • *See* SERP.

systematic risk • a risk that affects the entire market, not just one business or industry. Examples are market risk, inflation risk, interest rate risk, reinvestment risk, and currency risk.

take-home pay • *See* after-tax income.

target-benefit pension plan • a hybrid retirement plan that uses a benefit formula like that of a defined-benefit plan and the individual accounts like that of a defined-contribution plan. The contribution is derived from the benefit formula in a target-benefit plan, but once determined, the plan resembles a money-purchase plan in all other ways.

target market • an identifiable and accessible group of people with common characteristics and needs who regularly communicate with one another. The group must be large enough that the advisor does not run out of prospects.

tax-advantaged retirement plans • retirement plans that provide favorable tax treatment by meeting stipulated legal requirements. These plans include individual retirement plans (such as the traditional and Roth IRAs) and employer-sponsored retirement plans (qualified plans, SEPs, SIMPLEs, and 403(b) plans).

tax-sheltered annuity (TSA) • *See* 403(b) plan.

tax-qualified policy • *See* qualified LTCI contract.

testamentary trust • a trust that is created by the terms of the grantor's will

time value of money (TVM) • the concept that a specific amount of money received (paid) in a specific time period has a different value than the same amount received (paid) in a different time period

top-heavy plan • a plan that unduly favors key employees by providing 60 percent or more of the benefits or contributions to these employees

total disability • the inability to engage in any substantial gainful activity because of a medically determinable physical or mental condition

traditional IRA • an individual retirement account in which contributions are made on a pretax basis and qualifying distributions are taxable. *See also* Roth IRA.

transfer agent • an entity that handles a mutual fund's record keeping. It issues shares and confirmation statements, redeems fund shares, and sends out fund distributions

trust • an arrangement in which a person or entity holds legal title to property and manages it for the benefit of another person or group of people

trustee • the person or legal entity that holds legal title to the property in a trust

TVM • *See* time value of money.

underwriter • the entity responsible for marketing the mutual fund shares to the public and compensated by adding a sales charge to the price of each share sold (also known as the fund sponsor or distributor)

unfunded • a type of nonqualified retirement plan in which the employee's contractual right to the payment of deferred benefits in the future is unsecured. These funds are subject to the claims of the employer's general creditors.

unlimited marital deduction • a provision that allows up to 100 percent of a decedent-spouse's estate to pass to the surviving spouse without being subject to federal estate tax, and unlimited lifetime gifts to the donor's spouse without being subject to federal gift tax

unsystematic risk • a risk that is unique to a single business or industry. Examples include business risk, regulation risk, financial risk, default risk, and country risk.

variable deferred annuity • an annuity in which the owner receives varying rates of interest or capital growth on the annuity funds, depending on the investment options chosen. The annuity typically has two investment accounts: a separate account and a general account.

vesting • the acquisition by an employee of his or her right to receive a present or future pension benefit

Answers to Questions

Chapter 1

Answers to Review Questions

1-1. The eight steps in the retirement planning process from the advisor's perspective are as follows:
  - Identify the prospect.
  - Approach the prospect.
  - Meet with the prospect.
  - Gather information and establish goals.
  - Analyze the information.
  - Develop and present the plan.
  - Implement the plan.
  - Monitor the plan.

1-2. The five phases of retirement planning from the client's perspective are the
  - savings phase. During this phase, which starts as soon as possible after the client's career begins, the client is preoccupied with other competing savings objectives such as buying a home and starting a family. The advisor should encourage the client to begin to save for retirement and stress the importance of starting early and not dipping into retirement savings to fulfill other more immediate goals.
  - increased preparation and visualization phase. In this phase, planning intensifies as retirement seems less remote. The client is self-motivated to save, rather than spurred by the advisor. The client now sees the need to increase 401(k) contributions or pay off the mortgage, for example, and begins to understand that limiting expenses can be just as important a goal as increasing savings.
  - decision phase. This phase usually occurs when retirement is imminent and the client is preparing for a nonwork environment or phased retirement. In this phase, the client needs counsel on pension distributions, Social Security benefits, and how to convert his or her assets into retirement income.
  - retirement transition and lifestyle phase. This phase follows immediately after retirement, sometimes accompanied by increased spending on travel and leisure activities. The advisor must help the client adjust his or her spending plans as the client becomes more asset rich but income poor. As the client focuses on a changed environment in which psychological and emotional needs are different from preretirement, the client-advisor relationship goes beyond simply financial solutions.
  - frailty phase. At this stage, the client is concerned with health issues, coping with loss, and dealing with loneliness. The advisor can help the client by directing him or her to the appropriate social services.

1-3. A variety of factors influence the client's decision about when to retire. In addition to government and employer programs that affect the client's financial security in retirement, the advisor and client must evaluate the client's personal financial situation and risk tolerance, and they must consider inflation and changes in legislation that will have an impact on retirement plan distributions. For most clients, nonfinancial factors carry the most weight in the retirement decision. It is the advisor's responsibility to ensure that the decision is financially viable.

1-4. Eight common roadblocks to retirement planning are
  - the tendency to spend all income rather than save
  - having to handle unexpected expenses
  - not having adequate insurance coverage
  - divorce
  - not having an employer plan available

Answers.1

- changing jobs frequently
- the lack of financial literacy
- having to deal with other accumulation needs

1-5.   Retirement planning is a multidimensional field, which demands that the advisor—or team of advisors—be educated in the various aspects of numerous financial planning specialties. Specializing in only one area of retirement planning is too narrow; providing such limited assistance is a disservice to the client. Thus, the holistic approach, which encompasses a diversity of interrelated needs, is the only way to truly meet the client's retirement planning objectives.

1-6.   The retired population is increasing because the proportion of older to people to younger generations is growing, called the "graying of America" or "population aging." As the 78 million baby boomers reach retirement, the numbers of retirees will swell. It is estimated that by 2040 more than 20 percent of Americans will be aged 60 or older. In addition, Americans are living longer. It is forecast that by 2050 the number of those aged 85 and older will quadruple and the number of centenarians worldwide will reach 1.1 million. Seniors are also taking better care of themselves, which means they are living longer and healthier lives than previous generations.

1-7.   The characteristics of the four American generations are as follows:
   a.   silent generation—hardworking, frugal, cautious, and self-reliant
   b.   baby boom generation—spenders, inheritors, image conscious, and youth oriented
   c.   generation X—risk takers, self-oriented, and practical
   d.   millennial generation—technologically astute, affluent, consumption oriented

1-8.   The four criteria that identify a qualified prospect are that they
   - need and value your products and services
   - can afford to pay for your products and services
   - are insurable or financially suitable
   - can be approached on a favorable basis

1-9.   The three age-based market segments are the following:
   - under age 45. A common need in this segment is asset protection; thus, relevant products for these prospects are life insurance and deferred annuities in the context of retirement and/or estate planning.
   - ages 45 to 61. This market segment is interested in annuities, mutual funds and tax-favored plans, such as IRAs, as they seriously plan for their retirement.
   - age 62 and older. Because the people in this segment are concerned with protecting their nest eggs and not outliving their assets, they are prospects for immediate annuities, fixed-interest deferred annuities, and long-term care insurance.

1-10. Seven prospecting sources are
   - existing clients
   - referrals from clients and prospects
   - centers of influence
   - networking
   - worksite marketing
   - seminars
   - lists

Answers to Self-Test Questions

1-1.   B
1-2.   C
1-3.   B
1-4.   C
1-5.   A
1-6.   A
1-7.   D
1-8.   C
1-9.   C
1-10. A

Chapter 2

Answers to Review Questions

2-1. To be *fully insured*, a person must have earned 40 credits (completed 40 quarters) of covered employment since 1936 or have earned at least one credit for each year after 1950 (or after the year in which the person reaches age 21, if later) and before the year of his or her death, disability, or 62d birthday. To be *currently insured*, an individual must have earned six credits in covered employment within the last 13 quarters prior to his or her death, disability, or retirement.

2-2. People who are eligible to receive Social Security survivor benefits are the covered worker's dependent child(ren), dependent parent(s), and surviving spouse who is caring for the worker's dependent child(ren). A divorced spouse is eligible for benefits if he or she is caring for the covered worker's child who is under age 16 or disabled and who is also receiving benefits on the covered worker's Social Security record. A divorced spouse is also eligible if he or she and the covered worker had been married for at least 10 years and the divorced spouse did not remarry before attaining age 60.

2-3. To be eligible for benefits, a worker must be fully insured. Retirement benefits under Social Security are available as follows:

- A retired covered worker is entitled to a monthly benefit equal to his or her primary insurance amount (PIA) at full retirement age (FRA). Reduced benefits are available to workers who elect to retire before their FRA.

- The spouse of an eligible covered worker is entitled to benefits beginning at age 62 or earlier if he or she is caring for a child who is also entitled to benefits. The nonworking spouse is entitled to up to 50 percent of the covered spouse's PIA if they both retire at FRA. If both spouses have worked throughout their lives, the spouse whose PIA generates the smaller benefit is entitled to the higher of 50 percent of his or her covered spouse's PIA or the benefit generated by his or her own work history.

  A divorced spouse can receive benefits if the marriage to the former spouse lasted at least 10 years. The divorced spouse must be aged 62 or older and unmarried. If the spouse has been divorced at least 2 years, he or she can receive benefits even if the worker is not retired; however, the worker must have enough credits to qualify for benefits and be 62 or older.

- An eligible worker's children under age 18, or under age 19 if they are still in elementary or high school, and children who are over age 18 if they become disabled before age 22 are also entitled to benefits. The amount of the benefit is 75 percent of the worker's PIA.

2-4. All Social Security benefits paid are coordinated so that they do not exceed the family maximum amount. For example, suppose there are three dependent children who are each entitled to $884 and the surviving spouse is also entitled to $884, but the family maximum amount is $2,164. Instead of receiving a total amount of $3,536 ($884 x 4), the family will receive a maximum of $2,164 in benefits.

2-5. If a worker elects early retirement, his or her benefits are permanently reduced by a fraction of a percent for each month before the worker's full retirement age.

2-6. Under the earnings test, there is a $1 reduction in Social Security benefits for every $2 the individual earns. This test has now been eliminated for retirees at or beyond full retirement age, which will encourage individuals to work after reaching their FRA.

2-7. a. The higher the interest rate used in calculating the FVSS, the higher the future value will be.

b. Likewise, the higher the number of years used in the calculation, the higher the future value.

2-8. Using table A-1 in appendix A, the interest factor used to compute the amount to which $1 will increase in 20 years at 8 percent compound interest is 4.661. The future value of $10,000 in 20 years is calculated as follows:

FVSS = $10,000 (4.661)

= $46,610

2-9. The future value interest factor used to determine the amount to which $1 per year paid at the beginning of each year for 25 years will increase at 7 percent interest is 67.676, as shown in table A-2 in appendix A. Thus, the future value of periodic deposits in 25 years consisting of annual deposits of $1,000 each, earning 7 percent interest, is calculated as follows:

FVPD = $1,000 (67.676)

= $67,676

2-10. Using table A-4 in appendix A, the PVPP factor for periodic payments of $1 payable at the end of each year for 15 years at 6 percent interest is 9.712. Thus, your client will need $242,800 in the account today to be able to take $25,000 from it annually, calculated as follows:

PVPP = $25,000 (9.712)
      = $242,800

2-11. The key components of a financial position statement are as follows:
- assets—items the client owns. They should be subdivided into asset categories; at a minimum, they should be divided into financial assets and personal (nonfinancial) assets.
- liabilities—the client's debts, usually grouped in the financial statement according to the time period in which they must be repaid
- net worth—the client's wealth or equity as of the date of the statement. It is calculated by subtracting total liabilities from total assets.

2-12. A client's net worth can increase for any one of the following reasons:
- The client's assets appreciate in value.
- His or her assets increase through retention of income.
- Assets increase because of gifts or inheritances.
- Liabilities decrease because of debt forgiveness.

2-13. a. Paying off a debt has no effect on net worth because the cash account declines by the same amount that the liability declines, which leaves the difference between total assets and total liabilities unaltered.
b. Buying an asset with cash has no impact on a client's net worth because cash declines by the same amount that the other asset category increases.

2-14. A cash flow statement is used to summarize a client's financial activities over a specified period of time by comparing cash inflows and cash outflows. It indicates how such financial activities changed the client's net worth from what is shown in the beginning of the client's financial position statement to the end of the financial position statement. The three basic components of a cash flow statement are income, expenses, and net cash flow.

2-15. a. Cash flow analysis is the process used to gather data about the client's cash flow situation, present the data in an organized format, and identify strengths, weaknesses, and patterns.
b. Cash flow planning is used to determine courses of action to help the client optimize net cash flow (the difference between income and expenses).
c. Budgeting is the procedure of creating and following a specific plan for spending and investing the resources available to the client.

Answers to Self-Test Questions

2-1. C
2-2. A
2-3. D
2-4. C
2-5. C
2-6. A
2-7. D
2-8. C
2-9. D
2-10. B

Chapter 3

Answers to Review Questions

3-1. Goal setting is important to the retirement planning process because it enables the financial advisor to determine clearly definable, measurable, achievable, and realistic financial and personal objectives toward which the advisor and client can target the client's efforts and resources. It provides the basis for the subsequent planning process.

3-2. The six assumptions that an advisor must make in the retirement planning process are as follows:

- the rate of inflation the client will experience
- the age at which he or she will retire
- the age at which he or she will die
- the income replacement ratio the client will need
- the applicable marginal income tax rate (current and future)
- the investment return the client can expect

3-3.   Inflation is difficult to forecast for many reasons. Among them are the following:
- Published statistical data focus on the annual inflation rate, although long-term inflation is the appropriate variable.
- There are significant regional variations in inflation.
- Medical inflation is twice the national average of the general rate of inflation.
- The average "market basket" of goods and services that a retiree buys differs from what is used in measuring the consumer price index.
- Retirees buy more services than goods.
- A retiree's personal buying habits will affect his or her actual inflation rate, regardless of what statistical data the advisor selects.
- Inflation accounts greatly for housing costs. Many retirees, however, own their homes or live in rent-controlled buildings.
- Planning for a younger client can be especially difficult because the length of the planning period can span 60 years or more.

3-4.   A retiree's reduced living expenses make it possible to maintain his or her standard of living on a lower income. Some expenses that may be eliminated upon retirement are as follows:
- work-related expenses. After retirement, there are no longer the costs of appropriate clothing for work, commuting, and meals during working hours. Other expenses, such as association membership dues, are also eliminated.
- certain home ownership costs. Many retirees own their homes outright and thus have no mortgage payments.
- costs of caring for dependent children. Usually, by retirement, a client no longer has dependent children to support.
- saving for retirement. Frequently, a retiree will discontinue saving once he or she reaches retirement.

In addition, senior citizen discounts are often available for prescriptions, clothing, and restaurants, for example.

3-5.   Expenses that may increase for a retiree include
- medical expenses. Aging and its associated health problems increase medical costs for retirees. Those higher costs are further intensified by increases in the medical inflation rate.
- travel, vacation, and other lifestyle changes. Many retirees take advantage of their increased leisure time to travel more, take more vacations, and pursue activities they did not have time for before retirement.
- dependents to support. Although, in general, retirees no longer have children to support, some retirees still have dependents to care for, such as children with mental or physical infirmities that will require long-term custodial care or aged parents who need long-term care.
- payment for services that the retiree used to perform. Sometimes, retirees will hire others to perform activities they used to handle themselves such as housecleaning, cutting the lawn, making repairs to the house, or shoveling snow. Activities may also include caring for an infirm family member or providing transportation services.

3-6.   The replacement-ratio approach can be used to estimate a retiree's income by calculating the level of income the retiree needs to sustain his or her current standard of living, measured as a percentage of final salary. Many advisors use a replacement ratio of 70 to 80 percent.

3-7.   The expense method can be used to estimate a retiree's income by determining the expenses that the retiree will have in the next year and calculating the amount of income necessary to maintain that amount of purchasing power.

3-8.   The main purpose of the initial interview is not to make a sale but to establish the foundation for a collaborative relationship with the prospect. In this interview, the advisor seeks to
- create rapport and build credibility
- utilize effective communication techniques

- identify the prospect's needs, wants, qualifications, and concerns
- reach an agreement with the prospect to work together to address those needs, wants, and concerns

3-9. The components of steps 3 and 4 of the retirement planning process are to
- meet with the prospect
- explain the need for retirement planning
- discuss the inadequacy of traditional retirement funding sources
- review financial products as part of the retirement planning solution
- qualify the prospect
- gather information (fact finding, feeling finding, and financial information)
- identify the need
- quantify the need
- secure a discovery agreement

3-10. The four social styles are driver, expressive, amiable, and analytical. A driver is motivated to achieve by a desire for power, an expressive is motivated by a desire for recognition, an amiable is motivated by a desire for approval, and an analytical is motivated by a desire for respect.

3-11. Some presentation tools and techniques that an advisor can use to keep the prospect actively engaged in the presentation are
- visuals
- third-party substantiation
- statistical evidence
- real-life stories

3-12. The three basic methods to qualify prospects are to
- use the Personal Retirement Planning Review to make a general retirement planning assessment and attempt a preliminary discovery agreement prior to a full analysis
- use an abbreviated or modified fact finder to address a concern or dominant need that does not require a full retirement planning analysis
- proceed directly into personal information gathering using a comprehensive retirement planning fact finder

3-13. The four components of a formal retirement planning fact finder form are the following:
- personal data and retirement goals
- quantitative data
- retirement income sources
- calculations and interest tables

3-14. The implied contract that represents a mutual agreement for the advisor and prospect to continue to work together following the initial fact-finding interview is the *discovery agreement*. This agreement summarizes the prospect's retirement planning goals and concerns, and it confirms his or her willingness to seek solutions that meet those goals and concerns within the prospect's budget and time horizon. Although the discovery agreement can be verbal, it is usually written and provides a blueprint for the next steps in the selling/planning process.

Answers to Self-Test Questions

3-1. C
3-2. A
3-3. A
3-4. C
3-5. B
3-6. D
3-7. A
3-8. D
3-9. C
3-10. A

Chapter 4

Answers to Review Questions

4-1. Common examples of specialized financial planning needs that can create obstacles to successful retirement planning are as follows:
- college education funding
- divorce
- terminal illness
- nontraditional families
- job or career change
- job loss (including severance package)
- dependent parents who need long-term care
- other dependents who have special needs
- buying a first home
- purchasing a second (or vacation) home

4-2. Financial products that can help fund a college education are savings accounts, certificates of deposit, mutual funds, brokerage accounts (which include stocks and bonds), annuities, and life insurance policies.

Legal instruments that can be used to fund a college education include Uniform Gifts to Minors Act accounts, Uniform Transfers to Minors Act accounts, Sec. 2503(b) trusts, and Sec. 2503(c) trusts.

4-3. Employer-provided medical expense insurance primarily covers acute medical care for illness or injury, sometimes including very limited benefits for services provided by licensed medical practitioners. Medical expense policies often contain an exclusion for custodial care, which is the most common form of care the elderly and others with chronic physical and cognitive impairments require. This exclusion eliminates coverage for assistance with activities of daily living, services that do not attempt to cure the patient or are offered when his or her condition is not changing, and services that do not require administration from trained medical personnel.

4-4. Medicare pays for the following long-term care benefits:
- skilled-nursing facility care—inpatient care in a Medicare-certified skilled-nursing facility following a hospital stay if the person's condition requires nursing or rehabilitation services that can be rendered only in a skilled-nursing facility. Medicare-approved benefits are fully payable for 20 days and subject to a copayment for the next 80 days. No benefits are payable after 100 days.
- home health care—covered home health services provided in the home by a Medicare-certified home health agency that specializes in skilled-nursing and other therapeutic services. Medicare will also pay for 80 percent of the cost of durable medical equipment such as walkers and wheelchairs.
- hospice benefits—health care benefits to treat a terminally ill person in a Medicare-certified facility or in the patient's own home. Hospice benefits also include drugs, bereavement counseling, and inpatient respite care for family members who need a break from caring for the ill person at home.

4-5. Standard Medicare supplement insurance policies provide limited benefits associated with long-term care. For example, some policies provide up to $1,600 per year of at-home assistance with activities of daily living but do not pay for more than seven 4-hour visits in any week or more than $40 for any one visit.

4-6. LTCI policies provide for the following type of care:
- facility care (nursing home). This type of care encompasses
  - skilled-nursing care—daily nursing care ordered by a doctor and provided continuously by skilled medical personnel
  - intermediate care—occasional nursing or rehabilitative care that must be performed by skilled medical personnel
  - custodial care—assistance with activities of daily living
- assisted-living facility care—care provided in facilities for individuals who are no longer able to care for themselves but to not need the level of care provided in a nursing home
- home and community care—benefits for individuals who remain in the community, such as home health care, adult day care, homemaker companion or home health aide, caregiver training, respite care, hospice care, and therapeutic devices

4-7. Basic benefits in today's LTCI policies are as follows:
- elimination period—the amount of time the insured will pay for services before policy benefits begin
- maximum daily benefit—a daily amount up to which the policy will pay benefits for covered services
- inflation protection—an option whereby policy benefits increase automatically each year to counter the eroding effects of inflation on benefit amounts
- maximum duration of benefits—the benefit period, usually stated as years but sometimes as a dollar amount, for which LTCI benefits will be paid
- renewability—guarantee that coverage cannot be canceled except for nonpayment of premiums

Optional benefits include the following:
- waiver of premium—the requirement that the insurer will waive payment of premiums during the term of the insured's disability
- shared benefit—the ability for one spouse to access the other spouse's LTCI benefits
- nonforfeiture options—the policyowner's right to receive some value (most commonly, a shortened benefit period) for an LTCI policy if it lapses because the premium is not paid
- restoration of benefits—reinstatement of full benefits if the insured has not received long-term care for a certain period of time
- alternative plans of care—benefits for other plans of care even though the policy does not cover that type of care, as long as benefits are provided in an appropriate and cost-effective alternative to long-term care and approved by the insurer, the insured, and the insured's physician

4-8. Six common risks to consider in insurance planning and risk management are medical care expenses, long-term care expenses, premature death losses, disability income losses, property and liability losses, and unemployment.

4-9. Life insurance can provide retirement income for the insured, if living, or for the insured's spouse-beneficiary if the insured dies prior to retirement. Disability income insurance protects against the interruption of the steady flow of earnings due to accident or illness. In both cases, a person's earning capacity has an economic value that can be measured and protected. This protection can guard against the devastating consequences of an interruption in savings if the insured dies or becomes disabled.

4-10. Unearned income in many of the financial vehicles clients may use to save for retirement is taxed each year as the funds within them grow. This income taxation directly reduces the net amount of money that clients would accumulate for retirement. In addition, income taxes on the clients' wages reduces their income and thus reduces potential retirement savings.

4-11. Six income tax reduction strategies to minimize income taxation are as follows:
- taking advantage of adjustments to income, such as contributions to qualified retirement plans, to reduce current their gross income
- reducing taxable income by taking certain allowable deductions that recognize needs (such as health care) or to encourage positive social action (such as donations to charities)
- becoming familiar with and utilize income tax exemptions such as allowable personal exemptions, the cost basis of immediate annuity payments, interest on bonds issued by states and cities, and life insurance death benefits
- using tax credits rather than deductions to further reduce income tax liability
- taking advantage of income tax deferrals, such as 403(b) tax-deferred annuity programs and 401(k) salary reduction plans, to allow the growth in money to compound without being reduced by income taxes
- shifting (transferring) the obligation to pay income tax on specific items from a taxpayer with a high marginal income tax rate to another taxable entity with a lower marginal income tax rate

4-12. Inflation erodes purchasing power. The effect is most damaging to retired people who are living on fixed incomes. For example, if an individual retires today with a monthly income of $1,000, he or she will need $1,480 in 10 years to keep up with inflation and $2,191 in 20 years. The purchasing power of that $1,000 will have eroded to $665 in 10 years and to $442 in 20 years.

4-13. Among the numerous strategies to limit exposure to inflation are the five that follow:
- Save consistently. Regular, consistent savings are key in combating the effects of inflation.
- Reposition assets. Transfer savings that exceed the emergency fund into a well-diversified portfolio of assets whose rate of growth outpaces the rate of inflation.
- Reduce income tax withholding. By reducing the number of exemptions used for withholding taxes from paychecks, the extra money can be deposited into mutual funds that can grow and still have the asset remain liquid.

- Review insurance coverage at least annually. As the value of assets increases, the need for higher levels of homeowners and other property insurance also increases. As the level of income rises, so does the need for disability income insurance that protects this higher income level. Long-term care coverage should contain an inflation rider to adjust the maximum daily benefit annually to keep pace with inflation.
- Manage all investments wisely. Managing investments carelessly is particularly dangerous in inflationary periods where mistakes can be more costly and take longer from which to recover.

4-14. Procrastinating costs money at retirement. To make compound interest work and to enable funds to grow for the long term, it is critical to begin saving early. The cost of waiting is far more than the loss of whatever amount of savings the client may have put into the account. It is that amount plus the compounded earnings accumulated over the years during which the funds were allowed to grow.

Answers to Self-Test Questions

4-1. B
4-2. C
4-3. D
4-4. A
4-5. C
4-6. A
4-7. A
4-8. C
4-9. C
4-10. C

Chapter 5

Answers to Review Questions

5-1. The six criteria that an investor can use to choose from various savings, investment, and insurance products are risk, time horizon, liquidity, transaction costs, tax consequences, and competing investment opportunities.

5-2. The four categories of saving and investment vehicles are as follows:
- pretax. Pretax retirement savings, or qualified plans, meet IRS nondiscrimination, funding, and fiduciary guidelines for employer-sponsored retirement programs. Contributions to the fund are made with pretax dollars. No tax is paid on the money until it is withdrawn from the retirement plan. Profit-sharing plans, 401(k) plans, 403(b) plans, SEPs, and qualifying contributions to IRAs fall into the pretax category of savings and investment vehicles.
- tax-free. Money placed in a tax-free investment can be withdrawn any time income tax free. Deposits into this type of plan, however, are not income tax deductible. Sec. 529 plans, Coverdell education savings accounts, certain interest on Series EE savings bonds, and Roth IRAs are tax-free vehicles.
- tax-deferred. Contributions to tax-deferred plans are typically purchased with after-tax dollars, but income taxes on accumulated funds are deferred until the funds are withdrawn. Examples of tax-deferred plans are permanent life insurance, deferred annuity products, and noncoupon bonds.
- after-tax. These investment products are ones in which contributions are made with after-tax dollars and thus have no favorable income tax advantages; interest on after-tax investments is taxed each year. Their advantage is that they offer a flexible source of cash because of their liquidity. Examples are savings and money market accounts, as well as CDs.

5-3. a. Suitability is the appropriateness of a specific investment for a particular prospect or client.
  b. Risk tolerance is the degree to which the prospect or client is willing to accept risk.

5-4. Systematic risk is a risk that affects the entire market, not only one business or industry. Some examples are market risk, inflation risk, interest rate risk, reinvestment risk, and currency risk. Unsystematic risk is a risk that is unique to a single business or industry. Examples are business risk, regulation risk, financial risk, default risk, and country risk.

5-5. Diversification is a technique to minimize the impact of any one particular security, investment, or asset category on the client's overall portfolio performance. Three ways the client can accomplish diversification are by holding
- a variety of assets across several categories of assets
- alternative assets within each category of assets
- assets that mature or can be sold at different times

5-6. Asset allocation is a technique to spread investment risk across different categories of investments in a planned and predetermined manner. It depends primarily on the client's
- investment goals
- risk tolerance
- investment time horizon

5-7. Dollar cost averaging is an investment strategy to minimize risk by leveling off the ups and downs in the market through methodical, periodic investing. Its success depends on discipline and consistency—that is, investing the same amount of money in the financial product at regular intervals over a period of time, regardless of market performance.

5-8. Mutual funds enjoy an exemption on net investment income and realized gains. Mutual fund shareholders, however, must report all distributions in the year in which they are received; these distributions are subject to ordinary income tax.

5-9. Transfers within a mutual fund family may create a taxable event. Thus, even though a fund may impose no charge or penalty for this exchange privilege, any gain on the funds being transferred is taxable when the exchange is made.

5-10. An immediate annuity typically guarantees that payments will continue for the rest of the annuitant's life, regardless of its length, or for a specified period of time. This type of annuity is usually purchased with one single premium. A deferred annuity is a contract in which premiums paid into it are left to accumulate and grow into a larger sum of money over the course of many years. The invested premiums plus the contract's growth create the fund from which future immediate annuity distribution payments can be made.

5-11. The three types of deferred annuity products are as follows:
- fixed-interest deferred annuity—an annuity in which the owner's principal is guaranteed and the account is credited with a set interest rate that is guaranteed not to change for a certain time period, ranging from 1 month to 10 or more years. At the end of that period, the company can raise or lower the interest rate. The minimum guaranteed rate of interest is usually 2 or 3 percent. Because the insurance company assumes the risk in a fixed-interest deferred annuity, it is the most conservative of the three types of deferred annuities.
- equity-indexed annuity—an annuity in which the amount of interest earned is linked to changes in some type of securities index, most commonly the Standard & Poor's 500 Index. Principal and earnings are guaranteed not to fall below a certain specified level, regardless of securities market declines.
- variable deferred annuity—an annuity in which the owner receives varying rates of interest or capital growth on annuity funds, based on the investment options he or she selects. Of the three types of deferred annuities, variable deferred annuities are the least conservative.

5-12. Five advantages to using life insurance as a source of funds for retirement planning are as follows:
- tax-deferred cash accumulation
- financial flexibility
- freedom from management responsibility
- safety of principal
- return of investment

5-13. A stock is an ownership share in the corporation that issues it. Stockholders share in company profits but are generally free from any liability beyond their investment in the purchase price of the stock. Profits, however, are not guaranteed. A bond, on the other hand, represents a loan of money to the corporation. Bondholders receive regular, fixed interest payments, whether or not the company has positive or negative earnings.

Answers to Self-Test Questions

5-1. D
5-2. B
5-3. C
5-4. A
5-5. B
5-6. C
5-7. A
5-8. B
5-9. D
5-10. C

Chapter 6

Answers to Review Questions

6-1. Qualified plans differ from other tax-advantaged retirement plans in that qualified plans must meet the following legal requirements specified in IRC Sec. 401(a) to be eligible for favorable tax treatment. The qualified plan must

- cover a significant number of employees (not just the business owner and/or key employees), and it must meet IRS nondiscrimination requirements
- have a vesting schedule that gives employees a portion of the benefits if they immediately terminate from the business before they reach full retirement age
- require that assets be contributed in a way that the employer no longer owns the assets, which can be used only to pay retirement benefits and remain safe from the employer's creditors

The advantages of qualified plans are that contributions are made with pretax dollars, and all contributions and earnings accumulate on a tax-deferred basis. A disadvantage is that, although there are certain exceptions, withdrawals from a qualified plan are generally 100 percent taxable as ordinary income to the taxpayer.

6-2. A defined-benefit plan promises the employee a specified benefit at retirement; a defined-contribution plan provides a variable benefit, depending on the investment growth in participating employees' individual accounts. Hence, the employer bears the investment risk in a defined-benefit plan, whereas the employee bears the investment risk in a defined-contribution account.

6-3. A pension plan requires the employer to create a definite and ongoing commitment to fund it, usually by making annual contributions to the plan. Its sole purpose is to provide retirement income to participants. This means in-service distributions are not allowed. A pension plan can invest only 10 percent of plan assets in employer stock.

A profit-sharing plan, on the other hand, does not require that the employer maintain a specified level of annual contributions. Rather, the employer can determine how much to contribute and can even elect to make no contributions for 1 or several years. The purpose of a profit-sharing plan is to share profits on a tax-deferred basis, not to provide retirement funds. Thus, in-service distributions may be allowed. Finally, unlike the pension plan, there are no restrictions on the amount of company stock in which the plan can invest.

6-4. A 401(k) plan is called a CODA because it includes the option for the employees annually to receive a portion of their compensation in cash or to have that portion paid into the plan on a tax-deferred basis.

6-5. In 2006, the maximum amount a 55-year-old worker who earns $35,000 can contribute to his or her 401(k) plan is $20,000 (the $15,000 maximum plus an additional $5,000 catch-up contribution).

6-6. An employer can choose either a 5-year cliff vesting schedule or a 7-year graded vesting schedule. Under cliff vesting, the participant has vested rights to 100 percent of employer-provided benefits after 5 years (but none before then). Under the 7-year vesting schedule, the minimum required vested portion of benefits increases from 20 percent after 3 years of service to 100 percent after 7 years of service.

6-7. A SEP operates like a profit-sharing plan—that is, the employer decides whether or not to make a contribution each year to the plan. Employees cannot contribute. In a SIMPLE, employees can make contributions through salary deferral.

6-8. The 403(b) plan works like a profit-sharing plan. The employer, employee, or a combination of the two can make contributions to the plan. Individual accounts are established for each plan participant. The amounts contributed are excluded from the participant's income and grow tax deferred until they are withdrawn at retirement.

These plans are available only to 501(c)(3) organizations and public school systems. A 501(c)(3) organization is a corporation, community chest, fund, or foundation that operates solely for religious, charitable, scientific, public safety testing, literary, or educational purposes, or to foster national or international amateur sports, or to prevent cruelty to children or animals.

6-9. The three basic types of nonqualified deferred-compensation plans are as follows:

- SERP (supplemental executive retirement plan)—a plan in which the employer agrees to continue the employee's salary at retirement, death, and sometimes disability. The plan is funded as an additional employee benefit, not as a deferral of the employee's income.
- salary reduction plan—a plan in which the employer and employee agree either to reduce the employee's salary or to defer a bonus in order to postpone receipt and taxation to a future year. The employee bears the full cost of the plan by deferring the compensation that he or she would have otherwise received.
- death-benefit-only plan—a plan in which the employer provides a death benefit to the employee's heirs in either a lump sum or installments. There are no living benefits.

6-10. If neither spouse is an active participant in a qualified plan, all IRA contributions are deductible. If one or both spouses are active participants, however, the contribution is fully deductible only if the individual's AGI does not exceed the applicable dollar amount. In 2006, that limit is $60,000 or more for single taxpayers and heads of households, and $85,000 for married taxpayers filing jointly.

6-11. Distributions from traditional IRAs attributable to deductible contributions are taxable as received, but only part of the distribution that is attributable to nondeductible contributions is taxable (the other part is not).

Premature taxable distributions (those taken before age 59 1/2) are subject to the IRS 10 percent penalty tax for early withdrawals except when the distribution is

- made to a beneficiary or the individual's estate because of the individual's death
- the result of the individual's disability
- part of a series of periodic payments based on the life expectancy of the individual or joint life expectancies of the individual and a beneficiary
- for educational expenses
- for a first-time home purchase (up to $10,000)
- to pay medical expenses
- for health insurance for the unemployed
- to pay an IRS levy on an IRA

6-12. Owners of Roth IRAs who have earned income can make contributions beyond the age of 70 1/2 and do not have to begin making withdrawals at that age. In a traditional IRA, the owner must begin to withdraw benefits by April 1 of the year after the year in which he or she reaches age 70 1/2. Furthermore, required minimum distributions (RMDs) are mandated, whereas there are no RMDs for Roth IRAs. Unlike traditional IRAs, all contributions to a Roth IRA are non-tax deductible (made with after-tax dollars); thus, distribution penalties and restrictions are less of a burden to the taxpayer than they are with a traditional IRA. Withdrawals of contributions from a Roth IRA can be made free of taxation at any time; qualified distributions of earnings are also tax free, which differs from a traditional IRA in which distributions are taxed as received.

6-13. An IRA rollover is a transfer of funds from one IRA to the individual who then reinvests those funds in a second IRA. This type of transfer can result in tax problems when the funds originate from a qualified retirement plan because the custodian of the funds being rolled over is required to withhold 20 percent of the total amount as federal tax. The individual must provide the withheld 20 percent (which he or she later receives as an income tax refund) from other funds to complete the rollover. A direct transfer is a rollover directly from the custodian of one qualified plan to the custodian of an IRA or other qualified plan. No amount is withheld because the transaction is conducted between two account custodians.

Answers to Self-Test Questions

6-1. A
6-2. C
6-3. B
6-4. A
6-5. D
6-6. C
6-7. B
6-8. A
6-9. D
6-10. D

Chapter 7

Answers to Review Questions

7-1. The main reasons to retire early are
- financial independence
- real or perceived health issues
- corporate downsizing

Additional reasons are the retirement of the spouse, the death of the spouse, family responsibilities, the inability to handle physical demands of the job, problems in the workplace, a willingness to compromise financial goals, and health and pension incentives.

7-2. Reasons against retiring early are the
- decrease in Social Security benefits
- negative impact on pension benefits
- increased exposure to inflation
- necessity to pay off fixed long-term liabilities
- loss of employer-provided health insurance

7-3. Because of changing technologies and economies, an employer may offer an incentive to retire early as a cost-effective way to remove excess layers of management and restructure or reduce the company's total work force. To achieve downsizing but avoid layoffs, some companies encourage longer-term employees to leave voluntarily so that the companies can use more outsourcing or hire part-time, less highly paid workers.

7-4. An employee who is deciding whether or not to accept an early retirement offer should consider whether or not
- the available benefits will be enough to support the retiree and his or her family
- benefits will be sufficient to provide for the family until Social Security payments begin
- the necessary ancillary company benefits (for example, health insurance) will be available

7-5. The client could earn the following amounts in 2006 without affecting Social Security benefits:
 a. $12,480 annually for the year in which he is 62 until the year in which he reaches full retirement age
 b. $33,240 for the months January through August in the year he reaches full retirement age, after which there is no reduction on earnings above that amount
 c. an unlimited amount after the year in which he attains full retirement age

7-6. Calculating the taxable Social Security benefit amount involves adding the individual's adjusted gross income (excluding Social Security), tax-exempt interest and other excluded income, and one-half of his or her Social Security benefits and comparing that total to certain threshold amounts. The threshold at which 50 percent of benefits are taxable is $32,000 for married recipients and $25,000 for single recipients. The threshold at which 85 percent of Social Security benefits are taxable is $44,000 for married recipients and $34,000 for single recipients.

7-7. Generally, benefits under a defined-benefit plan are paid as a fixed monthly amount for as long as the retiree lives, and they are calculated as a percentage of final pay multiplied by the number of years the employee was with the company. According to the plan formula, early retirement benefits are then reduced by a certain percentage for each year the retirement date is before the full-benefit retirement date. Because benefits are based on average earnings, retiring early eliminates a number of high-earning years from the calculation. Many defined-benefit plans also build a Social Security offset into their plan formula, which reduces the amount of plan benefits according to how much in monthly Social Security benefits the retiree receives.

In a defined-contribution plan, the employee is not guaranteed a fixed amount at retirement. but instead receives the value of his or her account. Although the early retiree reduces the number of years that contributions are made to the plan, he or she still controls the amounts accumulated in the account and must make decisions regarding their investment and distribution. The retiree can select an annuity option or a lump-sum payout.

7-8. The advantages of rolling a lump-sum distribution into an IRA are that the IRA account will avoid current income taxation and defer income tax on the growth and appreciation of funds until the retiree must begin to take required minimum distributions. One way an individual can make an IRA rollover is to receive the money from the retirement account and deposit it into a new IRA account. There can be significant tax penalties in this approach. The other way to make an IRA rollover is via a direct transfer, whereby the plan trustee sends the money directly to the IRA. In this approach, no withholding is required and there are no tax penalties.

7-9. Most people, no matter how well prepared they are for retirement, find the transition disorienting for three primary reasons: It is a time of psychological, social, and financial change; it moves them from the known and familiar to the unknown and unfamiliar; and it may cause them to feel a sense of loss and loneliness. Some retirees experience diminished self-esteem and pride. Family and social relationships change. Many retirees are less active and have no financial compensation. They may have had an idealized picture of retirement, which is far different from reality. Generally, the retiree goes through four stages: the honeymoon phase, disenchantment, reorientation, and stability.

7-10. The preretirement mentality is characterized by a need to ensure a comfortable and financially secure retirement. Financial planning goals are directed toward accumulating a large amount of money. Because they have the advantage of time being on their side, preretirees show less concern about stock market downturns and have a more risk-tolerant outlook toward investments.

The postretirement mentality is driven by a need to ensure that retirement funds are never depleted. Postretirees fear running out of money and may deprive themselves of modest luxuries even if they can afford them. Time is not on their side, so their investment objectives are carefully balanced and monitored to remove excess risk.

7-11. The advisor can recommend the following strategies and planning considerations to retirees who fear running out of money during their retirement:

- selling their home, trading down to a smaller home, refinancing, taking a home-equity loan, or obtaining a reverse mortgage
- diversifying their investment portfolio
- allocating savings and investments in both tax-advantaged plans and fully taxable vehicles
- varying maturity dates on bonds and CDs
- resisting the urge to panic if the stock market experiences a downturn
- purchasing annuities to provide guaranteed retirement income
- making sure that they have adequate life insurance in place

7-12. Adequate life insurance enhances retirement planning because it removes some of the uncertainty about the future. It can ensure that funds are available to the family if the worker dies or becomes disabled. During the accumulation phase of retirement, life insurance proceeds can be used to replace income, make mortgage payments, and educate children. Having adequate life insurance in place during retirement can allow retirees to use more of their liquid assets that they might otherwise have been reluctant to spend for fear of disinheriting heirs. In addition, life insurance can be a source of tax-free loans or withdrawals of the policy's cash value to provide supplemental income for the retiree.

7-13. The seven steps in developing retirement planning solutions for a prospect are as follows:

- List and value assets and cash flow.
- Identify goals and objectives.
- Prioritize the goals and objectives.
- Assess the current retirement plan.
- Outline recommendations.
- Compare the current and recommended plans.
- Develop an implementation plan.

Answers to Self-Test Questions

7-1.   A
7-2.   D
7-3.   D
7-4.   A
7-5.   B
7-6.   B
7-7.   B
7-8.   A
7-9.   C
7-10.   C

Chapter 8

Answers to Review Questions

8-1. If the life insurance policyowner reserves the right to change the beneficiary, the designation of beneficiary is said to be *revocable* and the beneficiary is known as a revocable beneficiary. A revocable beneficiary has no rights under the policy—only an expectation of future benefits. Ownership of the death benefit does not vest in the revocable beneficiary until the insured dies. Thus, policyowners can take out loans, stop paying premiums, change dividend options, and assign or surrender their policies without the beneficiaries' knowledge or consent.

In an *irrevocable* beneficiary designation, the beneficiary's ownership rights are vested immediately. What this means is that the policyowner can no longer take out loans, stop paying premiums, change dividend options, change beneficiaries, or assign or surrender their policies without the knowledge and consent of the irrevocable beneficiaries.

8-2.   Ways that property can be transferred at death are by contract, will, survivorship, trust, and intestacy laws.

8-3.   The four elements of a trust are the grantor, trustee, beneficiary, and trust corpus (or principal).

8-4.   A trust is an arrangement in which a person or entity holds legal title to property and manages it for the benefit of another person or group of people. A trustee holds property for the benefit of another person. This arrangement separates the legal interest from the beneficial interest. Typically, this might involve ownership of property by the trustee (the legal interest), with income from the property being given to the beneficiary (beneficial interest).

8-5.   The federal estate tax is a tax on the right to transfer property at death.

8-6.   Deductions that can reduce the gross estate include death costs, administrative expenses, debts, the state death tax deduction, charitable bequests, and the marital deduction.

8-7.   Four estate tax credits that can reduce the estate tax are the applicable credit amount, the gift tax credit, a credit for estate taxes on earlier transfers, and a credit for foreign death taxes paid.

8-8.   The estate and gift taxes are offset by the applicable credit amount. This cumulative credit is applicable for both federal estate and gift taxes due on taxable transfers—that is, whatever amount of the applicable credit amount someone uses during his or her lifetime against gift taxes will reduce the amount of the total remaining credit that can be applied against estate taxes after death.

The applicable credit amount is $780,800 in 2006, which exempts $2 million from estate taxation. It is now impossible for a donor to fully exhaust the applicable credit amount by making lifetime gifts. Even if the amount of the credit allocated to satisfying gift tax liability is fully used, some of the credit will remain to use against estate taxes.

The marital deduction permits a 100 percent deduction for all property transferred between husband and wife. This means that an unlimited estate can be passed to a surviving spouse with no estate tax.

8-9.   Income that was earned by a decedent prior to death, but received by another person following death, is referred to as income in respect of a decedent (IRD). In general, the present value of survivor benefits payable to a third-party beneficiary under employer-sponsored tax-qualified pension plans, lump sums from profit-sharing plans, SEPs, SIMPLEs, traditional IRAs, and nonqualified deferred-compensation plans in which the decedent had no cost basis are considered to be IRD.

IRD is includible in the decedent's gross estate and potentially subject to estate taxation. These survivor benefits are also includible in the decedent beneficiary's income and subject to income taxation.

8-10.   The major issues that state regulations of insurance companies and advisors address are as follows:

- licensing of agents and advisors within each state
- authorization (licensing) of insurance companies to do business within each state
- consumer protection against possible misrepresentation of insurance products and their benefits
- use of illustrations in the sales process. Most states subscribe to NAIC model legislation that describes procedures for the proper use of illustrations within the entire sales process.
- safeguards against unjustified replacement of existing policies in order to sell new policies
- what advisors call themselves and the kinds of advice they give their prospects and clients. In many states, financial advisors, planners, and consultants are considered separate professional groups, and specific licenses are required.

8-11.   In the 1980s, the Securities and Exchange Commission (SEC) issued three tests to determine whether or not an individual must register as an investment advisor. If all three tests are answered in the affirmative, registration is required unless specifically excluded or exempted. If any of the tests is answered in the negative, there is no need to become a registered investment advisor. According to the SEC's three tests, the individual or entity must

- give advice or analysis concerning securities (security advice test)
- be engaged in the business of advising others regarding securities (security business test)
- be in receipt of compensation (compensation test)

8-12.   The NASD, which was established under authority granted by the Securities Exchange Act of 1934, provides voluntary self-regulation of broker/dealers under SEC oversight. The NASD has the power to require and monitor compliance with standardized rules of fair practice for the industry. NASD regulatory responsibilities include registration and testing of securities professionals, review of members' advertising and sales literature, and services such as arbitration of investor disputes. Registered representatives must provide the NASD with personal information, including prior employment and any history of securities-related disciplinary action.

8-13. The apparent conflict between doing what is legal and doing what is ethical in dealing with prospects and clients involves situations when fair business practices, legal requirements, and company rules seem to conflict with the advisor's best efforts. How this apparent conflict is resolved is a matter of ethics, which goes beyond compliance with the laws. Ethical behavior is doing what is right and putting the prospect's or client's best interests before the advisor's. It is maintaining the highest possible standard of behavior in all business dealings.

Answers to Self-Test Questions

8-1. D
8-2. A
8-3. C
8-4. C
8-5. C
8-6. A
8-7. A
8-8. B
8-9. C
8-10. D

Index